T0295772

The Age of Capitalism, Consumer Culture, and the Collapse of Nature in the Anthropocene

Environment and Society

Series Editor
Douglas Vakoch

As scholars examine the environmental challenges facing humanity, they increasingly recognize that solutions require a focus on the human causes and consequences of these threats, and not merely a focus on the scientific and technical issues. To meet this need, the Environment and Society series explores a broad range of topics in environmental studies from the perspectives of the social sciences and humanities. Books in this series help the reader understand contemporary environmental concerns, while offering concrete steps to address these problems.

Books in this series include both monographs and edited volumes that are grounded in the realities of ecological issues identified by the natural sciences. Our authors and contributors come from disciplines including but not limited to anthropology, architecture, area studies, communication studies, economics, ethics, gender studies, geography, history, law, pedagogy, philosophy, political science, psychology, religious studies, sociology, and theology. To foster a constructive dialogue between these researchers and environmental scientists, the Environment and Society series publishes work that is relevant to those engaged in environmental studies, while also being of interest to scholars from the author's primary discipline.

Recent Titles in the Series

The Age of Capitalism, Consumer Culture, and the Collapse of Nature in the Anthropocene, by Jack Thornburg
Sustainable Energy Development: Technology and Investment, edited by Kimarie Engerman, Elizabeth A. Keenan, Dmitry Kurochkin, Elena V. Shabliy
Making Nature Social: Towards a Relationship with Nature, by Rembrandt Zegers
Earth Polyphony: Law, Ecocriticism, and Eco-Activism in Postcolonial India, by Suhasini Vincent
Staying Together: Natureculture in a Changing World, Edited by Kaushani Mondal
Learning in the Anthropocene: Reimagining Education in the Twenty-First Century, by Carl A. Maida
The Social Life of Unsustainable Mass Consumption, by Magnus Boström
Everyday Life Ecologies: Sustainability, Crisis, Resistance, by Alice Dal Gobbo
Environmental Legacies of the Copernican Universe, by Jean-Marie Kauth
Anticipatory Environmental (Hi)Stories from Antiquity to the Anthropocene, edited by Christopher Schliephake and Evi Zemanek
Mapping the Environmental Humanities: The Emerging Role of GIS in Ecocriticism, edited by Mark Terry and Michael G. Hewson
The Bangladesh Environmental Humanities Reader: Environmental Justice, Developmental Victimhood, and Resistance, by Samina Luthfa, Mohammad Tanzimuddin Khan, and Munasir Kamal
Loren Eiseley's Writing across the Nature and Culture Divide, by Qianqian Cheng
The Saving Grace of America's Green Jeremiad, by John Gatta

The Age of Capitalism, Consumer Culture, and the Collapse of Nature in the Anthropocene

Jack Thornburg

LEXINGTON BOOKS
Lanham • Boulder • New York • London

Published by Lexington Books
An imprint of The Rowman & Littlefield Publishing Group, Inc.
4501 Forbes Boulevard, Suite 200, Lanham, Maryland 20706
www.rowman.com

86-90 Paul Street, London EC2A 4NE

British Library Cataloguing in Publication Information Available

Library of Congress Cataloging-in-Publication Data

Names: Thornburg, John C., 1950- author.
Title: The age of capitalism, consumer culture, and the collapse of nature in the anthropocene / Jack Thornburg.
Description: Lanham : Lexington Books, [2024] | Series: Environment and society | Includes bibliographical references and index. | Summary: "This book examines how modern society arrived at such a destructive environmental and social stage, suggesting that three great crises have converged: climate change, capitalism as a logic system, and questions of consumer society and social identity"—Provided by publisher.
Identifiers: LCCN 2024028501 (print) | LCCN 2024028502 (ebook) | **ISBN 9781666958782 (cloth) | ISBN 9781666958799 (epub)**
Subjects: LCSH: Capitalism—Environmental aspects. | Consumption (Economics)—Environmental aspects. | Climatic changes—Effect of human beings on. | Environmental degradation. | Environmental responsibility.
Classification: LCC HC79.E5 T485 2024 (print) | LCC HC79.E5 (ebook) | DDC 304.2—dc23/eng/20240809
LC record available at https://lccn.loc.gov/2024028501
LC ebook record available at https://lccn.loc.gov/2024028502

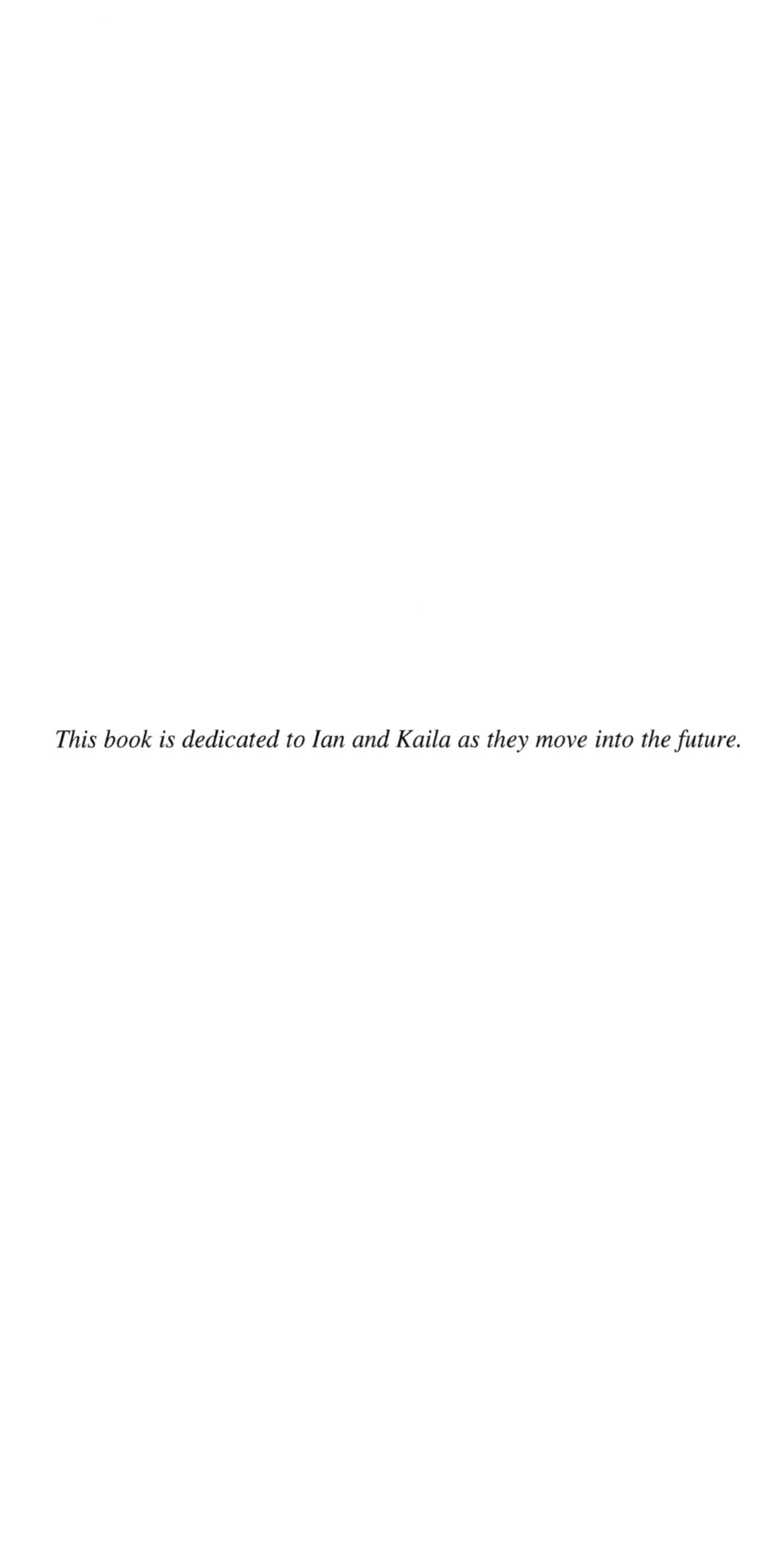

This book is dedicated to Ian and Kaila as they move into the future.

Contents

Acknowledgments

A book in many regards is a collaborative effort. It takes more than the author of a book to bring a manuscript to life. Comments, insights, and ideas for a topic are generated through readings, discussions, and experiences with many people. I am indebted to a number of individuals who helped bring this volume to the public. As a graduate student, I took classes with two particular sociologists, Drs. Eugene Havens and Russell Middleton at the University of Wisconsin–Madison, academics who taught me the responsibility to bring to the public the concerns of our research interests. They both believed that the defining role of a social scientist is not only to understand social reality but to use that understanding in the struggle for social change and the betterment of humankind. They impressed upon me the need to move beyond the academic ivory tower to include the broader public in our discourse. In my studies, I found Dell Hymes' call in his book *Reinventing Anthropology*, who asked of anthropology what they ask of themselves to find "a clear connection between what is to be done and the interests of mankind." The tenor of this book developed in those early encounters. The genesis for this book, however, began with a reading of Gustav Speth's *The Bridge at the Edge of the World*, where he wrote of a clear link between environmental problems and capitalist economic activity. I must also acknowledge the significance of Christopher Lasch's pessimistic prognosis on social loneliness and the narcissistic self in his books, *The Culture of Narcissism* and *The Minimal Self*. Though written more than forty years ago, they remain prescient for our own troubled times and have influenced my thinking on contemporary American society and culture. Speth and Lasch's volumes motivated my interest in developing an inclusive perspective, eventually leading to the three interrelated crises found within these pages.

More recently, I have to thank Benedictine University professor William (Bill) Scarlato for the years of discussion on what it means to be human and the absolute need to have a spiritual center when contemplating the human condition. As an art professor, Scarlato brought to our meetings a keen philosophical insight into the meaning of truth in the perspective of the natural wonders around us. Through those discussions, we searched for and debated the meaning of humanity, especially in its relationship to the sentient world of animal life, primarily in the context of who we are in relation to who they are. We frequently discussed the essence of beauty and truth to be found, we agreed, in the wonderment of the sentient world of life beyond the human endeavor. Our exchanges taught me a more humanist perspective on our physical world. It was those discussions that sensitized me to life beyond the immediacy of the practicality of our social lives, to behold the spirituality and majesty in all aspects of nature. Our relationship over the years sensitized me to move beyond the conventionality of the times and absorb what many indigenous people know that we cannot be fully human without an abiding presence of nature within us. Bill alerted me to the writings of Thomas Berry, who believed we are the consciousness of life itself and, as such, need to be celebrated by honoring all life as essential in the creation of Gaia, Mother Earth.

I also must give recognition to Dr. Jon Lewis, a colleague in the Department of Sociology at Benedictine University, for his years of debate over the social evolution of modern society. It was his skepticism of my ideas on postmodernism that compelled me to examine and strengthen my understanding of the sociological concept that had lost its explanatory power in endless academic debate over the conditions of modern society. It was his thorough understanding of the history of social evolution that helped, especially through the early classic sociologists that reinforced my thinking. But we did come to agree that contemporary American society, followed in various ways globally, was undergoing sociopolitical change unlike previous social eras. In our back-and-forth debates and exchanges, we developed an understanding of what Marx and Antonio Gramsci were telling us, that social members are expressions of the socio-political values of capitalist culture and not of any inherent nature. In discussion we examined advanced post-industrial society's ideological creation of Marcuse's "one dimensional man" of false needs and Zygmunt Bauman's views on consumer society. Through our interchanges, it became clear that late capitalism played an essential role in the social transformation of its social members. I must also thank Dr. Lewis for his time and effort in reading various chapters, looking for clarity and consistency in my argument. Many of his suggestions improved the flow and clarity of the manuscript.

A recognition must also be given to Dr. Patrick Polasek, the chair of the Department of Society, Justice, and Politics, for giving me access to office space and technological resources for the research and writing of this book. He was frequently at my door, encouraging me to complete the manuscript and get into the public. Grateful acknowledgement must also go to Dr. Chez Rumpf of the University of Illinois for her support and encourgement to complete this project. A better colleague would be hard to find. To my colleague at Benedictine University, Dr. Jean-Marie Kauth, professor of literature, I am grateful for her support and close reading of this book. Her laser focus and attention to detail and her incisive comments to clarify various points aided in the completeness of this project.

To Dr. Norberto Valdez of Colorado State University, a friend and colleague of many years, a debt of gratitude for our discussions as anthropologists on the intricacies of capitalism and its immense power to shape cultural lives. Finally, thank you to Drs.Tammy Sarver and Phil Hardy, political science professors, and Chair of the Psychology Department, Dr. Brian Patterson, all at Benedictine University, who encouraged me to keep on and finish this work.

Research and writing is a lonely business that requires a serious degree of solitude, of commitment by those to give that needed space. I have deep gratitude to Mirna Fernandez for giving me the time to complete this task. I also appreciate her comments on the clarity of various statements I wrote. I also have to thank Hatuey for providing company during my late-night research at home.

Of course, for the limitations found in this book, I alone am responsible.

Introduction

A World in Change

This is a cautionary tale, a warning about where a given way of life collides with the three great crises outlined in this book. The evidence is clear that nationally and globally this is a troubling era in human history. Like many people, I worry about the fate of both this planet and humanity.[1] The fact that I worry about the dynamics of this troubled planet is why I wrote this book. I look around me and feel something is lost, that somehow, we have lost our sense of what it means to be human, an exceptional sentient being on this one colorful, vibrant planet in our part of the cold, dark universe. Although violence and chaos seem part of the human experience, somehow the present seems different and troubling. While the focus is primarily on the United States, as the most advanced individualistically inclined consumer society, the dynamic of these three crises is increasingly global. This book attributes many of today's seemingly endless problems to the impact of capitalism and its logic. The underlying question of this book is, "Is this the best we can be, is this as good as it gets?" How do we answer this?

We face enormous issues that need not only to be confronted but addressed, yet these are problems without easy or comfortable answers. For instance, current warning signs over the lack of ice and snow during recent U.S. Midwest winters that affect agriculture due to warm weather and changing precipitation patterns are alarming. A headline in a recent Chicago newspaper read, "It's Summer in February." There is also growing fear that glaciers in Greenland and West Antarctica are rapidly losing vast amounts of melting ice, threatening sea level rise. At the other end of the spectrum, there are indications of societal dysfunction as social "diseases" such as depression, suicide, personality disorders, and forms of road rage, gun violence, and sociopolitical polarization are provoking havoc in a society of strangers more concerned about personal rights and privacy than the common good. Clearly, there appears to be troubling problems without easy solution. Therefore, it is incumbent upon me to be honest and deliberate in providing explanations about pressing issues and events. As it happens, this approach of forthright writing is nothing new to my field of anthropology. Witness this 50+ year old preface by Dell Hymes in his book, *Reinventing Anthropology*:

> This book is for people for whom "the way things are" is not reason enough for the way things are, who find fundamental questions pertinent and in need of personal answer, those for whom security, prosperity, and self-interest are not sufficient reasons for choices they make; who think that if an official "study of man" does not answer to the needs of men, it ought to be changed; who ask of anthropology what they ask of themselves—responsiveness, critical awareness, ethical concern, human relevance, a clear connection between what is to be done and the interests of mankind. (1972)

Today, we face appreciably more existential problems, many without easy solutions, giving one pause and a sense of foreboding. Edmund Leach, a British social anthropologist, many years ago referred to a runaway world, a place where we have played God in meeting our desires and wants while ignoring the implications of our yearnings (1967). The philosopher Jacques Ellul, a contemporary of Leach, felt it was a technological imperative that was impacting society. He described a "technological man" driven to develop technology but lacking understanding of the deep impact technology would have on society (1964). We have in many ways bought into a world ruled by science, technology, and the idea that the world is ours to do with as we see fit. But our relationship to the Earth, as to each other, is more than only technical and pragmatic. We are also creatures born of this Earth and have spent most of our existence immersed in its beauty. Technology and science cannot offer us the enjoyment of the mysteries life offers. Only a spiritual sense of oneness with the Earth can do that. Be that as it may, it seems that an idea of beauty, aesthetics, and an abiding philosophy of life is secondary in this expedient, practical world, if it is considered at all.

Thinking about this world we have created and our approach to it can lead one to ponder questions concerning the meaning of life, of the human trajectory. One can legitimately question what it means to be human within the chaos of endless calamities of the contemporary world. Travel the internet and numerous definitions of what it means to be human can be found. Most definitions do not question the possibility that the human direction of social change may be off course, that we have become something different from what we aspire to be. What we don't see, Stephan Harding believes, is that we cannot comprehend an all-encompassing love of self within a broader context of all living beings. He writes that "Experiencing our full humanity requires us to attenuate our self-centeredness by enfolding it within a much wider sense of self in which we experience genuine love and compassion for all beings, both living and non-living" (n.d.). In one of his daily meditations, Franciscan priest and author Richard Rohr summarized what is an important sentiment governing this book, the loss of connection with the natural world. He wrote,

> The very land itself meant something quite different to the newcomer than it did to the host people. Something was missing. The difficulty, as the Natives saw it, was with the settlers themselves and their failure to tread lightly, with humility and respect, on the land. The settlers wanted to live *on* the land, but the host people lived *with* the land. Living on the land means objectifying the land and natural resources and being shortsighted concerning the future. Living with the land means respecting the natural balance. (2021)

Should being human on this living planet mean we all share in the great mystery of how a Monarch butterfly born in Canada finds its way two thousand miles to winter sanctuaries in the *Oyamel* fir tree forests of Michoacán, Mexico, a place it has never visited? Or that cliff swallows travel three thousand miles from a winter habitat in South America to summer homes in North America only to return south three to four months later. What does it mean when research suggests that certain species of whales may have culture, that some behavior is not genetically based but learned in matrilineal clans? Or the fact of recent research indicating that bumble bees' lives are much more sophisticated than was long believed? In his research, Stephen Buchmann writes that

> we now know that bees are sentient, they may exhibit self-awareness, and they possibly have a basic form of consciousness. Some bees plan for the future by cutting resin mines into fresh bark, to which they return again and again. They think and may form mental maps of their foraging routes. (2023, xvi)

From my perspective, understanding and appreciating these examples should be part of our assessment about the meaning of life on Earth beyond simplistic public definitions.

Since the Enlightenment, Western culture has generally approached nature from an adversarial relationship, emphasizing domination rather than from any celebratory perspective. No corner of this planet has been left untouched, including the most remote and inhospitable places, such as Antarctica, the North Atlantic, the Chilean Atacama Desert, and Salar de Uyuni in Bolivia. Areas such as the vast wilderness of the Arctic National Wildlife Refuge (ANWR) in Alaska are under constant threat of petroleum development. Even when protected by statutes, such areas (e.g., Bears Ears National

Monument in Utah) are under relentless pressure for development. In *The New Yorker*, Elizabeth Kolbert comments that from the perspective of other life forms, what is frightening is our species' "remorseless vigor" as we go about the business of life. She cautions, "And if we are just thinking about ourselves, then we are failing as ethical agents, which is to say as human beings" (2017).[2]

This is not to say that some cannot see through the "artificiality" of modern life. For example, Henry Thoreau, John Muir, Wendell Berry, and Thomas Berry all have written extensively about nature and our role in it. Many do see the all-consuming beauty of this world. Others, recognizing the brutality of the bureaucratization of society and relentless consumerism, are moved to mitigate our impact on nature, if not society. But the problem, however, is not personal but social. What is required is an honest appraisal of how we view ourselves and how society is currently organized and operates. What needs to be examined is our sense of place, time, and responsibilities in the web of life. The fate of the Earth demands nothing less.

As a society, the question of who and what we are a part of is not a frequent topic of popular discussion that informs broader public discourse. As a society, we do not question who we are or what kind of people we have become. We do not recognize how much a narcissistic materialism has become a prevailing ethos of modern life. We have become so cynical and sense a powerlessness over our mutual fate as a society. Yet, it need not be so. We are born with the potential to embrace the world around us and celebrate all that there is within it. Children are born as vessels to be filled with the capacity for whatever a given culture deems fundamental. Early in life, young children exhibit a wondrous attitude and interest in the world around them and are enthralled by even small things such as birds, insects, or fish in babbling brooks and streams. Years ago, while on a camping trip, sitting beneath a canopy of windblown trees, my young son exclaimed, "Dad, listen to the wind song." Children are not born to be competitive or to crave possessions but instead are filled with the capacity to accept, to wonder, and to love.

Clearly, modern society is not so much a simple binary of good and bad, but this contemporary era does appear chaotic, full of moral ambiguity, relative compassion (depending on what side you are on), and a dearth of understanding of the human plight. Children are socialized into an environment to become what society and the corporate world need them to become if the system in place is to work. Those small instances of wonder give way to strategies and logics of acceptance, accommodation, and survival. In a sense, we have lost the ability to imagine a different, more nature-embracing way of life. As I write these words, it is difficult to project a positive future, a different kind of life beyond division, competition, fear, and insecurity.

In the early period of industrialization and emerging mass society, Max Weber foresaw and worried that freedom (too much?) and individualism (the sovereignty thereof) would lead to value fragmentation. He concurred with Emile Durkheim's view that individualism and the increasing separation of the individual from any intimate collectivity would usher in greater social dysfunctions. The sovereignty of individualism may be emancipatory, but it also leads to vulnerability, confusion, and uncertainty. The collective solidarity of earlier times afforded one too much "repressive" security, Durkheim believed. But in a competitive world of struggle over access to important social resources, the "free" individual is not left with much time to muse over the beauty of the natural world except possibly in short stints of vacation. Thus, beyond the divorce of culture from nature brought on by the Enlightenment, the ability to escape the duplicity of human ingenuity is limited by the individual's need to meet the demands and expectations of current society, our own modern form of "repressive law." Although David Levy was thinking about contemporary scholarship, his essay *No Time to Think* applies as well to the distractions of social media, smartphones, entertainment, and other demands confronting most people (2007).

Taking the time to think about the condition of this world is difficult in what Thomas Eriksen refers to as an "overheated world." By this, he means we are witnessing a sensory overload of information that is difficult for the human mind to accommodate. New information (and entertainment) technologies have quickened the pace of life, demanding to be recognized. Eriksen asserts that "Excess of information may well be regarded as a kind of waste. It pollutes not only minds, but also time, filling the gaps and turning slowness into a scarce resource," leaving little time to reflect (2016, 127). As I discuss in later chapters, information overload and insufficient time to ingest what confronts us lead to a loss or breakdown of narrative that explains who we are or directions where we might be heading. The result is social and personal confusion and fear about little-understood possibilities about the future or prevailing everyday conditions of life.

How did we get to this point, divorced from the world and divorced from each other? The narrative presented here addresses the problem of our runaway world from several perspectives: a focus on indigenous conceptions of nature, the development of science and objectivity stemming from the Enlightenment era, the growth of a new economic system evolving out of feudal Europe eventually leading to a new type of society characterized as consumerist, and the psychological and cultural effects of a modernized social system of mass urban society.

The analysis of how we came to this point begins by outlining the transition from traditional communities where individual identity, "I," was immersed within a web of communal relationships of kinship, abiding friendships, and nature, where "we" was paramount for survival, identity, and security. One was part of something larger than oneself that provided a sense of social and psychological invulnerability and freedom from doubt. Durkheim believed that in such social systems, expectations and assumptions of conformity to the degree of sameness were expressed in repressive informal laws and communal sentiment to enforce acceptance of the natural order of society. Certainly, most people did not question the operation of their society because such agreed-upon conformity seemed natural and provided benefits of belonging and security not found at the isolated individual level.

Indeed, most of human history has revolved around such tight-knit community dynamics. Many indigenous societies and their cultural perceptions viewed culture and nature as intertwined into a single element of reality. For example, Enrique Salmón, an anthropologist and member of the Rarámuri culture of Chihuahua, Mexico, describes the Rarámuri, including other Native American cultures, as "kincentric" ecologically, meaning that "indigenous people view themselves as part of an extended ecological family that shares ancestry and origins. The kin, or relatives, include all the natural elements of an ecosystem." Salmón further explains that "To indigenous people, humans are at an equal standing with the rest of the natural world; they are kindred relations. In addition, indigenous people believe that the complex interactions that result from this relationship enhance and preserve the ecosystem" (2000, 1332–1331). This perspective of inclusion is different from the Western world where culture is deemed dominant over nature and the individual superior over community.

The position assumed in this book is that humanity has moved beyond the bounded community of shared identities and collective representations in which humans and the natural world developed an intimate relationship. With the advent of a new economic system came new ways of thinking and organizing, which developed into modern urban life informed by rationalism, objectivity, and universal truths. We conceive of ourselves in terms of subjective individuality rather than exhibiting an ethos of a shared common good and social solidarity. Continued social change has brought affluent, postindustrial society to a new social era of consumerism and the sovereign individual immersed in a world consisting of an avalanche of competing facts and truths, of greater subjectivity and fluid social identities. One's center was no longer a close-knit community but instead materialism as an element of self-identification and self-assurance. It is this free-wheeling consumerism that propels the search for increased production of goods that is linked to climate change and environmental degradation. The increase in greenhouse gases reflects corporate production's creation and manipulation of the environment to promote consumption: they exploit, produce, we consume. It is apparent that humanity, Will Steffen and colleagues assert, is "becoming a self-conscious, active agent in the operation of its own life support system" (2007). Advertising serves as the tool to convince individuals that desires are needs and the means to an unrealistic happy good life. Advertising diverts our focus on ourselves rather than the negative effects of our wants. The systemic existential crises we face, in other words, are much greater than any individual or group of individuals realizes. Personal attempts at mitigating the negative effects of our environmental activities will not solve the problem of continuing environmental degradation. The environmental crisis is structural and cultural in nature—the scaffold of capitalist-oriented political-economics—and thus demands a structural and cultural solution around a collective social movement rather than a personal, individual response.

Prevailing environmental issues and the inability of individuals to understand the juggernaut of mass society call for substantive change to our way of living. The idea that we are hardwired for social connection, exemplified in traditional communities as well as in our attempts to connect with each other in cafes, pubs, and book clubs, suggests we need each other. This need is also expressed in indigenous cultures and their relationships with nonhuman nature, seeing various animals enfolding kinship. This book advocates adopting a new way of life to embrace that which has attenuated over time. The underlying philosophy of this book sees the meaning of the good life found in the depth of community, including the natural world. Thomas Berry once said, as a metaphor beyond our practical life, we need to look at the evening sky as darkness descends. He wrote that "It is a moment when some other world makes itself known, some numinous presence beyond human understanding. We experience the wonder of things as the vast realms of space overwhelm the limitations of our human minds." He goes on to say, "At this moment, as the sky turns golden and the clouds reflect the blazing colors of evening, we participate in the intimacy of all things with each other" (2006, 137). Berry sees the Earth as primary and the human as subsidiary, commenting, "The Earth is our primary community. Indeed, all particular modes of Earthly being exist by virtue of their role within this community" (43).

Recognizing this, I submit, is the great challenge for overcoming the existential issues raised in this book. The attempt here is to explain how we got to this point in history where both society and nature are jeopardized by this stage of human activity. This book provides no clear answers to the perplexing problem of postmodern rearrangements in the era of the Anthropocene and climate change. It does alert to the collapse of the grand capitalist-influenced meta-narrative expressing an inherently positive future. The attempt here is to elucidate the difficult challenges of a transformative social era. The hope this book offers is a future direction to think about human life and suggests a way to think about possibilities leading to a new habitable and sustaining world for all life.

NOTES

1. I would like to thank Dr. Jon Lewis for his insightful comments and suggestions regarding this introduction.

2. Franciscan Richard Rohr of the Center for Action and Contemplation (CAC) quotes an elder attending the 1999 Global Forum on Environment and Development for Survival who pleaded with delegates, "We have jeopardized the future of our coming generation with our greed and lust for power. The warnings are clear, and time is now a factor. . . . We speak of our children, yet we savage the spawning beds of the salmon and herring and kill the whale in his home. We advance through the forests of the earth felling our rooted brothers indiscriminately, leaving no seeds for the future. We exploit the land and resources of the poor and indigenous peoples of the world. We have become giants, giants of destruction. . . . We must return to the prayers, ceremonies, meditations, rituals, and celebrations of thanksgiving which link us with the spiritual powers that sustain us and, by example, teach our children to respect" (2021).

Chapter 1

Standing on the Fault Line of a World in Crisis

Climate Change, Consumer Capitalism, and Postmodern Culture

This book is about change and the future. It is also about choice and risk. The focus is on advanced post-industrialized consumer society exemplified by the United States. Although the emphasis is on the United States, the wake of contemporary change is lapping the shores of all countries and cultures of the world. It is believed here that U.S. culture and society are but the harbingers of things to come globally. The near horizon is witnessing the gathering of a series of dark, troubling phenomena that require action regionally and globally. From the perspective of today, it appears there are three potentially catastrophic events developing and moving toward convergence: climate change and severe environmental degradation, capitalist consumer political-economy, and sociocultural change to a postmodern society. This book is a review that suggests an understanding of climate change must go beyond questions of the politics of fossil fuel production and its environmental consequences to include the entangled issues of culture, consumerism, and social identity in a world of changing communities and social relationships. Our environmental problems cannot be solved unless we have a clear understanding of the proximate and ultimate causes of climate change. Environmental exploitation and industrial production exist to fulfill the demand for material goods. But why, in an advanced industrial nation, do individuals need or desire so many material goods? In other words, we cannot solve our environmental problems without also solving our psychosocial problems.

Climate change is well-recognized by many, and some now see the exploitation of natural resources and degradation of habitats as equally serious. Many people are now beginning to recognize that our current economic system, its operation and the logic of capitalism, is also problematic, creating dysfunction and social alienation. Nationally and globally, progress has been made to alleviate poverty, yet chronic hunger and malnutrition remain, and too many lack adequate health care, housing, and education. Climate change and environmental degradation are related to capitalism, and some researchers are beginning to see a problematic relationship between the kind of consumer culture promoted by capitalism and the psychological-cultural effects on social identity and relationships that modern societies are creating. The increase in mass killings, terrorist attacks, and the rise of various forms of fundamentalism are emblematic of some sort of social pathology in modern society. It is perplexing but should not be too surprising to see an increase in various psychological disorders such as suicide, eating disorders, myriad addictions, depression, and anxiety in affluent societies as loneliness and alienation become prevalent in a fast-paced, technologically driven world. The thesis presented here is that the dynamics of an earth in peril are global, structural, cultural, and psychological—it is both material and ideational—and not easily defined nor located but recognized by many in the scientific community.

There is among many an undercurrent of thought that maybe the human trajectory has gone off course. That is, for tens of thousands of years, humans needed and relied on intimate and direct human relationships and connections, a compact that brought all group members into an amity that included the broader world of nature and animals. We sat around campfires and lodges to tell stories and share experiences, we gathered as kinfolk to participate in public rituals and ceremonies, and we all shared in the direct intimacy of a vibrant nature around us. Wealth, as we understand it, was not as important as one's social reputation and social prestige. Today, however, we find ourselves increasingly socially isolated, alone in a world of strangers driven by commercialism and political-economic expediency. Is living as a cog in a mass urban technologically driven society what we are meant to do?

The world in all its complexity—physically and socially—is changing in ways that are difficult to anticipate and understand, yet these changes must be addressed. The growth in population, how people make a living and live, the assumptions about the technologies we employ, and our general conception about life present challenges to the way things are and to what we take for granted. Most people live in the world of "now," believing that things will remain relatively the same as they have always been, but perhaps with a crisis or problem to be overcome. For young people, the belief has been that life will be better for them relative to their parents. The reality of the way we live seems so concrete, permanent, and natural that it is hard to conceive that our way of life may be in jeopardy if attention is not paid to the existing crises. The two components of this reality revolve around a socioeconomic system that absorbs our attention and, in many ways, influences our lives, and a natural reality that humans are the dominant and divine species on this planet, and that we are exempt from sharing a fruitful niche on the tree of life. Yet in this modern world rather than a celebration of our ascendancy, a growing sense of loneliness, alienation, and anxiety has taken hold as if, somehow, we have lost our way into the future and that reality is not what it seems.

After tens of thousands of years of human evolution, do we know why we are here—to what purpose? Not what it means to be human, although we will discuss this later, but what does it mean to be a cohabiting species in the evolution of life on this planet? Do we even understand that this is not our planet exclusively? We are so removed from our ancient and natural history by the consequences of sociocultural development that we are adrift, unable to understand who we are. Such a lack of understanding of ourselves also translates into a lack of recognition of the needs of other species, even those beneficial to our survival. Many people, it seems, have a hard time understanding that humanity is but one element, albeit a very significant one, integrated into the tree of life on this planet, whose fate is intertwined with that of many other species in this era of climate change. On the other, many share a concern that involves the sustainability of an increasingly global neoliberal social structure and culture that produces income and social inequality, increasing alienation and Emile Durkheim's *anomie*, and an ideology of consumerism and technology that increasingly replaces human connection and relationships.

As we look back, our path to the contemporary world can clearly be seen. Cultural evolution has witnessed a seemingly linear progression from simple foraging societies to politically centralized agricultural and urban states to a "modern" society, developed out of the Enlightenment, centered on scientific and rational thought processes. Social institutions developed under these conditions to promote social order, conformity, stability, and social structures based on class, power, and acceptable prescriptions of social truth. The rise of modernity gave primacy to the economy to govern the social process of labor and lifestyles, and a power-knowledge center of science, control, and technology developed to guide choices in thinking and action within a meta-narrative of progress, conformity, and appropriateness. At the same time there is an "oppressiveness" of jurisdiction over thought and behavior by modern institutional arrangements, there are also possibilities of emancipation and self-actualization exemplified by the countercultural movement of the 1960s.

Modernity radically broke with the previous epoch of feudalism, leading to an unconstrained capitalized economic system and new organizational forms of social relations that Karl Polanyi wrote about so elegantly as the "great transformation." After several centuries of growth, individuals such as Jean Baudrillard, Zigmunt Bauman, and Frederick Jameson see a new sociocultural development taking hold, referred to variously as postmodernism, high modernity, or liquid times. Perhaps what reflects the postmodern state or condition is the nihilistic question, "What is the point of this?" The question takes on meaning in a contemporary vacuum of narrative and history in which the sovereign individual and his or her wants, personal opinions, and ideas are beyond reproach.[1] Underlying this sovereignty is the question of identity of the self. As we move further and further from our ancient history of close community, common values, and the intimacy of abiding social relationships, we find ourselves without substantive identity markers. A void is created that today is filled with the material values of consumer society and whatever we want to be. It is within this unanchored milieu that the "political and historical event always reaches us in a fictionalized form, in a narrative, messaged by the more or less hidden hand of political or economic purposes," comments Christopher Butler in his exploration of postmodernism (2002, 144). It is in this condition of the here and now of hyper-materialist consumerism that climate change has taken hold and our haphazard responses to it. At issue here is what are the prospects for the future cultural evolution of *Homo sapiens* given these converging crises?

This book will examine these three critical crises led by a capitalist-oriented socioeconomic system that is destroying the environment and causing changes in culture and society. The impact of capitalism has created a consumer society driven by new wants and desires promoted by increasingly individualistic orientations. We are witnessing, therefore, a fracturing of society in its many dimensions. While there is debate about whether modern society has entered a new cultural era, the world today is very different from that of only three or four decades ago.

CLIMATE CHANGE

The focus of this book is on Earth's physical changes related to human activity, especially since the arrival of the Industrial Revolution, and more recently, the consumer revolution. We have, consequently, entered the Anthropocene, a new epoch no longer governed by geological or biological time and dynamics but now by the actions of human beings. In their seminal essay in AMBIO, Steffen, Trutzen, and McNeill sum up much thinking on this new era of climate change writing, "Human activities have become so pervasive and profound that they rival the great forces of Nature and are pushing the Earth into planetary *terra incognita*" (2007, 614). Echoing their conclusion, Ian Angus, in the opening pages of his book *Facing the Anthropocene*, explains that "Earth has entered a new epoch, one that is likely to continue changing in unpredictable and dangerous ways. That's not an exaggeration or a guess: it's the central conclusion of one of the largest scientific projects ever undertaken" (2016, 29; Zalasiewicz 2010). Bill McKibben likewise recognized this change by entitling a recent book *Eaarth*, placing a second "a" in the word denoting that we now inhabit a new earth, a potentially more hostile world of our own making (2010). We have, in essence, destroyed that environmental "sweet spot" of the Holocene that allowed for civilization to form and flourish. We are now, it appears, at an experimental stage to see what consequences our actions have on various planetary systems and, in turn, on us. The year 2023 gives us a sample of those consequences with the hottest summer in world history.

The U.S. government in 2017 released its current assessment report on climate. The report concludes that the increase in major greenhouse gases is caused by anthropogenic activities.

> The atmospheric concentrations of CO_2, CH_4, and N_2O are higher now than they have been in at least the past 800,000 years. All have increased monotonically over the industrial era and are now 40%, 250%, and 20%, respectively, above their preindustrial concentrations. . . . Tropospheric ozone has increased in response to growth in precursor emissions in the industrial era. Emissions of synthetic GHGs have grown rapidly beginning in the mid-20th century . . . (Fahey et al. 2017, 87, IPCC 2022)

The essential characteristic of this new era is termed the "Great Acceleration," where rates of carbon dioxide and methane in the atmosphere rose rapidly to levels not seen prior to the beginning of the twentieth century.[2] The greatly increased acceleration of impact since the end of c II includes all aspects of human life, from the number of cars we drive, increased freshwater usage, overfishing of marine life, ocean acidification, energy consumption, and general habitat destruction.

The IPCC (Intergovernmental Panel on Climate Change) released a special report in October 2018, highlighting the threat of reaching 2°C by contrasting this increase with the 1.5°C it appears we are destined to reach (IPPC 2018). The report states that we are already seeing the consequences of a 1°C increase (over preindustrial levels) with more extreme weather, rising sea levels, and less ice and snow cover. This conclusion is supported by the recent 2021 6th IPCC report, *Climate Change 2021: The Physical Science Basis*. The report concludes in no uncertain terms, "The scale of recent changes across the climate system as a whole and the present state of many aspects of the climate system are unprecedented over many centuries to many thousands of years." That is, "Changes across a greater number of climate system components, including changes in regional climate and extremes can now be attributed to human influence" (2021, 1–8, 12). A more recent IPCC report states in no uncertain terms that climate impacts continue to worsen:

> Widespread and rapid changes in the atmosphere, ocean, cryosphere, and biosphere have occurred. Human-caused climate change is already affecting many

> weather and climate extremes in every region across the globe. This has led to widespread adverse impacts and related losses and damages to nature and people. (2022)

The conclusion is a dire clarion call that drastic increases in emissions must end immediately; otherwise, 1.5°C will be reached and surpassed on the way to 2°C with unimaginable consequences.

This 6th IPCC publication warns that further global warming cannot be stopped over the next several decades without immediate global coordinated mitigation efforts to stop carbon emissions. Of greatest concern are the rapid increase in global warming and severe weather changes, which make the time for substantial mitigation efforts now, not later. The conclusion that emissions of carbon dioxide needs to decrease by 45 percent by 2030 to reach net-zero, or nine years from now, rather than 2050 (at which point emissions must be zero and possibly necessary to pull carbon out of the atmosphere) suggests time is of the essence. The 2023 report continues, "Climatic and non-climatic risks will increasingly interact, creating compound and cascading risks that are more complex and difficult to manage." The experience of the Paris Agreement in 2015 illustrates that pledges made to mitigate emissions by various countries, especially the major industrialized countries, were not implemented. At the COP27 meeting in the Egyptian coastal city of Sharm el-Sheikh, UN secretary-general António Guterres warned that humanity is digging its own grave by not moving fast enough to bring emissions under control. Clearly, given the political-economic circumstances found in many countries, such a large and immediate decrease will present a great challenge. Any promises made at the COP 27 UN Climate Change Conference are not binding, and there is no enforcement mechanism to ensure pledges are met.

Volumes have been written about global climate change and the possible consequences for the way we have organized life on earth. Less pronounced, however, but just as significant for society are other environmental issues such as the degree of resource exploitation and habitat destruction due to economic development and urban growth. More recently, acknowledgment is offered but in a non-specific language. The IPCC Summary for Policymakers states, "non-climatic human-induced factors exacerbate current ecosystem vulnerability to climate change (very high confidence). Globally, and even within protected areas, unsustainable use of natural resources, habitat fragmentation, and ecosystem damage by pollutants increase ecosystem vulnerability to climate change" (IPCC 2022, 12). For political purposes, market-based logic and economic development are not directly addressed as drivers of climate change and environmental degradation. Yet the IPCC platform is where a critical narrative of market economics should take place.

Increasingly around the world, the debate is not exclusively about climate change but also who is responsible, what to do about it, and at what costs. The economic system and the modern way of life are taken as given by many as the embodiment of socio-cultural evolution and the hallmarks of progress. This is the essence of those who don't believe capitalism can be reformed or modified to accommodate the Green New Deal proposed by progressives. Joel Kovel, for instance, believes it is impossible to save capitalism and thus a need to transform into an *ecosocialist* society (2007). David Schweickart thinks it can be transformed into a steady-state economic democracy. He concludes, which most progressive thinkers would agree, "I have argued we must move beyond capitalism if the human species is to flourish to the full degree that our modern technologies make possible" (2010, 6750). In both cases, the authors argue for environmental sensitivity and social and economic justice through a socialist model, yet say very little about the consumer ideology that "infects" modern affluent society. A major point of this book is a critique of the power of not only capitalist production but also the development of a technologically based consumer society built primarily on material possession to define the meaning of a "good life."

Studies of the environment have become something of a cottage industry with new books coming online every year. With all the attention and discussion, most American and global populations accept, even with some skepticism, that something is crucially wrong with the Earth's environment, in particular climate change. The confusion lies for many people with the causes and, most importantly, what can be done to mitigate the negative effects of environmental change. The continuing political debate as to whether climate change is human-caused or part of a natural cycle adds to the confusion, even though it is conclusive that the degradation of the Earth System is caused by human activity. Considering the power and influence of the office of the American president, many look to the president for guidance and understanding. Former President Trump, however, professed to doubt climate change commenting, "I don't think there's a hoax. But I don't know that it's man-made" believing that China created it to hurt U.S. manufacturing. Questioning the motivation of climate scientists, he added, "Look, scientists also have a political agenda" (*New York Times*, October 15, 2018). He had on occasion commented that he didn't think it was a hoax but questioned the scientific community's consensus that climate change is not a natural phenomenon. Nevertheless, in either case, the end result most likely will be the same—a more difficult world to live in as expressed by McKibben's book, *Eaarth*.[3] The challenge for environmental writers, social scientists, and philosophers is how best to counter false claims, communicate the issues driving environmental degradation, and address possible solutions as the planet, and therefore human society, moves closer to passing the threshold of planetary boundaries of a stable, sustainable planet.[4]

The stories being told run along a continuum from the darkly apocalyptic leading to the doom of civilization to the very positive, suggesting that through new technologies and/or each individual household, neighborhood, and city doing their share to be environmentally friendly, a greener world can be created. Is doom inevitable and is individual responsibility—as citizen or corporation—enough? The question is how best to reach and then motivate people to take seriously the implications and possible consequences of changes to the Earth, and how to respond. Are the problems primarily political, economic, or cultural? Should the approach be to convince people by focusing on the problems—on the environmental, economic, or the cultural—and solutions or on our moral responsibility as the creative force impacting the planet? However the approach, and it is a combination of all three, there are serious and substantive risks involved as to how we presently live our lives if, in fact, it can no longer be business as usual.

There is a complicated set of issues at work when discussing the environment and change. The Earth is a dynamic arrangement of synergistic and interrelated systems that have throughout its existence experienced cataclysmic and devastating events. It appears stable but only from our limited timeframe of the development of agricultural civilizations 10,000 to 12,000 years ago. The Earth has had long periods of ice and snow, mass extinctions, and occasional hothouse loads of carbon dioxide in the atmosphere and the oceans. The main difference between then and now is that this latest dynamic period (since the Industrial Revolution) is primarily anthropogenic in nature, with unknown but growing consequences for the Earth System. At the same time, we have put in place a global economic system that sees the Earth as a cornucopia of infinite natural resources to be exploited with little regard for the environmental and social consequences of such actions. In our social development, society becomes alienated from the natural world, and consumers have lost a sense of the relationship between the consumption of things and the consequent degradation of nature. The idea that, somehow, as in the past, the Earth can absorb our effects and we can continue into the future behaving as we have in the past. Among many individuals, however, there is growing doubt that we can continue ad infinitum as we are presently doing.

THE IMPACT OF CAPITALISM ON NATURE AND PERCEPTION

As will be further discussed in the following two chapters, the Western world has a long history of efforts to transform nature into a cultural imaginary of order from chaos, and light from darkness. The project of civilization in many ways continues to erect an impermeable border against the natural condition or inclination of "natural man" and his animal existence. The use of the trope of "otherness" was a common approach between such early Europeans and indigenous cultures. Carolyn Merchant sees the West's "recovery project" transforming the savagery of the "Other" and Hobbes' "state of nature" into a civilized condition of a pastoral scene of farms and villages dominated by the Church and the "social contract." "[T]he primary narrative of Western culture," she writes, "has been a precipitous, tragic Fall from the Garden of Eden, followed by a long, slow, upward Recovery to convert the fallen world of deserts and wilderness into a new earthly Eden" (2004, 20). The social contract outlined by Locke was to insulate humanity from the state of nature, that is, as Tennyson put it, "Nature, red in tooth and claw," and the wildness assumed lying in the human heart. Today's developed urban and rural landscapes, in the minds of many, testify to the fruits of the recovery project.

The history of the contemporary estrangement from nature has a long pedigree indeed. One can consider a series of milestones in the history of humankind, but it was the Enlightenment of the seventeenth and eighteenth centuries that brought forth new ways of cultural, political, and economic thinking. Within such thinking physical reality was considered a machine of interrelated parts that could be understood and manipulated to serve various scientific or economic purposes, primarily the development of a new conception of an earthly Eden. Growing in consequence was awareness of the natural world, and those less civilized "Others," as service to the needs and desires of the descendants of Enlightenment thinking, those who believed they had a responsibility to realize the new Garden.

In this process a new way of existential philosophy and way of life in the West, different from our universal past, was created to support the operation of a new economy and the institutions and philosophy that underlie it. Over time, Western culture in general and American society and economy in particular gave birth to a new relationship between people and things rather than between people and nature.[5] A cultural ethos took hold, most strongly after World War II, in which the focus of social life began to revolve in earnest around the purchase and ownership of greater quantities of material possession. A major effort by business through advertising began, promising better, happier lives through the ownership of a host of labor-saving appliances and personal consumer goods. Thus was born consumer culture and the consumption society. This, in turn, has led to a greater impact on the environment than at any other time in human history as production systems extract more and more resources from the Earth, leaving behind a trail of toxic wastes, barren soils, deforested mountainsides, and polluted river valleys as testament to human ingenuity. As we developed great cities and sophisticated technologies, we have over time moved further and further away from an intimate contact with the natural world that has been a profound part of our history as a species. We have become estranged from the natural world and its rhythms through our self-imposed exile and thus often unaware or little understand the nature or extent of our impact on our world or on ourselves. That is, until now.

What have capitalism and our desires done to get us to this point? As we will discuss later in this book, capitalism is not just about making money but perhaps, more fundamentally, about changing the world, both physically and socioculturally, through the quest for the accumulation of capital. The world and all in it are affected primarily because all—people, habitat, and animals—can be turned, magically it appears, into a valued commodity to meet some designed market need. We have modified animals, such as industrialized chickens that cannot exist in the wild, in order to meet economic objectives. Through genetic engineering new versions of a species can be created, such as a new, faster-growing Atlantic salmon with two DNA sequences from Chinook salmon added to its genome. Mining, deforestation, agro-industry, water reclamation projects, and suburban sprawl have transformed nature in ways that increase human alienation from it. "Increasingly larger and larger dimensions of what was once the natural world," writes Howard Harrod in the introduction to his book, *The Animals Came Dancing*, "have become cultural artifacts and are now made available for large-scale manipulation and exploitation" (2000, xxiv). Ironically, our search for an earthly Eden has resulted in an ersatz and alienated world, one increasingly composed of strangers searching in a strangely artificial world for something, but what?[6] The main point of any discussion of environmental or social change is that we are not helpless in whatever the coming difficulties entail. We are not prisoners to the future nor just passive victims. We are agents with the capacity to think and decide what to do about the future. But it takes a firm understanding of how we got to this point and why we think the way we do. The future could be unbearable, leading to more severe climatic conditions and the collapse of society as we know it. In his recent book *The Uninhabitable Earth*, Wallace-Wells examined the possibilities of economic breakdown over worsening climate conditions. Perhaps somewhat dramatically, and perhaps not, he concludes,

> We have gotten used to setbacks on our erratic march along the arc of economic history. . . . What climate change has in store is not that kind of thing—not a Great Recession or a Great Depression but, in economic terms, a Great Dying. (2019, 119)

If one outlines various global warming scenarios, it is easy to paint a picture of deep depressions. In *Falter*, Bill McKibben likewise outlines the precarious state of the Earth, a lesson many, especially policymakers and business leaders, have yet to learn. He remarks that, "nothing slows us down—just the opposite." We worry for a while, but then other distractions pull us away from such concerns. He sees the earthly hell of Alberta's tar sands complex and the "grey, grim purgatory" of Delhi, India, but little is done to alleviate the vast problems they entail (2019). And the list goes on to add to an ever-increasing crisis and enlists an ever-increasing pessimism.

But nothing is foreordained. The future, as trite as it may sound, is up to us and what we want it to be. We just need a clear understanding based on knowledge of who and what we moderns are. There are organizations and groups that cannot fathom the idea of change from what they see as the natural outcome of human nature and creative intelligence. From this perspective, we are a materialistic and competitive species that inherently maximize our goals and outcomes, and, in this case, capitalist economy and society are the natural outcomes of our nature. Members of the corporate elite, such as the Koch brothers and the Club for Growth, are willing to spend millions of dollars in defense of the status quo. Yet, there are also numerous organizations that push back, that see history yet to be written about our present world and consider possible futures. Many (such as David Korten) believe that we can design new possibilities for a more humane-centered, less technologically and materially driven world. The contours of resistance are both of a political-economic and cultural nature, but also increasingly seen as ethical and moral issues.

POSTMODERNITY, SOCIAL RELATIONSHIPS, AND SOVEREIGN IDENTITY

Pre-contact groups such as the Tallness of Ghana, Gabra of Kenya and Ethiopia, Hmong of Vietnam, Lakota Sioux of the Great Plains, and the Kuna of Panama all exhibited a close set of intimate relationships based on community and kinship expressed in various socio-religious rituals. Raymond Firth focused on a small island horticultural society in the Solomon Islands of Melanesia called the Tikopia. As found in most horticultural societies, at the heart of the Tikopian culture was the intimate connection among kinship descent. It was the sacred relationship between mother's brother and guiding his nephew through his manhood ceremonies within a web of kinship (1936). Under such pre-modern or traditional circumstances, there was a taken-for-granted notion that the everyday reality is fixed, shared, and stable. While there was a great sense of security and belonging, it also did not allow much deviation from the instituted norms. Escaping the strictures of conventional expectations and developing a consciousness of freedom is the birth of modernity. If the traditional world of community, tribe, and heritage was one of established identity-giving authority, as Ron Eyerman put it, the modern one is of active, rational individual agents now open to new influences (1992). The fixed world of feudal Europe, for example, began over the seventeenth and eighteenth centuries to give way to greater openness and expression of possibilities, at least for certain classes and regions.

Whereas production for accumulation was the cornerstone of the modern period, the focus today has shifted to an emphasis on consumption. Core values such as individualism, choice, and freedom are enhanced by new technologies and accessible commodities. The automobile, microwave, TV, the personal computer and internet, the transition from tenements and apartments to the single-family home in the suburbs (Levittown), the credit card, the i-everything, and big-box department stores all supported by massive advertising ushered in modern consumer society and the celebration of individualism through materialism. Culturally, to ask those in the advanced affluent countries to change their ways and means of living will confront the conventionally accepted narrative of what the "good life" means, yet it is here where an opportunity to confront the consumerist narrative lies since research suggests materialism does not bring happiness nor satisfaction. Additionally, the growth of consumer society expressing the values of materialism plays a significant role in the environmental crisis. In order to consume, production must take place. Mineral extraction, processing, and transportation, as well as manufacturing, all depend on the exploitation of natural resources and fossil fuels. Nevertheless, as will be discussed later, the consumer goods owned become part of the signifiers of who the individual is, especially under conditions of weak social relationships, institutions, and personal socio-historic legacy.

The problem at hand is convoluted and perplexing due to variations in environmental change—from global warming to resource and habitat depletion—that is taking place during a period of both the globalization of the dominant economic system of capitalism and a global transformation in culture, society, and identity. There appears a vast and substantive movement of ideas, perspectives, and social relationships away from a world of tradition, psychic security, and predictability, leading to social change, anxiety, and uncertainty found within a world of consumerism and the immediacy of an individualistic sense of "this moment, of me." Zygmunt Bauman refers to this present era as "liquid times" in which fear and anxiety rule our "delinked" lives in terms of our relationship to each other and society (2006). This anxiety is made more palpable or profound as the innate human connection of one to another is weakened by the transit of society across a threshold into a postmodern world increasingly governed by tertiary relationships; that is, relationships mediated by social media and technology delinked from family, kin, and physical community.[7]

In *The Art of Loving*, Eric Fromm paid tribute to the costs of our socioeconomic system. From his perspective, the inhabitants of our modern world are "transformed into a commodity, experiencing his life forces as an investment which must bring him/her the maximum profit obtainable under existing market conditions. Human relations," he goes on to articulate,

> are essentially those of alienated automatons, each basing his security on staying close to the herd, and not being different in thought, feeling or action. While everybody tries to be as close as possible to the rest, everybody remains utterly alone, pervaded by the deep sense of insecurity, anxiety and guilt which always results when human separateness cannot be overcome. (1956, 72)

In the search for meaning, money and power become a utility for a variety of "escapist addictions," such as material indulgence and increased isolating self-centeredness.

As we drift into the "loneliness of an unlived life" that Fromm wrote of so elegantly, we find a social world little understood. Sociopolitical institutions, for instance, operated in "pre-liquid" times to provide a degree of stability, security, and certainty regarding social norms, values, identity, and knowledge. These institutions in their stability and acceptance by most as legitimate have given way to a new reality. The value of social institutions (such as universities) is increasingly called into question.[8] The political system and its parties are increasingly ideologically rigid and partisan, calling into question the legitimacy of the U.S. presidency itself and the bedrock of democracy. This includes the foundation of the rule of law, the Supreme Court, now seen as radically partisan. The certainty of knowledge itself is challenged where feelings, skepticism, and opinions are taken as equal to factual knowledge and truth. It is as if the descendants of the Enlightenment have turned on the creators of this world of science, empiricism, and, as Kant phrased it, *supere aude* (the dare to know). Too many have hunkered down into an insular worldview bordering on an inability to engage the world as it truly is. This has been most popularized with the term "fake news." How difficult it will be to evaluate and offer solutions to the critical problems of culture and environment we face under such conditions of fear, doubt, and mistrust, and mediated increasingly through impersonal social media technology, ideological belief, or political rhetoric.

We need a firm grasp of the extent of the issues that relate to the Earth's precarious condition. One of the primary challenges in understanding the issues is to get beyond ideological assumptions about climate change or the motivations of those who work within climate science. Likewise, we must recognize that capitalism and the market do not and cannot provide all the answers we seek. Corporations and the market are driven primarily by the self-interest of profit. Ideology as a set of abstract ideas and concepts supporting a worldview or a way of interpreting aspects of reality can have a profound impact on people's thinking and judgment. The problem with much ideology is that it generally provides a binary opposition of viewpoints; that is, yes-no, I'm right and you are wrong, regardless of what the facts may be. This is exacerbated by media, especially social media and the information bubbles they create (we only listen to people who agree with us). Such a dogmatic approach to the matters in question leads only to incontrovertible (but questionable) truths at a time when we need honesty, clarity, and the acceptance of empirically based scientific evidence. There is a compelling need to move beyond received truths and realistically see the world and our place in it, not as we think it is.[9] Beyond ideology and dogma lies truthfulness, and it is through probity and objective appraisal of the world that we can develop a vision of what kind of world we want and quite literally need. Recognition of urgency, most environmentalists and others would say, means time is of the essence. It is possible now or never to begin debate and reach for transformative solutions.

Unquestionably, the point is that we face a series of significant challenges, all of which are either directly or indirectly related. Beyond physical science, related environmental challenges include the economic, cultural, and political realms. Pope Francis recognized the challenge to the present state of the world, writing in his encyclical *Laudato Sí*,

> But a sober look at our world shows that the degree of human intervention, often in the service of business interests and consumerism, is actually making our earth less rich and beautiful, ever more limited and greyer, even as technological advances and consumer goods continue to abound limitlessly. We seem to think that we can substitute an irreplaceable and irretrievable beauty with something which we have created ourselves. (2015)

As the Pope seems to suggest, it is difficult to remain positive and optimistic considering the state of the world, if only because the future seems so confusing and uncertain.[10]

THE REALITY OF FUTURE POSSIBILITIES

However, the most fundamental and serious of challenges are imagining and thinking about future possibilities. It is difficult to think about substantive change to our philosophies of life and living when the consequences of today may not be realized for years to come, although the new special IPCC report believes the future is not that far off; in fact, it is here now. This includes a growing sense of social, psychological, and political dysfunction. Far too frequently, we tend to think primarily in present-tense terms and short-term goals. Why sacrifice for an uncertain and distant future? Yet, among many people, there is an uneasiness, a feeling that something is wrong, our trajectory for the future in doubt. Our everyday world is full of uncertainty, seemingly chaotic, relentlessly complex, and, if we give it enough thought, one which leads to feelings of disquietude or misgivings. We need the world to make sense, to be complete and orderly; yet, it seems too many to be now a series of fragmented and unrelated parts. Of this situation Bauman remarked, "no sailor can boast of having found a safe, let alone risk free, itinerary" (2001, 62). The prevailing ideologies and meta-narratives that stitched a relatively holistic and stable worldview, while deeply believed in by many, now seem to be far less satisfying and convincing than in the past. Or as Baudrillard noted, somehow, in some fashion, the world appears a simulacrum of the real thing rather than the real thing, a facsimile or unidimensional (1988). Who are we and where are we going are the unspoken questions to which there are no readily compelling answers. This leads to the rise of various strains of fundamentalism of a more pejorative type. Rather than a reliance on tradition or external verities, here fundamentalism is seen as dogma, the exclusive source of incontrovertible truth. This could be seen as all immigrants are a threat, liberals hate America, socialism is bad, or America is, with apologies to Candide, the best of all possible worlds, yet unwilling to see reality as it really is.

Upon what rests the fate of the Earth and the viability of human society? Technology can certainly play a problem-solving role, but technology must be immersed within a paradigm of enhancing the social good and a deeper appreciation for the richness of all life forms rather than technology for its own sake or "just because we can." Technology is generally more about control rather than enhancing or embracing humanity for the common good, as Michael and Joyce Huesemann write in their book, *Techno-Fix.* They conclude that, "The direction of science and technology must no longer be guided by the outdated values of power, control, and exploitation but rather by the values of social and environmental harmony, cooperation and mutual enhancement" (2011, 285). Their review of the history and progress of technology suggests that technology, unless tightly controlled and focused, cannot solve the problems we face without creating new and often unforeseen problems.

The economy likewise has an important role to play beyond an increase in GDP and profit-making. Rather, the economy should focus on meeting the basic needs and well-being of every individual beyond some algorithmic cost factor. Is human life, then, an emergent property that finds its fullest or ultimate expression in a complex yet intimate relationship with the natural world of which we are a part? Or are we nothing more than competitive material animals ever in search of the next convenience or greater profit? A broader and interrelated difficult question to ask is whether technology and our present social order enhance or detract from the social and psychological evolution of our species? Clearly, capitalism has brought a degree of material comfort to many people but not without social and environmental costs. Without looking objectively at the costs, many subtle yet profound, of a capitalist-oriented world, it will be difficult to develop effective thinking on the meaning of those costs or how to counter them.

The American federal administration under Donald Trump added an additional layer of difficulty to many people's ability to synthesize the profound environmental changes already in place or the future consequences of such change. Even though his administration pulled out of the Paris Accord and members such as the former Attorney General Jeff Sessions, and former EPA Administrator Scott Pruitt are climate change skeptics, the government did release the fourth National Climate Assessment in November 2017 (although the administration downplayed it). The basic conclusion of the report was that human activity is responsible for the increased greenhouse gas emissions leading to an increase in global warming and significant changes in the earth's physical operating system. Yet science met with skepticism and denial, and in many social quarters still does. Much of the opposition, Dunlap and McCright are convinced, comes from efforts to defend the fossil fuel basis for the development of Western civilization. This involves, they write, "A staunch commitment to free markets and disdain of governmental regulations reflect the conservatives' political ideology that is almost universally shared by the climate change denial community" (2011, 146). In other words, deniers are defending a system that has provided great rewards for corporate interests but, admittedly, also provided the basis for a higher standard of living for many in a very unequal, poverty-stricken world. Nevertheless, denial also confronts the fear of social change in values, narrative, and cultural meaning of new identity formation, in other words, the growth of humanism.

We are at a point in human history where the human condition needs answers or at least a direction to focus upon to deal with the cul-de-sac of fear, anxiety, and confusion over the meaning of the life we have created and is now threatened. We have reached a point in our intellectual development that warrants an assessment of our accomplishments and what they offer in our search for meaning. In *Laudato Sí*, Pope Francis also articulates this present situation. "Many things must change course, but it is we human beings above all who need to change. We lack an awareness of our common origin, of our mutual belonging, and of a future to be shared with everyone." Francis believes, "This basic awareness would enable the development of new convictions, attitudes and forms of life. A great cultural, spiritual and educational challenge stands before us, and it will demand that we set out on the long path of renewal" (2016). We have, in other words, tremendous amounts of data and information but, one might argue, not the wisdom of what to do next—but we have the potential.

The genesis of this book is an attempt to locate *the ultimate source or engine* that has propelled the global community into the environmental crisis we now face. Although the environmental issue is most obvious, it is not, however, the only crisis humanity faces. We also have a crisis of culture and society, as outlined earlier, of individual confidence and meaning in an increasingly alienated world. The elements that compose modern mass society have grown in complexity to seemingly take on a life of their own beyond human subjects. David Bidney, writing in the aftermath of World War II, outlined the modern condition of who or what is in control. In the *American Anthropologist*, he wrote, "Once human ideals, social institutions and technical inventions are regarded as impersonal 'superorganic' entities with a force of persistence and development of their own, independent of their human creators, it seems plausible to disregard human agents as the primary determining factor" (1946, 535). In the movement of history we have shifted, seemingly out of control, from an intimate world of kinship and community based on the interconnected web of social relationships to one where humans become increasingly the object of external bureaucratic, technological, and institutional forces. What should be of concern is what happens to those human ideals and sense of humanity if the promises of the seemingly uncontrollable forces of computerization and artificial intelligence are, rather than liberating, a prison.

To generalize capitalism as the cause or that we think of nature from a utilitarian viewpoint may be valid, but we need to understand the relationship between capitalism as an economic system and consumerism as a cultural process. Modern societies and culture evolved over time with capitalism as the driver, but how did we move from general basic needs for improving our lives to what is thought of by many today as hyper-consumerism, where desires become needs?[11] It seems clear that beginning in the 1950s, advanced post-industrial society, such as the United States, crossed a divide into a cultural landscape governed by the desire for and ownership of material possessions that provide psycho-cultural comfort and security. One hallmark of capitalism is the need to accumulate wealth via profit and to increase profit it is necessary to increase commodity production. Today, such a landscape is contoured by advertising and marketing to convince society of its new needs and wants, on the one hand, and, on the other, that growth and expansion of our consumer world is inevitable and good. The point here is that while this book focuses mainly on the culture of consumerism, it is not the consumer that is the primary culprit of environmental degradation but the system of corporate over-production in search of profit. In the search for profit we can account for other "human losses" such as the estrangement from nature, tradition, and the intimacy of social relationships. The present era of globalization in association with sociocultural evolution of mass industrial society has created the conditions that drive the need for consumption encouraged by production. This, then, is the hegemonic ideology in which we are entrapped.

We have invested so much in our present reality that it is difficult to imagine a different, let alone better, world. How can we move from a consumption-based capitalist system, convinced of the comfort it brings? What would happen to all the jobs and incomes, and how do we think about ourselves? What does it mean to say we need fewer material possessions and more intimate social connections? According to Bidney, an anthropologist who focused on modern culture, there are two types of crises that relate to survival. One crisis relates to survival or the existential question of "to be or not to be," while the other is what he terms an "axiological" or value crisis. Here the pertinent question, and one relevant to the theme of this book, is "*how to be, what kind of life is worth living and preserving*" (1967, 355). The question of "who we are" is linked to the value system we hold. He adds that, "A society may also experience survival crises when its culture is inadequate to cope with the problems of its social or natural environment," as we see today in American society. The axiological crises, in contrast, develop when there are conflicting social interests or divided cultural epistemology systems. The climate crisis, from Bidney's perspective, occurs in a divided society and the "unwillingness of various groups to co-operate for the common good soon makes for the suspension of normal, social life and imperials the life of the community" as it appears to be the case globally and in the United States in particular (356). As the crisis of modern living deepens and the environmental problems continue to grow, we must begin a dialogue and develop a new narrative of human agency and decision-making based upon a new set of values that, many would say, recaptures the basic elements of our humanity. Bidney, following the German philosopher Ernst Cassirer, reminds us that culture is (or should be) a "value-charged term connoting the spiritual life of man and comprising all moral, aesthetic, and intellectual achievements," all else an "embodiment" of cultural values and thus secondary (383).

Cynicism seemingly runs rampant in our thinking about such possibilities. What happens to identity as it revolves around wealth, power, and status centered on the economic status quo, involving physical and social mobility, and the symbolic appearance of status being more significant than the actual status? Consumerism operationalizes our aspirations to be seen as successful and powerful. But humanity today, led by the advanced affluent nations, finds itself now at a crossroads, an intersection for decision-making regarding the efficacy of such aspirations. As the various trends outlined in this book suggest, a discussion of future possibilities is imperative if we are not only to survive because the human species will survive, but how we will survive and what kind of new world we will inhabit. Given contemporary national and international politics and vested economic interests, many assume climate change and environmental degradation will continue, as will the status quo of social change. The choice for humanity is to begin the process of adaptation now or wait until it is too late for rational discourse and planning, at which point it will be every nation and society for itself. Can the few winners survive in a world consisting mainly of losers? That is, Is Speth's scenario of a "fortress world" of the affluent drawing a figurative moat around their affluence releasing globally all others to their fate viable (2008)?

The global environmental crisis has forced us to confront the stark reality that capitalist economics and related cultural values are a destructive force that not only consumes natural resources and destroys animal life but also our common humanity. But, perhaps more importantly, the constructed reality brought forth by capitalism—its economics, philosophy, and science—has broken our relationship with and integration into the natural world. This is reminiscent of C. P. Snow's two divided cultures, the sciences on one side of the divide and the arts and humanities on the other shore.

One of the more profound ecological philosophers of the late twentieth century is Thomas Berry. Berry's *The Dream of the Earth* is an examination, or ultimately a search beyond the "pathology of our times," for the true measure of what it means to be human on a living planet. It should not be the self-indulgence of our superiority over this planet and its life forms. Berry sees this dream of our ascendence, at the same time cultural and spiritual, as problematic since the "dream" is now infused within our particular cultural construction under capitalism, what he refers to as a pathology or a false human nature. "Whatever our gains in terms of scientific advances or in our industrial economy, neither of these is very helpful," he maintained, "in establishing an integral presence to the more profound depths of our own being or into the more powerful forces shaping both the universe and the planet on which we live" (2006, 199).[12]

Given the dire nature of the trend of climate change, Is geo-engineering and science the only alternative solution to atmospheric carbon loading as some suggest (see Schneider 2008 for an overview of geo-engineering)? Geo-engineering's attraction is that it is technological and scientific in nature, in support of the status quo, and limits the need for substantive cultural or economic change. This is in contrast to an Earth Community approach argued by many others. The future is pointing the way toward ecological and cultural principles of personal relationships that meet the needs of both humanity and the Earth Community of co-inhabitants. This is expressed, anticipating Pope Francis' *Laudato Sí,* by Thomas Berry in *The Great Work*, as a "mutually enhancing human presence within an ever-renewing organic-based Earth community" (1999, 201). Berry, who lived to the age of ninety-four, believed he was witnessing a "terminal" era of rapacious economics and human indifference to the realities of a spiritually induced physical world that will eventually lead to the "ecozoic" era of human and environmental sustainability. He adds in *The Dream of the Earth* of our special responsibility, not just to ourselves but to the magnificence of creation:

> The excitement of life and the sustaining of psychic vigor are evoked by our participation in this magnificent process. Even before we give expression to any intellectual statement about the natural world, we stand in awe at the stars . . . , at the earth in its shaping of the sea . . . the human as that being in whom this grand diversity of the universe celebrates itself in conscious self-awareness. (2006, 198)

I can personally testify that I stand in awe of the power of life as I witness the ever-ongoing chase of the seasons by wedges of wild geese flying overhead, a behavior they have exhibited for millions of years. As the only consciously self-aware species on Earth, the challenge we face is the special responsibility to confront what we have done to this planet and what we need to do to save the rich diversity of the tapestry of life unlike anywhere else in the known universe. Berry reinforces this prescription in his essay "The Viable Human" where he believes, "to be viable, the human community must move from its present anthropocentric norm to a geocentric norm of reality and value" (1995, 8).

In the last chapter, we will discuss the need for a change in consciousness, a new meaning for being a social being and a new way of living. To realize Berry's Earth Community, it will necessitate a vast global movement, not of resistance but more importantly of transformation. A mass movement of resistance is important to confront the powerful elite forces of great influence and determination, but there needs to be a concurrent mass movement of transformation informed by an awareness, philosophy, and demand for a new way of ordering a more satisfactory integrated life. Can we get back to celebrating the complexity and mystery of the diversity of life on Earth and recreate a wonderment of the cycles of life that continue to flow and link all life into a tapestry we call Earth as our ancestors once did? Or are we forever shackled to the latest iPhone and Hollywood blockbuster inside our artificial cocoon of "human nature?" The great challenge is not only to bring climate change under control but also to change our way of thinking about ourselves and our place in the universe.

The following chapters attempt to outline the significant issues as we confront a changing environment and social world. This book is a journey that begins in chapter 2, examining the pre-modern world where community encapsulated both human and nonhuman life forms with little separation between them. Animals, for example, were important food sources but were seen through a prism of spiritual meaning as fellow kin with agency and personhood. The following chapters take us from our perception of reality as a machine to changes in the climate and environment due to the search for something beyond the practicalities of resource extraction for production that capitalism's participants possibly do not understand. For example, Elon Musk, beyond making cars, cares about his wealth and its increase. Why? It is impossible for him under any circumstance to spend even a fraction of it. Why the need for more, to what unfathomed end? The chapter on consumer society illustrates the basic dynamic underlying social structure, and the next chapter attempts to explain what has happened to the individual's identity and social relationships as all the preceding falls at his/her doorstep. Finally, the concluding chapter summarizes our journey and attempts to point to future possibilities.

NOTES

1. Zygmunt Bauman references Cornelius Castoriadis and asks, "What is wrong with the society we live in that it stopped questioning itself." Furthermore, he wonders, "This is a kind of society which no longer recognizes any alternative to itself and thereby feels absolved from the duty to examine, demonstrate, justify (let alone prove) the validity of its outspoken and tacit assumptions" (2007, 22–23). Opinions no longer need to be supported by facts; feelings and beliefs are enough; that is, my faceless opinion is as valid as facts are.

2. See Angus' *Facing the Anthropocene* for a discussion of when the Anthropocene began (2016). The importance of this recently defined era is exemplified by new journals such as *Anthropocene* and *The Anthropocene Review*.

3. A recent article by David Abel of the Boston Globe records the Arctic changes in the town of Barrow, Alaska. His report clearly illustrates the environmental and Arctic Ocean changes due to warming weather and ocean conditions. The Heartland Institute can argue that these changing conditions are not due to human activity, but the changes are real nevertheless for the inhabitants of Barrow and other Arctic zones.

4. Johan Rockstrom and colleagues at the Stockholm Resilience Centre identified in 2009 nine processes that influence the stability and resilience of the global climate system. Each boundary is associated with thresholds of risk: zone of safety, zone of uncertainty and increased risk, and zone of high risk. Reaching the ultimate threshold, it is believed, will generate large-scale precipitous or irreversible environmental changes (2009).

5. As mentioned earlier, this book is not Eurocentric in its intention. The issues raised are found most advanced in the post-industrial consumer societies of the West, primarily most notably in the United States. It is in these societies where

climate change and shifts in social relationships, conceptions of self, and capitalist political-economy dynamics are most pronounced and offer the greatest object lesson.

6. In the *Ecologist*, Bill McKibben recognized the challenge. He wrote, "The environmentalist Alan Durning found that compared to 1950, the average American family now owns twice as many cars, uses 21 times as much plastic, and travels 25 times farther by air. Gross domestic product per capita has tripled since 1950 in the US. We obviously eat more calories. And yet—the satisfaction meter seems not to have budged. More Americans say their marriages are unhappy, their jobs are hideous, and that they don't like the place where they live" (2007).

7. Increasingly, people are communicating through technology and social media such as Snapchat, Instagram, Twitter, and Facebook. As many students have indicated, the preference is to text messages and keep the message short and to the point. Actual talking by phone is considered "messy" and ultimately too time-consuming. Many students agree that social media communication gives the individual a degree of power and control over both the message, its delivery, and the interaction.

8. Greg Lukianoff and Jonathan Haidt summed up their research in a current *Atlantic* essay, stating, "A movement is arising, undirected and driven largely by students, to scrub campuses clean of words, ideas, and subjects that might cause discomfort or give offense" (August 2015).

9. Of course, in a postmodern world, it has been pointed out, what "truly is" is itself controversial. As Graham Greene once quipped, reality in our century is not something to be faced.

10. Clearly, progress has been made in many areas. Global poverty has decreased, and many have found middle-class lifestyles, health care, and disease control markedly improved over the last couple of decades. Technological achievements have benefited businesses and consumers alike. On the other hand, political instability internationally and hyper-partisan politics nationally, terrorism, domestic violence, and mass shootings give many apprehensive feelings of anxiety and gloom. More than ever, the world seems dominated by disruptive impersonal forces beyond the comprehension and control of most people. It would not be unfair to ask what all this portends for the future.

11. For example, during the holidays, an urgent need is created in which parents in department stores will fight over obtaining the latest toy for their children as if the child does not receive that particular toy, the parent has failed. Or consider the after Thanksgiving stampede to purchase discounted consumer goods. One would be hard-pressed to say these events have no meaning beyond the desire to purchase gifts for loved ones. A question we will tackle is why do people, more so in the United States than possibly elsewhere, feel so compelled to engage in such a frenzy of shopping. What ulterior motives are there for such behavior?

12. Berry believes that we no longer control the forces we have unleashed under the pathology of capitalism. The dream of progress and a reformulation of the Earth, "Use of the term supreme pathology can be justified by the observation that the

change that is taking place in the present is not simply another historical transition or another cultural transformation. Its order of magnitude is immensely more significant in its nature and in its consequences" (2006, 206). Before the word took on its meaning today, Berry was thinking of the Anthropocene: "We are indeed closing down the major life systems of the planet" (206).

Chapter 2

Nature as Projection and Construct

The Meaning of Nature in the Mindscape of Culture

Although humans have, since the beginning of our species, interacted with the natural world, how we approach nature has always been subject to different interpretations and meanings. To appreciate the contemporary relationship with nature and understand what needs to change, it is important to review the cultural history of the meaning of nature in the actions of various societies in time and space. This chapter reviews the human–animal nexus, that is, how animals and nature were (and remain in many cases) perceived by various indigenous communities. How indigenous communities related to the animal world suggests they had a deeper appreciation for the natural world in general. Given the dire straits of our environmental crisis, we may learn from indigenous cultures what is required to repair our relationship with nature. With a fuller understanding of the human–nature connection, we may find new ways to govern environmental policies to protect the natural world and its living and non-living resources.

The history of the Earth can be read in the sedimentary upheavals of canyon lands or in the drilled ice cores of Greenland or Antarctica. Just as importantly, the history of the Earth is in the thinking by *Homo sapiens* who have physically confronted the earth for hundreds and thousands of years. The story of the Earth cannot be told without telling the story of humanity and its search for order and meaning on the one hand and survival on the other, as it approached nature. For much of our history, this story was mediated through direct experience, folklore, and religion, followed much later by philosophy and science. In his comprehensive overview of Western civilization's quest to understand its relationship with nature, Clarence Glacken sums up, in *Traces on the Rhodian Shore*, the West's unique search. He observed that from the early Greeks through eighteenth-century Europe,

> Even in antiquity some thinkers viewed cultural development in terms of a series of stages from a presumed remote origin to the present, a view that implied that cultures could be understood with only casual references to the physical environment. The chief emphasis was on man, his mind, his senses, his techniques, his inventiveness, which, in the acquisition of the arts and sciences, led him from one stage to the next. (1967, 6)

We have paid today a price for such a perspective given the environmental crises we have created. But for most of indigenous history, the environment could only be mediated through an animistic belief that animals, and indeed nature itself, existed and shared some existential qualities that absorbed them all into a single holistic tapestry.

THE HOME WORLD

The majesty and sumptuousness of our home are often lost among the distractions and noise of the practicalities of everyday modern life. The bubbles we live in have, essentially, no horizons beyond the next demand for attention. Yet, there are questions to be addressed as we think about the human impact upon nature, given the precarious state the planet is in. History suggests that with the development of civilization, humans became aware of their power to modify the environment and control the animals found within. Greek and Roman philosophers' ideas about nature recognized that culture was in many ways intertwined with environmental change but generally in positive ways. For humans to survive nature, they had to experience the power of human endeavor to change, but the consequences of such actions are qualitatively different for a foraging society relative to an agriculturally based hierarchical social system such as the Greeks, Romans, or Egyptians. Differences yet again come into play when considering the beginning of industrial society and capitalism, where nature is transformed into a valuable market commodity to realize monetary gain. Glacken understood that with the advent of the rise of human culture at whatever station of development, nature lost its "naturalness," its own rhyme and reason and began a journey of forced transformation, more integrative in many indigenous communities and more dominated in the developing cities and states of the world (2008).

For most of human history, the physical earth was only as big as the distant horizon, and its splendor and majesty were only as sight or imagination allowed for our thinking. If the horizon was transcended, it was through myth and apocryphal stories imagined in the minds of shamans and elders, as among the Greeks and their stories about Pan, the goat-man lord of the woods one dreaded to meet along a forest path. Then on December 7, 1972, a crew member of the Apollo 17 voyage to the moon turned around and took the first full-view photograph of planet Earth. Against the inky backdrop of space Earth stood out in blue and white, the image of a vibrant and living planet. All the other planets of our solar system—from the remote, cold depths of Pluto to the stark contrast between night and day, hot and cold of Mercury—are relatively empty and without the spark that makes the home planet alive and unique. As far as we know from our science and exploration of the solar system, the tree of life, as Holmes Rolston has phrased it, has taken hold only on our planet. We are, essentially, alone against the blackness of the universe and are, in this regard, special.

A brief look at our world illustrates the depth and complexity of its uniqueness. Over the millennia life on Earth has evolved into tremendous diversity, from the stupendous 170-ton blue whales to the nearly invisible microorganisms that live in the conjunctiva canal of our eyes. The uniqueness of life on Earth is not only in size or function but also in the mystery of how some species live out their life cycles. The human species essentially swims in a sea of life's mysteries and wonders. The female Green turtle, for instance, after ten to twenty-five years of ocean living to reach sexual maturity, will return to her natal beach exclusively to lay her eggs where the cycle will begin anew, a process that is estimated to be almost 150 million years old. Of all the sandy beaches available in all the world, she will return to the exact beach where she hatched so many years before. The mature salmon is a saltwater fish that, after five years of open sea life, will return to its freshwater natal stream, sometimes hundreds of miles upstream, to lay her eggs.

These great events can be duplicated many times by other species such as the bar-tailed godwit. In 2007, bird migration specialist Robert Gill with the U.S. Geological Survey implanted transmitters on godwits (that weigh only twelve ounces in the palm of your hand) and found they travel over 7,000 miles non-stop across the Pacific Ocean. How do they manage to do that remains a great mystery! Since then, ornithologists have found that many birds routinely fly several thousands of miles during their migration pattern. The four-generation stage of the Monarch butterfly's 2,000-mile migration cycle between Mexico and Canada remains a mystery yet to be uncovered. The fourth generation born in Canada finds its way to the Sierra Madre Mountains in Mexico, a place it has never been, and starts the cycle once again. So too is the wonder of the communication dance of the bumblebee. How is it we should think about the existence of multicolored parrots that inhabit tropical forests? There are, in essence, encyclopedias full of the wonders and mysteries of animal life on this world. These wonders of nature should, in some fashion, be important to our understanding, as co-residents, of how we should approach placing meaning on all life, not just our own.

More than anything, Earth is a water world. Most of the world is covered with water, about 71 percent of the Earth's surface. Of that number 96 percent is ocean, a saltwater world for tens of thousands of species. Of the 4 percent that is freshwater, only half of that amount is readily available for terrestrial life; the rest is held captive in ice caps, glaciers, and permanent snow. Glaciers are enormous rivers of frozen water covering about 10 percent of Earth's landmass and store about 75 percent of the world's freshwater. The largest glacier is the Lambert-Fisher Glacier in Antarctica, which is 250 miles long and in places 60 miles wide. The Taku Glacier near Juneau, Alaska, is the world's thickest glacier at over 5,000 feet thick. What is interesting about glaciers for climate scientists is that they contain a frozen record of climatic and atmospheric events covering hundreds of thousands of years.

Although glaciers are frozen rivers that travel at various speeds toward an exit, the world's populations rely on running rivers such as the Nile or Mississippi Rivers for transportation, energy, irrigation, and other uses. The Mississippi, for example, is over 2,000 miles long, stretching from a tiny creek in northern Minnesota to the Gulf of Mexico at New Orleans, Louisiana. The Nile River is 4,200 miles long and the longest in the world. Along its banks empires and civilizations have risen and fallen for 5,000 years. With the Mekong, Amazon, Indus, and Yangtze (among many others), rivers are the arteries along which humans have built cities, trading posts, and culture and its attributes have spread and diffused among various peoples over thousands of years.

Over the eons of time vast forests have also grown to cover valleys, river plains, and mountainsides, providing habitat for untold thousands of species. Interspersed among the forests and mountains are huge, seemingly unending grasslands, and where land meets the sea, estuaries, swamps, and wetlands where so much life begins. The grasslands of the American Great Plains provided habitat for the American bison that, according to Francis Parkman, one of the first whites to witness the buffalo herds on the Great Plains of Missouri and Kansas in 1846, in his book *The Oregon Trail*, claimed they migrated by the millions from horizon to horizon. He reported feeling the ground shake and then hearing the thunderous herds as they moved from prairie grass fields to new pasture (1985). The early seventeenth-century colonists of Virginia reported seeing passenger pigeons blacked the skies above Chesapeake Bay for hours on end. In 1614, Ralph Hamar of the Chesapeake Bay colony declared, "in winter beyond number or imagination, my selfe have seene three or foure houres together flockes in the aire, so thicke that even they have shaddowed the skie from us" (quoted in Wright 1911, 430). Each year for thousands of years, caribou in Canada and wildebeest in Kenya move as living rivers from season to season in search of calving grounds or new grasslands.

This story of the fecundity and exuberance of life found in forest, plain, and bay can be recounted around the world and celebrated for its vastness and diversity. Writing of the celebration of life on Earth, Thomas Berry, an early proponent of deep ecology, recognized the Earth as an unparalleled and remarkable planet. "The more we learn about the Earth the more clearly we see it as a privileged planet, a creation and the homeland of a multitude of living beings . . . a world of wonder, magnificence, and mystery for the unending delight of the human mind and imagination," he wrote in *The Great Work* (1999, 22). Berry also believed that human beings, as that species most self-aware and exhibiting a consciousness unlike any other species, has a special responsibility to the planet, one to uphold the majesty and grandeur of creation. Indigenous animists of many cultures see such a connection between themselves and living species around them, recognizing a commonality of personhood and a "responsibility" of respect through ritual and ceremony.

The natural world exudes a grandeur in its complexity and relational intricacy between species. What we see around us today is the legacy of millions of years of a dynamic Earth and the evolution of life form diversity taking hold in every conceivable niche, from the black, oxygen-deprived ocean depths to the boiling, toxic waters of Yellowstone's geysers. Our approach to this singularly dynamic living planet is twofold: a rational, scientific, and positivist view that sees inter-related ecosystems (either in an instrumental or environmental science sense) and those seeing our world as a community of co-inhabitants sharing an organic common good (in an environmental ethics or metaphysical sense). In a letter to Olaus Murie, the naturalist Sigurd Olsen professed a need to broadcast the importance of maintaining a spiritual connection to nature. He wrote that his charge was to "keep the faith alive, give people something to hold to, something to fight for that is bigger than politics, bigger than the problems the world is constantly facing, something in the way of a philosophical concept that lies at the root of any happiness the race can find." He believed his charge was to bring back that sense of curiosity and wonder of the natural world that we are born with yet often lose as adults, writing, "I also know that, being deep within us, their latent glow can be fanned to flame again by awareness and an open mind" (1997). From his vantage point in northern Minnesota, he felt he could hear the "music of the spheres." Even though we have great science, most of us have lost that urge that moved Olsen.

THE MULTIVALENCE OF NATURE

Anthropologists have been engaged either directly or indirectly for much of their history in the debate over the position of humans in nature. In Western culture, the separation of nature and culture into distinct and immutable spheres is informed by the Western tradition of conceptualizing reality in a series of binary oppositions, such as mind–body, civilized–savage, and subject–object. The most fundamental opposition is nature as chaos versus civilization as order. Indigenous communities are likewise thought of as oppositions, either noble environmentalists or indifferent exploiters of resources. The reality of the pre-modern, traditional world is much more nuanced with the dichotomous boundaries between nature and society being less clear. Many indigenous cultures used nature as a resource but approached their use of it with a different attitude, one of respect or caution or both.

One significant difference between the societies of the pre-modern and the industrialized, capitalist world we inhabit is that these older more traditional societies had a relative balance between relatively inefficient technologies and various ideas (cultural, religious, spiritual) about their relationship to the world.[1] Greatest connection between nature and humans was found in societies engaged in hunting and foraging as a major subsistence activity, but so too is such intimacy found among pastoral and horticultural societies with their deep knowledge of the properties of animals and plants. During periods of pig slaughter, for example, among the Tsembaga Maring of New Guinea, such actions only took place under ritualized and ceremonial conditions of special circumstances, conveying a significance to the animal.[2] As animists, the Maring believed there were many spirits found in streams, trees, and the forest that needed to be propitiated through care and ritual. Care had to be taken so as not to anger the animistic spirits; otherwise, they could withhold their gifts (i.e., resources).

The experience of being human in this world tends to reflect the inconsistency of mind and contradiction as we attempt to make sense of the realities we confront. Modern science and much environmental studies rest upon a priori assumptions regarding nonhuman life. Donald Griffin argues in his book *Animal Minds* that assertions of animals as "mindless automatons" are but unproven dogma that require degrees of empirical evidence (2002). The anthropological approach to human–animal relations has been, until recently either a functionalist or symbolic form of analysis. Functionalists view animals primarily as meeting subsistence needs, whereas symbolic analysis considers animals as symbols for metaphors about human society. A more recent approach is recognizing and accepting animals as intelligent, sentient beings with agency. That is, indigenous knowledge regarding human–animal social relations is being granted by many environmentalists and others as an alternate reality beyond the accepted understanding of science that utilizes only certain types of knowledge and methodology centered on animal population distributions or functional roles in ecosystem maintenance.

There are two ways we can approach an understanding of animal life on Earth. One perspective is examining the ontology of animal life, that is, investigating scientifically the life of animals to further our understanding of the meaning and complexity of life. The second perspective is comprehending ethnologically the various ways in which humans, through magic-religious and spiritual means, interacted with animals, creating complex relationships. Recent scientific research illustrates the complex lives of non-mammals such as bees, which Stephen Buchmann refers to as "fringe" research in his book *What a Bee Knows: Exploring the Thoughts, Memories, and Personalities of Bees*, since suggestive findings are far beyond conventional understanding. Research indicates that bees are not instinct-driven robots but exhibit cognitive skills such as facial recognition, innovation, and emotional responses. "Today, biologists understand that humans are not completely different from other animals," writes Buchmann, countering Enlightenment thinkers such as Descartes. "Especially in relation to cognition, sentience, and learning, we are enmeshed within a broad animal continuum, not better than or somehow set apart from the rest of the animate world" (2023, 5). Considering bees, he states, "We now know that bees are sentient, they may exhibit self-awareness, and they possibly have a basic form of consciousness" (xvi).

From a different point of view and closer to the topic of this chapter, Griffin addresses the question: Do animals have consciousness? He quotes H.S. Terrace, a psychologist at Columbia University, "Now that there are strong grounds to dispute Descartes' contention that animals lack the ability to think, it is appropriate to determine just how an animal does think" (2002; org. Terrace 1985, 126). Such studies caution the need for further research on animal feelings and conscious thought: "We cannot be certain how common this additional feature actually is, but suggestive evidence such as that reviewed in this book makes it at least plausible that simple forms of conscious thinking may be quite widespread" (272). Whereas Griffin is positive yet cautious in his assessment of animal cognition and consciousness, many indigenous communities recognize and accept his general conclusions regarding the abilities of animal awareness and would not be surprised by Buchmann's understanding of bee behavior.

Prior to the scientific revolution and capitalism, the ethnohistorical record suggests a more intimate relationship between human communities and nature. In many cases, animals played a central role in how people thought about the world around them and recognized the intrinsic value of animals as sentient beings. However, this does not imply that they were conservationists but, in a contradictory fashion, saw animals as they saw themselves and engaged in predations for survival, sometimes in extreme ways. Indigenous Americans, who bear the brunt of this binary opposition in environmental thinking, were both brother and hunter, kinfolk and exploiter. In other words, they were complex humans operating in an ocean of motivations, desires, and yearnings yet trying to make sense of the world they lived in. In her broad overview of the human–animal interface, *Humans and Other Animals*, Samantha Hurn, an anthropologist specializing in anthrozoology, outlines the often complex cross-cultural relationship humans have with animals (2012). For example, she discusses the well-known case in anthropology of the Bororo's comment "we are Red Macaws." The history of analysis of this comment has moved from the "primitive mentality" of Lévy-Bruhl to a more nuanced debate over the Bororo phrase. One interpretation suggests that upon death, the Bororo's soul is reincarnated as a parrot, as in "We will become red macaws." The macaws play a central ritual role upon the death of an individual, whereupon the human soul enters the bodies of parrots. Bororo men don macaw feathers to become spirits in ceremonial form to ritualize the reproduction of their society.

Others find a more gendered interpretation wherein their matrilineal society, just as macaws are kept as pets by women feeding them bananas, so men live apart from their wives but return home to be fed by their wives. Thus, red macaws are symbolic of men's place in the social structure of Bororo society. Animals such as macaws are not seen as food but as symbolic conduits between lifeworlds. The pre-modern era, as exemplified by the Bororo's relationship with macaws, illustrates the complexity of such relationships with animals over time by various cultures. They were used but encompassed in a ritualistic and spiritual context rather than one of outright exploitation.

In chapter one of his book, *The Perception of the Environment*, Tim Ingold uses the behavior of reindeer of Lapland to illustrate the gulf between a modern perception of reindeer behavior versus how Cree hunters explain it. When a reindeer senses the presence of a wolf, rather than immediately running, it will stop and stare at the predator who stares back. From a biological interpretation, this is a tactic to allow the deer a head start: stop, stare, standoff, run. This tactic, however, does not work with a human hunter, making for an easy kill. The Cree have a different interpretation of the stop and stare. The animal stops to offer itself in sacrifice to the hunter. "The bodily substance of the caribou is not taken," Ingold writes, "it is received. And it is at the moment of encounter, when the animal stands its ground and looks the hunter in the eye, that the offering is made" (2011, 13). Ingold adds that biologists would react with a degree of incredulity and scientific smugness, and who would not in our modern world, seeing a convenient excuse for the hunter placing the animal's death outside the responsibility of the hunter. Many animistic people would see the animating force in this encounter, the deer as a spirit with its own intentionality.

Harvey Feit's research among the Cree supports Ingold's illustration of Cree hunting belief and behavior. The Cree see animals as part of the same social world humans inhabit and thus Cree hunters consider that many "kinds of animals have distinct families . . . and are capable of willful action and responsibility for the things they do." It is not natural law that explains animal actions but "where habit and learning explain the actions of animals and other nonhuman persons" (2001, 421). An outsider would ask why an animal, a reindeer or other, would willfully allow itself to be killed. Cree belief comes in two parts: "The Cree answer with similar kinds of reasons to those they would offer for why a human gives food away to another person." It is because of the perceived need of the other, "it is the responsible thing to do as a moral social being" which the Cree see in the reindeer, in this case. Furthermore, Feit writes there is a love between animal and hunter and if in the proper killing of an animal with respect, its soul will want to be reborn. Hunters take only animals that are given; otherwise, the health and survival of the animal will deteriorate, endangering the survival of its "kin." From the Cree's understanding of the world of animals and humans, a degree of reciprocity with animals is necessary if both animal and human are to survive.

Many anthropologists believe it is not about the validity of the explanation but its meaning. In the cosmology or lifeworld of many traditional hunting communities, animals are, as humans are, invested with agency and intentionality as sentient beings. The reindeer, Ingold reminds us, did not offer itself because of some inner determination, although the notion of agency is evident. This telling of an eye-to-eye encounter is more in the way of a performance by the hunter, relaying the feeling of intimate proximity and connection to another sentient being. At this moment, "the hunter felt the overwhelming presence of the animal: he felt as if his own being were somehow bound up or intermingled with that of the animal," according to Ingold (25). A retelling of such intimacy suggests the animal is more than just food, but a fellow sentient, spiritual traveler bound together in a particular moment in a particular relationship. Such an encounter and the retelling relay a moral and ethical significance, a reframing that intimately links hunter and animal in time and space in a mutual, in the hunter's mind, meaningful reality.[3] Myths, stories, and meaningful conceptions centered on such thinking by the Cree or Koyukon, and other cultures, make up a unique worldview for a people, a unified set of assumptions, appraisals, and values about the world. Myths are a characteristic way of looking outward on the universe and how it works. Beyond myth, for the past twenty-four years, I live with a Severe Macaw and understand my parrot is more than a mere animal but one aware of his own intentionality and agency. I have learned Hatuey's ability to manipulate his environment, including manipulating me, to get what he wants, whether it is food, a bath, attention, or just wanting a break from me. I am convinced he knows his world, within the limits of his intelligence, as well as I know mine, and the gulf between us is not nearly as great as I once assumed. At times when I become angry with him, for example, he understands my emotion by getting on my hand to offer me a kiss. Does he know what a kiss is? Probably not, but I believe he understands emotions and what they mean and a way to convey, that is, intentionality, his feelings.

As anthropologists began to engage in ethnographic research with many different cultures, it was clear that various cultures did not divide the world as experienced by Western culture. For some cultures, there was no hierarchy of superior beings similar to the medieval European *scala naturae*, the great chain of being. The Danish anthropologist Kaj Århem's work among the horticultural Makuna of the Brazilian Amazon led him to believe that the notion of nature and society are seen as a holistic, single entity. Together they constitute an integrated order, alternatively represented as a grand society or a cosmic nature. Humankind is thus seen as a particular form of life participating in a wider community of living beings regulated by a single and totalizing set of rules of conduct (1996, 185). For much of human life on earth, at least until the advent of urban society, most groups had a cohesive cosmological model that included a "kinship" of reciprocal relationships between themselves and the species they depended upon for survival. This culturally specific relationship expressed itself in song, ritual, dance, totems, and clan names that helped organize perceptions and a holistic worldview by blurring the lines of distinction between humans and other living things.

To be human means to be involved with, or immersed in, the natural world, whether in relational or domineering terms. My relationship with my macaw, Hatuey, has taught me that to dominate him, to treat him as a "mere" animal, would rob him of an intangible quality that makes him an aware and unique creature deserving of respect. As a species, we spent most of our history intimately and directly involved with nature, using our culture to interpret the world around us and then to manipulate it to our satisfaction, not so much in terms of wants and desires but in cosmological, ritualized, and personal ways. Whatever "nature" is, it is always provisional according to interpretation. The answer is to be found within our mind's conceptions and perspectives, our experiences, aspirations, and fears of how we look at the world.

While post-Enlightenment Western culture tends to consider humans unique among animals, one interesting area of research and debate concerns the perception of the nature of animals. Among many indigenous cultures that rely on hunting as a major adaptive strategy, ritual preparation for a successful hunt is essential. The Cree of northern Canada believe that proper respect in the killing and consumption of the animal is essential, according to Ingold. "Above all, animals are offended by unnecessary killings: that is, by killing as an end in itself rather than to satisfy genuine consumption needs. They are offended, too, if the meat is not properly shared around all those in the community who need it" (20001 67, 71). The assumption on the part of the hunter is that those hunted are sentient beings and as such deserve respect for a mutually beneficial relationship.

Many anthropologists interpret such relationships through the lens of personhood and agency among animal species. Can animals have personhood? For many individuals, the answer is no; animals are but animals. Hurn defines a person as "an individual, animate, self-conscious being who becomes a person in a social context in which their individuality and intentionality are recognized and acknowledged by another" (30). Can animals be so categorized? Animal behavior in this case can be thought of much as we think about other human beings; personhood is thus linked to "embodied interactions." Among the Cree, hunting is regarded as an interplay between human and animal within their identities and intentions. Ingold considers, "The ways in which the animal behaves in relation to the hunter influence whether or not that individual is accorded personhood," in other words, just as humans observe and regard other humans (32). This should not be too surprising since many cultural groups do not necessarily consider strangers to be persons until known.

Parallel to personhood is the issue of agency among animals. Agency generally requires intentionality and judgment in action, something many see as an exclusively human trait. Ingold argues that "Animals act as conscious, intentional agents, much as we do; that is, their actions are directed by practical consciousness" (quoted in Pearson 2013, 134; cf. Dennett 1995). For example, common knowledge suggests the capturing and raising of wolf cubs led to a symbiotic relationship and the domesticated dog. Research suggests that wolves patrolled Mesolithic human settlements, exploiting the remains of hunting kills and allowing themselves to be domesticated. In this regard, wolves acted as agents, different from human agency to be sure, but nevertheless, as Ingold argues, wolf agency with purpose and intent.

The debate over personhood and agency among animals demonstrates, in a non-Cartesian manner, that the human–nonhuman divide is more porous than once thought. As I learned dealing with my macaw, we must get beyond our "anthrocentricity." Animal research indicates the full spectrum of human attributes such as culture, feelings, agency, etc., albeit in animal form. Central to the Yup'ik of Alaska worldview animals are conferred personhood because they share certain characteristics with humans. They both have decomposable flesh, a cycle of birth and rebirth, and awareness (Fienup-Riordan 2001). Informants told Fienup-Riordan that animals observe how humans treat the carcasses of dead animals and communicate this to others of their kind. She notes that informants believed animals "were believed to distain the approach of a hunter who seemed careless in either thought or action" (544). The implications of this dialogue over the meaning of animality may at some point force contemporary humans to reassess our perception and understanding of how we treat animals, and in particular, industrialized animals.

As humans, meaning must be placed on events, experiences, and the elements of the world we confront. Likewise, indigenous peoples such as Native Americans gave the nonhuman world meaning by conceptualizing animals in social and spiritual ways. The close proximity and dependence on animals were defined in ways similar to how native people defined themselves. For instance, the Koyukon of Alaska tell in their Distant Time stories that animals were once human, speaking human language and were thus kin to human communities (Aftandilian 2010, 82). David Aftandilian summarizes many Native American belief systems that considered animals as powerful spiritual beings because they came upon the earthbefore human beings. Ceremonies and rituals established reciprocal relationships with animals, as humans do with each other, so that humans could survive and animals to thrive.[4] Nevertheless, native communities did exploit their resources, especially animal resources, often to excess.[5] Before the introduction of the horse, Plains Indians constructed narrow chutes to drive herds of buffalo off cliffs. The Western Shoshone engaged in communal drives called *fandangos* to herd rabbits into enclosures (decimating the rabbit population for years afterward). Likewise, did the Creek Indians, as one example, prey quite heavily on the white-tailed deer, Stacy Krech asks? Yes, is the answer, but the hunters ritually sing their indebtedness to the deer, "Awake, arise, stand up! It is raising up its head, I believe. I walk about. Slowly it raises its body, I think; I walk about. It has now risen on its feet, I presume, I walk about. Awake, arise, stand up!" Krech writes (1999, 163–164).

Even though native communities relied quite heavily upon various animal species to the point of overuse, this does not necessarily preclude thinking of the power, majesty, and spiritual significance of the animal as a cohabiting living being. Paul Nadasdy's research, for example, illustrates that native people did kill animals that were seen as sacred. "Shooting a wolf is not blasphemy or sin. On the contrary, First Nation people's concept of respect is based on the need to kill animals. As long as hunters behave properly toward wolves and their remains, killing them can be a perfectly sensible and respectful act" (2005, 320, 310).[6] This is not to say, he adds, that the Kluane people of the Canadian Yukon did not punish those who do not adhere to the beliefs and values of how and when to hunt and kill (307, 315).[7] Among the Eastern Algonkin, for example, hunters feared spiritual reprisal if they engaged in injudicious overkill (Martin 1978). The Northern Plains tribes likewise employed various hunting rituals to make communion with their prey prior to the hunt. It was believed that rituals would have animals give themselves as food and later successful hunts tended to sustain such beliefs.

Traditional indigenous communities generally believed that nonhuman entities, according to E.B. Tylor in his book *Primitive Culture*, who first developed the concept of animism, had souls and bridged the spiritual and physical worlds (2010). Discussing the French experience in "New France" in the early seventeenth century, for instance, Thomas Altherr writes that the Jesuit LeJeune noted that "the Montagnais believed that each species of animal had an "elder brother," a spirit that 'was the source and origin of all individuals' of that species" (1983, 271). But even as animists, this did not preclude traditional cultures from modifying or transforming the environment around them. Careful observation would lead to adaptive strategies that would allow exploitation and sustainability. The Jesuits encountered various animistic and totemistic ideas and rituals among Indian tribes that controlled their hunting relationships with important animals like beavers and moose. Among East African pastoralists, the movement of cattle would mimic wild ungulates based on several cultural rules regulating pastoral behavior. The Kayapo of the Amazon developed small island mounds of important plants that over years began to resemble unmodified forest. The point is that traditional cultures did transform or modify their environments but often did so in a sustainable manner, replicating natural environmental rhythms and cycles; that is, working within the constraints of nature rather than against it.

This is not to assume that ritual activity functioned in all cases to maintain a stable relationship with the environment. William Cronon, professor of environmental history at the University of Wisconsin, cautions, "If we assume a priori that cultural systems tend toward ecological stability, we may overlook the evidence from many cultures—even preindustrial ones—that human groups often have significant unstable interactions with their environment" (1983, 13). The human nature relationship is variable and dependent upon population growth, rainfall and seasonal changes, and intervention by outside forces. Cronon comments that for many Atlantic coast native communities, for instance, there was little incentive to hunt more animals than necessary for survival or trade for fear of upsetting the spiritual balance between humans and animals. The emphasis by native Atlantic coast communities on fur trading with European settlers led to the decline in fur-bearing animals, agricultural activity, and the regrowth of dense forests. Historically, this idea of nature as a commodity associated with economic value can be seen in the early trade relationships between English colonists and Native Americans along the middle Atlantic and New England coasts. By the mid-seventeenth century, a thriving trade in animal pelts, particularly beaver fur, existed between Indians and colonists along the middle eastern seaboard. The trading of various furs and skins for a variety of practical and prestige European items induced Indians into a market exchange that commercialized what had heretofore been adjuncts to native subsistence and material culture (Cronon 1983; Cornell 1988; Krech 2000).

The demand for furs for top hats and other prestige items in Europe was such that by the end of the seventeenth century most fur-bearing animals had been hunted out of the region east of the Appalachian Mountains and into the Ohio River Valley. “By 1800, the joint efforts of Indians and colonists had decimated many of the animals whose abundance has most astonished early European visitors to New England,” comments Cronon (1983, 107). In the middle Atlantic region, it was trade commercialization that ultimately realized native land transfers to the colonists (Cornell 1988; Fagan 1998; Krech 2000). Europeans then assumed that the lack of agriculture was an indication that Native people did not have “ownership” of the land due to a lack of modification and thus the land was for the taking by whoever desired it. Ironically, the importance of the fur trade for native people in controlling the expansion of settler colonies could not in the end save them from dispossession of their ancestral lands by colonial forces. The point is, however, the overt exploitation of animal furs by eastern Indian tribes was due, in part, to the arrival of European traders and settlers, and native immersion into a transatlantic trade network.

The idea of a spiritual connection to animals yet at the same time killing them is seen as a contradiction by many people. But native people were not conservationists in the sense of awareness of “actions that prevent or mitigate biodiversity loss and are designed to do so,” according to Hames in his review of the debate on Indians as ecologists (2007, 180). Much rests on the understanding of the meaning of conservation and who determines the meaning of the term. We must be careful not to use present-day concepts and definitions to depict the actions or motivations of pre-modern traditional people. This could lead to a misunderstanding of what indigenous people thought or did, as David Pepper notes, “when examining pre-modern perceptions, we must not apply modern criteria to them, in some kind of misguided attempt to judge their “validity” in absolute terms” (1984, 38). In attempting to pigeonhole native people into pre-ordained categories, too many in the environmental movement envision a noble Indian as the antithesis of our indifferent environmental ways, who offer as a subversive example the way to a better approach to nature. Native people could have been, Hames articulates, inadvertent conservationists through their spiritual belief system regarding animal behavior but were hardly the equivalent of a modern conservationist engaged in careful management (184).

It is within this context that an intimate interconnection between human and nonhuman takes place and is given meaning in terms of identity as a “relational self.” That is, the relational self offers recognition and respect for all life within which the individual is immersed. In many cases, there was a respect for life found within the predation of animals as Silko’s Laguna native Tao in the novel, *Ceremony*, found out (1978). Fikret Berkes notes that, “The hunter’s obligations towards animals are intertwined with social obligations, so that the environmental ethic of the Chisasibi Cree is an integral part of a comprehensive philosophy of life" (2018, 110–111). Keith Basso's landscape, for example, takes on a holistic and inclusive relational aura among the Apache; that is, a spiritual and cultural respect for the physical landscape of rivers, mountains, and other natural features (1996).

William Cronon sees a dichotomy in worldview between indigenous Americans and the arriving Europeans developing their settlements along the Atlantic coastal areas of New England. This dichotomy, he says, is a "choice not between two landscapes, one with and one without a human influence; it is between two ways of living, two ways of belonging to an ecosystem" (1983, 12). This is not to say Native Americans were spiritually inclined ecologists as we understand the term, but they did possess a land ethic of careful consideration of the natural world that transcended the practicalities most indigenous cultures confronted.

The state of nature and the systems that sustain it are under growing stress from human activity that also threatens the viability of all life-form communities, including our own. The global environmental crisis brings the nature of the relationship between capitalism and the environment into full focus and is contested by various narratives outlining a different or alternative set of relationships, some realistic and others difficult to imagine being implemented. For example, while most people today would agree that nature is more than just the sum of its natural resource parts, yet how many would agree that humans are a non-privileged species of the Earth community sharing with beings that have an inherent right to exist even at our displeasure? The problem here is what does this mean for how humans live. This is something most people cannot conceive—how do we live our lives, yet respect and allow other species and ecosystems to thrive as well? We are so used to thinking in binary terms. In other words, how do we bridge the gap between the ideas of the Enlightenment and its step-children of capitalism and the age of science and technology, and yet embrace a new sustainable worldview of an Ecozoic Era?[8] Understanding this challenge is perhaps the greatest one our species has ever faced beyond climbing down from the trees to taking those first faltering bipedal steps onto the savanna grasslands of Africa.

A FRACTURING OF PERCEPTION

Among academic disciplines, anthropology in recent years has reengaged in a debate on dualistic thinking regarding the interpretation of indigenous peoples' relationship to nature (Howell 1996; Århem 1996; Descola and Pálsson 1996). Did indigenous societies live in harmony and balance with the environment and consciously develop conservation strategies to prevent overexploitation, or did they use resources to the best of their abilities given their limited technologies? Such questions, Howell notes, are so ingrained in our thinking that many people feel that a nature–culture divide must exist. Our contemporary separation from the natural world is so instilled in us that it is difficult to conceive of either no separation from nature or, if one existed, then it had to express exploitation.

Among non-European pre-capitalist societies, both kinship-based and state-organized, the metaphor that expressed relationships, such as *Pachamama* or "World Mother" among the Quechua, was generally "relational" and "integrative," in that society was thought of as an aspect of nature. Native Americans in general lived close to the land and were influenced by seasonal and climate changes in immediate and intimate ways. They thus defined themselves within such limitations and recognized the power of land and physical forces. Their rituals, oral traditions, and origin myths all worked to connect them with the natural world and the cosmos. This is likewise true for many other pre-modern cultural groups. For example, among the Ituri Forest Pygmies (the Bambuti) of Central Africa, the forest, as the source of all necessary resources, was religiously personified as the spiritual parent of humans, and religious rituals, such as the christening ceremony and *molimo* ritual, emphasized the tie between humans and the forest (Turnbull 1962). Among the sophisticated urban Mayans of ancient Guatemala, the cities of Tikal and Copan were designed to mirror the earthly seasons and the movement of the cosmos. Chichén Itzá in southern Mexico, for example, has two structures that link the Mayan city to the cosmos. El Castillo and El Caacol are buildings constructed to highlight certain celestial events such as the spring and fall equinoxes. From the Maya to the Navajo of the American West, and far beyond their borders, nature was a force that absorbed their consciousness, creating a non-binary and synergistic relationship. Nadasdy quotes Richard Nelson's experience among the Koyudon who believes,

> Nothing struck me more forcefully than the fact that [the Koyukon people] experience a different reality in the natural world. This can be viewed as belief, of course, but it also goes firmly beyond belief. For the Koyukon, there is a different existence in the forest, something fully actualized within their physical and emotional senses, yet entirely beyond those of outsiders (Euro-Americans). (2008, 36)

Many people are beginning to realize that modern culture has created an imbalance between society and nature, and it is for this reason that environmental crises exist as they do. How did this come to be, that is, what is the history that led to the modern estrangement from nature? It is instructive to examine a brief overview of this history. This separation began in the early depths of Western history, beginning with the Greeks who differentiated between the ordered nature of a pastoral setting and the chaotic wilderness. The Old Testament of early Christianity saw Adam and Eve expelled from the Garden of Eden into the howling wilderness with the command to be fruitful, multiply, and subjugate nature to the command of humankind. Yet at the same time, both the early Greeks and many in Renaissance Europe believed the earth to be a living organism. Stephan Harding, a major proponent of Gaian theory, notes that the Greeks saw Gaia as a most powerful deity, "The earthly presence of *anima mundi*, the vast and mysterious primordial intelligence that steadily gives birth to all that exists" (2006, 40–41). Over time, in the West, the idea of Gaia was buried beneath an otherworldly Christianity and later the scientific rationalism of the Enlightenment.

In *The Death of Adam*, John Green outlines how meticulous observation of physical phenomena over many centuries led to new insights into the structure of evolutionary reality, further removing it from religious dogma (1959). A major threshold in a new conception of reality took place one dark night in 1572 when Tycho Brahe, a Danish astronomer, looked upward and witnessed the arrival of light from a supernova in the constellation Cassiopeia. His observation of a changing heaven challenged the Aristotelian belief in a set, motionless celestial sky and instituted a cosmological revolution (Christianson 2020). The developing science of astronomical observation, later physics and mathematics, led people such as Tycho Brahe and Copernicus in the sixteenth and seventeenth centuries to allow empirical facts to interpret the motion of the stars and planets, opening cracks in the Catholic Church's monopoly over thought and seeing the Earth as both stable and of divine expression. Green carefully constructs how during the early Middle Ages in Europe, observation and inductive reasoning of the geological strata of simpler to more complex fossil forms were initially perplexing to the excavators. But such examinations and questioning laid the foundation for the theory of evolution centuries later.

This century-long process of liberation from liturgical doctrine through observation, experimentation, and reasoning became known as the Enlightenment. From this period came the development of science and the mechanistic "natural laws" that governed the universe. The multi-valence of reality, formally understood then as female, is now seen as a male-dominated machine, one that can be dismantled, understood for its dynamics, and then manipulated, serving new (masculine) ends. This is a reality that does not recognize the nurturing interrelationship between humans and the nonhuman world. This led to a rift producing a binary way of thinking of dominance versus submission and rationality versus an emotional relationship to the world, a "cold" way of thinking rather than a warm embrace of all things.

Emerging out of the Enlightenment, an examination began into the nature of things through observation and experiments that unlocked what appeared to be a mechanistic reality of component, interrelated parts. Discrete new methods of examination called physics, biology, and mathematics discovered the inner dynamics of both nature and humans. Merchant considers Roger Bacon as the epitome of the search for and then control of nature's reality. She quotes Bacon, "The end of our foundation is the knowledge of causes, and secret motions of things; and the enlarging of the bounds of human empire, to the effecting of all things possible" (2015, 90). Opening the mysteries of nature to rational order finally separated human society (read culture as masculine) from nature (read feminine as in Gaia). The chaotic or wild *natura naturans* could now be predicted and controlled. The laws of God, so to speak, now resided in the hands of those willing to accept the responsibility and challenge to control reality in the same manner that men accepted the responsibility and desire to dominate women.

Nature and all within it now became an object, a thing to be examined, dissected, and its usefulness ascertained. Under these men of science, the power of the intellect—synthesis, essentialism, rationality—came to dominate the natural world to reveal its secrets. One outcome of this development was the notion of boundaries, followed by taxonomies and classifications as declared by the Swedish botanist, Carl Linnaeus. While the Christian *Scala Naturae* also broke life into discrete parts, the mathematicians and physicians of the seventeenth and eighteenth centuries developed objective and empirical means to construct a particular image of reality. This scientific movement justified in new ways the alienation of humans from the chaotic natural world.

Yet centuries later, science, technology, and modern economic thinking have not produced an integrated nor satisfying way of conceptualizing our relationship to nature. But Stephan Harding, an ecologist at Schumacher College, believes that who and what we are is located within the "very materiality of our planet," beyond the self-centeredness of our preoccupations. Agreeing with Arne Naess's ecological self, Harding sees the human self intimately connected to a larger self, "The Self or soul of the world, the *anima mundi*, that awakens us to our full humanity when we know, palpably, in our very bones, that there is a selfhood far vaster than our own in which we live and have our being, and to which we are ultimately accountable." He adds a comment from the psychologist C. G. Jung who wrote, "At times I feel as if I am spread over the landscape and inside things, and am myself living in every tree, in the splashing of the waves, in the clouds and the animals that come and go, in the procession of the seasons" (n.d.). This comment of location, of immersion, is something that Keith Basso's Western Apache would certainly understand given that landscape and nature are something that, from the experience of the Apache, enfold human consciousness. As the Western Apache are aware, landscapes are repositories of symbolism and meaning. Landscapes, then, they add, are reflections of cultural identities and thus speak to our personhood as members of a community. Landscape from the Apache perspective is a way of seeing encapsulating intangible values and feelings.

The meaning of nature is an emergent human construct, of course, one that is devised to meet the circumstances of various human groups as they go about the act of placing meaning on the world around them and living their collective lives. Our relationship to nature and the meaning we place upon it are conditional and will vary from culture to culture, from epoch, to epoch and at the individual level, from experiential engagement. This is true even though the natural Earth and its nonhuman inhabitants have always existed as they are. In other words, animals do not change, but our perception and relationship to them does.

William Cronon quotes Raymond Williams, who once opined, "The idea of nature contains, though often unnoticed, an extraordinary amount of human history" (1995, 25). Over time, this relationship has moved from the spiritual to the scientific and from the immediate to the distant abstract and today comprises contested terrain of transcendence as we argue over nature's contemporary meaning. As much as we shape the natural world around us, it too shapes us in sometimes subtle, if not imperceptible cultural and psychological ways. For those indigenous inhabitants, walking the physical landscape was to encounter a veneer of unified meanings signifying history, identity, and place.

As Cronon argues, nature and culture have always, as an imaginary, coexisted in intimate dialectical relationship whether it was a gathering society, horticulturalists, or an industrial society such as ours. "Calling a place home" does not prevent us from using nature as we must; there is no other alternative. But we do decide how we want to approach and use nature to make our home. Contemporary culture, however, has classified animals differently from earlier humans and views landscapes as either dead or a backdrop for mundane pleasures, as in visiting national parks as photo opportunities or using wilderness trails for cross-country cycling challenges.

Yet, nature exists in modern urbanized society but in less organic ways. We have zoos and arboretums, national parks and wilderness areas, and we can watch nature documentaries on the Nature Channel. Many people encourage birds to nest or feed in backyards. Nature has always been an artifact of human intention and intervention, but now it is a commodity by design, and its meaning has changed into something other than direct human metaphysical experience. We ride our mountain bikes along wilderness trails to test our endurance and take pictures at Rocky Mountain National Park to show we've "been there." We thrill at seeing a wild bear, but it does not imprint on our consciousness as a sentient being operating in its world as we do in ours. We see the bear as momentary exciting entertainment within the frame of our camera. Our worlds are separate and placed in a hierarchy of significance and importance, with the human world as agent astride the bear as objectified subject.

Paul Taylor, an environmental ethicist, for example, asks a very central question: "Why should moral agents regard wild living things as possessing inherent worth" (1981, 202)? He answers his own question, stating that all living things have intrinsic value by simply being members of the Earth Community, regardless of whether we recognize them as sentient beings. On the other hand, it can be argued, as many indigenous people do and that many modern people are beginning to understand that all animals are sentient in some sense. If all animals, as Amy Weigand argues, likewise invest to some degree in "in meaning-making based on whatever needs, desires, and experiences it has, then by definition it is sentient" (2008, 52, 57). This recognition of intrinsic value and thus inherently worthy of our consideration and account can be thought of as organizing principles, as many deep ecologists do, in the mapping of a more sustainable and livable world of the future as it has been in the past.

Such organizing principles will not be found either in the metaphor of nature as a machine, the Cartesian dualism of nature versus culture, nor in nature as pristine, virginal, paradisiacal, but rather in thinking about the human–nature relationship guided by the metaphor of co-inhabitants of an inter-relational "garden." We will return to the ideas expressed here in more detail in the last chapter as we think about a future world of social and physical possibilities.

THE LIMINALITY OF NATURE IN HISTORY AND EXPERIENCE

The human species evolved in relation to the environment, and human societies cannot be understood apart from their adaptation to environmental conditions. This is not to suggest environmental determinism but, as anthropologist Julian Steward understood, an interplay between culture and environment. Anthropologists and biologists view human populations and their environments as interacting ecosystems (or human ecology). The environment, or surroundings, of a human population includes both a physical and a cultural aspect. In its physical aspect, the environment includes climate, soil quality, existing plant and animal life, and the presence of vital resources such as water, minerals, and forests or grasslands. In considering the capacity of various environments to support human life, both the quantity and the quality of natural resources must be considered. While a society's technological capacity is a significant factor in the utilization of a particular environment, humans also impact the environment through cultural meaning. In his study of the Southwestern landscape, Keith Basso remarked, "Long before the advent of literacy . . . places served humankind as durable symbols of distant events and as indispensable aids for remembering and imagining them" (7). Looking at a landscape and its features offers not only potential physical use but, additionally, the movement of human events surrounding those features offers a cultural impact on how they are to be approached and considered. Landscape, then, supports the continuation of social identity.

A traditional assumption in much of Western industrial culture and society is that nature is independent of human understanding, a thing apart, and is rather only something to be confronted and dominated by technology and human desire. However, the reality of nature is not something divorced from human consciousness and intent, as global warming is teaching us. William Cronon understood, agreeing with Basso, "We cannot know the world or nature 'out there.' We always approach the world/nature through the lens of our own ideas and imaginings." He adds that, "Ideas of nature have never existed beyond or outside a cultural context, and the meanings we assign to nature cannot help reflecting that context" (1996, 35). Natural landscape allows for historical and cultural awareness standing as symbols of experience. In this context, there is no "pristine" or "authentic" nature, only a transactional nature informed by human meaning and activity. Yet the natural landscape is that which throughout most of our history inhabited our awareness and consciousness, or as Merleau-Ponty once phrased it, the "homeland of our thoughts."

Today, it is interesting to think of the social evolution of our species as moving further and further away from the natural world toward an ever-changing, more artificial world of technology and the bubble of an inward-absorbed culture. As our understanding of many indigenous cultures suggests, memory is bound to animals and landscape in ways that are more permanent—the Hopi pueblo atop a mesa, for example—unless there is radical geographic change or human intervention. Until the advent of the recognition of climate change, we assumed that the outward boundary of culture was not nature but the infinite possibilities of our fantasies of technological domination and consumer desire. The "homeland" of our postmodern thoughts is found more in the storefront, our smartphones, social media, and various forms of entertainment. Research illustrates that the Apache were intimately at home, integrated into the physical landscape because that was where experience and the signifiers of cultural identity were found. The landscape of nature today is certainly "out there," but in a place alien for many modern urbanized people, estranged from our everyday lives and consciousness unless found on a vacation postcard or documentary.[9]

In its socio-historic aspect, the environment—nature—was used in earlier civilizations as a metaphor for thinking about people and culture. The flora and fauna of the New World suggested a young continent and as such were occupied by human groups themselves small, hairless, and naked. In other words, a form of environmental determinism led to the perception of inferior New World people. For Francis Bacon, Sepulveda, and many others, these people had to be savage children living in a young wilderness filled with small, weak animals (Jahoda 1999). For Cristóbal Colón and the many who followed him, the native people of the New World were naked savages since it appeared to the Europeans that they lived in a state of nature, like the dense endless forests, untouched by the working hand of civilization as understood by the Europeans.

The British, as did the Spanish, felt justified in conquest and colonization since the indigenous peoples of the New World or Africa did not transform their environments in ways recognizable by Europeans. "The belief that such societies could only be understood within the context of their physical environments, and that these shaped their moral and material characteristics to a degree unmatched in Europe itself, was a recurrent theme in Enlightenment thought," writes David Arnold, which justified possession of such lands by Europeans (1996, 24). From the perspective of these early "mission" driven visitors, chaotic wilderness needed development, and native people were in need of civilization.

Recent research, however, suggests that indigenous communities were actively engaged in transforming their environments, not just passive occupants, but not in a way recognizable by visiting European explorers. Based on recent research in the Brazilian Amazon, William Balée of Tulane University believes that hunting and horticultural groups were agents actively terraforming their environment rather than just conforming to the found environment (2015, 34). Balée responds to researchers who suggest that soil infertility, for example, would be a limiting factor in population and sociopolitical growth. He realized through his research that the evolved landscape was part of a social process of terraforming the natural landscape into a cultural one for human purposes. He comments that a type of soil, *terra preta do indio*, was employed by local villagers to increase the nutrient value of relatively infertile soils. Such soil is charcoal black and an artifact of human action resulting from forest burning for cultivation. He estimates that around 12 percent of forests and nut plantations were of anthropogenic origin that predates European arrival (50). Balée adds that, "Given anthropogenic forests of such scope, most indigenous groups, even foraging peoples, seem to exploit 'natural' environments that display cultural components" (51). Balée's research demonstrates that many Amazonian societies transformed nature into cultural artifacts, into new forms of environment relevant to the physical needs of the community. Transformations by pre-modern cultures incorporated not only land and biomes but also animals to be absorbed into a cultural matrix of kinship, cosmology, and spirituality, to be worshiped and at the same time exploited.

Århem's work among the Makuna, or Yeba-masã of Colombia and Brazil, illustrates the human propensity to place meaning on the world to make the unknown known. He employs the term "eco-cosmology" to exemplify this human–nature interface. The Makuna see most living things, plants, animals, and human as undifferentiated moral beings. Animals, for example, are considered "persons" exhibiting human attributes and agency, constructing their own "culture." Yet such animals are necessary to exploit as a food source. "Men supply the Spirit Owners of the animals with 'spirit foods' (coca, turf, and burnt beeswax). In return, the spirits allocate game animals and fish to human beings" (1996, 192). Both animal and human must die for another to be born for the reproduction of life; the instrumentality of death is required in Makuna's cosmological order. Yet such animals are necessary to utilize as a food source, but with return gifts offered so that the cycle of life continues.

The Makuna employ a shaman-mediated reciprocal exchange relationship between humans and animals of mutual dependence. Each is essential for the reproduction of the other. In order to eat animals, they must first be deprived of their "humanity" through ritual activity. Food shamanism, Århem details, must convert the animal-person from a potentially dangerous being into food through ritualistic food blessings. By failing to do so, "people in effect refuse to return the life-sustaining and regenerative powers of the animals to their birth houses, thereby denying the species its capacity to reproduce" (196). In this regard, Århem states there is an ideology of reciprocity expressed through ideas and rituals which limit the over-exploitation of local resources. The Makuna do not recognize a supremacy over other beings allowing for mindless exploitation, but have constructed an ideological-ritual structure that "emphasises man's responsibility towards the environment and the interdependent of nature and society" (201).

Among many indigenous groups that focus on gathering, hunting, and horticulture (but not necessarily excluding agricultural societies), their approach to the environment is twofold: a physical approach that includes adaptation and a cultural approach that places cultural meaning on a living sentient environment. Among Northern Plains hunting cultures, rituals were carefully crafted to ensure that animals were always available as a food source. Without proper ritual preparation for the animal spirits, there was a danger that existed, that is, the animals might withdraw as a food source. Howard Harrod notes in *The Animals Came Dancing* that many oral traditions among Plains cultures gave careful adherence to proper ritual behavior. "If it was not, then there was the real possibility that the animals would be withheld, and the people would suffer" (2000, 116). Seeing reality in a "holistic" manner does not necessarily imply such cultures were conservationists in any overt sense as we think of the term. It is argued that communities engaged in sustainable practices that were (or are) incidental or aspects of a larger cosmological order, not necessarily intentional.

For example, Omar Khayyam Moore's analysis of divination practices among the hunting Montagnais-Naskapi of Labrador points to magical practices, in this case, reading the cracks in burnt caribou shoulder blades that the practitioner employs to divine where to locate game. The ritual also acts to randomize hunting so as not to deplete the game population, thus sustaining the animal population (1969). However, the hunter also realizes that the caribou are aware of the dangers that hunters present and will adapt to those dangers by changing their behavior and routines. Randomization is not only to prevent overhunting an area but also to keep the caribou from "guessing" what the predator will do next. In other words, the caribou, as sentient beings, also understand their environment and the conditions found within it and will change behavior accordingly. Only in an objective sense could this be construed as a conservation act, but not subjectively from the hunter's point of view.

On the other hand, resources can be exploited extensively and given the species, with little significant impact. The pre-contact Western Shoshone of the Great Basin, for instance, held rabbit drives in which large numbers of rabbits were driven into nets for slaughter (Steward 2002 [org. 1938]). As commonly known, rabbits are prodigious in their reproduction. In an arid environment of limited resources, the rabbit drive, as with the collection of pine nuts, was generally preceded by communal dances and ceremonies paying homage to the spirits of the natural world. From the point of view of the Shoshone, rabbits did not die per se but were given rebirth through death. Ritual was a prevalent feature among Plains cultures such as the Lakota, Cheyenne, and Arapahoe, as Sun Dances with prominence given to buffalo skulls where the animal's potency resided. Among the Lakota Sioux, for example, it was believed that the spirit of a killed buffalo would reemerge from a lake to be born again if proper spiritual ceremonies prepared the hunt. In all these cases, Harrod writes, "The belief that the animals would be renewed and would come to the people for food was deepened, and the confidence that life would flourish was given fundamental support" (113). But, cautioned Harrod, this did not mean animals were inexhaustible and could be summarily slaughtered.

Beyond a spiritual approach to nature, the physical approach involves social organization and the degree or nature of adaptation to local resources. The challenge for many groups was, and remains the nature of adaptation to effectively employ environmental resources. In most circumstances, the more general the adaptation, the more likely a society can withstand changing environmental circumstances such as drought or insect predation. Many horticultural societies fit this description by mimicking the forest structure. They plant several different types of crops, some with the ability to survive drought conditions, others planted in case of excess rainfall. A variety of crops ensures that as circumstances change, some will survive to be harvested. In the 1950s, Harold Conklin engaged in research among the Hanunóo, a horticultural people of Mindoro Island in the Philippines. The farmers grew as many as forty different crops on the same plot, a multi-cropping strategy that allowed the farmer to account for any weather change throughout the year (1975, org. 1957).[10]

Many pre-California indigenous communities understood a spiritual relationship with nature but also burnt large areas to create new ecological space to promote environments meeting their needs. Native Americans, like people everywhere in time and space, had and continue to make choices based on resource availability and the needs of the moment but, in a contradictory fashion, then go on to give meaning to those choices. The image of Native Americans promoted today as a spiritual people in tune with the rhythms of the natural world is very much akin to the "noble savage." Recall the TV image of the Native American crying over a despoiled land, crying for the sins of modern culture's disregard for the environment.[11] Part of this image reflects an assumed religious and philosophical sensitivity to "Mother Earth" that is fueled by ideological belief (promoted by Hollywood, New Ageism, and spiritual ecologists) rather than by seeing Native people as they really were (and are). People, however, can be spiritual and have a deep connection to nature but at the same time exploit it, as we discussed above. Subscribing to the indigenous as a "holy" people living in harmony with the natural world robs them of their humanity and creates a one-dimensional people generally outside of contingency and the practical needs of survival.

Sylvester Lahren, a Shoshone tribal ethnographer, considered "Round dances punctuated the yearly cycle with Spring dances being held for abundant plant growth, Summer dances conducted to assist with the ripening of plant growth and Fall dances were held for rabbit drives and pine nuts" as ceremonies of rebirth (2010, 14). Many cultures exploit local natural resources but also entertain sacred areas that prohibit human interventions. "Key to their sanctity in the outlawing of hunting and other uses of natural resources . . . unintentional nature conservation is often the outcome," conclude Mulder and Coppolillo (2004, 88). On the other hand, there is considerable evidence that many indigenous cultures exploited various species to extinction (Diamond 1989). They suggest, however, that indigenous-based extinctions are more nuanced. They write, nevertheless, that "Pleistocene extinctions cannot be attributed exclusively to hunting pressures per se, but to the multiple ways people modify that environment, such as the burning of hunting grounds and the introduction of predatory exotics like rats" (92).

That beliefs and cultural patterns held by local native people operated within an ideology of at least conditional respect for the natural world is not questioned. For pre-scientific peoples, nature was seen as a determinant power over much of their lives and thus in need of deference and respect. But to proclaim the Noble Ecological Indian suggests that Indians are more "natural" than cultural beings, which in itself is dehumanizing as it is demeaning. Writing of his experience in the New World in 1500, Pietro Martire d'Anghiera believed he had encountered what Rousseau would go on to think of as the "Noble Savage."[12] d'Anghiera characterized Indian culture as,

> The land belongs to all, just like the sun and water. Mine and thine, the seeds of all evils, do not exist for those people . . . they live in a golden age. And open gardens, without laws or books, without judges, and they naturally follow goodness. So, in harmony with their surroundings that they all live justly and in conformity with the laws of nature. (cited in Mulder and Coppolillo 2004, 98)

Historically, not everyone agreed with such an assessment but rather questioned the humanity of such newly encountered people. For example, Gustav Jahoda writes that some sixteenth-century intellectuals regarded native people as little more than semi-human. He refers to Boningo de Betanzos, Gil Gregorio, and Garcia de Loaysa, whose assessments were of new world people as "talking animals" or "soulless parrots in human guise" (1999, 18). Rousseau's noble savage was one operating outside of civilization on instinct and amorality, without a sense of justice and reason but aping true humanity, considered earlier by Buffon as crude as was the land.

It was the measure of "man" to transform and create a new "garden," Buffon believed, anticipating Carolyn Merchant's "recovery project" thesis. The early European settlers of New England cleared, burned, and built their way to an ordered and disciplined environment. Glacken quotes Jared Eliot's recognition of such development,

> Behold it now clothed with sweet verdant Grass, adorned with the lofty wide spreading well-set Indian-Corn, the yellow Barley . . . a wonderful change this! . . . a Resemblance of Creation, as much as we, impotent Beings, can attain to, the happy Product of Skill and Industry. (1967, 693)

John Winthrop, the first governor of the Massachusetts colony, declared building a "city upon a hill," a new Garden, for all to gaze upon and wish to emulate.

Early colonists could not understand the "wandering" behavior of local Indians as they shifted their gardens from plot to plot, abandoning the older in favor of new, more fertile soils. Thus, early English colonists viewed native land use patterns of foraging and horticulture as not sufficient evidence of Indian land ownership. Without a sense of "fixity" or orderliness, that is, without transforming the land into an obvious sociocultural space, the land was deemed "*vacuum domicilium*," or an empty space legitimately ready for occupation by another. To enter the condition of civilization meant settlement, improvement, and a defined space that also suggested a place in a sociopolitical hierarchy. This process of finding place, Jean O'Brien writes, "symbolized a way of both ordering the landscape in an overwhelmingly agricultural society and replicating what the English viewed as the divinely-ordained social order" (1997, 206). John Winthrop arrived as governor of the Massachusetts Bay colony in 1630 and quickly concluded that the native Indians of New England, "inclose noe Land, neither have any settled habytation, nor any tame cattle to improve the Land by" which meant the Indians therefore had no natural right of claim to the land (1996, 39). Anthony Hall notes John Cotton's conclusion, "In a vacant soyle, hee that taketh possession of it, and bestoweth culture and husbandry upon it, his Right it is" (2005, 309). Cotton was a firm believer in the Biblical command of Psalms 2:8, "Ask of me, and I shall give thee, the heathen for thine inheritance, and the uttermost part of the Earth for thy possession." Individual and exclusive use of land was seen as superior to any collective arrangement, a principle that informed English colonists of the seventeenth century and later Western settler movement. For Puritans, such as Cotton, it was essentially inconceivable that Indians, who were but pawns in the hands of the Devil, could have legitimate claim to the lands they lived on. The land thus was for the taking.

It was the cleared and settled field of individual use that gave the occupant inherent rights to the land, a condition that was absent among the kinship-oriented native inhabitants of New England. In her book *Ceremonies of Possession in Europe's Conquest of the New World, 1492-1640,* Patricia Seed notes that Englishmen occupying the New World believed that both God (Genesis 1:28) and natural law declared that it was the duty of man to subdue and improve the Earth (1995, 32–34). Under English law, she writes, "erecting a fixed (not movable) dwelling place upon a territory . . . created a virtually unassailable right to own the place" (ibid, 18). For the Earthly ethnocentric European settlers, then, to demonstrate ownership one had to demonstrate possession, and possession was shown through the transformation of the land.[13] To transform the land was seen as an act of creation, an Earthly exactitude of Eden.

Europeans saw "landscapes in terms of commodities meant something else as well," according to Cronon. They "treated members of an ecosystem as isolated and extractable units . . . with mercantile possibilities" (21). As many have pointed out, most indigenous communities recognized a totally different reality. Ingold adds that the "Domain in which human persons are involved as social beings with one another cannot be rigidly set apart from the domain of their involvement with non-human components of the environment" (61, 62).[14] As Basso wrote, landscape, which includes all living beings, is where the interaction between the human and nonhuman has taken place over our racial history. The symbolic meaning of landscape as a place

> possess a marked capacity for triggering acts of self-reflection, inspiring thoughts about who one presently is, or memories of who one used to be, or musings on who one might become. And that is not all. Place-based thoughts about the self-lead commonly to thoughts of other things—other places, other people, other times, whole networks of associations that ramify unaccountably within the expanding spheres of awareness that they themselves engender. (1996, 55)

For many groups such as foragers and hunters, it was not the land but what moved on it that was important. Mobility, following the seasons, vegetation, and animals, was the significant adaptive strategy. It was imperative to understand the cycles of nature and the animals, their movements or "intensions" both physically and spiritually. Many Native cultures did have a spiritual connection to nature, but they also needed to utilize the environment in various ways to physically maintain themselves.[15] Krech maintains that many Plains Indians had complex relationships with animals beyond exploitation that included conversation, sexual intercourse, and spiritual belief. He adds that for many Plains Indians the expectations and obligations between Indian and buffalo, for example, were like those that governed kin and community. From a non-Indian point of view, this may not make sense, writes Krech, adding, "Perhaps conservation and waste should be construed in other than narrowly utilitarian terms. It may be that wasting one's total relationship with buffaloes—a relationship expressed in religious and kinship idiom as well as in other ways—was far more risky than wasting a hide or an entire herd" (1999, 149). Harrod concurs, adding that spiritual and symbolic intimacy between human and animal, constrained as they were by ritual obedience, kept exploitation within reasonable limits. Krech's analysis offers to make the Indian whole again, a true person with needs and wants found within a system of environmental meaning yet utilizing environmental resources to the fullest but within a ritualized context.[16]

The sense of spirituality or kinship with the land and its inhabitants was more than just an element of spiritual bonding with living beings, but also a relationship placing meaning on identity through *place*. Going beyond the geography of landscape as an assemblage of physical features, many scholars view landscape as a process of cultural meaning people use to think about themselves and their place in time and space. Various features of the landscape were (and continue to be) considered to be "living" or having "personhood" since the landscape contained or mediated the residue or intentionality of human action and thought. Roger Keesing noted in his research on the Kwaio the cultural nature of landscape as a place of "imputed meaning." He wrote,

> The landscape of the Kwaio interior appears, to the alien eye, as a sea of green, a dense forest broken periodically by gardens and recent secondary growth, and an occasional tiny settlement. . . . To the Kwaio eye, this landscape is not only divided by invisible lines into named land tracts and settlement sites, it is seen as structured by history. (quoted in Hirsch and O'Hanlon 1995, 1–2)

Keith Basso's ethnographic work found that among the Western Apache of Cibecue "The past lies embedded in features of the earth—in canyons and lakes, mountains and arroyos, rocks and vacant fields—which together endow their lands with multiple forms of significance that reach into their lives and shape the way they think" (1996, 34). In this case, place and self are enmeshed, linking landscape, individual, and community into a complete whole. The landscape, in other words, can be thought of as an ideological text to make a deeper sense of the world in which the individual finds herself as a historical and social being. As we shall consider later, contemporary consumer society conceives of landscape in more practical terms, not as a living embodiment of thought and perception but as a backdrop or investment.

The recognition of place, practically and spiritually, locates history and meaning within a cultural community and thus the identity of the individual born of it. In landscapes reside the stories and the moral imagination that link the past to the present and the future through sacred place. "Sensing places, men and women become sharply aware of the complex attachments that link them to features of the physical world," Besso believes (53). The survival of society is of course paramount, but as Basso points out, "social life is more than just surviving" (67). Landscape is a cultural construct and as such, so too are the living beings—animals, plants—found within it. It is in this sense that one can be spiritually connected to nature, have reverence for it, and yet at the same time under proper conditions utilize it for the continuation of memory, community, and identity.

CONFRONTING THE NATURAL WORLD

In contrast, the early European settlers such as John Winthrop, William Bradford, and John Endicott saw their project as one carving a new Jerusalem out of a chaotic and wasteful wilderness, one that demanded intentional and complete transformation if there was to be an earthly Eden of farm, village, and garden. It was "man's" (read Western civilization) sacred duty to bring the order of a garden to God's gift. Matthew Hale, a seventeenth-century English lawyer, believed it was the obligation of man's "usufructuary of this inferior World to husband and order it, and enjoy the Vegetables, to preserve the face of the Earth in beauty, usefulness, and fruitfulness" (Glacken 1967, 481). The mission was clear and the goal understood, but it took the intellectual revolution in science and technology of the eighteenth century to develop the tools for substantive transformation of nature to take place. The proponents of this transformation embraced a dispassionate worldview as they went about doing the work of God.

In his book *Wilderness and the American Mind*, Roderick Nash attempted to explain American culture's antagonism to wilderness (1967). He outlined the history of thinking about the meaning of wilderness, suggesting the foundation began in ancient Greece, as outlined earlier. The ancient Greeks had a reverential relationship with nature, but their ideas fell into two categories. Nature was the gentle parkland of cultivated order determined by the actions of the Greeks, on the one hand, and nature as untamed wilderness, dark and forbidding where the "lord of the woods" Pan lived, an uncivilized being to be feared. For the ancient Greeks unkept nature was seen as something alien to them upon which to engage in continuous struggle to overcome and defeat. The relationship toward the environment became adversarial due to its threatening nature. The control over nature and the transformation of wild lands into a reflection of civilization's desire for order was the hallmark of achievement and advancement toward civilization. This notion of the relationship between the condition of the landscape, transformed or wild, and the state of culture was a legacy passed on in the social development of Europe and eventually, the new land of America. The impetus for settlers in the New World, as with European imperialists later in the nineteenth century, was progress and "improvement."

The age of European exploration up through the nineteenth century was often expressed in terms of the supremacy of European achievement and the progress of plentitude. Those the Europeans encountered fell into at least two broad categories: a form of corrupted civilization such as the Mexica of Mexico or the West African kingdoms such as Dahomey, or the "child-like" cultures of true "primitives" illustrated by the Khoikhoi of the Cape of Good Hope. In all cases they were judged according to the institutions and values that ethnocentric Europeans accepted as the pinnacle of progress and enlightenment. The idea of cultural adaptation to the opportunities or limitations of the environment was understood only by a small group of natural philosophers and scientists such as Charles Darwin. Thus, most encountered people were in need of education and through colonial occupation and conquest, whole societies were destroyed and then reconstructed according to Euro-American principles.

By the nineteenth century, existing alongside a sense of doing the work of Providence, others such as Cecil Rhodes considered the taking of land in need of economic or political development the right of the superior nation. In 1895, at the height of imperial ambition, Rhodes said, "we colonial statesmen must acquire new lands for settling the surplus population, to provide new markets for the goods produced in the factories and mines" (Beaud 2001, 159–160). Whether Native American or various African tribal groups, Europeans, and Americans began to justify such takings through the lens of imperialist economic ideology wrapped in the guise of progress and the promise of a better life for their citizens. Looking at Africa and Asia, the racism of colonial ambition is clear in a relationship of subject and object. Leroy-Beaulieu, a professor at the Collège de France in the 1880s, declared, "It is neither natural nor just that the civilized people of the West should be indefinitely crowded together and stifled . . . and that they should leave perhaps half the world to small groups of ignorant men . . . without energy and without direction" (161). Industrialists needed new resources and additional markets to meet the needs of factories, capitalist owners, and investors. Colonial intervention in Africa dispossessed traditional African adaptive strategies for new forms of colonial exploitation through resettlement, engineering projects, and Western ideas of natural conservation. Visiting Europeans to the Khoikhoi of the South African coast could not understand why these cattle herders moved their cattle around from area to area. Once the Dutch settled the Mossel Bay region, transhumance pastoralism gave way through violent confrontations and defeat to corralled cattle farms and feedlots. As Jan Van Riebeeck, in the 1650s, recorded in his journal,

> They [the Khoikhoi] strongly insisted that we had been appropriating more and more of their land, which had been theirs all these centuries, and on which they had been accustomed to let their cattle graze, etc. . . . [E]ventually they had to be told that they had now lost the land as the result of the war and had no alternative but to admit that it was no longer theirs. (quoted in Guelke and Shell 1992, 807)

By the beginning of the eighteenth century, the ability to dissect reality into functionally interrelated parts and the perspective of natural resources and human labor as augments of industrial enterprise and cultural superiority continued in the name of economic development, itself but another name for Merchant's Eden project characterization. The mission and goal of the westward movement of settlers was to overcome the wild country and those who lived within it, bringing forth a new civilization and the narrative of conquest and business opportunity. Landscape lost its meaning, and as native people lost their lands, memory of place and heritage likewise became more problematic once various native communities were exterminated or sequestered on isolated gulags. With the advent of capitalism and its need for various resources, the idea of nature morphed into one of multifaceted exchange values based on utilitarian principles rather than a drive to create an earthly facsimile of paradise. As individuals moved further and further into developed cityscapes, technology, and the market world, and further away from the environmental landscape, society likewise created a greater human separation from a holistic relationship with nature.

The prevailing narrative continues to reside in capitalist culture, an illusion of economic determinism and progress but now increasingly under critique and resistance. The search for paradise will continue but now under the guise of economic growth for jobs and the search for wealth as the measurement of paradise. For most people, paradise is to be found, they have been taught, in the Eden of the shopping mall and in the aisles of consumer goods offering a cornucopia of plenty. The illusion is that all can be accomplished in an environmentally controlled clock-like manner with limited social or physical consequences. We now issue commands and move mountains with machinery, level forests without thought or effort, and redirect rivers in the name of progress. But the costs to human moral value, social justice, and global environmental degradation belie the illusion, though for many difficult to see.

This chapter illustrates that for most of human history, cultures had to deal with the natural world as it existed. Given the level of sociocultural development, the degree of technological achievement, and empirical understanding of the physical properties of the Earth and its living inhabitants, nature was known through patterned experience and codified in symbolic form into categories of meaning about how the world worked. The chapter suggests that premodern cultures did not, indeed could not, divorce themselves from an intimacy with nature. Myth, ritual, and a spiritual ethos helped not only to understand the world but also how to engage it for physical and cultural survival. They did so in a manner that respected not only the power of nature but also infused the human imagination with meaning beyond themselves.

The state of nature and the systems that sustain it are under growing stress from human activity that also threatens the viability of all life-form communities, including our own. The global environmental crisis brings the nature of the relationship between capitalism and the environment into full focus and is contested by various narratives outlining a different or alternative set of relationships, some realistic and others difficult to imagine being implemented. For example, while most people today would agree that nature is more than just the sum of its natural resource parts, yet how many would agree with Paul Taylor, who argues that humans are a non-privileged species of the Earth community sharing with beings that have an inherent right to exist even at our displeasure (1981)? The problem here is what does this mean for how humans live. This is something most people cannot conceive—how do we live our lives yet respect and allow other species and ecosystems to thrive as well.

What caused the break between the natural world of animals, landscape, and nature in general in Western culture? The break between culture and nature gained the greatest currency with the growth of scientific thinking during the seventeenth-century Enlightenment that consumed much intellectual life in late medieval Europe. The next chapter outlines the Enlightenment breach with nature most profoundly by thinking of the natural world like a machine of many interrelated parts that can be investigated as discrete units of a unified whole. In turn, our techno-scientific knowledge, although producing wonders, has culminated in a worldview that sees the natural world in cold, dispassionate, and utilitarian terms. The result is human mastery over nature and its reconstruction to meet the ever-expanding needs and desires of modern society, forever restless and unsatisfied. It is this approach that has led to the sixth great extinction, the collapse of critical ecosystems, and an overheated planet.

NOTES

1. Many tribal societies, however, did exploit their environments and at times to excess. Beinart's review of African environmental history leads him to state, "When control and accountability do break down, often under pressure from social change, population growth, markets, war or drought, then there is scope for degradation or ecological stress" (2000, 290). One example is fifteenth-century Great Zimbabwe where, according to one theory, overexploitation, drought, and population growth led to the Shona culture's collapse.

2. The point here is that among hunters, horticulturalists, and many simple agrarian societies, the use of animals was conditioned by various representations and symbolic meanings. The pastoral Nuer of Sudan considered their cattle as they considered themselves. Evans-Pritchard wrote that the Nuer identified with cattle and animistically, cattle identified with people. "They depend on the herds for their very existence," he observed, "Cattle are the thread that runs through Nuer institutions, language, rites of passage, politics, economy, and allegiances" (1969). This contrasts with modern consumer society, where animals as food are decontextualized and wrapped in plastic as industrialized products.

3. In many African cultures, fables played an important role as coded moral or social messages. "Many fables illustrated perceived animal characteristics and abounded with metaphors and observations drawn from nature, but also offered a mirror to human society. They could be moral tales, explanatory myths, or more

open-ended narratives," outlining encounters and understanding of the natural world, writes William Beinart (2000, 300).

4. Through ceremonies, honor and respect were paid; otherwise, believing animal spirits had the ability to "exact a spiritual revenge as well, taking away a hunter's 'luck,' that indefinable spiritual quality that alone allows success in hunting. Without luck, even the most skilled hunter will pass right by a game animal without seeing it," according to the Koyukon (84).

5. The historian Stephen Cornell discusses in his book *Return of the Native* that Eastern seaboard Indians engaged in a lengthy trade in furs with English colonists. Whereas there was a balance between Indians and beaver due to technology, need, and a sense of spirituality, once integrated into the European economy, new technologies and new needs led to Indian predation and depopulation of fur-bearing animals east of the Appalachian Mountains by the middle of the eighteenth century (1988). Calvin Martin cautions that the technology of many hunting-gathering groups was adequate for the exploitation of animals. What limited their hunting, including for the fur trade, were ideas revolving around need and gift exchange (1978, 10–11, 14–15).

6. Respect for the deer was a lesson Tayo, a young Laguna boy, learned from his uncle in Leslie Marmon Silko's novel, *Ceremony*. His uncle engaged in a ritual sprinkling cornmeal on the deer's nose to feed its spirit. "They had to show their love and respect, their appreciation; otherwise, the deer would be offended, and they would not come to die for them the following year" (1978, 47).

7. Nadasdy also reminds us of the cultural misunderstandings between indigenous religious beliefs and concepts such as the environment and those of Euro-Americans and the attempts at the imposition of Westernized beliefs on native people. They are, Nadasdy argues, "simply people with a complex set of beliefs, practices, and values that defy standard Euro–North American schemes of categorization" (2005, 321).

8. "Ecozoic" is a term coined by Thomas Berry to refer to a (potentially) emerging and mutually beneficial relationship between humans and the Earth community. This begins, according to Berry in *The Dream of the Earth*, by recognizing the "universe, by definition, [as] a single gorgeous celebratory event."

9. In our urban world today, it is the "homescape" (the home as castle and refuge) that is most significant, followed by the cityscape (the artificial urban environment). We occupy a world of human-made artifices in which most things, such as plastic-wrapped packages of animals sitting on a grocer's shelf, have little or no relationship with the "natural" animal. Such "structural alienation," as Howard Harrod phrases it, means, "The living animal as well as the blood, entrails, and hair out of which meat products emerge are matters far from the consciousness and practical experience of most people, especially those who live completely within the web of an urban culture" (2000, xxiv). How far removed we are from the testimony of our ancient embrace of the natural world.

10. J. Peter Brosius et al. point out that horticultural farmers are very aware of the ecological system in which they operate, including plant and animal interactions and soil conditions for various cultigens. They report, for example, that in Northeast Thailand, "an area of unpredictable rainfall and frequently dry conditions, farmers

often rely upon a variety of faunal and floral clues to help them predict patterns of precipitation. For example, some farmers observe the fruit-bearing patterns of perennial crops such as tamarind, custard apple, kapok, and mango trees to predict how soon the rainy season will start and how much rain there will be" (1986, 195).

11. The "crying Indian," as the ad is called, was played by a character actor named Iron Eyes Cody, a non-Indian whose specialty was playing Indians in Hollywood westerns.

12. Rousseau, however, never actually used the term "noble savage" but rather, like Michel de Montaigne, described the characteristics of "natural man" that would later apply to the noble savage (1964).

13. In a sense, it isn't the dwelling that is significant but the labor that resides in it. Labor bestows ownership as John Locke believed in his discourse, *Of Property*. He wrote that labor conferred ownership: "Though the Water running in the Fountain be every one's, yet who can doubt, but that in the Pitcher is his only who drew it out? His labour hath taken it out of the hands of Nature, where it was common, and belong'd equally to all her Children, and hath thereby appropriated it to himself" (*Second Treatise of Government* 1689).

14. Western history produces a false perception of separation between the natural and cultural worlds. "Humans . . . are different because the essence of their humanity transcends nature" (Ingold 2011, 63). Ingold goes on to suggest that the Western notion of dualism between humans as sentient agents and nonhuman animals is invalid. He considers that "animals participate with humans as real-world creatures with powers of feeling and autonomous action," and that we are interacting cohabitants of the same world (52). Do humans, he asks in an earlier work, see the world through their own senses? "Surely not," he answers, adding, "For the hills and valley, the tree, the corn and the birds are as palpably present to them (as indeed to you too) as are the people to each other (and to you)" (1993, 171).

15. See, for example, Charles Mann, *1491: New Revelations of the Americas Before Columbus*. Mann discusses various "anthropogenic" environmental manipulations by Western Hemispheric indigenous cultures. His book is an examination of recent archaeological debates that bring anew the question of the "pristine myth," an untouched hemisphere until the arrival of Europeans.

16. The excessive predation on important species such as beaver and buffalo may have been the result of contact with European colonizing populations. The hunting of beaver or the white-tailed deer to practical extinction was due in part to native people incorporated into the European colonial fur trade system. Stephen Cornell's treatment of the fur trade between eastern seaboard native communities and Europeans illustrates how assimilation into such a system led to the collapse of the ecological balance for these communities. He concludes, "It [the trade] gave some groups unprecedented power and even, for a while, the means of survival in the face of European invasion. But it also transformed their environments, their cultures, and their lives, and linked them irrevocably to an evolving economic order that ultimately had no use for them" (1988, 19).

Chapter 3

The Great Transformation of *Anima Mundi* as Environment

The Political-Economic Divide between Culture and Nature

What does hubris mean? As commonly known, it pertains to arrogant self-importance and a degree of assumed superiority. Over time, our self-awareness and ingenuity have given us a world to own and to transcend. Seemingly dissatisfied with our accomplishments in the contemporary era, we have moved beyond the confines of natural selection to investigate new lifeworlds and new lab-designed lifeforms. "How beauteous mankind is! O brave new world, that has such people in't," wrote William Shakespeare in *The Tempest*. It appears that we have crossed a threshold into a new reality as creators as we remake the world with implications we cannot yet even imagine. The essential question to address is whether this technological world of human "mastery" is sustainable or even desirable. This chapter examines the consequences of the Enlightenment, the Age of Reason, and the imprint of Western culture's metaphor of reality as a machine and the institution of power and control over nature. The chapter concludes with an overview of the great transformation of the world as it used to be and what it has become.

What do we make of this Earth and nature found within it? When seen from afar, our planet Earth is the only planet in the solar system that gives the impression of a rich and inviting place. It appears as a garden of blue, white, and green in a solar system of cold, deep black set against the twinkling of distant stars. It has taken over 4.5 billion years to reach this dynamic phase in Earth's history. Our species, *Homo Sapiens*, emerged on the savannah of East Africa about 200,000 years ago into a world that was rich in a diversity of resources and life, but never more inviting than since the end of the last Ice Age 12,000 to 10,000 years ago, the environmental "sweet spot" as Bill McKibben characterized it. For most of the 200,000 years, modern human groups searched for opportunities as gatherers, hunters, and fishers. Due to a limited technological base, small populations, and spiritual beliefs, the impact on the environment was minimal or localized.[1]

Among the early Greeks, there resided a belief in a designed Earth in which humans were a part along with plants and animals, an ordered world. Nevertheless, the Greeks, seeing themselves as the premier of creation, felt a responsibility to bring those regions encountered beyond their borders into the pantheon of civilization. Glacken goes on to examine the later complexity of Christianity's perspective on the relationship between nature and humans. "Man" is the "climax of God's work, set here as a steward, responsible to his Creator for all he does with the world over which he is given dominion" (1967, 152). But in the perfection of the world, God gave humans mastery to satisfy needs, which Augustus in 384 AD explained: "Formerly, the earth did not know how to be worked for her fruits. Later, when the careful farmer began to rule the fields and to clothe the shapeless soil with vines, she put away her wild dispositions, being softened by domestic cultivation" (199).

In untamed nature lurked the miasma of disease and moral decay exemplified by human cannibalism, threatening the order of European society. In Western history and culture, the divorce of civilization from nature was a "prerequisite for the smooth functioning of society . . . preventing humanity from existing in a "state of nature" with all its Hobbesian implications (Heyd and Brooks 2009, 272; Arnold 1996). With increasing empirical knowledge and observational powers, this would eventually lead to the discovery of nature's laws. The drive to subdue nature and put its resources to use is referred to as the "recovery project." The project saw nature not as something to celebrate but from which deliverance was sought. The recovery project, Merchant remarks, was a Western effort to reinvent the natural world (and the people within it) into an earthly garden of cultivated fields and orderly human settlements. The evolution of civilization, including capitalism's development, is seen as an attempt at an earthly Eden to please the Father for disobeying the command not to eat of the Tree of Knowledge of Good and Evil and the consequent expulsion from the Garden of Eden (2004).

A significant underlying ideological approach to this need to dominate and transform nature is found in various biblical interpretations. The English philosopher and scientist Francis Bacon in the late sixteenth century felt Europeans had a moral duty by providence to place nature in a yoke of servitude to society. Merchant quotes Bacon, who states that humans could "recover that right over nature which belongs to it by divine bequest," and should endeavor "to establish and extend the power and dominion of the human race itself over the entire universe" (1996, 136). The recovery project, an unconscious projection of Western insecurity overlaid with piety, is reflected in John Winthrop's 1629 pronouncement that "the whole earth is the lords Garden & he hath given it to the sonnes of men, and with a general Condision, Gen. 1.28: Increase & multiply, replenish the earth & subdue it" (Nash 1967, 31). Sixty-eight years later, once English settlements are firmly established in New England and the native people either dead or subdued, John Higginson could claim with confidence that God's "blessing upon their undertakings, . . . a wilderness was subdued. . . . Towns erected, and Churches settled . . . in a place where . . . there had been nothing before but Heathenism, Idolartry, and Devil worship" (37). The pronouncements of Winthrop and Higgins illustrate that the new science was a call to action to remake the world, or as Bacon saw it, to improve the moral condition of (European) civilization.

The simultaneous development of capitalism in Europe and America, in conjunction with exploration beyond their borders, embraced this new metaphor of mastery and rebirth. Within the paradigm of European culture, the ideas of nature to be controlled were used to explain and justify conquest, slavery, and racial superiority. For example, the arrival of the Spanish in the Caribbean in the late fifteenth century had them confront, in their ethnocentric minds, a savage cannibalistic people because of the wild and chaotic conditions of their adaptation to the natural world around them. Just as the ancient Greeks believed one could not think rationally if one did not speak Greek, so too the early European arrivals to the New World believed one could not have civilization if a people lived in a state of nature. Indeed, Cardinal Garacía de Loaysa considered native people more like soulless parrots in human guise given their lifestyles.

Our journey beyond an abiding and intimate relationship with nature began with agriculture and urban civilization within John Locke's framework of private property and in recent centuries was driven by the idea of progress and betterment. Following biblical scripture of dominion over "beasts in the field and the fowl in the air," individuals such as Bacon believed it was God's desire that nature be subdued and brought to order. Progress implies a destination and a linear sense of advancement and accomplishment. Progress is only realized through some means of control over the process of development. This can only be accomplished by recognizing nature as resource "parts" to be manipulated and utilized. Merchant succinctly sums this process, stating, "The domination of nature depends equally on the human as operator, deriving from an emphasis on power and on the human as manager, deriving from the stress on order and rationality as criteria for progress and development" (1992, 55). The past several centuries since the beginning of the Scientific Revolution has witnessed the power of the mechanical perspective and the great advances in science and industrial development.

We now possess superhuman powers to straighten rivers, level mountains, manipulate the genetic code, and travel beyond the confines of Earth. These past centuries of what is called progress has given us powers unimaginable just one hundred years ago. Whereas once humanity was conjoined with nature, modern society has launched itself into a vast void filled with human desire, mastery, and conceit of all else. There is literally no place on Earth that has escaped the unfolding nature of modern forms of development and social transformations. Of course, it is legitimate to ask what have we accomplished with such power? A vast improvement in the human condition but at the expense of immense misery to various life forms and natural habitats?

At the end of his book *Sapiens: A Brief History of Humankind*, Yuval Noah Harari asks, Through all our progress have we decreased the amount of suffering in this world? "Time and time again," he concludes, "massive increases in human power did not necessarily improve the well-being of individual Sapiens and usually caused immense misery to other animals" (2015, 415). All that has passed since the Enlightenment, the question has yet to be considered in any concise or consistent manner, let alone answered: "What do we want to want?" As we witness this world, is it valid to ask what our destination is? Where are we going? Is there an endpoint? Does anybody really know?[2] What does progress mean in terms of what we have given up, what we have lost to realize it? We will discuss later the consequences of the drive for progress, which has morphed into the need for profit, alienation, and a tendency toward self-absorption.

The concept of mastery is deeply embedded in Western culture and science, leading to a paradigmatic shift in how we view reality. For much of human history in indigenous cultures and emerging civilizations such as Christianity or Islam, what was needed to know about the world was already known. Through scripture or myth and storytelling, knowledge was offered as complete and settled. Such truths were not subject to inspection or critical thought. The scientific revolution of the eighteenth century, however, ushered in a compelling desire to know why the world was as it was. Precision in understanding and control came from the rational, liberating growth of specialization in knowledge, method, and application beyond religious dogma and superstition. It is from this perspective of mastery over things that technological fixes can answer our environmental, political, and social problems without jeopardizing the status quo of business as usual. However, the idea of a clock-like apparatus with laws of cause and effect that can be examined and manipulated in a controlled manner has today, apparent to many, run its course given the present state of disrepair of nature and increasing social dysfunction. The various realms or ecosystems of nature are, it appears, in destructive retreat from the full onslaught of human activity.

THE DIVORCE OF NATURE AND THE BIRTH OF THE MACHINE

By the Enlightenment of the seventeenth and eighteenth centuries, the metaphor of nature became a filter for various ideas about the meaning of nature and whatever it contained. Metaphors operate as mechanisms that explain and structure a constructed factual basis to reality, allowing, in this case, order over chaos. People do not begin their lives devoid of meaning and received truths, nor do they think about the world in exclusively idiosyncratic terms. Society provides a framework for how to think and interpret the world around them. Over time, unifying themes are created to explain and interpret how the world operates, which are generally accepted as truths. A master narrative enfolds history, experience, and philosophy, making comprehensive and natural a lived reality. Such narratives are profoundly consequential since they provide a sense of understanding and security for the individual.

The sublime of nature now fell under the clinical gaze of an evolving science of physics and mathematics, leading to one of the master narratives of the primacy of civilization over chaotic nature. Johannes Kepler was an early proponent of viewing reality as a machine operating like clockwork. Kepler considered, "My aim in this is to show that the celestial machine is to be likened not to a divine organism but rather to a clockwork" where motion, such as the planets and the sun, "are carried out by means of a single, quite simple magnetic force, as in the case of a clockwork all motions (are caused) by a simple weight" (Popper 1984, 47). Rather than a single tapestry as medieval European cosmology believed, science began to discern individual threads, each of which could be dissected and studied to discover their hidden universal principles, mysteries, and potential usefulness. The Enlightenment's Descartes' celebrated aphorism, *I think, therefore I am*, led to the belief in a dualism between mind (subject) and matter (object). Unlike the mind, objects were reducible to mathematical laws but humanity, by contrast was "defined as a rational thinking being—the subject who observed the object and could impart, in his mind, secondary qualities to nature" (51). With the rise of science in the Age of Enlightenment came the metaphor of the machine that there are natural laws that govern both society and nature, laws that can be understood and engineered.

The discovery of these natural laws offered a mechanistic worldview, defined by Carolyn Merchant, as a unifying model for science and, by extension, society. Consequently, the metaphor of the machine of power and order infused human consciousness so completely that it is accepted by most as unquestionable. Science can now approach nature, society, and the human body as a series of interchangeable parts for repair or replacement. Within this mix lies capitalism. "The mechanistic worldview," Merchant concludes, "continues today as the legitimating ideology of industrial capitalism and its inherent ethic of the domination of nature. Mechanistic thinking and industrial capitalism lie at the root of many of the environmental problems" (1992, 59). This has led to a very anthropocentric view of nature and a cold view of the human being. Humans stand outside the metaphor as makers and controllers, on the one hand, and subjects, on the other. Foster, Clark, and York characterize this as the Human Exceptionalism Paradigm, that "The notion that human beings were not only exempt from nature's general laws but could transcend them in almost infinite ways, given ingenuity," including transcending the human via artificial intelligence (2010, 33).

It is such a mechanistic perspective that has led to the environmental problems and challenges that we face today. Research and thinking about the state of the planet indicate that the Earth is more complicated—and more nuanced—than the mechanistic metaphor suggests. It is also clear that the environmental crisis is more than just climate change; it is about our whole approach to the meaning of life—in its broadest sense—from the perspective of PETA (People for the Ethical Treatment of Animals) to Greenpeace, from Aldo Leopold, Carolyn Merchant to Thomas Berry. As a counterpoint to the supremacy of humanity, there is a small but growing revolution taking the place of how to think about life on Earth. Organic life, including planet Earth itself, is not merely the sum of parts but a fuzzy holism of interrelated animated life.

Animism is a belief that all material life has a spiritual essence (or *anima,* Latin for breath of life), which developed, according to the nineteenth-century anthropologist E. B. Tylor, as an expression of the immediate connection with the natural world as well as to understand and take advantage of that world (2010). This essence, sentience, or life force, Tylor understood many cultures believed, is found not only in all animal life but also in trees, mountains, etc. For many of these cultures, there was little of a border between themselves and the natural world since animals, for example, showed their sentience through their awareness and reaction, their animal spirit, to human beings. All life in this regard shared an organic wholeness. Consequently, human groups created a bond of identity between themselves and nature and, in the process, created a singularity in which there was no division between human and animal (nature); in other words, to the animist, the relationship is not one of subject-object but subject-subject. In discussing the currency of animism in the premodern world, Stephan Harding quotes Thomas Berry's summation of this view, that all things were seen as "a communion of subjects rather than a collection of objects" (2009, 21). With the development of settled agriculture, the *anima mundi*, or "soul of the world," as Plato phrased it, gave way to fearful attitudes and the dangers of nature's power. This power was realized in crops "susceptible to pests, floods, droughts and other natural misfortunes, and because these early farmers had to expend a great deal of effort to prevent wild vegetation from taking over their fields and pastures" (22).

In his work *Timaeus*, Plato also recognized this oneness, believing the world to be part of a Living Creature. He wrote,

> that whole which encompasses within itself all intelligible living beings, just as this world is made up of us and all other visible beings. For by choosing as his model the most beautiful of intelligible beings, perfect and complete, the god made the world a single, visible, living being, containing within itself all living beings that are naturally akin to it. (quoted in Honorata and Malgorzata 2010, 14)

Other Greeks such as Empedocles, however, felt that if the world was perfect, then there could be no development, an observation that proved the world imperfect and thus the need to build and create perfection (20, 21).

Over time, the social evolution of organized society led away from the necessity and spirituality of *anima mundi* to the development of agriculturally based urbanized civilization and the beginning of a different interpretation of nature. Such civilizations developed forms of state religious ideology and organization to appease or propitiate the unseen forces or gods that were believed to control the reality upon which human life was centered. Unlike other regional civilizations, from the earliest moments in Western civilization, wild nature was a problem that had to be addressed. Early Christianity approached raw wilderness as a cursed condition that needed transformation, believing, as the Greeks did, in nature as pleasing and non-threatening pastoral settings. The foreboding of the dark unkempt wilderness was clearly expressed in Dante's *The Divine Comedy* written in 1320. He wrote,

> Halfway upon the road of our life,
> I found myself in a dark wilderness,
> The path of righteousness lost to me.
> Oh, to talk about it is difficult,
> That wilderness. So brutal and harsh and unrelenting,
> The very thought of it brings back my fear!

From the earliest days of Western civilization, uncontrolled and wild nature was something to avoid, if not from highwaymen, then from malevolent forces. For the Greeks, it was the Akepheloi and their deformed and monstrous kind that inhabited wild nature. In early medieval times of Europe, the *Liber Monstrorum* catalogued monstrous beings such as gorgons, skiapods, and cyclopes roaming the wild lands. Many centuries later, the early Spanish and English conquerors and settlers would share the same perspective as they confronted new, unanticipated peoples and such dangerous creatures as *Ursus arctos horribilis*, the American grizzly bear. From their perspective, the world was a new and mysterious place. Besides cannibals of Colón's time in the writings of Dr. Chanca in Brazil, writers in the sixteenth and seventeenth centuries were still reporting monstrous humans with rabbit ears, tails, and lion-like legs or men with scaly bodies and ass-like heads (Ritvo 1995, 491–492).

Monsters notwithstanding, it was the authority of God that gave Europeans legitimation and justification over both nature and its human inhabitants. From Carolyn Merchant's perspective, the sacred was the initial Garden from which Adam and Eve were expelled for disobeying the Christian God's command to eat not of the Tree of Knowledge of Good and Evil (1996, 2004). Once expelled, the mission from that misfortune was to dominate and transform the wild world (and all savages found within) to seek redemption in the eyes of their Lord. In Joel 2:3, "The land is like the Garden of Eden before them, And behind them a desolate wilderness." The mission is clear: seek favor by transforming the wilderness. God promised in Isaiah 35:1 that "The wilderness and the dry land shall be glad for waters shall break forth in the wilderness and streams in the desert." Thus, untamed lands were an arena for either punishment or reward, but in the eyes of those looking toward Heaven, the land and all in it was something that had to be conquered. Nature considered as female meant subordination to male control, analogous to the gender subordination of women. Merchant quotes Francis Bacon, who uses the metaphor of gender, writing, "As woman's womb had symbolically yielded to the forceps, so nature's womb harbored secrets that through technology could be wrested from her grasp for use in the improvement of the human condition" (2006, 515). Indeed, many sixteenth-century woodcuts symbolically depict the newly encountered lands of North America as female, naked and vulnerable, confronting, for example, Cristóbal Colón, fully clothed and holding technology ("America," [c. 1600], by Jan van der Straet).

It was the growth of the Age of Reason that began a more substantive rift between culture and nature, from *anima mundi* to *machina mundi*. It was, for example, "René Descartes's contribution to the development of modern science [that] contains the deterministic segregation of mind and matter and the method of reductionism that led to a purely mechanistic worldview" (Pattberg 2007, 6). René Descartes, exalting in the divinity of the human soul, asserted that through mathematics and science society could allow humans to take possession of nature and assert mastery. Thus, rendering possible the construction of a new Eden. Through the scientific revolution, nature could be fragmented into constituent and simplified parts, metaphorically conceived as a machine, for exploitation and understanding as one would understand the workings of a clock. The new method of examination through science led to a superior belief in a greater way of knowing the world divorced from Church dogma. For example, the Swedish botanist Carolus Linnaeus engaged in the 1750s in cutting-edge biology by classifying the animal kingdom in a rational order of Families, Orders, and so on. Unlike *Scala Naturae*, his scientific observations placed humans within the animal phylum alongside other primates. Such understandings would, over time develop into the idea and metaphor of evolutionary progress as the clarion call for human thought and activity, and through a Western drive for a greater scientific understanding of reality, transform the world with European scientific understanding as the centerpiece.

The use and abuse of the natural world is a consequence of the divorce between nature and culture expressed in much Western thinking. Nature as disordered wilderness was seen as a threat to the virtues of civilization and is a theme that runs throughout Western history, from the ancient Greeks, as in the story of Odysseus, to the fight over natural resource use in the Arctic National Wildlife Refuge in Alaska. Wild nature was seen from a biblical perspective as an expression of a fallen world from God's graces. This can be seen from the moment of the first landing by Pilgrims as the mission to push back the darkness of natural and savage chaos, bringing the light of order, beauty, and reason through the efforts of development. From the vanquishing of native people to the development of Yellowstone National Park as controlled space, the remaking of the land had to conform to the image of a pastoral garden outlined in the imagination of Euro-Americans. Through biotechnology and the knowledge of genomes, life itself can be re-engineered to create new or better plants, animals, and humans. The benefactor of the modern design of an earthly garden was the development of science.

By the end of the sixteenth century, Enlightenment thinking broke reality into two opposite modes of thought and perception. On the one hand, such thinking brought forth critical or analytical thinking, moral political ideas about human freedom and the social contract, and, on the other, a scientific methodology to allow for a more intricate and positivistic examination of reality. The perception of reality as a machine coincided with the growth of specialized knowledge supported by repetitive experimental and observational activities, culminating in precise outcomes, principles, and conclusions.

The shackles of superstition, myth, and fear were displaced by new liberated modes of inquiry focused on objectivity, experimentation, and replication. The old order of hierarchy and religious orthodox dogma was slowly replaced by rational and dispassionate discourse. Humans and their societies may also be objects of study, but humans were innovators and agents of change while nature—its flora and fauna—became mere passive, soulless objects in need of study and change, a perspective known as "speciesism" (see Singer, Chapter Two for examples of animals as objects of research [2023]). Science, both physical and social, followed by technology, was to ensure the primacy of humans over reality. We can now delve into the most intimate secrets of nature to develop knowledge useful to human endeavor.

From an environmental point of view, thinkers of the Enlightenment period were determined to enforce the dualism between human society and the natural world. With the command of new analytical tools, it would be possible to create a new garden to mirror the lost Garden of the Father. These early thinkers believed scientific understanding would realize the divine bequest of control over nature. The command of nature through the arts could lead to the repair of the world in the image of an orderly garden as it existed prior to the Fall. René Descartes, exalting in the divinity of the human soul, asserted that through mathematics and science, society would allow humans to take possession of nature and assert mastery over it, "render ourselves the masters and possessors of nature." Thus, rendering possible the construction of a new earthly Eden.

The division between humanity and nature also has a corollary within human societies, between the savage and the civilized, or Levi-Strauss' "the raw and the cooked." The boundary marking this division centered on the degree of manipulation and domination of the natural world. Civilized people manipulate and build as agents, whereas "savages" only exist passively in the natural world. This division was considered by many, such as Hippocrates, to be an expression of environmental determinism, the influence of climate on the development of society. It was thought, for example, that temperate climates, fertile soils, and abundant resources produced weak and shiftless people. Civilization developed in demanding climates, it was thought, that required struggle and resilience.

Given the degree of ethnocentrism, Westerners did not recognize that indigenous groups developed their own institutions to meet their perceived needs for order, predictability, and a sense of the world around them. Among hunting and gathering groups, nature dominated and hunters focused on maintaining a relationship of understanding with it. In a sense, there were no "filters" governing thought and perception dividing such human groups from nature. The anthropologist Tim Ingold writes: "Human beings do not inscribe their life histories upon the surface of nature as do writers upon the page; rather, these histories are woven, along with the life cycles of plants and animals, into the texture of the surface itself" (Ingold 2011, 198). With the advent of agriculture, forms of domestication entailed and demanded by force of circumstance a separation and mastery over and control of nature.

It was the scientists in Europe—Copernicus, Kepler, Newton—who began employing mathematics to investigate the world beyond the Catholic Church's dogmatic assertion of a divinely inspired world. Religious truths began to give way under the assault of Bacon's ideas that observation and empirical facts lead to inductive reasoning and objective truth. Economic development projects are the recipients of their thinking and dreams about creating a human impact upon nature.

THE CONTROL OF NATURE

Science, engineering, and technology unlocking the secrets of nature could now be used to redesign nature in ways conforming to the needs of humanity. The metaphor of nature as a machine-like reality that can be broken into its constituent parts has proven to be the lynchpin for the operationalization of economic development and progress. In many cases, projects require the transformation or destruction of local environments into "sacrifice zones" for a project to be realized. The environmental devastation brought on by such projects, even with federal EPA review, exemplifies the estrangement of society from nature. The prior federal administration in Washington, for instance, continues to push for opening forested areas, including wilderness areas, for extensive logging and mineral extraction. The Environmental Protection Agency (EPA) under Scott Pruitt sought to undo the Obama-era Clean Power Plans to phase-out coal-fired plants and to remove science-based decisions from environmental policy. Following Donald Trump's orders, Pruitt systematically began to dismantle the EPA. Today, the Biden adminstration, as other administrations, is conficted between environmental protection and resource use for development.

On the surface, the evidence seems clear. The howling wilderness and vast empty grasslands of the Central Valley of California and the Great Plain's Great American Desert had to be transformed into America's breadbasket of irrigated farms and ranches. Limited or erratic rainfall meant the engineering of dams, canals, and irrigation systems to feed water to cropland. Wild undeveloped lands had to be transformed, leaving unkept remnants as nature reservations of diminished habitat for remaining wildlife. By the mid-twentieth century, it seems a new Eden was realized. Such development, however, also meant agricultural chemical pollution, destruction of important habitats and river wetlands, new forms of erosion, and other problems. The problem of passion to conquer and control nature does not guarantee any sort of new garden. Underlying the surface of desire, we find an environment teetering on the brink of collapse.

The next chapter will examine in more detail climate change and various environmental issues of degradation. Here are the following three brief examples of the illusion of Edenic recovery, thinking that complex systems can be modified to create new systems in service to human needs without consequences. These examples and those in the next chapter give a sense of urgency that awareness and action are necessary now.

The Dying of the Aral Sea

The domination of human will and action over nature can be seen in early Soviet attempts to develop an agricultural Eden over the arid wastelands of Soviet Central Asia. In the 1960s, the Soviet Union decided on a major project to transform the arid landscape of Kazakhstan and Uzbekistan into an agricultural region growing cotton, rice, and other important crops. To do this, the government diverted two major feeder rivers, the Amu Darya and Syr Darya, from the Aral Sea, then the fourth largest inland lake in the world (Glantz 2005). The lake was bordered by forests and wetlands and had a large fishing industry that has since vanished. The consequence of this was the drastic decrease in the size and eventual disappearance of the lake basin and the desiccation of the surrounding region. The lake has decreased volume by 90 percent and the lake has shrunk by 74 percent and "In some places, salts have accumulated on the surface forming solonchak (salt pans) where practically nothing will grow" (Micklin 2007, 54). It is estimated by Bosch et al. that over 12 million acres of agricultural land have been destroyed due to salinization and desertification, affecting a regional population of 60 million people (2007). The area is prone to salt windstorms of sodium bicarbonate, chloride, and sulfate, and is laced with heavy metals and pesticides. The consequences, according to health officials, are respiratory illnesses, eye problems, and various cancers (56).

With the collapse of the Soviet Union in 1993, the region's nations have worked with international agencies to restore the Aral basin to a degree of environmental health. One substantial improvement would be to reduce water withdrawal for crop irrigation, especially cotton. There are attempts to substitute less water-intensive crops, but cotton remains a significant source of foreign exchange (Micklin 2007; Glantz 2005; Bosch, et al. 2007). One means under discussion since the Soviet period is water diversion from Siberian rivers to Central Asia, but unlikely due to expense and probable environmental costs. Lessons appear hard to learn, as Bosch believes, writing,

> The Aral Sea situation is a perfect example of the consequences of the disregard of precaution, of a blind faith in the ability of science and engineering to extract on demand Nature's bounty and of how short-term gains can have deleterious impacts if they are pursued without consideration of or care for the adverse impacts in the long term. (324–325; also Micklin 2007, 61–62)

Various international agencies have played a role in helping restore the Aral basin to a semblance of its original state. The United Nations Development Program, the U.S. Agency for International Development, the European Union, and others continue efforts at water retention and infrastructure projects. One mitigation method would be improved irrigation technology and new dikes and dams. But as McKibben once quipped, destroying an ecosystem is easy, but to rebuild one can be most difficult and involve a lifetime of work, money, and effort. Micklin points out that efforts at restoration of the basin would involve considerable economic costs. As is so often the case, human and environmental health and well-being involves a tradeoff.

As Seen from Space: The Tar Sands of Alberta

For a vast amount of time, the northern arboreal forests (also known as taiga) of Canada, Russia, and Alaska consisted of coniferous trees such as black spruce and larches, interspersed with marshes and bogs. This landscape of long, cold winters is also home to moose, caribou, and the predators that track them, primarily wolves and bears. Numerous indigenous First Nations cultures also call this region home and depend on it for subsistence activities. These ancient forests and their dwellers now face industrial development and a changing climate regime. Climate change has brought warmer weather, thawing the permafrost in the far north, forest fires, and new insect outbreaks. Development has brought environmental degradation, itinerant laborers seeking a living, and social change to local communities.

Perhaps the world's greatest environmental hotspot or sacrifice zone is found in the fossil fuel development of Alberta, Canada's tar sands. As seen from the International Space Station, the 345 square mile (as of 2013) tar sands development appears as a sore, a blight, a wound upon the arboreal landscape of otherwise endless forest. Captured in the sandy soil is bitumen oil that requires considerable water and energy to extract, either from the top layers of soil or from deep underground. Running alongside mine operations and toxic tailings ponds are the Athabasca and Peace Rivers. NASA estimates that "The mines . . . emitted more than 20 million tons of greenhouse gases in 2008—a product of both oil production and electricity production for the mining operation. The effort produced the equivalent of 86 to 103 kilograms (about 227.08 lb) of carbon dioxide for every barrel of crude oil produced" that in 2015 was 2.4 million barrels per day (2016). The impact of this development has led James Hansen to quip that this development was a carbon bomb for the planet.

The extraction process demands an enormous number of natural resources. Large haulers move 720,000 tons of sand every day for processing. The vastness of this operation is hard to visualize. Ian Urquhart flew over this area and described it:

> Hectare after hectare of clearcuts in the boreal forest lay in advance of expanding tar sands mines, delimited aspens stacked like matchsticks. Deep in the vast open-pit mines . . . 400-ton trucks scurried like ants at a picnic. Fed by

> mammoth 100 ton-plus shovels, they disgorged their one-million-pound payloads of tar sands into crushers that, in turn, spit chunks of the sand out onto conveyor belt systems. Some of those systems were more than three football fields long. (2018, 127–128)

It requires 2.4 gallons of water (hot and cold) to process two tons of sand for each gallon of crude oil extracted. Additional water is turned into steam to liquify the underground tar sand for pumping. A major long-term hazard is the liquid waste generated in the extraction process. The NRDC (Natural Resources Defense Council) reports that the 20 tailings ponds store more than 300 billion gallons of toxic waste (arsenic, ammonia, chloride) with the potential to seep into the water table, lakes, and rivers (2019). All operating with machine-like precision, moving millions of tons of sand, water, and oil from the Earth to processors, pipelines, and refineries, and the eventual despoliation of the environment, as empty and barren as a moonscape. This environment will take tens of thousands of years to recover, if ever.

The Florida Everglades in Crisis

The Everglades is a vast subtropical 4,000 square mile (about half the area of New Jersey) terrestrial sea of water moving through South Florida composed of wetlands, swamps, and shallow lakes teeming with wildlife and unique flora. Beginning north of Lake Okeechobee, water moves slowly toward its final destination, Florida Bay, and the Caribbean Sea. Evidence suggests that humans have lived in the Everglades region since the Late Archaic, around 5,000 years ago. Although the Everglades National Park was established in 1947 to protect the uniqueness of the area, overall, the Everglades Basin has lost almost 50 percent of its area to development and/or water control projects (Ingebritsen 1999).

In the mid-nineteenth century, southern Florida was considered open for agricultural development once the Everglades were drained by a hydrological system of dams and canals. The first attempts at settling were by Hamilton Disston in 1881, who hoped to drain 12 million acres (about twice the area of Vermont), opening the area to farmers. Poor drainage schemes did not solve the water problems, problems that were not solved by later projects until the Army Corps of Engineers began a concerted program of new dikes, canals, levees, and pumping stations in the 1930s that continued into the 1950s (Lemaire and Sisto 2012). The point of these efforts was to control the Everglades for agriculture, to move water as efficiently and effectively as possible to the sea: "Turn-of-the-century mentality dictated that the Everglades be subdued, populated, and used, rather than preserved" (Heitmann 1998, 42). Hydrologists, engineers, chemists, biologists, and soil specialists put the

Everglades under the development microscope to solve the water problem. By the 1970s, "all the power of modern agricultural science was harnessed to improve soil fertility, reduce insect crop destruction, and minimize weed control" (61). A national park notwithstanding, the Everglades region is the focus of agriculture, primarily sugarcane and rice, not preservation.

Whatever the success of sugarcane production and urban development, the Everglades have experienced serious degradation and contraction due to development activity. The drying out of the land through water diversion has caused several feet of subsidence or the shrinking of the mucky peat soils. The soil becomes compacted through dehydration and the oxidation of organic matter (Ingrebritsen 1999, 102–103). Fertilizer runoff, primarily phosphorus, from sugarcane fields results in algae blooms in waterways, and various herbicides affect indigenous plant life. The severity of environmental degradation and its consequences over the decades has led to various restoration plans and projects, most significantly the Comprehensive Everglades Restoration Plan passed by Congress in 2000 (Lemaire and Sisto 2012). Considering the economics and politics of such endeavors, lobbyists for special interests influence the contours of restoration plans and cleanup costs (see SunSentinel 2014). As McKibben once said, it is most difficult to reproduce the exact pristine state of environmental conditions previously destroyed or modified. In other words, we do not have the capacity nor wisdom to create new rainforests or wetlands once destroyed.

Many low-income countries find themselves squeezed by climate change on the one hand and by economics on the other. Countries such as Haiti, Honduras, most of tropical Africa, and south Asia are extremely poor. Naomi Klein described such zones as, "They were poor places. Out-of-the-way places. These zones are valued only for the profits they realize. Places where residents lacked political power, usually having to do with some combination of race, language, and class. And the people who lived in these condemned places knew they had been written off" (2014b, 310). Whether it is petroleum extraction, industrial air pollution, or coastal degradation, these areas are sacrificed in the name of economic development, reacting more to neoliberal economic policy than to broad national interests. A case can be made that the whole world has now become a sacrifice zone all in the name of economic growth.

A "GREAT TRANSFORMATION" IN A CHANGING CULTURAL WORLD

And thus, we come to today: the Age of the Anthropocene or, the Age of "Man." "The term Anthropocene," Steffen, Crutzen, and McNeill write in their seminal essay, alerting us to a new reality, "suggests that the Earth has now left its natural geological epoch, the present interglacial state called the Holocene. Human activities have become so pervasive and profound that they rival the great forces of Nature" (2007, 614). Human groups have always manipulated the environment to secure resources, but until recently, the impact was localized or temporary in nature. There is, having said that, considerable evidence that humans contributed to various animal extinctions, that "Preindustrial societies could and did modify coastal and terrestrial ecosystems, but they did not have the numbers, social and economic organisation, or technologies needed to equal or dominate the great forces of Nature in magnitude or rate" (615).

With the advent of the eighteenth century, industrialization and technological efficiency set a new stage for human impact on the Earth. Industrialization was the first stage of the Anthropocene, with the human impact spreading globally and consistently moving beyond natural variability, for instance, in CO_2 concentrations in the atmosphere. The Great Acceleration, as the second stage is termed, began with massive production and hyper-consumerism after 1945. The global impact of industrial production to meet the demands of the market without regard for environmental consequences reflects that now humanity is the active agent of environmental change. As we witness global warming and its effects harming various ecosystems and the nine planetary boundaries worrying scientists, it is clear we are jeopardizing our own life support system (see McNeill and Engelke 2016).

It is human activity and enterprise, primarily economic in nature, that now rules the world and affects the physical operation of the world's environmental natural ecosystems. Action and ingenuity are governed by the logic of capitalist economics and the market. From the capitalist perspective, nature is, as Bacon proclaimed, nothing more than dead resources to be understood and used. From the perspective of the Anthropocene, there is a need for a friendlier, less destructive touch; to change our technologies, increase our awareness of green power, and to stay within the confines of the planetary boundaries. Jason Moore, however, sees from the beginning of capitalism a world-praxis, or a remaking of the world in capitalism's image beginning with the Enlightenment, as we have discussed.[3] "The new knowledge regime," he writes, "prized dualism, separation, mathematization, the aggregation of units. At the core of the new thought-structures was a mode of distinction that presumed separation [of] Humanity/Nature . . . [now] fundamental to the rise of capitalism" (2016, 87). The Capitalocene is an ontology that organizes the world in its totality for the endless accumulation of capital. Capitalism is, in a sense, a black hole that engulfs all that falls within its orbit in its remorseless pursuit of profit. There is no avoiding the Anthropocene without escaping the Capitalocene.

The state of the present environment necessitates a series of questions, reflections, and assumptions that express the modern condition. In her now classic essay "The Historical Roots of Our Ecologic Crisis," Lynn White, foretelling Merchant, wrote, "As a beginning we should try to clarify our thinking by looking, in some historical depth, at the presuppositions that underlie modern technology and science" (1967, 1204). Even at the dawn of pervasive environmental awareness, White questions, as many of us do, whether we can survive what we have become. We have largely boxed ourselves into a set of received truths—the idea of the goodness of unquestioned progress, that human nature is one of materialism and wealth, individualism as the highest order of socio-psychological achievement, more is inherently better than less, and that culture is separate from and superior to nature. It is clear how we got to this point but much less clear how we get out of the predicament we created. White is correct when she states, "I personally doubt that disastrous ecologic backlash can be avoided simply by applying more science and more technology," a basic tenet of this book (1206).

The growing recognition of the consequences of global climate change and an uneasy awareness of the environmental repercussions of human activity has led environmentalists and philosophers of environmental ethics to propose a set of competing narratives explaining the relationship between culture and nature. At one end are those such as Bill McKibben's *The End of Nature*, where he outlines the destructive trend of human activity and advocates a "return to nature" which he refers to as a "humbler world" (1989; see also McKibben's *Falter: Has the Human Game Begun to Play Itself Out?* [2019]). He believes that we have already destroyed "nature" and are in the process of unmaking of life on Earth as we know it. The only thing left at this point, advocated here, is to walk away from the material and large scale and return to a smaller, more localized rural lifestyle. On the other hand, there are those such as Julian Simon who believe science and technology wrapped around human ingenuity will solve the consequences of our activities. Proposals have included cloud seeding to deflect solar radiation, carbon sequestration, and greater use of ocean desalinization to supplant a diminishing supply of freshwater sources (see Huesemann and Huesemann [2011] for a rebuttal to geo-engineering). A third position proposes developing green capitalism and green technology—in other words, a kinder, gentler version of what we already have.

It is hazardous to read the tea leaves of the future, yet various data today suggest that there are several converging dynamics beyond climate change that have profound implications for the prevailing structure of the contemporary world. Many social scientists worry about the continuing evolution of technology on society and culture, while others think of the consequences of the growth of the global population, or segments of it, moving across national boundaries in ever greater numbers as environmental crises such as drought or sea level rise increase. What these trends share is that they are all epiphenomena of the "Capitalocene" or "late" capitalism.

Late capitalism is characterized by advances in technology, trade, and production, including increased consumption, on a globalized market scale. Labor is fluid and internationalized, and a global culture is increasingly dominated by advertising, the market, and the commodification of life, the primacy of financial transactions, and the extraordinary power of multinational corporations. On his blog, the former Secretary of Labor Robert Reich characterizes an evolving sector of the postmodern economy as a "share-the-scraps" economy. The new economy involves work beyond the mechanization or robotization of labor. Increasingly, the jobs are "tiny tasks needed at any and all hours—odd jobs, on-call projects, fetching and fixing, driving and delivering" (2015). He adds, "They're Uber drivers, Instacart shoppers, and Airbnb hosts. They include Taskrabbit jobbers, Upcounsel's on-demand attorneys, and Healthtap's on-line doctors." (ibid). Many jobs are subcontracted, temporary, and part-time and offer no benefits, little job security, and few safety or health standards. Along with outsourcing labor to low-income developing nations, this is the new economy for the postmodern world. It is a fluid economy increasingly inhabited by fluid, as-needed "throwaway people," superfluous to the needs of the new economy.

But it is also a world of a consumer middle class, one that is growing as more enter the ranks as new consumers. In China, India, and elsewhere, millions of people are pulled into the middle class with varying amounts of disposable income to improve their lifestyles. Not only does this entail greater consumption and production but such movement also reorganizes society by jettisoning history, sense of place, and identity to make room for the ideology of materialism and the demands of the global economy. While the odd jobbers scrape by on low wages, the middle and upper classes continue to define much of their lives around the products enhancing their lifestyles. A corollary to this development is the growing economic and social inequality in the United States and global society. The movement of production to low-wage countries provides, through cheap labor and affordable products, an economic subsidy to low- and middle-income people. Cheap labor in conjunction with weak environmental regulations and access to developing nations' natural resources masks the growing inequalities by allowing limited access by labor to the market for minimally affordable food, clothing, and technologies.

The world we live in is, in many respects according to Frederick Jameson, a different world in structure, content, and meaning from the immediate pre- and post-World War II eras. In terms of economics and cultural production, something fundamental appears to have changed since then. Jameson defines this new era as late capitalism. In terms of a production-focused, consumer-driven culture, which provides meaning and narrative about life, and a political- economy hijacked by corporate wealth and power, we have tentatively embarked upon uncharted waters into a new kind of social world immersed within the Anthropocene. The orientation of this new world revolves around production and "cheap nature" to increase the accumulation of wealth, on the one hand, and a concomitant weakening of social relationships needed for deriving existential meaning, on the other. An inordinate amount of social life centers around private consumption and the individual ownership of things. Many years ago, W. H. Auden published in 1947 a long poem *The Age of Anxiety*, in which even then he captured the world we live in today, the fear of war, social change, and doubt. He wrote,

. . . life after life lapses out of
Its essential self and sinks into

Here, he is alluding to the fall into social isolation and, in the next line, the emptiness of disbelief, which leads nowhere. Without something to believe in, we fall victim to hearsay and distress. As belief in progress weakens, what should we do?

One press applauded public untruth
And, massed to its music, all march in step

The lie that we fall into is the false promise of technological progress to which we all march, exemplified by the escalator.

Led by that liar, the lukewarm Spirit
Of the Escalator

Referring to the endless movement of progress, Auden sees ever-moving upward and beyond, but to where? In *Another Time*, Auden's 1940 poem foretold the growing cynicism of modern life brought on by the onslaught of World War II. Yet it was not only the coming of war but the meaning found in modern, industrial, and impersonal urban life that he felt:

Faces along the bar
Cling to their average day:

As discussed in later chapters, in our age, we search for satisfaction, happiness, and comfort through the relentless purchase of things and entertainment; we also cling to the "music" of our expectations as we relentlessly move forward. His words suggest a sense of desperation.

The lights must never go out,
The music must always play . . .

Auden, sensitive to his extrapolation of where he felt modern society was moving, believed society was blind to its own meaning and, as such, lost.

Lest we should see where we are,
Lost in a haunted wood,

Is he speaking to us in our moment? Today's era of uncertain social change is not unlike the anxiety Auden faced heading into the unknown of war. As this book attempts to outline, we are likewise lost, but for our period, lost in a forest of consumerism, devoid of historical or symbolic depth.

Children afraid of the night
Who have never been happy or good.

Auden ends by expressing how frail, afraid, and uncertain we are. Yet we bravely push ahead, convincing ourselves that our postmodern life is most appropriate. As we will discuss in later chapters, individuals such as Auden and Eliot would be comfortable writing their prose for our time.

Auden's poems express the ideas formulated by social thinkers such as Emile Durkheim, Peter Berger, Anthony Giddens, and others who view modernity as leading to the collapse of networks of individuals and communities, resulting in a loss of intimacy. This nascent new era that Auden sensed was the growth of an undifferentiated mass of consuming individuals now influenced by capitalist interests and relegated to fending for themselves in an impersonal, fragmented, and bureaucratized world. In other words, as Max Weber expressed it at the beginning of the twentieth century, there appeared a "disenchantment with modern life without convictions." Modern culture's existential crisis began with the loss of connection to the intimacy of community, giving way to the fluidity of today's consumer culture of mélange and a hodgepodge of momentary experiences. Beyond the political struggle over the nature of capitalism and a changing economy, socioeconomic inequality, the persistence of pervasive racial division, and the relentless onslaught of advertising and commercialism, a degree of sociocultural fragmentation has taken hold, leaving people adrift in a world of relativism, a weakened public common, suspect institutions, a loss of community, and bereft of a sense of historical meaning in their lives. If history is dead, as some assert, along with a lost sense of cultural collectivity and moral absolutism, what is left to provide a sense of meaning and security but our belief in the value of materialism and the ability to obtain things we want in the here and now?

Why is this so? One of our most salient contemporary values is that of future progress, that we are embarked upon an escalator into the future in which the past loses its significance as we move forward toward better things. It is a common refrain that Americans look more to the future than back to the past. Much communication is via Twitter/X, Instagram, Facebook, and other social media for instant connection but via a disembodied technological filter. Unlike the landscape of the Western Apache, where embedded memory and identity reside over prolonged periods of time and generations, most social media is about the spontaneity of the moment and the contrived, individualized experience. Even movies are no longer a public experience but more and more the private domain of internet streaming via Netflix. Whatever history is, in one sense, it is now politicized as irrelevant or even reimagined to fit political ideology, expediency, or personal preference. The history of yesterday can be based on the "fake news" of today. As members of contemporary society, where and how do we find meaning and relevance that gives us a sense of purpose, continuity, and identity? This problematic is a major concern of Jameson (and others, of course), where he writes of the "disappearance of a sense of history, the way in which our entire contemporary social system has little by little begun to lose its capacity to retain its own past" (1992, 179). Not only is contemporary society delinked from social history but, as we will discuss, likewise delinked historically from the patterns, rhythms, and intricacies of the physical environment.

With the development and expansion of new computer technologies, mass communications and media, physical mobility, and new political-economic features, global society, but especially advanced affluent societies, has moved deep into a future world. The quest here is to understand how contemporary social formation, cultural production, and identity relate to a deteriorating physical environment. It is presently clear that the state of the global environment demands radical change in business and production, as well as social structure and cultural meaning if we are to construct a more sustainable world. What is less clear is how such radical change will take place, if indeed it can. Lenin once famously remarked that there is no hopeless situation from which capitalism cannot escape. Perhaps artificial intelligence or unlimited clean fusion power is the answer. I am extremely doubtful if the needed answers will be found in more technology. The capitalist system created the consumer society, and the project of much cultural production has been to create an imaginary where social members are convinced that consumption and lifestyle are the primary foundation of social meaning and existence.[4] It may yet escape its present crisis as it attempts to control the narrative of change by co-opting the language of the green movement, although there is doubt that capitalism can be tamed.

There are basic questions and possibilities associated with the future world. However difficult these questions are to answer, they must be asked. Given the prevailing economic development model pursued by most of the developing world, Can the Earth supply the required amounts of food, energy, water, and consumer goods that represent a promise of progress to a better life for a growing global population? And can this be accomplished in a sustainable manner? If the capitalist-consumer society is to persist in some manner, can it provide for the *communitas* and solidarity that many social scientists believe are necessary for a healthy social life? Second, given our faith in technology, Can we develop affordable and efficient means to recycle the wastes and pollutants of expanding economic growth without overwhelming the Earth's absorptive capacity? The technological question is significant given that technological development for the past hundred years has been part of a progressive movement into the future, as many believe will be the case with artificial intelligence. Many individuals recognize the challenge of environmental change but believe nevertheless that technological fixes can save the day—a business-as-usual approach. Proposals include carbon sequestration and atmospheric "seeding" to reflect sunlight back into space or great sun shields in outer space. It is not hard to conclude that such engineering responses reflect the metaphor of the machine, that we can control events. But is this a realistic assumption given that necessity is not necessarily the "mother of invention" or that one technological fix can have unforeseen and often negative consequences (see Huesemann and Huesemann 2011; Klein 2011, 2014a)? The globe's economic growth path of usage of non-renewable resources (including water, various minerals, land, and soil conditions) suggests that there may be, as mentioned, finite limits to such resources even if, given climate change, we go green.

A hallmark of late capitalism is the growth of corporate-controlled technology to harness more energy for development that leads to more consumption of natural resources. But of course, this is the nature and history of capitalism. The health of the economy is determined by both production and consumption. As innovative technologies allow for greater energy capture and efficiency, the result frequently is an increase in the rate of consumption. This is known as Jevon's Paradox. The consequence of such fossil fuel development is more energy usage. Daniel Bates, considering past development efforts, warns, "If we merely use this energy to support more people and to speed up consumption, the results are quite likely to be disastrous for the environment" (2005, 85). Available and cheap energy has allowed for greater materialism in cultural life but also for the growth of suburbs, megacities of urbanized mass society, and fossil fuel-based industrial agriculture. In affluent societies such as the United States, it is the growth of spreading suburbia that will present problems for mass transit, waste disposal, energy usage, and the loss of agricultural lands, local ecosystems, and habitat degradation and loss. In developing nations like Kenya or India, such problems exacerbate the growth of dense urban areas with concentrations of impoverished people often accompanied by poor waste disposal, lack of infrastructure, local deforestation (for charcoal), disease, and limited potable water supplies. In either case, affluent or impoverished, the amount of energy needed and the demand for various resources all contribute to a negative toll on the environment.

This book's general outlook about contemporary social change recognizes three great trends that are moving toward an intersection: environmental collapse (climate change, resource depletion), economic dysfunction (the inability to solve poverty and inequality, the problem of growth), and consumer-induced cultural alienation (the sovereign individual, demise of community, weakening of the common good). Is this new world trend, based on continual economic growth and consumer-materialist expansion into more facets of social organization and cultural life, sustainable for the social and psychological well-being of increasing numbers of people? If not, then the result may be the end of a capitalist-oriented hegemonic epoch, similar to the ending of European feudalism in the fifteenth century. We may be entering an era of another "great transformation," as the German economic historian Karl Polanyi put it. The capitalist age of a self-adjusting market that Polanyi wrote about in *The Great Transformation* has led to an ever-increasing exploitation of and alienation from the natural world, as well as from each other (1957).

Polanyi saw in the growth of the self-regulating market system a radically new economic organizational form unlike any witnessed by history heretofore, one that would break down the walls of an ancient feudal social order and create a new ideology of life. The Great Transformation brought forth wealth as an end, the individual divorced from generational relationships of community, and the primacy of economic interests over traditional hierarchy. He warned at the beginning of his book, "Such an institution could not exist for any length of time without annihilating the human and natural substance of society; it would have physically destroyed man and transformed his surroundings into a wilderness" (3). For our purposes here, the focus will be on how the converging trends affect our ability to counter global environmental degradation threatening our way of life. Continued environmental degradation is the change agent that ushers in a new stage of global development, creating a world quite different from that we now possess. Will the development be reactive or planned, induced by panic or calm rationality that recognizes a subliminal yearning for a different social world?

CROSSING THE DIVIDE INTO A WORLD OF UNCERTAINTY

Clearly, humanity has crossed many divides: the Anthropocene, the weakening of the international world order, and the transit to a postmodern social world of individualism as sovereign. Within the social, political, and economic uncertainty and instability, the world is spinning out of control. Or, if there is control, it is either at the personal level of everyday life or by unseen forces exercising great power, both political as well as ideological. Political power can be obvious, such as the elimination of environmental regulations to support business and industry. But power can also be more subtle. The power and influence of the corporate world and their political-economic supporters come in part from persuading citizens to think in either personal terms about solutions or through a controlled democratic process. Writing during what they considered their own dark times of the early 1980s, political scientists Joshua Cohen and Joel Rogers argue that American democracy is constrained in two ways. They write that political rights are procedural rather than substantive. That is, rights do not consider the inequalities influencing political rights and expression. They also consider that capitalist democracy tends to direct rights toward certain interests (1983, 50–51). "While capitalist democracy cedes workers [that is, citizens in our case] certain rights and liberties . . . it does not eliminate the subordination . . . to the interests of capitalists." Second, Cohen and Rogers add, "this structural subordination of the interests of workers is reproduced through the reduction of political struggle to struggle over short-term material gain" (146). In other words, the political system directs individuals to think in personalized terms or operate through approved measures such as voting or joining an organization. In any case, individuals are encouraged to think in ways that do not jeopardize the basic status quo of power and control of corporate-economic interests.

Stacy Thompson offers that capitalism's "deworlding" project has been to delink people from the macro issues of the world to the micro choices of the individual. He believes that "Our cognitive mapping abandons the systemic forces of our day as inaccessible and assumes, instead, the form of an exacting attention to the individual's choices" (2012, 900). Thompson adds that this focus on the "micro-ethics of everyday life" means many people have difficulty recognizing a common fate linking all humanity together.[5] Capitalists have designed a narrative to reorient people from concerns of the operations and outcomes of capitalism, to deny the relevancy of the commons, and instead to pay attention to immediate things surrounding their inner selves.

Capitalism engenders environmental concerns from macro structural processes to individual ethical concerns, that is, individualism, personal responsibility, and a parochial outlook on how things should be constructed and performed. Michael Maniates captures this shift in emphasis, writing, "Responsibility for environmental problems is individualized, there is little room to ponder institutions, the nature and exercise of political power, or ways of collectively changing the distribution of power and influence in society" (quoted in Thompson 901). "In this case," he adds, "the problem that capitalism seems to have created, the loss of local connections between people, is bound up in perfect symmetry with its own solution, and, best of all, I need do nothing else myself. I am already doing precisely what I need to do to address the problem: I should keep buying to keep safe my community" (ibid. 902).

Much of what global corporations do is far beyond the sight and awareness of most, especially affluent consumers. The effects or consequences of resource exploitation, for example, operate in exotic faraway lands such as Papua New Guinea, distant mountain regions, rural smokestacks, and waste disposal yards. Much degradation, whether in the United States or in foreign countries, is located among communities of color who are marginalized in civil society or among impoverished peasant or tribal communities, such as the polluted landscape of the Niger River delta in Nigeria. In both cases, international media attention regarding resource degradation, such as deforestation is random, sporadic, and in competition with other pressing events and issues. Resource extraction companies spend considerable effort to control what we see through media campaigns. In many cases, it is a question of an "out of sight, out of mind" mentality and awareness. Furthermore, many effects will not be apparent until years into the future. Additionally, the corporate world and its advertising work to convince us of the importance of their products if we are to enjoy the "good life." Things, after all, go better with Coke, or, Beyond Your Dreams, Within Your Reach.

Individuals, of course, are not solely to blame for the growing environmental calamity that is rapidly degrading the planet. Most of us just go about living the life that we have been born into and taught to accept as natural. We go to work, buy our groceries, and fill up a tank of gas while thinking of the weekend. To many, the values and norms that order our lives are natural and right. It is hard for many to link what seems natural and orderly with such dire environmental consequences, though awareness is growing.[6] While the environmental crisis necessitates, as might be expected, that everyone has an essential role to play in mitigating the effects of change, there are limits to what can be accomplished at the individual level. The crisis we face, however, is much greater than any individual or group of individuals. Personal attempts, in this view, at mitigating the negative effects of our environmental activities, though commendable will not solve the problem of continuing environmental degradation or slow global warming. Human agency is limited by political, economic, or social factors that constrain choice through regulations, normative practices, or ideological beliefs of what can or should be done. We are asked, mostly in advertisements, what we as individuals can do to help the environment. We are both consumers and voters, so we do have an impact on both political policy and economics. Yet individuals act within broader and more fundamental systemic structural constraints. The environmental crisis is, as mentioned, structural in nature—the scaffold of logic of a political-economy of power, control, and wealth built into various institutions and ways of thinking—and thus demands a structural solution rather than, or in addition to, personal individual responses. The structure is composed of values, rules, and regulations based on practice, experience, and the science of economics and political expediency. This includes various interlocking institutions woven into the very fabric of society. This logic is communicated through our educational and media systems to be a valid and natural way of thinking. From a conventional perspective, when change is discussed, it is often in terms of incremental change rather than radical change (the debate over health care is a good example).

Given the present state of crisis, not only must individuals change their cultural worldview but social systems must transform in radically new ways as well. New ideas regarding values and new conceptions of economics are necessary for environmental sustainability and for the growth and sustainability of a new equitable global social order. This was the intention of the 2019 House bill on a Green New Deal. This, of course, proved to be much easier said than done considering the dominant influence of an economic elite-driven corporate ideology to convince people of the need and benefits of continual growth through the production of traditional energy and consumption of consumer goods. The elite decision-makers have been very good at presenting a zero-sum game of jobs and lifestyles versus environmental protection.

It is instructive now to quote Paul Mattick of Adelphi University. In his book, *Business as Usual*, he contends that capitalism has run its course, yet it is difficult to see what could replace it even when the evidence points to a new direction. He writes,

> If the peaking of oil supplies and the catastrophes of climate change do not provoke a major transformation of social life, then it's hard to imagine what could. But this demonstrates only imagination's weakness, not the unreality of the challenges in store for us, as local disasters like the flood of oil that poured out from BP's drilling rig into the Gulf of Mexico in 2010 will perhaps make it easier to understand. (2011, 104–105)

This suggests that thinking about the future, without a broad-based social movement and a compelling narrative of change may yet be determined by those who already influence the prevailing yet dysfunctional system.

The question, then, is how to spark the imagination that would engage our thinking about a future sustainable and environmentally friendly world. Bill McKibben, in a gloomy if not accurate fashion, has told us the old world is dead, that, "The planet on which our civilization evolved no longer exists." He adds, detecting the faint vibrations of seismic change, "The stability that produced that civilization has vanished: epic changes have begun" (2010, 27). This, of course, does not mean the world will end but the real question is what kind of world will take its place. Will it be a "fortress world," as Gustav Speth terms affluent society's use of its power and technology to look out exclusively for itself, raising the drawbridge (2008)? Speth outlines other alternatives such as "market world" where faith is put in the free market and business competition to find solutions. Many politicians and economic elites have put their self-interests in the magic of a flexible and innovative market. None of these alternatives seem promising since they build on what has caused the problems in the first place. Only by the twin approach he refers to as New Sustainability World and Social Green World, Speth believes, can we "protect and reclaim natural and human communities with a concomitant change in values and lifestyles" and address "power within society and with equitable resource access and distribution" can we substantively resolve our maladaptation to the planet (44). What would this "green" world look like economically, politically, and culturally? And, more importantly, how would we get to that new world? Will we have to build on the ashes of the old world or can a transformation via planning create a chrysalis out of which something new emerges? How likely is it that the U.S. Congress will do something radical and creative to set the foundation for a new world?

This call for imagination is important to understand. Some would say we need imagination to develop new technologies as we go forward. But the planet's ecosystems are changing fast, and new technologies may not be relevant or might present new problems. Our technology, for instance, cannot refreeze the Arctic or regrow a rainforest once destroyed. The increasing acidity of the oceans will take centuries to undo—there is no technological fix that is affordable or doable. Furthermore, will new technologies limit or increase our ability or need to consume more and more of the Earth's increasingly limited natural resources? The call for imagination is to envision a world beyond economics, ever more technology and materialism, to develop a new philosophy of life and renewed relationship to our Earth. These trends, individually and collectively, represent significant challenges and risks. The major challenge is moving beyond the pressures of political systems under the influence of powerful economic interests.[7] The second challenge in the face of the first is to be realistic and honest about the risks involved between doing nothing and doing something—there will be social costs. The science of environmental and social analysis is clear in methodology and conclusions and goes through an objective process (a consensus concurring on conclusions) of the scientific method. However, the policies to manage these emerging problems uncovered by the environmental community are modified or tailored according to the degree of political and economic pressure by various interest groups. In other words, present systems for policymaking within government, institutions, and think-tanks are not totally objective or neutral in devising effective policy regardless of the costs to vested interests. There are many stakeholders on both sides of the climate divide driven by ideology or self-interest. The hegemony of capitalism is a powerful stakeholder with the most to lose, on the one hand, while, on the other, the general population is determined or limited by complacency, indifference, fear, or feeling of disempowerment. This reality will make it more difficult to tackle the increasingly obvious effects of global climate change, resource depletion and degradation, and a consumer-oriented social order increasingly at odds with itself and the world of which it is a part.

Naomi Klein, in an article in *The Nation* based on her book, *This Changes Everything*, offers a unique but important perspective that is limited but increasingly taking hold within the environmental community (2014a). Klein asserts that our polarized cultural-political climate has changed such that it is difficult to develop solutions to counter the effects of the growing environmental crisis. A common political and cultural foundation upon which to build an inclusive narrative runs aground against special interests or skepticism and doubt about the ability of any organization or government (think of Tea Party ideology or fake news) to be effective or work toward the "common good." Essentially, Klein's argument is that our notion of the public commons and the common good has been eclipsed by a deregulated, self-centered privatized world in which a robust public response is increasingly difficult to develop since there are limited means to engage in public debate and planning without devolving into "me versus you, I'm right and you are wrong." This sea change in American political life is underpinned by a fractured and disillusioned citizenry staring at each other across a politicized ideological divide. Social media may offer a means to organize a common ethos, narrative, and leadership but has yet to capture the broader general imagination in any sustainable way. According to so many commentators today, national consensus on critical issues is less and less likely under a concerted campaign of disinformation, politicization, and fear.

Rather than dwell on alternatives to capitalism, which seems unassailable, many find comfort in going green and buying efficient lightbulbs, organic food, and not wasting water. Individuals need to take responsibility for their consumption and waste to feel like they are doing something. Yet these actions do little to provide a counter-narrative to capitalism's impact on the environment or on our collective lives. As individuals, we need to be ethically responsible for our role in the environment, but saving the planet is not a personal problem. Wasting tap water here in Illinois did not lead the residents of Cochabamba, Bolivia, to lose their water rights and supply in 2000. It is not a personal choice by us to reuse hotel towels (as hotels urge us to do to "save" the planet) to save water that put water back into Bolivian mouths. It was a structural problem of privatizing municipal utilities controlled by a multinational company, Aguas del Tunari, that was confronted by a mass collective movement that forced collective ownership of the right to water back to the local government. While state and multilateral institutions devoted attention to the broader institutional issues of contracts and markets, various other actors at the grassroots level focused on more immediate relevant issues of human rights to water.

Suffice it to say, the delinking or "deworlding" of our perception and concern from a sociopolitical and environmental arena of common action is a serious problem in need of attention if we are in fact to save the world and ourselves. Recognizing that many see their lives in personal terms, C. Wright Mills argued for what he called the "sociological imagination." The sociological imagination . . . enables us to grasp history and biography and the relations between the two within society. . . . Man's chief danger today lies in the unruly forces of contemporary society itself, with its alienating methods of production, its enveloping techniques of political domination, its international anarchy—in a word, its pervasive transformations of the very "nature" of man and the conditions and aims of his life, he was convinced. (1959, 5, 13)

The understanding of the relationship between one's "personal troubles" and broader "public issues" would lead to critical thinking and consciousness. Critical thinking and an imaginative consciousness are required for the challenges ahead.

We are at a moment in history when collective and global decisions must be made. The consequences of our decisions will have broad implications for many decades to come. Environmentalists, including myself, speak of the need for new narratives; narratives that link our fate to the fates of diverse species, including humans on the far side of the horizon who do not occupy our attention or concern. The proposed Green New Deal is a first step, but there remains the need to develop an inclusive and believable narrative taking us into the future.

The previous two chapters focused on how profoundly the perception of nature has changed over the past several centuries. To understand the possibility of a new direction for human society it is instructive to have a contrast of what we were and why we changed. The process of social change has brought us to a new world beyond nature but at an environmental cost.

The following chapter will examine in more detail the impact of climate change, resource exploitation, and environmental degradation. Our environmental problems are complex, difficult for many to understand, and we are engaged in a haphazard approach to developing effective policy. Each day, new research supports earlier findings pointing toward probable environmental collapse. Recently, a report was published indicating that the Atlantic Meridional Overturning Circulation sea current may be reaching a tipping point that will have profound effects along the Atlantic seaboard and global weather patterns. Global scientists, citizens and activists, and many politicians call for an end to fossil fuel use and greater efforts at controlling greenhouse gas emissions. Yet, over the years of international environmental meetings, little of substance has been accomplished. As we have discussed in this chapter, the political economics of social and climate change are deeply entrenched and difficult to change even under dire circumstances.

NOTES

1. This is not to say that human groups have not modified their local environments, as discussed in chapter 2. Contemporary research in the Bolivian Amazon by anthropologists such as Clark Erickson has uncovered considerable indigenous construction that has created vast anthropogenic environments, changing but not destroying local ecosystems (2010). More recent work by de Souza and colleagues suggests that large and pervasive Pre-Columbian earthworks indicate dense populations over tens of thousands of square miles of the Southern Rim of the Amazon (SRA) (2018). A significant point to address is that even with substantive human modification and development by indigenous populations, the various ecosystems were able to recover in short order from such activity once halted.

2. These questions will be addressed in detail in the concluding chapter.

3. But as Moore points out, it is not general human activity per se but the foundational and transformational operation of capitalist activity. "The Capitalocene argument posits capitalism as a situated and multi species world-ecology of capital, power, and re/production." The Anthropocene, he maintains, obscures the "remaking of land and labor beginning in the long sixteenth century, ca. 1450–1640 . . . a new pattern of environment making" (94, 97). Environmental making that Moore refers to as "Cheap Nature."

4. This compares to the premodern world where religion and kinship were central to the identity and lives of people. See, for example, Peter Berger, *The Sacred Canopy* (1969) on the significance of religion in life and Marshall Sahlins's What Kinship Is-And Is Not (2014) on the "mutuality of being," or the imperative of kinship in human affairs. Yuval Noah Harari agrees with Berger and Sahlins, writing of our early ancestors, "Members of a band knew each other very intimately, and were surrounded throughout their lives by friends and relatives. Loneliness and privacy were rare" (2015, 46). Today, without that sense of community solidarity, the sovereign yet lonely individual has been normalized as a hallmark of modern society. The coronavirus outbreak has given the United States a temporary sense of solidarity, but even

here it is conditional and to an extent politicized by those who see health precautions as an infringement on their constitutional freedoms.

5. On the other hand, the recent ongoing massive demonstrations against police brutality, the killing of George Floyd, and racial discrimination led by Black Lives Matter have brought together various coalitions of interest groups to press against inequality and injustice.

6. Speaking to one individual regarding responsibility for the increase in the extinction rate, he replied, "What is my relationship to the endangered and, from my perspective, insignificant 36 amphibian species that I cannot even name? What can I even do about it?" It is difficult for many individuals trying to make it through the day to understand how they might be complicit in such environmental damage.

7. The Interior Department in the last administration proposed new guidelines to protect rivers and streams from localized mountaintop removal mining. This sort of mining has been the focus of environmental action for years due to the dumping of waste in or near water sources and erosion into rivers and streams. For some members of Congress and President Trump, this was part of the "war on coal" by the Obama Administration. Senator Mitch McConnell called such action an "all-out economic warfare on [coal-producing] communities" and the coal mining association's president, Hal Quinn, declared, "It has nothing to do with new science and everything to do with an old and troubling agenda for separating more coal miners from their jobs" (*New York Times*, July 16, 2015). The threat of eliminating jobs is used to defend the externalities of mining and capital accumulation by the mining industry.

Chapter 4

The Dismantling of the World in the Search for Paradise

Environmental Degradation in the Age of Science, Technology, and Human Desire

The Earth as we know it is in deep crisis, as many headlines in the media indicate. The Earth is clearly in trouble. This chapter offers a selective overview of climate change and environmental degradation, the twin dynamics of a changing planetary ecosystem. Even with the slowdown in economic activity due to the coronavirus of 2020, CO_2, nitrous oxide, and methane levels continue to rise. According to Climate Central, “Earth is like a plugged-up bathtub—slowing the flow doesn’t mean the tub will stop filling.” Add runaway global population growth and the politics of economic expansion, it seems likely that global warming will meet or exceed 2°C of warming unless drastic measures appear on the near horizon. In fact, according to the American Meteorological Society’s most recent report, this past decade was the hottest since record-keeping began in 1880. The most recent World Meteorological Organization estimates that the planet will exceed 1.5°C at least once over the next several years (WMO 2022). Each report results in dire warnings greater than the last one. The most recent IPCC 6th assessment, based on much more observational data to reduce uncertainty, is that climate change is unequivocally caused by human activity but that conditions will clearly worsen if mitigation efforts are not put in place immediately (2022). It is hard to find disagreement that fossil fuel industrialization has covered the atmosphere with heat-trapping gases. The point of this chapter, however, is that it is not exclusively climate change that jeopardizes our environmental “sweet spot,” but natural resources and ecosystem habitat exploitation and destruction as well. We continue to exploit, with little regard, the Earth’s natural resources even in the face of scientific evidence of environmental degradation that jeopardizes human well-being.

THINKING ABOUT THE ENVIRONMENT AND CHANGE

Numerous studies outline the challenges of responding to the deterioration of the Earth's ecosystems and the nine planetary boundaries associated with these systems. Human activity is diverse in its exploitation of Earth resources, from oceans to mountaintops, the humid tropics to the arctic, and from empty rural landscapes to megacities. Degradation is accomplished by poor farmers cultivating erodible hillsides and city dwellers without access to infrastructure such as sanitation. Degradation also includes "loving to death" areas of pristine beauty as multitudes of visitors bring their footprints, automobiles, and trash. But the more meaningful degradation, however, is corporate in nature as multinationals go about the business of using powerful technologies to efficiently exploit resources for production and consumption. No area is safe, not the depths of seabeds nor the arboreal forests of northern latitudes—the search for resources goes on. Global climate change and degraded ecosystems and animal/plant life are the by-products of corporate planning and bottom lines. For a long time, not much thought was given to the consequences of these actions, that is until the late twentieth century when the accumulating negative evidence was impossible to ignore. This one habitable planet in our solar system is now in jeopardy given our addiction to fossil fuels.

In the name of "progress" sacrifices must be made, and to many people, the "web of life" is but an abstraction, while the standard of living is real and of immediate concern. Thus, living with this conception of self-interest leads, as we discussed about Enlightenment thinkers, to humans at the apex of evolution or the vertex of divine inspiration. The result is a plundering of the Earth since what is not human has little intrinsic value. However we conceptualize and think about this perception and the values it presupposes, they regardlessly play an important role in answering the question of what kind of world we inhabit and what future world we want to live in. Nature, in one sense, is something "out there," far removed from our high-rise condos and daily lives or consciousness, either something processed and wrapped in plastic as we go about our business or found on vacation at the Grand Canyon. Wilderness may be appreciated, but possibly less as an intrinsic value and more so to test our endurance, for example, mountain bike racing. Whether animal cuteness as therapy or a National Geographic documentary on animal exploitation, the point is that in modern society, nature and environmental issues are abstract with little direct relevance to our increasingly urban lives. As one individual put it, how can the endangered California gnatcatcher be more important than people, arguing what about the importance of people and jobs who would benefit from development? In other words, we have developed a clouded perception regarding what is "real" or what is important. We do not, in essence, see an owl—we see through it to a horizon of our own meaning and making. Instead, we apply a homocentric filter in how we conceptualize the gnatcatcher or owl.

This same question can be replicated many times, as the decades-old fight over saving the old-growth forests of the Northwest from the lumber industry testify. How much water shortage should farmers in California's Central Valley suffer at the risk of their livelihoods to save the endangered delta smelt in the Sacramento-San Joaquin Delta? Many people cannot understand how the spotted owl justified the loss of lumber jobs in rural areas with scarce employment opportunities. The conflict was, and in other circumstances remains, over values that guide our perception. Modern capitalist society tends to approach the environment in terms of instrumental values. Instrumental values consider worth dependent primarily on its practical ability or utility to serve human ends. Intrinsic values, favored by many others, on the other hand, see worth independent of human needs. The spotted owl, for example, has a right, such as Thomas Berry would say, to habitat beyond human need because the owl is a cohabitant on this planet. The owl, the genera *Berruornis* and *Ogygoptynx*, have been on Earth since the Paleocene, 60 to 57 million years ago. But the owl, in essence, does not directly inhabit the "world of man" as Julian Marías phrased it. Unlike cars, smartphones, homes, and work, animals such as the owl are not a constituent part of our world. For many, the significance of intrinsic values is hard to understand due to capitalism's long history of promoting instrumental values to support its own ends toward the defined needs of individuals. In this regard, these creatures, indeed nature itself, are outside our "world-hood," or that area of our significance, experience, and meaning.

This challenge, for many, if not most people, is the uncertainty of meaning and implications behind approaches to global warming. This tension frequently revolves around the question of economic growth (i.e., jobs) versus the environment. Social movement formation is difficult under conditions where the tradeoffs are unacceptable to many people. Is saving the spotted owl more important than creating jobs so families can eat? What difference would it make if the owl no longer existed as I sit in my comfortable home, many might ask? Over time, we have moved further and further away from intimate contact with the natural world, which has been a profound part of our history as a species. As we have developed great cities and sophisticated technologies, we have fallen under the spell of the commodification of all things, including the contemporary sovereign self. We have become estranged from the natural world and its rhythms through our self-imposed isolation and enthralled with the creation of our artificial world. We have been, due to our distractions, unaware or indifferent to the nature or extent of our impact on our world.

The important things in life are not found in such abstract concepts as nature or the environment, or in the existence of the spotted owl, but rather in the office, home, the grocery store, or the important sense of self. So, with a limited understanding of the role of nature and with difficulty envisioning a different way of living, many, of course, choose jobs over owls, wolves, and bears. As so many people ask, "what is it good for," the essence of a utilitarian approach. For many, thinking about nature is thinking about resources, that is, nature as a storehouse of materials for our benefit. We could just as easily ask, "what are you good for"? This is not meant to be insulting but to "illustrate the absurdity of our presumption that one being's existence can be justified only by its utility to another" (Eyernden 1993, 12). As society has evolved, the divide between subject—us, and object—them, a question of the use or value of life (i.e., what's in it for me), has only grown more profound. As a reflection, most of the media focused on climate change tends to revolve around the material impact on human life (droughts, migration, rising sea levels, etc.). For example, recent reports warn of rising ocean levels and the thousands of homes at risk of severe flooding. But what about the multitude of animal species who, in many cases, have existed for millions of years?

Of course, this is a serious concern and deserving of national attention. But at the same time, biologists warn of a sixth great extinction of animal life (following on the 5th or the Cretaceous event of 66 million years ago). Gerardo Ceballos and colleagues' analysis of species loss suggests a modern mass extinction of mammals and vertebrates due to both climate change and habitat loss from human development. They conclude, "The evidence is incontrovertible that recent extinction rates are unprecedented in human history and highly unusual in Earth's history. Our analysis emphasizes that our global society has started to destroy species of other organisms at an accelerating rate, initiating a mass extinction episode unparalleled for 65 million years" (2015, 4). Species extinction and rising sea levels are serious developments but with a limited understanding of their significance, seemingly far removed from our everyday concerns.

According to a recent report by the IPBES (Intergovernmental Science-Policy Platform on Biodiversity and Ecosystem Services of the United Nations), environmental degradation has presented an accelerating rate of widespread species extinction (2019). In no uncertain terms, the authors conclude the extinction rate is proceeding much more rapidly than previously thought. Accordingly, "Ecosystems, species, wild populations, local varieties and breeds of domesticated plants and animals are shrinking, deteriorating or vanishing. The essential, interconnected web of life on Earth is getting smaller and increasingly frayed." The IPBES report makes clear that human activity is directly responsible for the state of the global environment and species loss.

We know the drivers are economic growth, increased population, and resource extraction, often with little accountability or governmental oversight of consequent results. The result, as mentioned earlier, is the Great Acceleration of human, in most cases, negative impacts since the 1950s on the Earth bio-systems.

A CHANGING PLANET: THE ERA OF THE ANTHROPOCENE

At the global forefront of climate change assessment is the Intergovernmental Panel on Climate Change (IPCC), a global organization founded in 1988 by the World Meteorological Organization and the United Nations Environmental Program. Recent IPCC reports warn that not only is the evidence of climate change beyond doubt but now includes likely impact assessments of the consequences of climate change. The general conclusion is that various changes in melting ice caps and Greenland glaciers, fresh water supplies under stress, increasingly more intensive storms, heat waves, and changes in agricultural regimes, among others, will be worse soon unless action is taken now to bring greenhouse emissions under control (IPCC 2021, 2022).

The idea of the Anthropocene first gained prominence with the publication of an essay twenty-three years ago by Paul Crutzen and Eugene Stoermer in the International Geosphere-Biosphere Programme (IGBP) newsletter. After reviewing the physical impact of human activity on planetary systems, they were among the first to focus on the growing impact of human activities and coined the term "Anthropocene" (2000). Of course, many observers recognized the impact of human activity much earlier, such as the Russian geologist Vernadsky and French Jesuit Teilhard de Chardin, but Crutzen and Stoermer's essay was a contemporary clarion call for greater dialogue and research. Today, almost five hundred years after the initial development of capitalism, the ceaseless need for natural resources in ever greater quantities is finally having a far-reaching impact on Earth's ability to accommodate our activities. Most important, they found, are changes to the global climate due to CO_2 (i.e., greenhouse gases [GHG]) emissions, which are increasing rapidly and in conjunction with a warming of the planet.

The degree or amount of GHG emitted into the atmosphere determines whether 1.5° C is surpassed. The IPCC employs five scenarios for mapping out the levels and consequences of actions governments take: very low emissions (SSP1-1.9), low emissions (SSP1-2.6), mid-level emissions (SSP2-4.5), high emissions (SSP3-7.0), and very high emissions (SSP5-8.5). The goal is to keep rising global temperatures below 1.5°C, at which even at this threshold would result in extreme heat, drought, sea level rise, collapsing ecosystems and habitats, and ocean acidification, severely threatening hundreds of millions of people. The data reflects that to achieve the more realistic low emissions scenario, it would require net zero CO_2 by 2050 and include forms of carbon capture (2022). The effects of future climate change is dependent on how aggressive governments can radically institute massive and expensive emission reductions over the next thirty years. It is a question of political will and the ability to confront entrenched interests in the business-as-usual capitalist mindset.

In 2007, Will Steffen, Paul Crutzen, and John McNeill continued to ask the question: Are humans the dominant force supplanting nature as the major force influencing the environment? Is human activity on the same scale as meteorites, volcanic explosions, and colliding continents? Criticism of those advancing a human-dominated geological era, the Anthropocene, asks if there is enough evidence for it to join the Jurassic and Pleistocene (among others) as a new element of the Geological Time Scale? Considering geological time, the Anthropocene has had a short life to date, and a search remains for the "golden spike" that will be the benchmark for the new geological era.[1]

Many environmental scientists believe that due to human activity we have left the geologic Holocene epoch, a 12,000-year period of climate stability, a period of the development of agriculture and state forms of civilization. Steffen and colleagues conclude that, "Human activities have become so pervasive and profound that they rival the great forces of Nature and are pushing the Earth into planetary *terra incognita*" (2007, 614). Although the stage for human-caused change was set at the beginning of the industrialization era early in the nineteenth century, it became apparent that after World War II, sometime around 1950, a turning point was reached. We have, they report, moved far beyond the historical upper limits of ecosystem and atmospheric variability. Over the last seventy years, the impact of human activity was illustrated by Michael Mann's hockey stick graph showing the dramatic upswing of consequences. At no time in human history have humans made such an impact on the environment as in these past decades.

Since 1950, the point of departure for the second stage of the Great Acceleration, resource exploitation, has greatly intensified (damming of rivers, water use, deforestation, huge mine excavations), urbanization, fertilizer consumption, population growth, motor vehicles, etc., have all sharply spiked upward (the famed hockey stick graphs illustrating the acceleration after 1950). At the same time, CO_2, methane, and nitrous oxides have likewise increased dramatically, leading to increased global warming, acidification of oceans, ozone depletion, and biodiversity loss. Steffen, Crutzen, and McNeill conclude, "The pressure on the global environment from this burgeoning human enterprise is intensifying sharply. Over the past 50 years, humans have changed the world's ecosystems more rapidly and extensively than in any other comparable period in human history" (617). Indeed, the recent IPCC assessment concludes, "Under scenarios with increasing CO_2 emissions, the ocean and land carbon sinks are projected to be less effective at slowing the accumulation of CO_2 in the atmosphere" (2021, SPM-25; UNEP 2021).

Over the past several years, many reports point in the same direction. The work of the Intergovernmental Panel on Climate Change, the Global Footprint Network, the various National Climate Assessment Reports, and a host of university and scientific organizations all conclude that the health of the planet is troubling at best. While climate change is of greatest concern, the ecosystems of a variety of natural resources are also under stress and change. The fear among many observers and researchers is that we have more than likely reached the carrying capacity of the planet. A report on the carrying capacity of the Earth by the United Nations Environmental Programme's Global Environmental Alert Service (GEAS) was introduced stating, "The size of Earth is enormous from the perspective of a single individual. Standing at the edge of an ocean or the top of a mountain, looking across the vast expanse of Earth's water, forests, grasslands, lakes or deserts, it is hard to conceive of limits to the planet's natural resources" (GEAS 2012).

The dynamic of economic and demographic growth is increasingly jeopardizing natural resource supplies and habitats, and the ability to deal with the waste byproduct of such growth. The demand for resources encourages fossil fuel exploitation, industrial production, and massive consumption, degrading the environment and exacerbating social health, especially concerning the disadvantage and poor. Recent scientific reports have shown that we are living in an era in which human activities are having a negative influence on the Earth's system on an unprecedented scale. The provision of ecosystem services, such as food production, clean air and water, or a stable climate, is under severe and growing pressure. The rate of global environmental change that we are currently witnessing has not been observed before in human history and has an increasing impact on human well-being. As a result, people and communities face growing climate change and environmental vulnerability (Kok and Jäger 2009).

In 2009, global leaders and policymakers met in Copenhagen for a climate conference to discuss the state of the global environment and specifically climate change. Climate economist Sir Nicholas Stern of Britain referred to the conference as the "most important gathering since the Second World War, given what is at stake." Yet it appears that little has been accomplished over the intervening years. More recently, the WMO published on its website, "The warmest seven years have all been since 2015, with 2016, 2019 and 2020 constituting the top three." Studies provide increasing certainty of the causes of global warming, "We find no convincing evidence that natural variability can account for the amount of global warming observed over the industrial era" (2022, 35).

The latest IPCC report concludes that it is quite likely that the last thirty years are the warmest consecutive years in the last 1,400 years in the northern latitudes (IPCC 2021). According to the National Oceanic and Atmospheric Administration's National Centers for Environmental Information (NCEI) Global Annual Temperature Outlook and data through July, it is virtually certain (> 99.0 percent) that 2023 will rank among the five warmest years on record, with a nearly 50 percent probability that 2023 will rank as the warmest on record (NOAA 2023). The implication is that the Earth will continue to warm significantly into the future, bringing more intense tropical storms, long-lasting droughts, intensified rainstorms, and rising sea levels.

Reports including the National Climate Assessment Report, The Royal Society, and the IPCC's recent release reach the same basic conclusions regarding carbon loading and global warming. The reports also outline where there are uncertainties in data analysis and interpretation, especially considering the variability in weather patterns and global warming feedback. Opponents or skeptics of climate change see in these uncertainties a means to deny that there really is change at work. For instance, data indicate that there is a slower rate of increase in temperatures over the last fifteen years (the "pause" or hiatus), whereas popular opinion (and earlier science) assumed a steady onward increase. Thus, many climate deniers assume climate scientists must have it wrong. The NCAR, however, addresses this issue, stating,

> Climate models are not intended to match the real-world timing of natural climate variations—instead, models have their own internal timing for such variations. Most modeling studies do not yet account for the observed changes in solar and volcanic forcing mentioned in the previous paragraph. Therefore, it is not surprising that the timing of such a slowdown in the rate of increase in the models would be different than that observed. (Melillo et al. 2014)

In Scientific Reports Number 5, Lewandowsky and co-authors countered climate skeptics (including the IPCC itself) regarding a "hiatus" or pause in global warming that was popularly reported. The researchers recognize that there is fluctuation in observations of warming but no change in the warming trend since the 1970s (2015). The confusion for the public is over the meaning of "hiatus." In science, this does not mean "stopped" but refers to observational temperature difference from the models employed.[2]

The observed slowdown in surface temperature is not unexpected since both observation and modeling recognize that surface air temperature does not project a steady linear increase, especially considering the effects of El Niño and La Niña. Nevertheless, the last decade has been the warmest recorded decade according to the UN's World Meteorological Organization (WMO 2023). The oceans absorb much surface heat (more than 90 percent) with a concomitant effect on general surface temperatures. Otherwise, surface and atmospheric temperatures would be much higher. "Globally, these carbon dioxide 'sinks' have roughly kept pace with emissions from human activities, continuing to draw about half of the emitted CO_2 back out of the atmosphere. However, we do not expect this to continue indefinitely," according to Pieter Tans, a climate researcher with NOAA's Earth System Research Laboratory (NOAA 2012).

Because climate change is very complex, with feedback loops and with such feedback loops, and under constant revised, rejected, or uncertain theories, data, and models, corporate interests use lobbyists and advertisements to throw doubt on the science of climate change among the population. In November 2009, the servers at the University of East Anglia were hacked, and hundreds of emails were stolen and made public. Portions of these emails were publicized to suggest that data were fudged and that ultimately climate change warnings were part of a vast conspiracy. For example, one email has a university climatologist writing, "I've just completed Mike's Nature trick of adding in the real temps to each series for the last 20 years (i.e., from 1981 onward) and from 1961 for Keith's to hide the decline" (Skeptical Science 2015). That the researcher was discussing a data handling technique was irrelevant to those who believe in a climate conspiracy. The Union of Concerned Scientists summarized the reaction to the suggestion of manipulation of data by listing six official investigations and other organizations that exonerated the East Anglia scientists of wrongdoing (2014). They used a statistical technique to uncover a true measure of the data, something any statistician would recognize as valid.

Skepticism in science is valid and part of the scientific method, with observations and conclusions challenged for their accuracy. But much of the work of climate scientists, never complete but under constant review, adding or subtracting ideas as new data are generated, has become politicized. Climate science represents a challenge to business as usual, and this in turn generates fear among those whose ideology, economic well-being, or sense of the meaning of the role of government is challenged. Climate research, from a conservative point of view, suggests creating a new world order with new global rules and expectations and may sound suspiciously like a leftist project to upset the status quo.

For many scientists, the question is how rapid global environmental change will occur as time moves on. If we believe change will be gradual or smooth, then it is quite possible society can adapt over time relatively well to these changes taking place. But it is also possible that change can come rapidly and radically as well. Earth history offers many examples of rapid and drastic change, sometimes over a few decades (see, for example, Adams, Maslin, and Thomas 1999). Spencer Weart provides a recent review of the history of the discovery of climate change, illustrating not only how the knowledge of global warming developed but also the increasing awareness that Earth's climate history is less stable than previously assumed and, "The accumulation of evidence, reinforced by at least one reasonable explanation (the reorganization of ocean circulation) destroyed long-held assumptions. Most experts now accepted that abrupt climate change, huge change, global change, was possible at any time" (2017).

Brian Fagan (2008) and Eugene Linden (2007) have written on the tenuous relationship between climate and the health of societies, particularly urban-based social systems. Looking at historic patterns of climate change in *The Great Warming*, Fagan illustrates the impact of climate, writing, "Far to the south, in Central America, great Maya cities tottered under medieval drought while Andean civilizations wilted in the face of an evaporating Lake Titicaca and faltering runoff in coastal river valleys" (229). Jared Diamond agrees with Fagan's analysis and argues in his book, *Collapse*, that for many earlier societies such as the Viking settlements of Greenland or the Rapa Nui of Easter Island, the collapse of local ecosystems played a significant role in the demise of those societies (2011). What history teaches us is that civilization is conditioned on an adequate, stable environment conducive to developing and expanding agriculture and the urban settlements on which it is based (the 12,000-year Holocene interglacial period). Fagan and Linden point out that changing patterns of precipitation, as experienced by the Mayans of Central America or the complex at Chaco Canyon in the American southwest, for example, led to the collapse of those societies. Anasazi culture, after hundreds of years, migrated due to the rapid onslaught of the Great Drought and their increasingly arid canyon, disappearing into the mist of history, leaving behind irrigation complexes and empty adobe cities. The great civilizations between the Tigris and Euphrates Rivers likewise befell the same fate as population increase led to agricultural expansion, which relied on intensified irrigation, resulting in increased soil salinity and declines in agricultural production. The conclusion is that it is difficult for societies to change in a way that meets the new challenges yet maintains a traditional way of life.

THE OPENING OF PANDORA'S RESOURCE BOX

A growing population not only brings pressure on food sources but also on a variety of other natural resources. Everything we touch began as a raw resource to be processed and manufactured to some endpoint. According to Erik Assadourian at the Worldwatch Institute, between 1950 and 2005, "metals production grew sixfold, oil consumption eightfold. . . . In total, 60 billion tons of resources are now extracted annually" (2010, 4; Worldwatch 2013a). Such resource use is rapidly growing beyond the Earth's capacity to absorb such exploitation with limits to the Earth's resilience capacity. A growing global affluent class manifests itself in new demands for various consumer products, leading to increased pressure on resource exploitation for manufacturing.

As mentioned at the beginning of the chapter, we are facing not only global climatic change but also pervasive resource exploitation and degradation on a scale never experienced in history. The United Nations Environmental Program's 2016 report on global material flows illustrates the growing use of materials (iron, steel, cement, copper, etc.). The increase in extraction, processing, and use is attributed to increased per capita income and consumption (UNEP 2019). The general reverberations on the environment have created an immense impact footprint. The Global Footprint Network sees the human imprint of resource use, along with population growth, requiring 1.5 planets to provide the ecological goods needed each year (2014; WWF 2018, 32). The consequence of contemporary environmental exploitation is pervasive: mineral mining and its waste, deforestation, desertification, water, soil and air pollution, and increasingly scarce water supplies. Such concerns are nothing new, of course, occupying the thinking of earlier environmentalists. Fairfield Osborn, president of the New York Zoological Society, and William Vogt, an ecologist at the Pan-American Union, both expressed environmental concerns as the Great Acceleration was beginning. Both published books in 1948 linking the post-war economic boom to environmental degradation. Both were concerned about how expanding production and resource use were fast placing limitations on the Earth. Seventy-four years ago, we were given notice that our behaviors were ill-adapted to the health of the planet, and yet in 2024 we still grapple with issues of environmental degradation.

In 1972, *The Limits to Growth* was published by Donella Meadows and colleagues, which argued a finite number of natural resources would be jeopardized by continual economic growth and consumption. The authors argued that "If the present growth trends in world population, industrialization, pollution, food production, and resource depletion continue unchanged, the limits to growth on this planet will be reached sometime within the next one hundred years" (1972, 23). The instant controversy had critics point out that science, technology, and innovation will solve the problems of depletion, pollution, and population. The doomsayers, it was thought, were alarmists employing simplistic logic, a trend that continues today. Critics of the report said the market would make corrections, and that rising resource prices would lead to conservation of resources. Critics reflected the basic problem that environment and resource limitations are in opposition to the ideology of progress as a dominant worldview, one pushed by economic advisors and politicians.

After centuries of indiscriminate use of the Earth's natural resources, from extraction to dumping of toxic chemicals, seemingly irreversible damage is apparent. Since the middle of the twentieth century, the growth of the technological capacity to locate and exploit natural resources to meet new production and consumer demands has had a profound impact on the planet's ecosystems. All environmental systems appear under critical stress. The degree of our impact and the difficulties of mitigating the effects of such impacts can be seen in the five resource case studies. The term "environmental crisis" encompasses more than global climate change but includes a variety of associated issues such as resource depletion, habitat loss, and chemical pollutants. There has been an incredible growth in human activity, remark Steffen, Crutzen, and McNeill. "Over the past 50 years," they write, defining the Great Acceleration in Ambio, "humans have changed the world's ecosystems more rapidly and extensively than in any other comparable period in human history. The Earth is in its sixth great extinction event, with rates of species loss growing rapidly for both terrestrial and marine ecosystems" (2007, 617; WWF 2020).

The degree of our impact and the difficulties in mitigating the effects of our impact can be seen in the following case studies. The selected studies illustrate the degraded nature of the environment. Yet, with numerous warnings of the effects of environmental degradation, serious resource exploitation continues unless concerted efforts are made to limit such consequences.

Unlike global warming, the "good" news is that many of these systems can be remedied through mitigating policy solutions and environmental enforcement.

Case Study 1: The Ocean of Life

The condition of global warming means that the oceans will continue to absorb carbon dioxide, but up to a limit, which in turn increases ocean warming and acidification. The 2021 IPCC states, "The heat content of the global ocean has increased since at least 1970 and will continue to increase over the 21st century (virtually certain). The associated warming will likely continue until at least 2300 even for low-emission scenarios because of the slow circulation of the deep ocean" (9–5). Research suggests that the increased acidic rate is possibly faster than any period in the last 300 million years. Additional research suggests as acidity in the ocean increases, its ability to absorb CO_2 decreases, weakening its ability to act as a carbon sink. Increased ocean acidification will also have a serious effect upon many marine species such as phytoplankton (a major food source for many marine animals), coral reefs, mollusks, and various finfish. Some species will win and thrive while others will find the changes too rapid to adapt and will most likely die out. A study of the growth and extent of marine heatwaves (MHW) by Smale and colleagues found that extreme ocean warming has stressed critical foundational species such as corals, seagrasses, and kelp (2019). The study concludes that birds and corals will be most affected. Some fish and invertebrates may be able to migrate to areas less prone to warming habitats. The three foundational species are particularly worrisome since they provide critical ecological services for other species.

In general, the globe's oceans are under severe stress due to atmospheric climate change and exacerbated by other human-caused actions. "Multiple stressors—ocean acidification, warming, decreases in oceanic oxygen concentrations (deoxygenation), increasing UV-B irradiance due to stratospheric ozone depletion, overfishing, pollution and eutrophication—and their interactions are creating significant challenges for ocean ecosystems," summarized in a report by the Third Symposium on the Ocean in a High-CO_2 World (IGBP 2013).

The problem is not only acidification but also the twin problem of mining the oceans for seafood and, increasingly, mining for mineral deposits. Due to industrial open-sea fishing, most fisheries are now in crisis, being fully overexploited or heavily depleted (Gjerde et al., 2013; Roberts, 2012). Multinational fishing trawlers engage in the excessive capture of non-market fish species, sea turtles, seabirds, and so on. Ocean floor net dredging has affected coral ecosystems, coinciding with the cumulative effects of fish technology. The decline in fish stocks is also due to a lack of any multilateral commons governance over international waters. Pollution such as plastics is a growing danger to many marine species such as turtles. The increase in deoxygenated dead zones likewise has a detrimental impact on marine habitats.

Camilo Mora and colleagues discuss the twin threats from ocean warming and marine life predation. They focus on overexploitation due to indiscriminate bottom trawling that captures vast amounts of marine life and habitat fragmentation that prevents the efficient migration of breeding populations of species from moving between groups. The inflow of marine immigrants is important for genetic exchange, "reduces the effects of inbreeding depletion, expands the geographical ranges of species, sustains populations that could not be maintained through self-recruitment and affects the probability of stochastic local extinctions" (2007, 1023). They conclude that warming waters negatively affect the ability of populations to counter limited species migration, thus contributing to population decline 1.4 times faster than nonwarming populations.

Various IPCC reports over the years indicate that marine degradation is occurring more rapidly than anticipated or predicted. In *The Ocean of Life*,

Callum Roberts outlines the impact on the world's oceans from the giant plastic garbage dump known as the Pacific Gyre (almost the size of Texas), the collapse of 80 percent of the major fish populations (such as grouper and red snapper), the amount of toxic metals and chemicals flowing into the sea (creating dead zones), and the dying of the major coral reefs (due to acidification and ocean warming). In his conclusion, Roberts states that the diminishment of ocean health should discomfort us all and warns that, "the disintegration of untamed nature reaches beyond aesthetics. It is undermining the ability of the oceans to sustain human needs and well-being" (2012, 228; see also Whitty 2009). The Second World Ocean Assessment of the state of the world's oceans offers a dire warning of oceanic collapse. The report concludes, "The lack of appropriate wastewater treatment and the release of pollutants from the manufacturing industry, agriculture, tourism, fisheries and shipping continue to put pressure on the ocean, with a negative impact on food security, food safety and marine biodiversity" (United Nations 2021, 7). An earlier review of the literature on the health of the oceans had J. Bijma and colleagues conclude, "Regardless of whether or not an extinction event has started, the current carbon perturbation will have huge implications for humans" (2013, 502). The outcome is difficult to foresee. How the trend toward large-scale extinctions will impact global societies, especially those most directly dependent upon marine harvesting, remains uncertain.

In a recent op-ed essay in the *New York Times*, Richard Spinrad of NOAA and Ian Boyd of Britain's Department of Environment, Food, and Rural Affairs wrote of the increasingly perilous oceanic conditions. They conclude that due to increased levels of global CO_2 ocean acidification is accelerating and will "almost certainly affect seafood supplies and the ocean's ability to store pollutants, including future carbon emissions" (Spinrad and Boyd 2015). New research recently published in Science Advances estimates a more rapid increase in ocean heat content and since 1990 greater heat content at deeper layers of the ocean (Cheng et al. 2017). Of course, increases in ocean heat content will increase glacial calving where glaciers and ice sheets meet warmer ocean waters, contributing to rising ocean levels.

Climate change and marine degradation are causing fundamental change and collapse in a variety of ecological niches. The human impact on the oceans is profound. The decline in marine ecosystems has had a dramatic impact on the seabird population. Research by Michelle Paleczny and her colleagues found that the global seabird population declined by 70 percent between 1950 and 2010. The causes are a laundry list: "The cause of the estimated overall decline in seabird populations is likely a suite of threatening human activities—introduced species at nesting colonies (e.g., rats, cats), entanglement in fishing gear at sea, overfishing of food sources by humans, climate change and severe weather, pollution, disturbance, direct exploitation (harvesting chicks, eggs, adults), development, and energy production" (2015, 7–8). Such a population decline is worrisome because seabirds are a major indicator of the health of marine ecosystems.

Natural ecosystems are changing due not only to changing climate and temperature conditions but also to various forms of economic development. More recent development and concern center on the increased interest and activity of deep-seabed mining (DSM). The global conservation organization, Fauna & Flora, published a new assessment concluding that deep-seabed mining potentially threatens the health and viability of various marine ecosystems. DSM is increasingly attractive as new technologies allow for the extraction of countless nodules of manganese, nickel, and cobalt important for the manufacture of electric cars and other products. Using ocean floor robots to dredge and pump the nodules up to surface ships, vast areas will be disrupted. The industry argues that to meet a clean energy future, deep-sea mining will support the transition to a low-carbon future. Fauna & Flora's 2023 assessment cautions that increased mining activity is premature without further research and safeguards in place. The report highlights growing evidence that sediment plumes from dredging and dewatering of the nodules will harm marine life:

> Deep-sea organisms are expected to be highly sensitive to the effects of sediment plumes as many exist in an environment in which the water is typically very clear. Plumes, which may contain elevated metal concentrations, can smother organisms, clogging respiratory and olfactory surfaces, and weaken organisms leading to mortality, reduce visual communication and bioluminescent signaling in turn affecting the ability of animals to capture prey and reproduce. (2023, 15)

Additionally, the report warns that such mining activity could release captured carbon dioxide, and other toxic chemicals, and negatively affect deep-sea food webs. Little is understood of the implications sea mining has on broader marine ecosystems. This includes coastal communities dependent upon fishing and other marine activities.

The above suggests the need for increased research and the development of new rules-based regulatory oversight of ocean mining. Presently, governance remains fragmented with uncertainties and scientific gaps in understanding the dynamics of deep-sea ecosystems. The need for greater research to close the information lacuna for effective policy to engage in industry oversight is paramount. Research and transparency are needed to create standards and rules governing the widespread impact of DSM.

While global warming has received most of the public's attention, the continual exploitation of natural resources such as marshes, wetlands, and tidal zones and the consequences of such exploitation likewise offer the potential to disrupt our conventional forms of development and ways of living. Many coastal areas are degraded by seaside tourist resort development. One estimate is that 50 percent of the world's mangrove swamps have disappeared. These ecosystems are important, providing habitat for many species, stabilizing coastal areas, and acting as energy buffers from storm waves. Much economic development, such as residential housing development, does not consider the costs of such environmental degradation. For example, much new residential development in Arizona's Valley of the Sun and southern California lacks a realistic assessment of the risks of decreasing water availability in what are water-scarce deserts.

Lester Brown alerts us to the fact of increased global population growth and its relationship to agriculture. The global population is expected to increase from the present 7 billion people to 9 to 12 billion by 2100. The growth of population, the increase in the number of affluent global consumers, and their demand for better standards of living and consumer goods will also add to environmental degradation. Brown warns that such a population increase is problematic, "given the difficulties in expanding the food supply, such as those posed by spreading water shortages and global warming," concluding, "We are fast outgrowing the earth's capacity to sustain our increasing numbers" (2012, 15). William Laurance reports on the relationship between population growth, conversion of ecosystems to agriculture, and the increase in the use of inorganic cultivation inputs. Laurance forecasts that by 2050 "global nitrogen fertilization is projected to rise by 270% where phosphorus use increases by 240%. Agricultural demands for irrigation water are expected to grow by 190% over the same period" but at a time of increased global drought conditions such as in Arizona and Kenya (2001, 532).

Population growth, urbanization, and urban sprawl continue to encourage habitat destruction, loss of arable farmland and wetlands, and, in some cases, armed conflict. The major obstacle is one of political will and changes in policy by governments and corporate enterprises. The difficulty here is that from a political and economic viewpoint, economic expansion is seen as imperative. Former President Donald Trump saw a zero-sum game in which climate change mitigation comes at the expense of economic and employment growth. Corporations may wish to engage in less exploitative activities, but competition and the profit motive are difficult issues to counter.

Case Study 2: The Chemical Revolution

As much as Earth is a water world, it is also a chemical world where a sea of natural chemical compounds makes life possible. Many of these chemicals are useful, such as the chemical trails used by ants, bees, and other insects, or the chemical secretions that alert members to changes in bodily function. Hormonal chemicals control when Macaw parrots are to molt older feathers and when it is time to seek a mate for procreation. But over the last several hundred years, a whole series of newly manufactured chemicals have entered the environment. Rachael Carson's famous 1962 warning call to environmental chemical pollution, *Silent Spring,* was an early and dramatic analysis of the indiscriminate use of inorganic chemicals and their fatal consequences for birds and insects. Our land, lakes, rivers, oceans, and air are now saturated with organic acids, hydrocarbons, nitrates, pesticides, fertilizers, and pharmaceutical wastes. The human body itself is a storehouse of various laboratory-designed synthetic chemicals. It is estimated that the human body contains seven hundred industrial chemicals, many of which have not been tested.

The Stockholm Resilience Center lists chemical pollution as one of the planetary boundaries of concern. The Centre warns about the effects of heavy metal compounds and synthetic chemicals, stating on their website,

> These compounds can have potentially irreversible effects on living organisms and on the physical environment (by affecting atmospheric processes and climate). Even when the uptake and bioaccumulation of chemical pollution is at sub-lethal levels for organisms, the effects of reduced fertility and the potential of permanent genetic damage can have severe effects on ecosystems far removed from the source of the pollution. (Stockholm n.d.)

Since World War II, research and manufacturing of a host of new chemicals have been released into society to fight various pests in agriculture or in creating new products. Rockström and colleagues cite an EPA report from 1998 suggesting that there may be between 80,000 and 100,000 chemicals available on the global marketplace (2009). It is estimated that 96 percent of all manufactured goods are touched by chemistry. Many chemicals, as by-products of manufacturing, migrate from waste dumps and industrial areas and find their way into rivers and streams, eventually reaching the oceans. For example, General Electric used polychlorinated biphenyl (PCB) in manufacturing and contaminated the Hudson River. The company has had to spend $1.4 billion to remove PCB-contaminated sediment from the river. Most of these chemicals have no counterpart in nature and are organic laboratory creations with deadly consequences for humans and nature. The environmental saturation of these chemicals, whose long-term health and environmental effects are unknown, is a cause for concern.

Christian Daughton, chief of EPA's Environmental Chemical Branch asks,

> Tremendous investments continue to be made in the prevention, control, and mitigation of environmental pollution by chemicals. Nevertheless, how can we be sure that these are the most important chemicals with respect to protecting humans and the ecology? Do we sufficiently understand the processes that

> dictate exposure to these pollutants and its aftermath? Is the introduction of new chemicals to commerce outrunning our ability to fully assess their significance in the environment or to human health?" (2005, 7)

With tens of thousands of chemicals that haven't been evaluated by the EPA, their global environmental impact is not known except in specific cases.

A recently released report by the U.S. Food and Drug Administration found that in 2017, numerous food commodities such as grains, fruits, and vegetables contained detectable levels of chemical residue. In grain samples, 41.7 percent contained residue, fruits 84 percent, and vegetables 53.1 percent (FDA 2017, 17). According to Hemler et al., "In the general population, low-level pesticide exposure is widespread, and the primary route of exposure is diet, especially intake of conventionally grown fruits and vegetables. In the United States, more than 90 percent of the population have detectable pesticides in their urine and blood" (Hemler et al. 2018, E1). The list of pesticides found in human food at any level is quite high, but most problematic are glyphosate (active ingredient in Roundup), 2,4-D, and chlorpyrifos, all known carcinogens. We are daily exposed to chemicals used in our gardens and lawns, as we clean kitchen countertops. However, they point out that violative residues in all samples were well below illegal levels. The Harvard researchers do caution that the health consequences of pesticides in humans are currently unknown.

The global population is at 8 billion and continues to increase at about 1 percent a year. As populations grow, there is a continual need to increase food supplies. The need to use a variety of inorganic inputs such as fertilizers, herbicides, and pesticides is important if food supplies are to keep abreast of population growth. Global population is projected to increase by billions by 2050, with a concomitant grain demand expected to double (Tilman et al. 2002). They add that "This doubling will result from a projected 2.4-fold increase in per capita real income and from dietary shifts towards a higher proportion of meat (much of it grain-fed) associated with higher income" (671). Although food stocks have improved due to chemical inputs, it has been at a price to the health of the land and local environments. Private family farms (in whichever country) need to survive, and industrial farms need to make a profit, and both are on a treadmill to increase input use to maintain or improve yields. There are thousands of farms, for example, in various watersheds along the 2,300-mile Mississippi River where excess fertilizer and other chemicals wash into the Mississippi and end up at the "dead zone" (due to hypoxia) at its confluence with the Gulf of Mexico. Mitigating such run-off would be very expensive and possibly offer little benefit to farmers. Profit-oriented corporate farms see little incentive since there is a bottom-line need to show profit growth (this reminds me of Perlman's book *Farming for Profit in the Hungry World* [1977], in which he said, "Farms today are designed to grow but one product: profit"). As we will discuss, how does the current market-based economic system get beyond the structural imperative of profit that is so instrumental to capitalism?

The intensive use of agro-chemicals has several consequences. Many agro-chemicals are exported to foreign markets where the buyers of a chemical may not understand the precautions if the warning label is not translated into a local language. There is also the additional problem that in the minds of many farmers, if a little application is good, a greater application is better, thus exacerbating the chemical's toxic effects or leading to runoff into neighboring water streams. In many countries such as India, where rural people live near the use of chemicals on local agro-plantations, exposure could lead to health problems. Matthew Power's research on the chemical endosulfan use on cashew plantations in Kerala, India, is a case in point. Power reported on the birth defects and harm to the central nervous system of villagers, the lack of health care, and the seeming incompetence or indifference of the local government to help the villagers or control the use of chemical spraying (2004). The problem is not the acute poisoning that is at issue, "It is the micro dose, a few molecules at a time, the chronic exposure of the community around the plantations over twenty years, that has visited upon them the wrath of a new and vengeful god" (60).

Heavy application of synthetic inputs can lead to soil erosion (bringing marginal lands into production by employing the inputs), loss of soil quality (decrease in organic nutrients, micro-fauna such as worms), and the elimination of pests and their predators. Modern farming, and especially monocrop industrial farming, though productive, is decreasing the diversity and viability of local ecosystems. The shift by Monsanto, Dow, and others to biotechnology and genetically modified plants does not solve the basic problem of ecosystem degradation. A major threat in this regard is genetic modifications (herbicide and pesticide-resistant crops) bleeding out into surrounding plants and animals. The possibility exists of the creation of super-resistant pests and weeds that will require ever more powerful chemicals or genetic modifications to control the new problem. It is within this context that cities such as Chicago struggle to recover wildflower prairie vegetation among lands that have been polluted.

Case Study 3: The Politics of Water: Rising Demand, Diminishing Supply

The Earth is composed primarily of water; however, most of it is saline and not fit for human consumption. Fresh water accounts for only 3 percent, and an estimated 2 percent of that is locked up in glaciers and the icy poles. As a critical resource for life on Earth, fresh water and its relationship to the global hydrological cycle is one of the nine planetary boundaries. Human activity and physical manipulation of water sources are now the driving forces for this boundary. "The consequences of human modification of water bodies include both global-scale river flow changes and shifts in vapor flows arising from land use change. These shifts in the hydrological system can be abrupt and irreversible" (Stockholm Resilience Centre n.d.). Agriculture, manufacturing, and a growing global population will put increased pressure on a limited water supply. As an increasingly scarce resource, water grows as a valuable commodity, in some cases public water privatized for sale, that will determine access to it, especially for low-income individuals and racial or ethnic minorities.

Many populations rely on glacial melt to feed rivers that are then exploited by local populations as a critical water source. Glaciers represent a large percentage of the planet's total freshwater source. Glaciers act as "water towers" by accumulating water as snow and ice over winter seasons and releasing meltwater during dry seasons for agriculture and drinking water for communities. As glaciers recede due to decreased winter snowfall, input into lakes and rivers decreases. La Paz and El Alto in Bolivia receive around 30 percent of their water from glacial melt. According to Wouter Buytaert of the Grantham Institute of the Imperial College of London, "in remote regions of Bolivia, Peru, Chile, Argentina, and to a lesser extent Ecuador, tens of thousands of poor rural dwellers rely on glacier-fed river water for irrigation and drinking water" (2021). Millions of people will face shrinking rivers, lakes, and groundwater, having trouble accessing water for domestic use and local small-farmer agriculture.

Water may not seem a likely candidate as a change agent or instigator of trans-boundary political conflict or within national borders. Water plays a unique role as an absolute necessity for life—we can only survive a few days at most without it. Yet water is becoming an increasingly scarce commodity, limiting access to clean potable water for hundreds of millions of people. Water is a progressively finite resource due to the Earth's slow ability to replenish aquifers, the shrinking of glaciers, and changing rainfall patterns. Models of climate change suggest that northern hemispheric areas and the tropics will experience increased rainfall, but the middle latitudes, already relatively arid, will become drier (Mexico City and Cape Town, South Africa relies on a diminishing supply of surface water and is in a recent water depletion crisis). Yet it is in these areas where large, dense populations exist and where agriculture is already pumping vast amounts of surface and groundwater (aquifers) to irrigate crops and serve industry. Recent analysis by James Famiglietti at the University of California, utilizing specialized NASA satellites named Grace, has moved to develop an inventory of global groundwater reserves. Famiglietti adds, in comments to *The Observer* newspaper, "What Grace shows us is that groundwater depletion is happening at a very rapid rate in almost all of the major aquifers in the arid and semi-arid parts of the world" (Goldenberg 2014). As groundwater supplies begin to diminish, water demand has to be compensated by tapping into river sources, and most rivers are already under stress due to excessive demand and decreasing rainfall runoff.

The pressure on water sources and supplies is due, in part, to a global increase in population adding an additional one and a half billion by 2050. Much of this increase will take place in areas that are already water-stressed, such as India and Arizona, adding to a desperate scramble to secure adequate supplies. This is particularly true in transboundary areas such as the Jordan River basin, the Nile, and the Indus River of north India. Growing populations mean more economic growth and activity, as well as intensified use and/or expansion of agriculture to meet food demands. Michael Klare points out that the history of major river basins is one of tenuous political relationships over water usage. He illustrates the difficulty of reaching equitable agreements when power differentials exist, such as between militarily powerful Egypt and the other less powerful riparian states, or when one nation controls the sources of the river, as exists between Turkey (the source of the Tigris and Euphrates) and Syria and Jordan (2001). North Africa and the Middle East are presently experiencing high water stress for most of their populations.

Peter Gleick and Matthew Heberger of the Pacific Institute, a research organization tracking water issues as they relate to international security, have found in recent years a fourfold increase in confrontations over access to water. Of grave concern is what happens as water becomes scarcer and untold numbers of people begin to suffer and migrate across international boundaries. While there is a history of agreements among states over water usage, Gleick and Heberger believe that there is a growing threat within countries, at the subnational level, leading to local water conflicts. Their fear, they conclude, is that mechanisms to mitigate the risk of transnational boundary disputes over water do nothing to control or reduce the risks of subnational ethnic, regional, or religious violence (2014, 161–162). For example, they report that two hundred foreign tourists were held hostage by farmers of the Abu Simbel region of Egypt as a protest over inadequate irrigation water. Subnational violence also can be instigated not only by local groups struggling over water rights, such as between pastoral cattle herders and farmers, but by international and Kenyan economic development plans to secure land for food and biofuel cultivation, thereby exacerbating distribution problems over scarce water supplies (167).

Even when there are historic river management schemes in place, such as among the river states bordering the Rio Grande in the American Southwest, the agreements can come under increasing pressure as circumstances change.

The critical variable is growing river basin populations with their concomitant pressures for economic development and agriculture. According to analysis by NASA's Grace data, the Southwest is experiencing groundwater depletion at substantial rates due to increased population, long-term drought conditions, and continued demand by agriculture and industry in a dynamically growing region (2013). Yet it is such growth and demand that can force riparian states to attempt (re)negotiations to effectively manage increasingly scarce water. The Colorado River Management Plan, covering seven states and Mexico, is an attempt to reach agreed-upon solutions to water usage under historic drought conditions.[3] The Jordan River provides one such example of a series of attempts to develop an equitable plan involving states generally at odds with each other in religious, political, and cultural terms. Yet despite such differences, Israel, Jordan, Syria, Lebanon, and Palestine have established several treaties, accords, and institutions to manage the river (Zawahri 2010).

For the Nile River Basin countries, assert Link and colleagues, "Cooperation is essential for a basin-wide increase of adaptive capacity and therefore reduction of vulnerability to climate change" (n.d., 35). It is a question of the right incentives for reaching an equitable management plan. They add that the need by Egypt for information on rainfall and upstream water flows in the Upper Nile countries could act as an incentive if Egypt is to efficiently manage the Aswan High Dam (36). On the other hand, they caution, regional climate change could affect upcountry hydrology and change water runoff, lessening those countries' ability to challenge "Egypt's hydro-hegemony." This in effect could upset any potential compromise and limit Egypt's willingness to cooperate and instead assert military-political pressure. Yet when countries define access to water in national security terms, the stakes in dispute outcomes increase and may lead to violence. In their analysis on international water conflict, Gleick and Heberger found indications that Egypt and Sudan entered into a secret agreement regarding a major dam project under construction by Ethiopia.

From Ethiopia's perspective, the historic agreement that gave Egypt the majority share of Nile water and veto power over other riparian states' demands is unjust and invalid. The GERD dam is necessary to meet Ethiopia's growing demand for energy and water to encourage economic development and to meet the demands of a population that has almost doubled in the last decade (Rahman 2014). Capturing water by damming the Nile is seen as essential by Ethiopia to address the growing problems of increased aridity due to drought, a population growth rate that needs access to land and food, and land degradation due to deforestation. These basic and growing problems and the primary means of addressing them are seen, by Egypt, Ethiopia, Sudan, Kenya, and others, to lie with increased Nile water access. In other words, all the states share the same problems and have designed the same basic solution that requires all states to increase usage of a growing scarcity of river water. With its own population already under stress due to poor infrastructure and delivery of adequate water supplies, the Egyptian government understands such circumstances, should they become worse, could lead to further social and political unrest. If no agreement can be reached in which all parties agree to adequate (and possibly decreasing) water delivery, military action may be the only available option. In this regard, Rahman is relatively pessimistic about the riparian states' ability to cooperate. Responding to calls for "water sharing" or "benefit sharing," he argues is idealistic, "given the power relations along the Nile, and the asymmetrical flow of water resources in the upstream and downstream countries" (2014).

On the other hand, Ethiopia has more recently moved aggressively to map its aquifers for groundwater availability. According to the British Geological Survey, research suggests the potential for much greater groundwater access for development and households exists, although contaminants such as fluoride, salinity, and nitrates must be removed (2001). In Kenya, the discovery of the Lotikipi aquifer in the Turkana region will help to alleviate the severe drought conditions of the northern region. Speaking to SciDev.net, Suresh Patel of the Kenya Private Sector Alliance remarked on the potential for the Turkana region's economic future (2014). New aquifer mapping of the entire North Africa area is underway, but it is already clear that many of the aquifers are small and often of poor water quality. They may help local populations but are not a major water source for large scale economic development or population growth.

The United States, a country blessed with plentiful water, likewise is beginning to experience a growing regional water shortage. California is amid a historic drought that presents serious economic and political problems, a circumstance facing many Western states as well. Adam Nagourney and colleagues wrote recently in the *New York Times* that California has confronted the limits to growth due to a limited water supply. "But now a punishing drought—and the unprecedented measures the state announced last week to compel people to reduce water consumption—is forcing a reconsideration of whether the aspiration of untrammeled growth that has for so long been this state's driving engine has run against the limits of nature," they wrote (Nagourney et al. 2015). The issue, however, is not necessarily about future growth but rather about existing economic activities already underway. There is the potential for political conflict as farmers compete for scarce water. As the supply of surface water allotments diminishes for farmers, many are sinking expensive tube wells to tap into aquifers. The repercussion of such widespread drilling is lowering the water table for other farmers, forcing deeper wells, as well as land subsidence interfering with the flow of water.

What is clear from such reporting is that, beginning in California but spreading throughout the Western United States and globally, lifestyles and economic activity will have to change. Instituting new values and behaviors, such as foregoing golf courses and swimming pools, affecting lifestyles, may be the easier adaptation to dry conditions. A recent research report published in Science Advances by Mesfin Mekonnen and Arjen Hoekstra concludes that up to 4 billion people will experience severe water shortages at some period during the year, especially in areas already water-stressed (2016). Much more difficult will be the economic and industrial fallout of drought. Infused as economics is with politics and power, how will the new climate regime play out among the economic actors? What is certain is that the less income one has and the poorer one's nation, the more dramatic will be water stress.

It may be difficult to find common agreement when population pressures exist on a foundation of ethnic, religious, and political differences between the border states. You can, so to speak, cut the pie into only so many pieces, especially once all conservation practices are in place. What happens as the pie becomes smaller yet the demand for a slice continues to grow? What determines the division of the pie are the driving forces of capitalism—class interest, profit, and property relations. The internationally known water conflict in Cochabamba, Bolivia, pitting the working classes against elite interests combined with international capitalism is a case in point (see, for example, Achtenberg 2013).

Case Study 4: Mining the Earth

Exploiting the Earth for its mineral and metal content is nothing new. Many indigenous communities took advantage of various natural elements to make work more efficient for hunting, cultivation, or security. It could be argued that true exploitation began when Europeans linked, in a significant way, mineral extraction as a commodity that could bring wealth and power. For example, in the sixteenth century, the Spanish mined the great silver centers of Potosi, Bolivia, and Zacatecas, Mexico, employing thousands of Indian peons in the name of creating wealth. Using mercury in the process of separating silver embedded in ore poisoned workers and despoiled the surrounding environment. Beginning with the aftermath of the conquest of Mexico in 1521, the Spanish exported by 1660 over 185,000 kg of gold and more than 16 million kilograms of silver (see Spate 2010 on this aspect of Spain in the New World). As manufacturing and industry grew, such as iron ore for building material, new markets and demand in Europe and elsewhere, the need for ores and minerals likewise grew.

Many developing nations have been promoted and developed by Western colonial nations as sites of natural resource mining and production for export.

In their need for foreign exchange to import various goods such as medical technology or pharmaceuticals, they invite foreign extraction companies with the technology, investment capital, market access, and management skills to develop this sector of the economy. Following prescriptions by the International Monetary Fund and World Bank (ie., structural adjustment), low-income developing nations must fully exploit their natural resources to meet their international debt obligations.

According to a fact sheet produced by the American Association for the Advancement of Science, over the twentieth century major ores such as iron, manganese, tungsten, and cooper extraction have produced, for many of these ores, a waste rate between 60 and 99 percent. The organization adds,

> In consequence, over the past century mining has removed an estimated 100 million people from their land and destroyed forests and farmland, either directly for extraction or to accommodate the waste. The extraction and refining of ores require the use of toxic substances such as cyanide and mercury, which are often allowed to pollute land and river systems. (aaas.org)

In his environmental overview of the twentieth century, J. McNeill relates one estimate that by 1994 over 42 billion tons of earth had been moved for ore and metals extraction (2001, 30). It is important to note that much mineral exploitation in developing countries is often accomplished with little oversight by governing bodies due to corruption, a lack of skilled, technologically proficient personnel, or the financial means of accessing or rehabilitating damaged exploited areas. In developed nations such as Canada, controlling mining activity or mitigating the effects of mining projects can be just as difficult. According to the newspaper Business in Vancouver, Seabridge Gold Inc. plans on developing a $3.5 billion KSM "mega-mine project" near the border with Alaska. The project entails twin 23 kilometer long tunnels for moving ore and miners between two locations, producing 130,000 tons of ore per day, most of it tailing ponds that would require constant monitoring. Guy Archibald, a mining and clean water coordinator for the Southeast Alaska Conservation Council, commenting on the project, said, "The KSM calls for the application of unproven technology applied on an unprecedented scale that will have to operate for eternity in order to offer any level of protection to downstream communities" (Business in Vancouver 2014). As of 2022, the project continues to advance.

As the United States, Canada, and other countries search for alternatives to Middle East oil, recent investments have focused on fracking for oil and natural gas, often in sensitive environmental areas. Much attention and criticism of developing these resources has centered on how much CO_2 would be released into the atmosphere. Of equal importance, perhaps, is the other environmental effects such as groundwater usage, earthquakes (in fracking areas), water pollution, habitat destruction, and the general degradation of regional ecosystems. These consequences have received much less attention yet play a vital role if any kind of environmental sustainability is to be entertained for these industries.

Oil replaced coal as the fossil fuel of choice after its discovery at Oil Creek, Pennsylvania, in 1859. As coal's reputation as a great emitter of sulfur, nitrogen, and carbon dioxide became controversial, new alternatives were found in tar sands. Tar oil, or bitumen are sands rich in heavy oil found underneath Alberta's northern boreal forests where the deposits have laid for tens of millions of years (see Worster 2016, 203–215, for a history of Alberta's oil sands). According to Ed Struzik of Yale University's School of Environmental Studies, the sands need great heat to separate the oil from sand, which in 2011, 370 million cubic meters of water was used to create steam in the separation process. As the tar sands industry expands and as more countries seek to exploit their own tar sands, the diversion of water from already tight global supplies will become worse, increasing local environmental degradation. Once removed, the water and sand are injected into deep aquifers or placed in tailings ponds which cover 66 square miles of northern Alberta (2013). Environmentalists are concerned that such massive diversions will exacerbate warming trends in Canada's arboreal forests, drying up wetlands and threatening riparian habitats for thousands of miles within the Mackenzie River basin. It is estimated that cleaning up the tailings ponds and reclaiming mined land will cost more than 50 billion dollars and, as Worster concludes, probably cannot be done (Swift 2017; Worster 2016, 214–215).

A recent paper examining the health consequences of hydraulic fracturing by Theo Colborn and colleagues at the Endocrine Disruption Exchange found that fracturing to recover natural gas uses 944 products containing 632 chemicals. Many of the chemicals have the potential to be very toxic to human health, stating that

> More than 25% of the chemicals can cause cancer and mutations. Notably, 37% of the chemicals can affect the endocrine system that encompasses multiple organ systems including those critical for normal reproduction and development. The category of "other" is more common, and includes effects on weight, teeth, and bone and the ability of a chemical to cause death. More than 40% of the chemicals have been found to have ecological effects, indicating that they can harm aquatic and other wildlife. (2011, 1046; cf. Murawski 2014)

In the Appalachian Mountain regions of the eastern United States, the exploitation of coal reserves employs a method known as mountaintop removal. This process involves removing the "overburden" of soil above the seams of coal and essentially dumping the overburden over the mountainside into the valley below (the acronym MTM/VF). A National Resources Defense Council paper claims that one major mountaintop mine may exceed 10 square miles and remove 750 million cubic yards of waste (NRDC). Studies indicate the negative consequences of MTM/VF on local ecosystems. Margaret Palmer and Emily Bernhardt, in a survey of MTM/VF sites, conclude that valley fills "causes permanent loss of ecosystems that play critical roles in ecological processes such as nutrient cycling and production of organic matter for downstream food webs . . . also support abundant aquatic organisms, including many endemic species," what are referred to as biological hotspots (2010, 148; Bernhardt and Palmer 2011). Bernhardt and Palmer write that the Environmental Protection Agency (EPA) predicted that by 2012 an area over 5,600 km² of Appalachian forests will be severely and negatively impacted by such mining (49).

Land surface projects of the sort outlined above lead to severe and dramatic changes in the ecosystems and landscape of areas impacted. Many landscapes have developed into complex systems of structure and function between flora and fauna over many thousands of years. Once destroyed, reproducing such complex systems is practically impossible. The reclamation and restoration projects required under existing laws are inadequate to replicate nature. Bernhardt and Palmer examined 38,000 projects between 2002 and 2005 and found little support for even minimal replication of the original landscape in riparian areas. They comment,

> we do not know of a single case (of 38,000 projects in our database) in which stream creation, as proposed by many MTVF compensatory mitigation plans outlined, has been shown to recreate stream hydrology, much less to support the ecological functions lost when streams are filled. No peer-reviewed scientific studies document a case where the critical features of stream ecosystems (flow, biota, and nutrient and material processing) have been created in a surface-mined landscape. (2011, 50)

The issues that affect bringing exploited landscapes back to health are twofold. One is the inability to replicate complex ecosystems. The science, technology, and corporate will to do so is nearly impossible. Palmer and Bernhardt, in U.S. Senate testimony, conclude that "An analysis of >75 channel reconfiguration projects overwhelmingly showed that restoration of biodiversity failed" (2009). Second corporations that engage in mining activities essentially see substantive reclamation as a cost and will limit, to the best of their abilities, such financial outlays. The result is environmental degradation whose long-term ability to fully recover its former complexity is very problematic.

Case Study 5: Disappearing Forests

Forests, which cover about one-fourth of the Earth's land surface, play a critical set of roles as habitats for wildlife, storehouses for biodiversity, water run-off, and prevention of soil erosion. The Stockholm Resilience Centre lists land system change as one of the nine planetary boundaries due to the critical role land use plays in the stability of the Earth system. Changing land use such as deforestation, urban sprawl, and patterns of agriculture, while taking place at the local level, have in the aggregate global consequences. The Centre declares, "This land-use change is one driving force behind the serious reductions in biodiversity, and it has impacts on water flows and on the biogeochemical cycling of carbon, nitrogen and phosphorus and other important elements" (n.d.).

In terms of immediate human use, forests provide lumber, pulpwood, areas of tourist attraction, and home to many global indigenous communities. Perhaps most importantly, forests act as carbon sinks as they absorb atmospheric carbon for growth. It is estimated that forests store about 80 percent of atmospheric carbon, but through their destruction, they also act as sources of carbon output into the atmosphere. Forests also play a major role in climate change since they "influence ground temperatures, evapotranspiration, surface roughness, albedo, cloud formation, and precipitation" (IPPC 2014, 99). Thus, the health and condition of the Earth's forests are of prime concern for the health and condition of all Earth's living communities.

The conditions of forests under climate change are subject to debate primarily due to the understanding that as atmospheric carbon load increases, trees benefit through increased carbon absorption and growth. A recent study published in *Nature* by Trevor Keenan and coauthors found that trees not only stored more carbon for growth but were also more efficient in their usage of water (2013). The research suggests that in semi-arid areas, where water is a limiting factor in tree growth, the intake of carbon increasing water uptake efficiency might lead to higher growth rates and, in the long run, contribute more to pulling carbon out of the atmosphere. Additionally, forests also emit tremendous amounts of water vapor that play a role in local and regional rainfall patterns that affect agricultural and water supplies for urban populations. When forests disappear due to land use such as deforestation replaced by soybean plantations, regional rainfall patterns also change. Last year (2023) witnessed boreal forests in Canada and northern California experience intense, immense, and essentially uncontrollable wildfires over vast swaths of land. Most experts agree that climate change had a large role to play in these fires.

The beneficial effect of carbon absorption remains subject to debate due to other negative feedback. According to work by Aaron Weed and colleagues, other factors such as drought-induced stress can likewise play a role in the health of forests (2013). As temperatures increase, the survivability of insects and pathogens increases due to milder winters as well as an increase in their geographic zones. Weed et al., comment that this pattern is "evident in the United States where invasive insects and pathogens are becoming an increasingly important component of forest disturbance" (2013, 449). Their research found bark beetle epidemics have increased in a variety of U.S. forest regions. They conclude that, "Given the climate trajectory, the strong ties between temperature and beetle epidemics, and the extensive mortality that has already occurred in some regions . . . we can anticipate continuing losses of these forests and the ecosystem services that they provide" (453). Research by Bentz, et al. agree concluding, "Bark beetle outbreaks driven by climate change may also result in trajectories beyond the historical resilience boundaries of some forest ecosystems, causing irreversible ecosystem regime shifts" (2010, 611). The results are vast swaths of western and northeastern forests being lost to insect infestation and local climate change.

Additionally, forests are under pressure due to deforestation from logging, changing land use patterns, and more intense forest fires. Much deforestation and habitat loss are due to land use changes to develop palm oil plantations, primarily in Indonesia, which holds the globe's third-largest intact rainforest (Vidal 2013). In Indonesia, such monocrop plantation development provides employment for poor workers and needed revenue for the government. According to a report published by the Worldwatch Institute, Indonesia has more than 7 million hectares (1 ha = 2.457 acres) in plantation-based cultivation, with plans for up to 24.5 million hectares available for plantation development (Worldwatch 2013b). The result of such development, beyond its effect upon habitat loss and species diversity, is an increase in greenhouse gas emissions due to the clearing and burning of tropical forests and less local CO_2 absorptive capacity. In terms of CO_2 emissions, Indonesia ranks third highest, behind China and the United States.

The little-known island nation of Papua New Guinea (PNG) is second only to the Amazon River Basin in intact tropical rainforest and biological diversity. Nevertheless, the forests of PNG are experiencing intense oil palm plantation development. In *On the Edge: The State and Fate of the World's Tropical Rainforests*, Claude Martin writes that about 14 million hectares have been allocated as logging concessions and estimates that by 2021, "83% of the accessible forest areas may be deforested or severely damaged" (2015, 87). He adds that much of Southeast Asian deforestation is destined for paper and cardboard products demanded by the Asian market in particular. If any of these areas are reclaimed it will be a monocrop of fast-growing trees for pulp or developed as plantations.

The need to economically develop means that countries such as Indonesia and Brazil fully exploit their natural resources as much as possible. Road building through the Amazon River basin opens new lands for cattle ranches, soybean and sugarcane plantations, and mineral extraction for both large-scale commercial operations and smallholder plots as well. The need to generate foreign exchange means that protecting the environment is a luxury ill afforded. NASA's Earth Observatory's special report on deforestation points out that the most severe cases of deforestation are taking place in the poor tropical countries of the developing world (NASA 2013). Brazil alone has cleared over 42 million hectares, an area the size of California, between 1990 and 2005. Lula da Silva's election as president of Brazil in 2023 quickly instituted policies that have led to a 22 percent decrease in deforestation, a five-year low.

It is estimated that the Amazon River basin has about 70 billion tons of locked carbon and emits 20 percent of the Earth's oxygen. New research suggests that the Amazon (and other vast tracts of forests such as the Congo River basin) acts as a "biotic pump" releasing vast amounts of water vapor into what amounts to "flying rivers" that impact rainfall. Sheil and Murdiyarso's examination of a new hypothesis suggests the global hydrological system experiencing change is due to deforestation and the release of diminishing amounts of water vapor. Research leads them to conclude, "deforestation has already reduced vapor flows derived from forests by almost five percent . . . with little sign of slowing" (2009, 341; Lovejoy and Nobre 2019). While much research yet remains to understand the relationship, deforestation is implicated in declining rainfall patterns in the Sahel, West Africa, areas of Amazonia, and India, placing added stress on regional agricultural regimes. On the other hand, large-scale plantations can act as water vapor pumps, as do intact forests but as research suggests, less effectively (346). Once these indigenous and original forests are gone, after millions of years of development or transformed they can never come back to provide the services they now offer.

In the search for new forms of energy sources, biomass is seen as a means of producing energy that is benign in its effect upon the environment. One of the newest sources of renewable, yet considered by some environmentally "friendly energy" are wood pellets. Wood pellets are produced by grinding down logged trees and compressing them into small hard pellets, then burned for electrical generation. Considered by the European Union to be carbon neutral, there is a growing demand for American-made wood pellets. There is, however, considerable controversy over the claim that pellets are carbon neutral. A recent research report by Climate Central concludes that rather than being environmentally neutral, wood pellets produce more carbon dioxide than coal (Upton 2015). The report states, "Burning wood pellets to produce a megawatt hour of electricity produces 15 to 50 percent more climate-changing carbon dioxide pollution than burning coal" Much of the growing development of this industry is from the demand for clean replacements as coal and nuclear energy plants are closed. The report goes on to claim, "But wood energy can accelerate climate change. Living trees absorb carbon dioxide from the atmosphere, and burning dead ones releases more carbon dioxide than coal" (2015). Without oversight regulations that balance global warming concerns with corporate business practices, there are indications that some pellet facilities are logging hardwoods and forested wetlands, which lead to a carbon deficit, especially considering the high demand (the U.S. is expected to export an estimated 6 million tons of pellets in the near future) (Drouin 2015).

Forests are important carbon sinks, but concern for the state of natural forests and biodiversity is warranted, given that it is estimated more than half of all animal and plant species exist in forested lands. The exploitation of hardwood forests for wood pellets or pulp mills in such huge numbers suggests that natural habitats for native species are under threat of degradation. One major concern is that natural forests are giving way to plantations with limited biodiversity for biomass production. Some observers, such as the World Rainforest Movement, believe that new tree plantations are essentially deserts of monocrop tree species with little habitat diversity. Brockerhoff et al. recognize the limitations of plantation forests, writing, "Plantation forests usually have less habitat diversity and complexity. For example, some forest bird species may not find their required food sources in plantations, or there may be a lack of over mature trees suitable for nesting" (2008, 929). They add, however, that the role of plantations is often context-specific; such generalist species may colonize long-rotation plantations. On the other hand, intensively managed plantation forests can reduce the likelihood of natural forest logging, and plantations established on formerly agricultural land offer greater chances of diverse species colonization. "While a plantation stand will usually support fewer native species than a native forest at the same site," they conclude, "plantations are increasingly replacing other human-modified ecosystems (e.g., degraded pasture) and will almost always support a greater diversity of native species" (945). Thus, the impact of forest plantations on biodiversity will be determined by the degree of forestry management practices that are sensitive to biological conservation.

The research and information blog Landscapes for People, Food and Nature lists several global initiatives to begin the process of reforestation. The Bonn Challenge is promoting the global reforesting of 150 million hectares of land. Robin Chazdon cautions that, "Finding this balance between forest conservation and reforestation, and the need for social and economic development in a global economy poses a seemingly insurmountable challenge for developing tropical nations" (http://peoplefoodandnature.org). It is not only political will and financial resources that are needed but also adapting to the shifting climate conditions and accommodating increasing demands for food. Yet it is clear that healthy and extensive forests provide numerous ecological and health/psychological services that can benefit significant numbers of people.

Planning should play a crucial role in meeting the future challenges of climate change and resource degradation, especially for such "lynchpin" resources as the Amazon. Chazdon also points out that various consortiums of international cooperation need to coordinate research and planning to save global resources. She adds, "The formation of a collaborative, interdisciplinary, international network of researchers represents the most plausible way forward to understand the coupled natural and human dynamics of reforestation. An integrated understanding of the causes and consequences of alternative reforestation pathways will promote effective inclusion of reforestation" and "help guide nations in their efforts to meet the CBD Reforestation Targets, and lead to longer-term sustainability of complex forest landscapes" (ibid). Lastly, reforestation is not the same as habitat restoration. Many would say it is not only more trees that are needed but protected or developed habitat for diverse lifeforms that presently exist and are threatened. And, of course, habitat restoration is much more difficult than simply reforesting a devastated area.

As we "run out of environment," the real possibility of serious future resource constraints sees the next series of armed conflicts not only over oil supplies but also over water supplies and other natural resources. It is not petroleum products exclusively that will lead to conflict, but an increasing demand for consumer-based commodities under conditions of growing shortages of various minerals and resources. A serious need for economic growth is a security matter, but given the global demand for significant natural resources, equitable cooperation is necessary. Without international cooperation to develop strategies to meet future resource needs in a globally equitable manner, conflict and political instability are inevitable, and the world's poor and powerless will find themselves as sacrificial victims at the altar of the affluent nations (Downey, Bonds, and Clark 2010).

THE INEQUITY OF CLIMATE CHANGE: THE GLOBAL POOR AND THE ENVIRONMENT

Since the beginning of European colonial adventures and imperial control over less powerful nations, indigenous communities or tribal areas, cheap labor, and accessible cheap resources such as land or minerals have been the course of history. With capitalism's continuing need for land, labor, and new markets, the peasant and laborer have always been and will continue to be the points of contact for exploitation. This process, examined in the works of Paulo Freire, Emmanuel Wallerstein, Karl Marx, Gunder Frank, and Frantz Fanon and many others, exposes the vulnerability of the poor and powerless to the needs and desires of the corporate well-to-do. The past several centuries record a history, as Peter Worsley remarked in his book *The Three Worlds*, "The spread of Western capitalism wrought a parallel transformation of social life across the globe at the cost of the immiseration of far more millions" (1984). The contours of inequality and a divided world of development and political-economic powerlessness seen today result from colonial imperialism transforming the new colonies, often if not usually racist in nature, into storehouses of cheap land, resources, and labor. This led in many cases to the "underdevelopment" of colonies and newly independent countries stripped of natural resource wealth without recourse to adequate environmental resource management or public welfare.

Climate change and environmental resource degradation today is an epiphenomenon of this history of conquest and exploitation. Many countries of the developing South are ill-equipped in financial or technological terms to confront and deal with radically changing environments. An earlier IPCC report concludes,

> Climate change will amplify existing risks and create new risks for natural and human systems. Risks are unevenly distributed and are generally greater for disadvantaged people and communities in countries at all levels of development. Increasing magnitudes of warming increase the likelihood of severe, pervasive, and irreversible impacts for people, species and ecosystems globally. (2014; Wobbles et al. 2017; SYR-24, 2021, chapter 5)

Without containing high emissions, biodiversity and ecosystem services would be seriously impacted, leading to increased food insecurity, the risk to various livelihoods, and harsher climate conditions.

Early discussions of climate change centered on the affluent Organization for Economic Co-operation and Development (OECD) countries since they contributed disproportionately to GDP and greenhouse gas emissions. Steffen and colleagues realized this, "By treating 'humans' as a single, monolithic whole, it ignores the fact that the Great Acceleration has, until very recently, been almost entirely driven by a small fraction of the human population, those in developed countries" (2015, 91). It is now apparent that the global poor are increasingly playing a greater role in emissions, yet still far below the United States, China, and OECD countries, resource exploitation, and a limited ability to contribute to mitigation programs.

Research examining the relationship between poverty and the environment points to not only an increase in global population but, more importantly, the large number of global poor with a direct and immediate impact on the environment and vice versa (Bremner et al. 2010). Most attention to climate change within low-income countries focuses more on the impact of climate change on the environment rather than the social impact among low-income people. Climate change on the poor, however, presents an impact cycle. The inequality suffered by the poor culminates into greater exposure and vulnerability to environmental damage and less ability to overcome due to lack of resources, education, and scarce assistance programs. This then perpetuates their poverty, and the cycle continues.

The global poor present two problems: the growth of the urban poor in developing world cities lacking adequate infrastructure and employment and the rural poor that rely on local natural resources such as firewood and potable water (see Davis 2007). The fifth climate assessment for the United States highlights the threats to indigenous communities that rely on natural resources use. Increased wildfires, drought, decreased snowpack, and rising sea levels affect indigenous subsistence and commercial activities such as tourism (USGCRP 2018, 2023). Without adequate access to new technologies or capital to adapt to changing conditions or take advantage of different opportunities, global low income and American indigenous communities may by necessity continue to exploit degraded resources.

Population growth is critical but not sufficient to explain the relationship between the poor and the environment. There are political, economic, and institutional elements impacting rural conditions to which the rural poor react. For example, the expansion of intensive cash-crop agriculture may drive small farmers into virgin forests or to marginal, hillside land prone to erosion, to develop new farm plots, especially when better arable land is monopolized by agribusiness. Based on personal research, this was clearly seen along the Caribbean Coast of Costa Rica where large agribusiness banana plantations, such as United Brands or Chiquita, monopolize valley bottomlands, forcing smaller farmers onto marginal lands (likewise in St. Lucia and Honduras where the majority of small banana planters cultivate erodible hillsides are in a constant battle to control erosion).

The Millennium Ecosystem Assessment (MEA) project by the World Resources Institute examined twenty-four critical ecosystem services (forests, marshlands, cropland, etc.) important for human needs and assessed that 60 percent were either used unsustainably or were in poor, degraded condition. "Poor people have historically disproportionately lost access to biological products and ecosystem services as demand for those services has grown," according to the report (MEA 2005, 5, 30). The MEA concludes that for the rural poor, biodiversity of ecosystems acts "as an insurance and coping mechanism to increase flexibility and spread or reduce risk in the face of increasing uncertainty, shocks, and surprises" within the rural or global economy (ibid, 30). Thus, as diversity and health of ecosystems degrade, the poor find themselves in a more tenuous situation.

Many of the rural poor in areas such as Africa engage in deforestation since they need wood as fuel (making charcoal) and as a building material. They erode hillsides since no other land is available, kill animal species for food or to earn money, and pollute water due to a lack of sanitation facilities (the United Nations Water for Life estimates 2.5 billion people do not use improved sanitation facilities and over 1 billion practice open defecation [UNDESA 2015]). The poor cannot help but degrade local natural resources because they are poor, lacking capital, technology, or access to governmental services. In the edited volume *Anthropology and Climate Change*, a series of papers outline local experiences with climate change. Crate and Nuttall summarize experiences from Papua New Guinea, Tuvalu, and indigenous Australians: "Everywhere, from high latitude taiga in tundra regions, to high altitude mountain ecosystems, from tropical rain forests to near sea level coastlines, there are compelling similarities in the narratives, accounts, and experiences of indigenous and local peoples who are already seeing and experiencing the effects of climate change" (2009, 9). For many rural and indigenous people, their dependence on the environment is immediate and direct. Whatever problems they face will be amplified by shifting rainfall patterns, changes in seasons, desiccated lands, and limited water sources. "To indigenous people this means that climate change is not something that comes in isolation; it magnifies already existing problems of poverty, deterritoriality, marginalization, and non-inclusion in national and international policymaking processes and discourses," Crate and Nuttall conclude (12). As I found doing research in St. Lucia, many rural farmers are not equipped nor receive much financial or technical help and are left on their own to confront often life-threatening problems. They are essentially on their own to figure out how to survive.

The result of the small farmer as well as the rural and urban poor's share in environmental degradation is reactive; that is, without adequate resources, skills, education, or a voice in policies affecting economic development, they react to the given circumstances around them as best they can. These circumstances are often determined or influenced by the class-based interests of the wealthy, corporate interests, and politically powerful individuals who are proactive in their own interests. Land loss due to a variety of circumstances, limited access to water, inputs, and extension help, basic to local communities, are now in many cases controlled by multinational corporations concerned more with exporting to foreign markets than with the needs of local communities.

The urban poor and near-poor will continue to contribute to the degrading quality of local ecosystems and the general environment unless substantive changes occur in development programs. It is estimated that by 2050, 67 percent of the developing world population will live in urban areas, often driven out of rural areas lacking in opportunities and infrastructure as climate change kicks in. In cities such as Lagos, Nigeria, Nairobi, Kenya, and Mumbai, India (among many more, what Mike Davis called megacities), the number of low-income and poor without basic services will continue to grow. The need for adequate sanitation facilities, potable water, and energy will exacerbate already inadequate conditions. The poor and marginal poor live primarily in slums, barrios, *favelas, katchi abadi*, and *pueblos jovenes* where essential services are submarginal or non-existent (Davis 2007). The Dharavi slum in Mumbai is one of the world's most densely populated areas with an estimated 1 million inhabitants under very poor sanitation conditions. The problems associated with dense populations of low-income poor communities encumbered with poor public services and resources will, one can assume, only get worse as environmental conditions continue to deteriorate. Davis concludes that, "Third World cities . . . are systematically polluting, urbanizing, and destroying their crucial environmental support systems" such as potable water sources, habitat destruction, and growing amounts of toxic waste (136–137). Yet the urban poor use fewer resources per capita than their affluent neighbors and possibly a smaller footprint than their rural counterparts.

In a recent paper produced for the European Parliament, the authors confirm the adverse effects of climate and poverty. In much of Sub-Saharan Africa and South Asia, agriculture is the predominant economic activity located in semi-arid regions. Development in these areas must be designed to accommodate the limitations faced by such groups. Ludwig and colleagues understand institutional support may be lacking to help react to climate change (2007). The possibility of new technologies needs to be appropriate and education available to use new methods of production or environmental control. For the poor, who number in the hundreds of millions, it is not a question of dealing with climate change as much as it is fighting for survival in an unequal world with few resources.

Many poor have struggled to cope with climate variability and extremes, but the climate challenges of today require greater articulation and coordination among local communities, national governments, and international agencies. New adaptive strategies are necessary for people of limited means to cope with or recover from changing environmental conditions. New technologies, development outreach programs, and financial assistance will be needed to identify and develop potential positive consequences of environmental change. For this to take place, the idea of a global commonwealth is necessary, one that commands greater equity in sharing global resources to adapt to changing environmental conditions. The condition of the planet today has already produced millions of environmental refugees. What part will they play in our unequal world of power and wealth under climate change?

The result of the quest for mastery over the environment to meet the perceived or actual needs to support social life has culminated in a global environment on the verge of collapse. We are beginning to understand that all life and Earth dynamics are interconnected, that their various elements, especially the human, are not sovereign or independent, and our actions do have consequences. Severe drought, disappearing lakes and rivers, massive flooding of coastal and riverine areas, and temperature spikes of extreme and long-lasting heatwaves suggest turbo-charged climate change, the result of all-out prodigious economic development and growth in affluent countries.

This chapter illustrates an era of restless capitalism continually in search of resources for profit, with little regard, in many cases, for the environmental consequences. The result of which Foster, Clark, and York describe as the "ecological rift" between nature and society and between the corporate affluent and local communities that are often left with environmental devastation beyond their ability to recover. The following chapter offers insight into the development and structure of capitalism. Without a deep understanding of what capitalism as an economic system is and the consequences of its integration into social structure and culture, it would be difficult to discern the magnitude of its influence on nature and global society or the embracing of alternative narratives of a more substantive culture–nature relationship.

NOTES

1. A golden spike would be a stratigraphic marker found universally that would mark the transition from one era to another. The International Commission on Stratigraphy has a working group charged with formally recognizing the Anthropocene as a new geological era. The search is for a universal marker in the rock record that would identify the new era, separate and distinct from the Holocene.

2. One congressional skeptic of climate warming, Rep. Lamar Smith, chairman of the House Committee on Science, Space and Technology, has demanded documents, including emails from NOAA (National Oceanic and Atmospheric Administration) scientists, that he believes adjusted the temperature data to fit their idea that there has been no pause in global warming.

3. Historically, the Southwest has experienced drought every several decades. According to the Environmental Protection Agency (EPA), "Since the early 1900s, the Southwest has experienced wetter conditions during three main periods: the 1900s, 1940s, and 1980s. Drier conditions occurred through the 1920s/1930s, again in the 1950s, and since 1990, when the Southwest has seen some of the most persistent droughts on record" (2021). The current IPCC report states, "high confidence (robust evidence and medium agreement) that anthropogenic forcing has made a substantial contribution (~50 percent) to the southwestern North America warming since 1980," that is, much of the ongoing drought is exacerbated by human-generated GHGs (2021, 10–76).

Chapter 5

The Anthropocene's Handmaiden

Capitalism's Impact on Remaking the World

If the present circumstances of climate change and environmental degradation suggest a shift in how we go about the business of life, then capitalism as an economic system must be understood since it presents serious impediments to needed socio-economic change. We may define capitalism as a system for the private ownership of capital (land, property, and the means of production [such as factories]) and free markets with the intent of marshaling resources to accumulate capital and produce wealth. The growth of capitalism has not only witnessed a physical transformation of society but has also induced a particular way of thinking, expressed in increased wealth as a fetish, with consumption and material possession as elements of social identity, including the disposition of nature as an exploited commodity. It has likewise created the conditions leading to environmental degradation and climate change.

As an economic system, capitalism has been a force for creating tremendous wealth, innovation, and unleashing the creativity of human effort. Notwithstanding the unevenness of its accomplishments within and between societies, it has brought forth a greater standard of living and comfort for millions of people around the world. Yet hundreds of millions live in poverty with little escape, and tens of millions of middle-class people living lives of quiet desperation, nevertheless. Growing income and wealth inequality remains a fundamental hallmark of our capitalist era. The foundation of capitalism, its sole purpose, Jerry Mander notes, is the "expansion of individual and corporate wealth. It has no other job, and no interest in 'right or wrong,' or human welfare, or communities, or in the well-being of the natural world, except as resources for itself" (2012, 13). As such, it is the most dynamic force for change in history. From its inception, capitalism has pursued a relentless quest for raw resources with disregard for the environmental or social costs. To understand the power of capitalism, we must review its historical development followed by a discussion of the operation of capitalism.

MASTER NARRATIVES AND HUMAN NATURE

Master narratives frame not only our stories and myths but also the questions we ask that interpret the world and its operation. A master narrative brings together a coherent whole of a variety of social, historical, and political puzzle pieces into a meaningful order to provide a comprehensive explanation of a particular reality. Narratives also suggest the natural order of things and a way of life. A master narrative in this case can produce an illusion of freedom, human nature, and prosperity that people deeply believe in. The power of the master narrative we are born into and many inherently accept as truth is that capitalism is the end of history and it is unimaginable that it could end.

The master narrative promoted by proponents of the present economic system sees human beings as economic animals striving for the greatest good (in personal terms) at the least cost, and constantly aware and appraising the cost-benefits of their actions; in other words, how to maximize utility. Individuals are genetically endowed, it is thought, to pursue self-interest in a Hobbesian context of all against all. Humans are also assumed to be inherently individualistic in their pursuit of material acquisitions. These ideas run deep in Western thought about human nature. Aristotle wrote in *Politics*, "The baseness of human beings is a thing insatiable. They always want more . . . for appetite is by nature unlimited and the majority of mankind live for the satisfaction of appetite" (Sahlins 2013, 106). Not only do we want more, but we are born to be independent and self-sufficient. The American narrative is found in many Hollywood movies, especially Western ones, where settlers built towns and livelihoods without government interference.

Donald Trump's ideological call to "make America great again" fits into this perspective of searching for a bygone golden age of rugged individualism. This line of thought believes humans are not communal animals by nature but rather free thinkers, independent, yearning for self-improvement, self-made. Essentially, we are, with a few exceptions, fundamentally islands onto ourselves.

Are humans basically economic animals in search of utility and profit (of some kind) or are humans more socially oriented? In other words, where do people find satisfaction—in maximizing self-interest or the comfort of being integrated into a community of primary relationships? Are we material, possessive, individualistic animals, or moral social beings? Do we define ourselves in the singular "I" sense or see ourselves immersed within a deep web of social significance? Anthropologists have long known that humans are plastic in the sense that we can be whatever social reality we create for ourselves, individualistic or collectively oriented. To be individualistic is adaptive in our modern economic system, but in a horticultural society, such as the Dugum Dani of Papua New Guinea, an individual is born into a matrix of social intimacy in which one's identity is infused in kinship and other collectivities (see, for example, Heider 1970).

The assumption that humans are utility-maximizing and rational choice individuals is seen as a gift of nature, and the economic system was designed to meet the expectations and needs of the "natural" propensity to consume. As Voltaire's philosopher, professor Pangloss, noted long ago, "all is for the best in the best of all possible worlds." Given the framework of this assumption of reality, which has taken us to the brink of environmental collapse and social dysfunction, the idea of human nature and society needs to be rethought and operationalized in new ways. There are many calls by radical ecologists, social philosophers, and social scientists to recognize the need to socially reorganize for a future of climate change, scarce resources, and environmental limitations. We now realize that Pangloss was overly optimistic in his assessment.

In this era of late capitalism, there appears a contemporary cultural-political struggle between the traditional narrative of American exceptionalism and a bifurcation of emerging narratives centered around a new socially oriented humanity sustainable within environmental limitations. Social scientists consider humans as social animals within a framework of profound cultural meaning and organized social environments. Human attributes and characteristics are not genetically specified but are related to the circumstances of human cultural meaning.[1] In this case, there is no universal human nature except that which is found within the history and experience of human groups in relationship to the social construction of their surroundings. Clifford Geertz, who spoke for the consensus of most anthropologists, famously wrote in *The Interpretation of Cultures*, "One of the most significant facts about us may finally be that we all begin with the natural equipment to live a thousand kinds of life but end in the end having lived only one" (1974, 45). Geertz goes on to counter the economist's assumption of a common human nature by stating the importance of culture in creating the nature of particular groups. He concludes that, "Men unmodified by the customs of particular places do not in fact exist, have never existed, and most important, could not in the very nature of the case exist," and that, "There is no such thing as a human nature independent of culture" (43, 49).

The eminent anthropologist Marshall Sahlins insisted that biologically, what evolved was the human ability to realize our capacities to fulfill needs through culture. For Sahlins, biology is the dependent variable offering, perhaps, very broad drives and needs such as the need for shelter and sustenance and the drive to procreate. But how these drives and needs are expressed and experienced is in the thousand different ways humans approach a solution using our diverse experiences. Over time, human groups figured out how best to solve their needs within their own particular social dispositions. In human history, most of the cultural arrangements to meet needs and control drives were found in face-to-face kinship-based communities and their associated values. Ella Cara Deloria, a Lakota Sioux anthropologist, noted that among the Lakota, kinship occupied a central location in the value system of the Sioux people. "I can safely say," she wrote, "that the ultimate aim of Dakota life, stripped of accessories, was quite simple: one must obey kinship rules; one must be a good relative. No Dakota who participated in that life will dispute that . . . every other consideration was secondary—property, personal ambition, glory, good times, life itself. Without that aim and constant struggle to attain it, the people would no longer be Dakotas in truth. They would no longer even be human. To be a good Dakota, then, was to be humanized, civilized" (1998, org. 1944, 25).

Sahlins uses the research of Maurice Leenhardt on the New Caledonians to illustrate his point on the social character of human nature. Leenhardt wrote that among New Caledonians, experience was not personal but infused in a community of kinship. "people suffered illnesses as a result of the moral or religious transgressions of their relatives . . . where kinsmen must be compensated for one's death, the injuries one receives . . . " Sahlins' point: "Here is the very opposite of bourgeois possessive individualism: in a community of reciprocal being, not even a person's body is his or her own; it is a social body, the subject of the empathy, concern, and responsibility of others" (2005, 100). This, from Sahlins' perspective, comprised most of human history and the evolution of our species. We had, in essence, nothing else to rely on, given the lack of technology and broad knowledge, but each other.

What this conveys is that there is no single way of being a human being, as Geertz and Sahlins rightly pointed out. Human behavior and thought are always contingent upon a context of meaning beyond the biological composition of our species. This idea of flexibility in what it means to be human offers the potential to allow us to adapt to new and possibly radical environmental constraints. The point of this discussion is that if future environmental circumstances are such that society (and all that implies) must transform, it is not our "human nature" that will stand in the way but the way we think, politically and economically, about human nature. As cultural beings, we do have freedom of choice to imagine and to be what we wish to be.

It is not surprising from an anthropological point of view that recent research by a team of specialists led by Kathleen Kline of Dartmouth University Medical School concluded that humans are "hardwired" in brain circuitry for intimate human connection. Kline and a panel of doctors, scholars, and scientists reviewed research which suggests that "we are hard wired for close attachments to other people, beginning with our mothers, fathers, and extended family, and then moving out to the broader community." The panel also suggests that humans have an innate capacity to derive meaning and a "drive to search for purpose and reflect on life's ultimate ends" (2008, 9; see also Liberman 2015). Kline and colleagues add that while attachment may have a biological basis, it is the social context that may be most significant, stating, "that the environments we create influence our children's genetic expression" for attachment, exactly as expressed by Geertz and Sahlins (13).

While our genetic heredity is significant, it is the nurturing environment allowing for the formation of diverse attachments that is most notable in the socialization process.[2] Of course, nurturing takes many forms and contains many meanings. The relationships and lessons taught lead individuals to a set of values and perspectives that influence behavior and how they think about themselves and the world they inhabit. Many of these values and norms develop to conform to or express the objective conditions brought on by both the physical and social environments. Adaptive traits of ideas, behaviors, and perceptions to changing circumstances operate to create new forms of social organization over time. As societies evolve, so too does the kind of human nature required to "fit" what is to become, or as Herbert Spencer once remarked, "Before he can remake his society, his society must make him" (1874, 35).

Through stories, myths, and experiences over time, people begin to think, perceive, and behave in ways relevant to new developing institutional forms or the a priori expectations of others. Joel Kovel uses the term "life-world" to explain the perspective within which individuals dwell. "The life-world is," Kovel writes, "what an ecosystem looks like from the standpoint of individual beings within it." A particular need of capitalism, he adds, is to alter life-worlds to benefit the accumulation of capital by "introducing a sense of dissatisfaction or lack—so that it can truly be said that happiness is forbidden under capitalism, being replaced by sensation and craving" (2007, 52–53). What was a want or desire under a non-capitalist life-world now becomes a need for the conduct of life. But these new wants and desires are devoid of meaning since they are created to serve a purpose beyond what individuals inherently need.

Prior to the rise of capitalism, most goods and needed services were distributed in society by various reciprocal (general and specific) exchanges and/or kinship/tribal obligations, as Polanyi and the French historian Marc Bloch pointed out. Polanyi summarized what many early anthropologists were discovering in their fieldwork: "structurally, the economy does not exist [in pre-modern societies]. Rather than a distinct and specialized organization, economy is something that generalized social groups and relations, notably kinship groups and relations, do" (1957, 48). Writing in *Feudal Society*,

Bloch detailed that the personal bond infused all medieval European society. All levels of society—family, peasant, lord—were governed by various ties of dependence, tradition, and obedience (1964). In *Stone Age Economics*, Marshall Sahlins declared in his introduction, "'Economy' becomes a category of culture rather than behavior . . . not the need-serving activities of individuals, but the material life process of society" (1972, xii). Sahlins, agreeing with Polanyi, expanded on this, offering that "Economy is rather a function of the society than a structure," by which he meant,

> The built-in etiquette of kinship statuses, the dominance and subordination of domestic life, the reciprocity and cooperation, here make the "economic" a modality of the intimate. How labor is to be expended, the terms and products of its activity are in the main domestic decisions. And these decisions are taken primarily with a view toward domestic contentment. (76, 77)

There were, throughout history, more advanced social systems where systems of redistribution of goods based on centralized collection via rent taxes or kinship or tribal obligations existed, such as among the Bunyoro of Uganda or the Kwakiutl of coastal British Columbia. In such kinship-based societies, commodities (C) were produced and exchanged for other commodities (C). The basic formula informing this system is C > C (in pastoral or horticultural societies) or C > M > C, where M is used in centralized redistributive chiefdoms by the paramount political authority to support the pre-state. In some cases, what was exchanged was the exact same commodity but exchanged nevertheless because the exchange expressed meaningful social relationships. In more advanced kinship societies, such as chiefdoms, C (commodities) could be used to obtain a form of monetary value (M) but only to buy more commodities to enhance the living standard of the chief and his kinsmen, gain social prestige, trade, or meet political objectives.

In these pre-capitalist systems, the economy as we understand it remained submerged within a web of social relationships, as Polanyi and Sahlins maintained. Profit was non-existent as we know it; however, social status and prestige were important and stood as "profit" through one's social obligations and general character.[3] Gift-giving and reciprocal exchanges did not necessarily mean that economic transactions were not functionally important. The function of the ceremonial exchange of precious gifts among the participants of the Kula Ring of the Melanesian Islands, made famous by Bronislaw Malinowski in his book, *Argonauts of the Western Pacific*, was to ensure a peaceful order for the trading of mundane but important economic commodities. The Kula was significant for the orderly movement of various unequally distributed resources among the various islands of the exchange network. But the ceremonial exchange was in itself a means of achieving social prestige (if only fleeting since significant objects had to re-enter the Kula Ring). Among the Kula traders, all prestige necklaces and bracelets could only be had temporarily. After a time, the item had to return to the trading ring to be "owned" by a new individual. Here, C. B. Macpherson's "possessive individualism" did not exist in the way the term is meant today.

It is hard for contemporary people to understand that the economy and contemporary economic thinking were not always a primary consideration of society. The pre-capitalist world, in many cases, had money and markets for the exchange of goods but, as pointed out earlier from Polanyi's understanding of economic history, in these societies the economy, in a sense, did not exist except as an aspect of general social behavior (1957, 54). The economic relations of "material provisioning," as he called it, were by-products of other forms of behavior and types of relationships. Bridewealth payments, for example, may be treated as an economic transaction by an objective observer, but for the Yoruba, Hausa, or the Nuer of East Africa, those payments from the husband's patrilineage to the bride's, balanced a transfer of a set of rights, obligations, and responsibilities that relate to sexual service, fertility, residence, and work service (see Evans-Pritchard 1969). It is not the economic interest that is primary but social interests such as prestige, status, and social obligation "man's economy is submerged in his social relationships," Polanyi noted, "he does not act so as to safeguard his individual interests in the possession of material good—he acts to safeguard his social standing, his social claims, his social assets" (ibid, 46; see also Bloch 1964). In most cases, it is social status and relationships that are the paramount forms of "wealth" in pre-modern societies.

Many goods move through society by reciprocal exchange relations or via redistributive systems that can involve religious and social ceremonies. For the tribal members of the Tsembaga of Papua New Guinea, for example, it was a funeral ceremony honoring the recently dead soon-to-be ancestors that contributed to the redistribution of goods. The significance here lies not in the actual operation per se but as a celebration of the ideology of group solidarity. Reciprocal relationships and "pure" gifts are pregnant with symbolism of social relationships but also function to equalize consumption among community members, sharing any unexpected windfalls, and spreading out the burdens of crop failures or individual catastrophes. Such systems insulate the individual from individual calamities by defining risk, uncertainty, and problems as group problems to be addressed by the collectivity.

John Beattie's research among the Bunyoro, a small African kingdom in Uganda, for example, illustrates not only how goods and services are distributed through society without a formal market but also offers an example of what wealth and power means in a non-capitalist setting. Power resided in the *Mukama*, the senior member of the royal lineage who claimed the ownership of farmland that was distributed to lesser chiefs or commoners in exchange for food, *corvee* labor (free labor service), and craft products. The power and prestige of the *Mukama* depended upon his redistribution of these goods back into the chiefdom. Beattie writes, "In the traditional system the king was seen both as the supreme receiver of goods and services and as the supreme giver" (1960, 34). However, a portion of what he received was kept by the *Mukama* to be distributed to his close kin, royal retainers, and to non-kin such as the military, religious officials, and a host of specialized kingdom-oriented functions (e.g., potters, musicians, various custodians) (31). Although the Bunyoro had a stratified system of status positions, the movement, capture, and differential use of goods and services were to maintain the status and prestige system through the nexus of social relationships, not necessarily to increase the physical economic wealth of the top echelon of the royal lineage for the purpose of greater capital accumulation activities. The *Mukama* did not think in economic terms but in terms of kinship or obligation and a particular standard of living associated with the rank of *Mukama*.[4]

Polanyi saw the idea of "commodity fiction" as the organizing principle necessary in a commercially oriented society if goods and services are to meet the mobility and flexibility requirements of this new capitalist economic capitalist system. Individuals as labor had to be an amenable supply and available at its determined true market value (cost versus productivity of labor) would have to be available for sale on the market, and thus had to be commoditized. Through this commodity fiction, the individual, reduced to offering his labor for sale in a competitive atmosphere, was pulled away from those social institutions which, while protecting him, restricted his freedom to sell his labor on the market. Individuals now had to think in economic terms. The basis of modern capitalism is that individuals are capable and do act regarding the costs and benefits of their actions that we rationally choose between alternate ends that offer the best payoff.

For Polanyi, Marx, and anthropologists such as Sahlins, Paul Bohannan, and George Dalton, economizing behavior and motivations of self-gain are innovations of the past few centuries in Western culture and society. The desire for profit and material gain driven by the relentless buying and selling of goods and services under the determination of competitive market price integration is an epiphenomenon of the historical period of capitalist development in Europe, although profit and gain existed well before in non-Western markets and many indigenous contexts, though for different reasons and different outcomes. Adam Smith's butcher looking out for his own self-interest represents a view of human nature in economic terms. *Homo economicus* view humans as rational actors who understand the need to optimize their behavior to realize the greatest return for their efforts, in many cases just to survive. Such an orientation by the individual will seem as real and natural, dependent upon the context of the circumstances, the *relative appetites*, as Marx once phrased it, will guide one's perspective on human behavior.

PART ONE: THE ANTECEDENTS TO CAPITALISM

Prior to the rise of capitalism, a rigid social system governed medieval Europe from the ninth through the fifteenth centuries. The economy functioned in part on a labor force tied to a land-owning elite through custom, obligation, and exchange. By the beginning of the sixteenth century,

A more dynamic system, based not on landownership and traditional labor arrangements but on international trade, mass production, and capital accumulation, developed. New forms of manufacturing efficiency, the shift from labor power to waterpower and eventually steam power, meant a continual search for resources as new machinery increased productivity. New resources had to be found and new markets developed as factories produced quantities of goods. The beginning of this new economy is captured in Ralph Davis' book *The Rise of the Atlantic Economies* (1973). By the beginning of the sixteenth century, Western Europe's resource base, especially arable land, faced both degradation and population pressure. The first phase of capitalist economic development was the increasing continental trade between the Western economies and those of the Baltic states. Davis wrote of the importance of long-distance trade, "The prosperity of Europe during the first half of the sixteenth century, grew out of the development of its internal resources" supporting international trade (73, 79). It was during this transition that the New World of the Americas, with its abundant resources, came into greater focus. It was Cristóbal Colón's encounter with a new continent, a "Second Earth" conceived of great possibilities of material abundance. Initially, the Spanish quickly realized the potential of sugar plantations on the island of Hispaniola by 1519. Later, further north, Steven Cornell argued in *The Return of the Native*, the initial importance of trans-Atlantic trade between Native Americans and Europe, in particular animal pelts and indigenous slaves in exchange for English finished goods, allowed for anchoring settlements in the New World (1988). For the English colonizers, it was an escape from old rigid feudal property rights and patrician privileges. Both commoner, prosperous Dutch burgers and English traders saw potential in the vast untapped resources of North America; the former looking for freedom and independence and the latter for greater wealth and social stature. But in either case, they had to move beyond the encumbrances of feudal society. Once the English began serious colonization efforts in North America, the focus turned to the political-economy of development and profit-making from cash crops, such as the tobacco plantations of Virginia in the south, and nascent industrialism in the north.

The Death of the Feudal Community and Emergence of the Market

By the sixteenth century, Europe began to experience a shift in economic orientation from a feudal system based primarily on subsistence needs, traditional rigid social hierarchy, and mercantile activity to a more market-oriented economy based on land as a commodity, untied labor, and money as capital for investment and profit. The economic transformation over many centuries began earliest in northwestern Europe and took the longest to affect Eastern Europe. In England, for instance, under the manorial system, whereby feudal landlords controlled large blocks of land shared with a variety of peasant tenants, land was viewed as a resource to satisfy subsistence needs (and sumptuous living for the lord) and for growing basic commodities for local and regional trade. Although it is difficult to capture all the subtleties of early European agrarian systems, two forms of land management stand out: common field agriculture, that is, "non-privately owned land found in common field townships and regulated by an assembly of cultivators" (Campbell and Godoy 1992, 119). Second, a more complex system consisting of large estates (*demesne*) and the landlord's dependents (*mansi*) (Bautier 1971, 44). Additionally, there were numerous individually owned smallholder plots scattered across the countryside. Markets developed, despite controls imposed by town councils or manorial lords, to lower transaction costs in production and trade to encourage greater land use in commercial crops for the landlord and peasant.

Many dependents or serfs worked on both the manorial demesne and the land allotted to them along with common areas where firewood, building material, and pasturage were located. The historian Maurice Dobb describes this early condition: "Historically it [i.e., feudalism] has also been associated with conditions of production for the immediate needs of the household or village community and not for a wider market" (1947, 37). Due to a limited projection of central political power, roving banditry, regional wars, and various endemic plagues and depopulations, intra-regional trade and the growth of a money economy were extremely limited until the mid-fifteenth century. Such constraints kept most economies local and subsistence-based. The economy was an instituted or embedded system of material means provisioning; that is, the processes of production, distribution, and consumption of material needs were expressed within the organizational forms of kinship, religion, politics, and social networks. Under feudal or kinship-based peasant social systems, interests that were protected were not necessarily economic interests to the actors but social interests such as prestige, status and morality, sexual rights, or social obligation. Both E. P. Thompson and James Scott referred to such a system as a "moral economy." Thus, "Man's economy is submerged in his social relationships," Polanyi tells us, "He does not act so as to safeguard his individual interests in the possession of material goods, he acts to safeguard his social standing, his social claims, his social assets" (1957, 46). Within the social environment of pre-industrial or indigenous societies, the individual was submerged within the identity of the community (Durkheim's mechanical solidarity). Individual peasant economic interests, indeed, the individual's personal identity was secondary to community identity and collective interests such as protection and welfare. This also insulated the individual from individual calamities by defining risk, uncertainty, and problems as group problems addressed by the collectivity as a whole. These systems were in effect in different areas of Europe until the transformation of society in the late fifteenth and sixteenth centuries as markets expanded alongside a growing ideology of wealth and power.

The seat of this evolving and dynamic economy that became the backdrop for much of Europe was the rich burgers of Amsterdam. Starting with the United Provinces of the Dutch under Philip the Good in the fifteenth century, laws were enacted that brought stability and certainty to economic activity. For instance, the creation of the States General, Douglas North suggests in his review of economic history, "Favored legislation that fostered the growth of trade and commerce and the granting and protection of private property rights that made such growth possible" (1981, 153). Richard Lachmann argues that conflict between several feudal English elite classes allowed the landed gentry to grab power as clerical and crown control over local social relationships diminished (1987). Due to the Dissolution of the Monasteries after the Reformation in England in 1534, the church lost its influence over or mediation of relationships between landlords and peasants. This opened, according to Lachmann, a vacuum where landlords could take Church lands, on the one hand, and, on the other, began to dissolve the land rights of peasants, eventually instituting the *enclosure* movement whereby peasants lost access to common land or traditional land rights on manor property. With such autonomy, Lachmann believes, the local gentry, comfortable in new property rights, established agrarian capitalism. "Gentry strategy," writes Lachmann, "was to prevent a reassertion by clerical courts of their authority to regulate manorial land tenure." Enclosure, for example, was in part a political strategy to gain control over manor lands from tenants, the reason being the "chief means for limiting crown and clerical authority over manorial land rights . . . to eliminate manorial structures and manorial tenant positions" (1987, 141). In England, with the growth of opportunity brought on by an emerging woolen industry and an external market based on money transactions, factor endowments such as land and labor began to be viewed as commodities for private investment purposes.

As trade and opportunity developed, landlords felt the need for cash income and began to substitute traditional social obligations and services for rent contracts. "For a fee, lords were willing to free their peasants of the . . . ties of personal service; and the manorial contracts, which had promised personal protection and a subsistence living in return for labor service, gave way to rent contracts" (Rice and Grafton 1994, 69). International trade with Asia and internal long-distance trade within Europe brought increased quantities of desired goods such as wines, olives, silks, linen, and jewelry to a growing class of merchants, bankers, and royalty. New perspectives on the meaning of power and property took hold among large landowners and a growing class of long-distance traders. Indeed, in Chapter IV of Book III, Adam Smith wrote in *The Wealth of Nations* of the changing nature of the meaning of ownership of productive resources. He noted that increased commerce and manufacturing induced in

> the great proprietors with something for which they could exchange the whole surplus produce of their lands, and which they could consume themselves without sharing it either with tenants or retainers. All for ourselves and nothing for other people, seems, in every age of the world, to have been the vile maxim of the masters of mankind. (1776, 224)

By the late sixteenth century, the transformation of the manorial lord into a capitalist entrepreneur was well established. With the idea of land as a commodity from which to make money, estates were consolidated through expelling common landholders to consolidate estate holdings to grow new products such as wool, olives, and wine for the growing market (Rice and Grafton 1994, 70). Although enclosures began as early as the Tudor period under Henry VII in the late fifteenth century, this movement was codified under the English Enclosure Act, where over 5,000 enclosures consolidated 6 million acres of common land after 1760. The idea of "enclosing" common pasturage and releasing peasants from traditional and generational servitude in order to plant vineyards or olive groves, pasturage for sheep, or other high-value activities gained currency. Peasants so released from community relationships stood naked before a new economy as vulnerable wage laborers. The result was dislocation, poverty, and social turmoil. "In village after village, enclosure destroyed the scratch as scratch can subsistence economy of the poor, the cow or geese, fuel from the common, gleanings, and all the rest" (Thompson 1968, 237). Thompson recognized the growing search for personal value, referencing the great proprietors,

> As soon, therefore, as they could find a method of consuming the whole value of their rents themselves, they had no disposition to share them with any other persons. For a pair of diamond buckles, perhaps, or for something as frivolous

and useless, they exchanged the maintenance, or what is the same thing, the price of the maintenance of a thousand men for a year (225).

The value to be derived from their resources was to be theirs alone without regard to others except in self-interest. Money and the wealth in attendance became a fixation with a power that transcended morality, responsibility, and the equalizing effect of the common good.

E. P. Thompson characterized this as class robbery, adding that there was no compensation for eviction and for those who could lay a claim, the land was often of marginal productivity and inadequate for survival. Peasant farmers and manorial serfs were in the slow process of transforming into workers toiling for a daily wage, and more and more alienated from those to whom they traditionally owed allegiance. While many peasants lost their means of livelihood, others were able to take advantage of the nascent industrial "putting out" system in rural areas. This system of commodity production brought much-needed income into rural economies and improved the standard of living for many peasant households. The putting out system of cottage production transformed over time into factories, and independent craftsmen evolved into guilds and eventually quasi-employees for long-distance merchants or manufacturers.

Those entering these emerging production systems were forced onto a market that bought and sold their labor and exposed them to the vagaries of the market. Once "freed," individuals within a market environment felt compelled to buy all necessities of life in the market with cash earned as wages from selling their labor in the market (Polanyi 1969, 64). As Polanyi summed it up, hunger and gain (and fear) are linked with the production process due to the need for one to earn an income. Here, then, is the beginning of the modern working class, those who "must sell themselves piecemeal," as Marx and Engels put it in *The Communist Manifesto*, into the waiting arms of the "satanic mills." Not only was market commoditization of land at work during this period, government policy also served to create landless workers. Consequently, the English parliament introduced the Poor Law of 1834 to ensure "life so intolerable for the rural paupers as to force them to migrate to any job that offered" (Hobsbawm 1962, 185; Marx and Engels 2010).

This was imperative, according to C. B. Macpherson's analysis. "If the market was to operate fully and freely, if it was to do the whole job of allocating labor and resources among possible uses," he observed, "then all labor and resources had to become, or be convertible into, this kind of [freed] property" (1978, 10). Land, and by extension the people bound to it, had to be freed from the fetters of traditional social obligation and tradition and develop independence to operate in an evolving market economic system, a system now regulated exclusively by market forces as self-regulating. The market principle of price control through market transactions of land, labor, and money resulted in the separation of the individual from his social group through competitive individualism in the market. Consequently, this process released and elevated the economy from its submerged function to become an autonomous force determining social organization. Increasingly, the morality of life was undergoing a transformation to the economics of life.

By the beginning of the nineteenth century, capitalism generated considerable wealth, making the idea of the superiority of single private ownership, supported by an expanding bourgeois an integral aspect of Western ideology. With the expansion of markets from which needed labor could be purchased, and the development of new labor-saving technologies, the need for common ownership with collective labor became less important or, in fact, an impediment to capitalism's ability to exploit labor. Additionally, there was a concomitant expansion in the number and scope of institutionalized rules and regulations generated by both state and economy in support of productive private property ownership. The era of a new political economy was in full force, creating a new kind of human being compatible with the maturation of capitalism, the human as an economic animal. New values and new assumptions about human nature and its concomitant behavior became the hallmark of this new force in social life.

Epoch of Capitalism: *Homo Economicus* as Capitalist Avatar

The capitalist economic system under which most of global society operates today is not, contrary to Ayn Rand, a product of human nature and thus inevitable, although many like Milton Friedman would like to think it is. Many follow a Western-oriented belief in a core notion of human nature as a sort of self-centered economic animal, that is, *Homo Economicus.* It is assumed to be a universal trait rather than an ideological belief found in Western values and ideals. We continually seek the essence of humanity when the answer is found in the epoch in which we are born, as Marx pointed out long ago in *The German Ideology* (1981). This is, of course, a serious philosophical question given today's debate over human nature and thinking about the future. But the question is something not asked by most people, at least not in a practical sense. The question arises because of the uncertainty of the meaning of life as guided by capitalist philosophy focused on the here and now, that is, the immediacy of being.

The answer to our basic "architecture" is a product of particular historic circumstances and expressed through a series of events, circumstances, and values deemed important through the consensus of groups of people. Marx believed we found ourselves in a matrix of history and environment that shapes our thinking. We are guided, he felt, by our early predecessors into the natural way of perception and being. In essence, we follow in the footsteps of those cultural others in the way forward. Or, as Marshall Sahlins put it, we manifest our humanity through a particular cultural way of life and then pass it on.

Capitalism can be thought of as a system of ideas expressed in a series of coherent political-economic actions. The basis of capitalist economics is the need for rational calculation by both the owners of wealth (corporate factory owners, hedge fund managers, etc.) and the average individual consumer (the assumed maximizing individual). Ayn Rand, famous for her novel *Atlas Shrugged*, argued in *Capitalism: The Unknown Ideal*, "The moral justification of capitalism lies in the fact that it is the only system consonant with man's rational nature, that it protects man's survival qua man, and that its ruling principle is: justice" (1986, 20). From an anthropological point of view, it would be difficult to suggest that pre-modern humans shared Rand's idea of "man's rational nature" expressed in the idiom of self-interest and must sell themselves piecemeal for maximization of benefit. Rationality is expressed differently in different societies under different historical and cultural circumstances. Yet all humans have the capacity to understand ends and means for attaining a goal and are guided by normative considerations and facts. Most anthropologists and other social sciences recognize and agree that it would be difficult to attribute all behavior or concepts, such as rational choice or "self-interest," to one universal but Westernized ethnocentric definition. Goals and means are relative and play out differently in different cultural and historical contexts, as suggested by Sahlins.

Nevertheless, from Adam Smith to Ayn Rand, capitalism operates through the mechanism of the free market, a system of dealings that is controlled by private producers looking out for themselves and unencumbered by government regulation or any sense of moral obligation. Most conservative proponents of capitalism believe that governments should employ a laissez-faire position, giving independence to the market and "human nature." Rand believed, following Smith, that unencumbered markets are "natural" systems based on the idea of natural law governing human actions, such as the inherent desire for self-determination of own's own fate. Relatedly, humans are believed to have unlimited wants (as opposed to needs) and must therefore rationally calculate choices between alternate ends to maximize their outcome.[5]

Natural law was a preoccupation for many Enlightenment thinkers such as Smith, Thomas Hobbes, and John Locke. They shared the belief that there is a set of rights and values that are determined by nature and thus inherent in humans and expressed in human reason. These ideas and values are progress, reason, individualism, and rational choice. By 1690, when John Locke wrote his *Second Treatise of Civil Government*, it was clear that qua "natural man" there existed a relationship between property, liberty, and the new economics of capitalism. Private property took on greater meaning, especially around production, which itself encouraged accumulation, innovation, growth, and expansion. Those such as Locke were beginning to understand capitalism as a natural system expressing economic logic and activity and firmly located in the idea of freedom and the sovereign individual. Locke claimed, "As much as anyone can make use of to any advantage of life before it spoils, so much he may by his labor fix a property in; whatever is beyond this, is more than his share, and belongs to others" Furthermore, he added, "Though the Water running in the Fountain be every one's, yet who can doubt, but that in the Pitcher is his only who drew it out" (org. 1691; 1992, 747). The product of the sweat of one's labor, Locke held, belonged to the laborer who had the freedom to do with that product as he saw fit. This was as human nature intended it to be.

Locke wrote of the need for private property if development (or, as he put it, "the greatest conveniences of life") were to be successful, but it was Adam Smith almost two hundred years later that directly linked property to the self-interest of individual effort, writing, "It is not from the benevolence of the butcher, the brewer, or the baker that we expect our dinner, but from their regard to their own interest. We address ourselves, not to their humanity but to their self-love, and never talk to them of our own necessities but of their advantages" (Book One: On the Principle which gives occasion to the Division of Labour 1776). Growth is realized not through communalism but through individual effort and free labor, according to Smith, where "His labour hath taken it out of the hands of Nature, where it was common, and belong'd equally to all her Children, and hath thereby appropriated it to himself" (Chapter V. of Property), a point that Locke and Rand most likely would agree with.

It is only through the natural law governing private effort that nature can be tamed and put to better use, transforming disorderly nature into something resembling, in Carolyn Merchant's view, the Garden of Paradise from which man was expelled. "We take freedom of the individual," Milton Friedman wrote, thinking about the market, "as our ultimate goal in judging social arrangements" (quoted in Derber and Magrass 2014, 148). Social arrangements around the market, centered on assumed human nature, encourage socioeconomic development, Friedman believed. This process can only be realized through the sanctity of individual rights and private property, two cornerstone values of American society (and, increasingly, the globe). In this case, then, from Milton Friedman to the Heritage Foundation, contemporary capitalism and its associated market is the purest expression of the ascendancy of human reason and nature, as Enlightenment thinkers presumed, and thus nothing can surpass it. Freedom in this case is to allow the innovation and ingenuity of individuals' free rein to solve social problems without the direct involvement of government policy. Freedom of the market and market behavior is the only thing, from Milton Friedman and Friedrich Hayek's points of view, that stands in the way of governmental central planning and, hence, the totalitarian state's stagnant economy and enslaved society. It is interesting how self-interest and wants as human nature represent the epitome of freedom in the rise of democracy as natural law. These elements make up a long-enduring history in the development of a uniquely American narrative that combines freedom and capitalism.

The basic components of the structure of the capitalist economic system are the role of competition and market share, a question of costs (production versus external costs), mergers and consolidation. The market is the point of exchange of commodities for money, which then is partially reinvested in production, and the rest as profit. Karl Polanyi, in his economic history of the development of capitalism, offered the formula M > C > M = M1 + M2, where M is money to produce a commodity, C is the commodity which in turn makes M, more money. M1 is that which is reinvested, and M2 is corporate, shareholder, and personal profit (1957). Magdoff and Foster quote Richard Levins summing up the basic perspective of capitalism (not capitalism as in what an individual capitalist thinks, but what the economic logic of capitalism demands). Levins states that, "Agriculture is not about producing food but about profit. Food is a side effect. . . . Health service is a commodity, health a by-product" (2011, 39). Essentially, investors and investment funds will invest where it is thought the greatest return exists, not necessarily for the good it does for society. Money in capitalist society is fetishized, in that money is seen as an agent that can do things; it has a power of its own. How else to explain why the super-rich continue to strive to make more, for what purpose if they cannot spend it all? What more can Jeff Bezos or Elon Musk do with their hundreds of billions of dollars? The social relationships which give money such power are obscured, lending money a sense of godlike independence. Money creates an overpowering rapture of its own. The logic and meaning of money evolved to create the "great transformation," the crossing of the Rubicon to leave behind the old feudal world in search of new wonders.

Yet for all its accomplishments, capitalism has exacted a high cost, both socially and environmentally. Globally, millions of impoverished people have been left behind in its wake, as Mike Davis pointed out in *The Planet of Slums* (2007). Capitalism as a productive force is a Janus-headed dynamic, acting as both creator and destroyer. As a side effect, as we will discuss in the next chapter, for many beneficiaries of this system, a sense of social alienation and isolation due to the greater commercialization of life via economic domination has become pronounced, as predicted many years ago by Marx, Weber, and Durkheim. Resources, including human labor, have been exploited and squandered as if there is an infinite supply always available when needed. Human beings themselves have become but images of the productive drive of capitalism's reinvention of the human as a commodity. It seems axiomatic to say that for the capitalist system to work, individuals must conform in ways compatible with that system. Ideas such as acquisition, competition, cost-benefit analysis, and possessive individualism are essential components for the operation of the system.

Considering the hegemony of capitalism's infiltration into the modern human psyche, it is far easier to accept the ecological destructiveness of capitalism than it is to imagine an alternative to capitalism. The essential question is not its effect but whether it can change in any substantive manner. The logic and principles of the economics of capitalism, or the laws of motion as they call it, are such that a no-growth economy is a contradiction in terms, in that endless growth is a fundamental feature of the system.

Capitalism thus must grow or die. But the ecological crisis is so pervasive and the physical impact of capitalism so dramatic that the ability of capitalism to transform into something more environmentally benign is as much an "undiscovered country" as is a new economic system based on a Gaia-centered ethical philosophy. At this point in history, it appears this is where we stand, and now we must begin to think about the future: Can capitalism be saved, or should the world reinvent itself anew? Capitalism, for most people today, is akin to a fish in the ocean. It is such a pervasive aspect of life that most rarely think about it; it just is.

PART TWO: THE PERVASIVENESS OF CAPITALISM

The underlying philosophy guiding the capitalist spirit since the decades after World War II is neoliberalism, which came to fruition in the 1970s. Neoliberalism is the center around which most economies revolve. At the center of this philosophy is the primacy of the free market, the rational competitive individual, privatization of public services, and the pursuit of capital accumulation. The basic freedom in this regard is for each individual to be responsible and accountable for their own well-being; success or failure is centered on individual action. As someone once put it, the market ensures that everyone gets what they deserve.

There are two outcomes of this neoliberal situation: one centers on the constrained notion of freedom and the other on the personal isolation of the individual. There are different ways of valuing freedom, and the idea of choice is one of them. For many people, choosing between various commodities—different cereals, smartphones, in part the meaning of freedom, in this case centered on the market. As will be discussed in later chapters, as individuals are lost in a bureaucratized mass society and disenfranchised from social institutions, a feeling of *anomie*, as Durkheim warned, sets in. The corporate world realizes that this void can be filled by advertising the joys (and sense of control) of consumption. And, as will be discussed, capitalist production requires a constant stream of consumption of produced goods; otherwise, capital accumulation stops.

The World of Capitalism

The political system is fraught with discussion of the role of government in the operation of the market. Many proponents believe government regulation distorts the market's ability to effectively use resources to create wealth and opportunity or to overcome socioeconomic problems. How capitalism operates and the effect it has on various aspects of society, culture, and the environment require awareness of how the political system is influenced by and infused with the imperatives of the economy and its actors. Capitalism is seen by many as efficient and effective in its acquisition and use of resources in ways that promote wealth, and the political system must support economic activity for the well-being of society.

What has led the globalization of capitalism and capitalist-oriented consumer culture is the multinational corporation. The global economy is largely organized and controlled by global corporations that have become an inescapable influence in the lives of global citizenry and political-economic policies. Multinational corporations since the late twentieth century have had the productive technology to produce globally and sell everywhere, including networks to penetrate every corner of the global, they are essentially world empires. In a mix of the political and the economic, corporate power gained the world through the design of several international organizations meant to oversee the spread of international production and trade. Following the end of World War II, a series of meetings took place in 1944 at Bretton Woods, New Hampshire, to map out a new international monetary and financial system. From these meetings came the World Bank and the International Monetary Fund (IMF). Recognizing that the last two wars were as much economic as political, economic stability through lower tariffs, free trade, and fixed exchange rates became the cornerstone of the agreement. The result was to open both French and English empires to American trade and investment in the ensuing years. A primary agreement that emerged from Bretton Woods was the General Agreement on Tariffs and Trade (GATT), a precursor to the World Trade Organization (WTO). GATT and the WTO that came after are the chief enforcers of free trade and labor, health, and environmental regulations instituted as policy. A sovereign nation's economic, labor, and environmental policies can be challenged through the WTO if they limited free trade. Bretton Woods was the gateway through which multinational corporate-led globalization would emerge.

The main role of the World Bank is to provide large loans for national infrastructure projects such as dams, highways, and other development projects that help to improve economic performance, promoting direct foreign investment and international trade. The IMF, on the other hand, aids in budgetary matters such as balance of payment problems and meeting international financial obligations. The economic philosophy that guides these institutions is neoliberalism, which holds that the best approach to a robust economy is market reform and economic liberalization policies such as deregulation. These institutions wield considerable power because for many heavily indebted or poorer nations, there are no alternatives to large development loans or relief from balance of payments problems except through these organizations.

The power of these institutions to influence national policy and the economy is through conditionalities, often referred to as structural adjustments that are enforced with respect to the loans. The idea is to bring greater market efficiency and productivity to the local economy through privatization of government-controlled industries and utilities, increased trade liberalization through abolishing tariffs, and eliminating subsidies to social programs. The goal is to increase the productivity of national resources and release government funds to meet their loan obligations and balance payment problems. Such measures, it is assumed, will lead to a healthier, more robust economy and increases in the country's GDP.[6] Promoted by the advanced industrialized countries and the Bretton institutions, neoliberalism's values and assumptions have taken on an orthodoxy difficult for policymakers to resist. The push of neoliberal principles by an international class alliance of institutions and corporations has led to a hegemony that appears as objective and natural outcomes of development. Global neoliberalism as policy and action enforced the idea of individualism and consumerism on the world. Its policies recognized private property, capitalist economic logic, and individual responsibility at the expense of communalism, collective thinking, and a life based on community rather than consumption. In advanced countries certainly, but more and more found elsewhere as well, a neoliberal "subject" of consumption becomes "an active agent," as Detlev Zwick understands it, "is yet another example of how personal consumption is constructed as an act of social action, moral duty and active political participation." Eventually, consumer interests become aligned with the market and multinational corporate economic policy creating a new economic-oriented trajectory in human history. The result means, according to Zwick, the subject as agent is morally and individually responsible for their relationship to the market and any other social circumstance. They need to employ "market-based principles" of rational choice and cost-benefit analysis without regard to ethical beliefs or standards (2011, 26).

Critics of neoliberalism believe that deregulation and government pullback from the local economy have led to a race for cheaper labor, ineffective environmental oversight, unencumbered access to natural resources by international corporations, and the spread of consumer culture. In many cases, the result is the shift of sovereign control of the local economy to international machinations with little accountability for those who are most affected by such actions. It is in poorer nations where neoliberal programs are most interrelated with environmental change and degradation due in part to the inability of poorer nations to determine their own fate. The interests of such entities, as well as many of the government policymakers and economic elites, lie not in environmental protection or elevating poverty per se, but in self-interest in resource and labor exploitation. Research trips to Mexico and Costa Rica by this author found little governmental oversight of industrial development and local conditions. Communities in both cases, in Puerto Viejo de Talamanca in Costa Rica and colonias outside Tijuana, Mexico, lacked information regarding development programs or their potential environmental impact.

The world of capitalism has historically promoted, more pronounced since Bretton Woods, a project to transform all economies in its image. After rising out of the ashes of World War II and the sacrifices and hardships of Mao Zedong's Great Leap Forward and Cultural Revolution, China today is emerging as a powerful state-led capitalist economy. According to Homi Kharas and Geoffrey Gertz's estimate, China's emerging middle class is 157 million people with a desire to consume and improve the objective conditions of their lives (2010, 7). American companies are not just in China for production purposes but also to develop markets for their products, to enhance China as a consumerist society. Citizens in all countries struggle to improve their lives, and more and more such improvements go beyond the basic necessities of life to include a host of modern conveniences and consumer commodities.

The Epoch of Capitalism: Profit Motive and Competition

The great push to rule the world is the pursuit of profit. The owners of such operations see certain opportunities to meet a demand for a commodity by bringing together investment capital, raw resources, talent, and labor, and production of the desired product. Earlier economic systems likewise needed to produce commodities and had to acquire the elements of production as well. A craftsman in feudal Europe also needed labor, talent, and investment resources to produce pottery or linen clothing. Likewise, the *Mexica* craftsmen of *Tenochtitlan* had to marshal a variety of resources to produce the high-status goods demanded by the *Mexica* aristocracy. In both these examples, natural resources—trees, silver, water, plant dyes, etc.—had to be exploited. The difference with capitalism is twofold: on the one hand, the European craftsperson generally sold for local households, while the Mexica had some produce household goods and others social prestige items. On the other, capitalism's continual expansion also meant a grander scale of resource exploitation and use of nature if eventually profit was to be realized. Among the former, the impacts were local or regional; among the latter, the impact is global.

A fundamental building block of capitalism is the relentless need for capital accumulation. This, from Marx and other's reference point, is the absolute general law of capitalism. To secure new production technologies, enter new markets, improve the production process, gain investment capital, and compete against business rivals, capital must be realized. Furthermore, the search for profit is expansionary. That is, as Marx declared, if profit is X in the original cycle, then in the next the profit realized must be X_2, and so forth. Thus, production and profit expand exponentially. Marx pointed out in *Grundrisse*, "If capital increases from 100 to 1,000, then 1,000 is now the point of departure, from which the increase has to begin" (1993). Marx believed that any original profit is but a starting point for a relentless expansion. In other words, to survive profit is not only exponential but the time frame to realize profit from investment must approach the immediacy of short-term goals. The drive for quick profit illustrates the short-term time horizon, one that must be met due to the competitive nature of the search for investment.

Competition among business is considered not only a "good," but is essential to its being. Without profit, there is no capital for innovation or expansion, and thus, it is believed, prosperity will suffer and economic growth will slacken. It leads to innovation in production and new products that advertising persuades citizens they need to acquire. Competition leads to greater creativity, output, standards, and falling prices to capture a greater share of the consumer market. The result is more people purchasing more and better goods. For example, Apple's iPhone is as good as it is due to the competition for customers between Apple and Samsung's Galaxy. Constant innovation and technical iterations from one generation to another secure greater market share and produce wealth for the company. Of course, such competition means that products become obsolete rather quickly. Not only must resources be exploited for the new iteration, but to replace the old, discarded item assumed to no longer be of any use or value. So, the perfectly good iPhone 4 gives way to the iPhone 5, the iPhone 7 and 8, and soon the iPhone 14 and 15.

Magdoff and Foster offer the example of razor blades to show how competition leads to innovation but in a rather empty fashion. The two major razor blade companies, Gillette and Schick, have been in intense competition for greater market share for years. They have moved from one-blade razors to four and then five blades, attempting to outdo each other. Now it is Gillette's Fusion ProGlide versus Schick's new Hydro Quattro blades (2011, 50).

Where is the social value (for the shaver, for society) of such competition other than raising the price of razors and increasing corporate profit? After all, how close of a shave can one ultimately get? On the other hand, the increase in business competition leads to greater corporate concentration. Competition can mean expansion into new markets (and revenue streams) or the absorption of innovative or "green market" niches through acquisition. For example, Exxon Mobil's $59 billion agreement to acquire Pioneer Natural Resources and Pfizer's purchase of Seagen for $43 billion have been recently reported in the news.

The nature of capitalism has evolved into a system of increased concentration and centralization of production and control over the market in the late twentieth century. The pressure on price has also shifted production to the lowest possible labor costs and environmental regulations found in countries such as India, Bangladesh, and Honduras. Cheap Global South labor and poor environmental regulations have given consumer society affordable products subsidized by such labor conditions.

The Epoch of Capitalism: Externalities and Market Operation

One means by which companies attempt to maintain control over the costs of business is by shifting certain operating costs onto the public sector. The market is an ineffective means of policing business activity's impact on the environment due to the problem of externalities. Externalities are effects from the production or consumption of goods and services in which cost is not factored into the consequences of production or consumption. The social and environmental costs are excluded from profit/loss thanks to lobbyists and political allies, allowing the public to bear the burden of cleanup. Such costs are often hidden from individuals unaware of shifts of costs that degrade various ecosystems or local communities. This shift leads to market failure because the price (or consequence of consumption) does not reflect the social or environmental costs of production (but externalities can increase profit). This leads to market failure because of distorted signals regarding resource value. Externalities distort those signals.

A negative externality related to production is an aspect of market failure if there is no built-in cost factor pricing the consequence. For example, mountaintop removal to access coal deposits in West Virginia requires sludge retention ponds holding billions of gallons of toxic waste (arsenic, ammonia, chromium, etc.), hillside erosion, habitat destruction, and increased turbidity of streams and rivers (Epstein et al., 2011). Yet the coal companies do not pay fully for the negative effects of their coal mining efforts. These costs are primarily absorbed by local communities and state/local governments or the federal government.[7] In fact, as Wright and Rogers argue, "The principal obstacles to solving the problem [of environmental exploitation] may be strategies of powerful actors, especially business corporations, in which they effectively use their power to block solutions" (2011, 81). Because of the market failing to account for these externalities, coal is much cheaper than it should be. Companies thus bear the costs of labor, technology, capital, and materials but not the costs of the pollution unless enforced by the courts or government. If the costs are not borne by the producer, then there is little incentive (if the market does not provide one or the government compels one) to invest in environmental conservation measures.

Hawken, Lovins, and Lovins argue in *Natural Capitalism* that "natural capitalism," if properly designed, can harness the creative energy of innovation and markets to create a sustainable world in which many of today's problems will be solved. They remark, "Protecting the climate is not costly but profitable, because saving energy costs less than buying it: efficiency is cheaper than fuel." Companies can become allies in the fight for environmental sustainability once they realize that "Environmentally sound practices . . . typically cost less and return higher profits than destructive ones" (2010, xiii). Most basically, they argue, natural resources, habitats, and ecosystems should be given true market value. They use terms such as "markets for their proper purpose" which, they add, is to "allocate scarce resources efficiently over the short term" (261). It is primarily a question of redirecting the values and energies of markets in new sustainable directions to deal with inefficiencies and waste, allowing for economic growth. Yet capitalism is a prisoner's dilemma game played as a political-economic power struggle over externalities.

Foster, Clark, and York, however, are skeptical of their analysis as an "eco-veneer." This, they believe, is a misreading of the nature of capitalism. From their perspective, "The capitalist market system is geared at all times to the concentration of economic surplus and wealth together with the displacement of the majority of costs onto society and the environment" (44). What's more, Magdoff and Foster believe the problem is the economic system as it exists: "It is precisely because ecological destruction is built into the inner nature and logic of our present system of production and distribution that it is so difficult to end" (2011, 30). It is understood that adaptations accepted do not jeopardize business as usual.

The present trend to deal with the environmental crises is to combine the logic of the market with affluent consumers demanding a gentler environmental impact. Much of the environmental movement appears to hold the view that along with policy changes, market corrections, and individual sensitivity to conservation, we can reverse global environmental degradation. Ted Steinberg questions this perspective, asking,

> It is hard to imagine that a system so good at producing wealth and so poor at distributing it, so steeped in the commodity form and bent on bringing everything from land to water to air into the world of exchange, is likely to be turned around to save the earth without a great deal of reform (2010, 9).

Reform necessitates serious and costly public policies of economic transformation and governmental oversight.

THE ROLE OF THE STATE UNDER THE INFLUENCE OF CAPITALISM

Recently, there is much discussion about what is termed the "environmental commons." In 1968, Garrett Hardin proposed a "tragedy of the commons" as an open common resource available to all users. Without rules to govern who and how a common resource can be used, over-exploitation and environmental degradation often ensue. For example, all marine resources are available to all users beyond national boundaries where nothing governs limitations on exploitation. In this case, what would stop a company from harvesting as much of the resource as possible? Are companies ethically obligated to limit their impact on a common resource? The answer depends on the circumstances. Without rules, overfishing results in lobster depopulation, as happened in Maine's lobster watershed. The tragedy of the commons can be prevented, as in Maine, where collective self-interest developed agreed-upon principles to conserve fishing stock through sustainable harvesting practices and management (Nordman 2021). The agreement developed locally among lobster boat captains in conjunction with state-sponsored co-management. This was not a top-down agreement but was determined locally by those with a vested interest in an important resource for collective livelihoods and community survival. Such an example would be more difficult for profit-driven large corporate interests beholden to shareholders or where the government has little or no role to play except through policy determinations.

In his book *Will Big Business Destroy the Planet?*, Peter Dauvergne makes two important points. He outlines the rise in the massive financial power of the 500 leading corporate organizations, with revenues of $27.7 trillion and profits of $1.5 trillion. With this wealth, he concludes, comes "increasing power over political systems and cultural understandings, with waterfalls of money cascading into political parties, lobbying campaigns, advertising, and branding" (2018, 28, 22). Dauvergne also points out that many companies recognize the demands to take greater social responsibility and have signed on to corporate social responsibility programs and actively promote greater environmental concern in their business practices. While many companies, such as Walmart and McDonald's, have designed very good programs (recycling, better packaging, sustainability), the result is, according to Dauvergne, companies engage "NGO discourses, governmental agendas, and global governance mechanisms toward solutions amenable to more growth, profits, and control for big business" (52). Without oversight, many businesses use "greenwashing" to limit costly environmental changes. Greenwashing involves businesses in superficial efforts of minimal environmental benefit to receive a green certificate, advertise their sustainable friendly practices, etc.

Importantly, given the history and makeup of our late era, Can the corporate world, as we asked earlier, willingly reform to develop a responsibility to the planet's environment? In *The Acquisitive Society*,R. H. Tawney criticized capitalism because it encouraged economic power without social responsibility. The right to property had become separated from any obligation to discharge a useful social function, he added (2004, org. 1920). Commenting on such economic actors, he said,

> They inherit the earth and change the face of nature, if they do not possess their own souls; and they have that appearance of freedom which consists in the absence of obstacles between opportunities for self-advancement and those whom birth or wealth or talent or good fortune has placed in a position to seize them. (ibid, 31)

Does the need, then, for growth and profit to meet head-on the competition eclipse the environment even with the best of personal intentions by corporate types? Economists would answer that there need be no choice, that a clean environment is like any other commodity and if people desire it enough and are willing to pay for it, the market will supply a cleaner, more efficiently used environment. The assumption which many state actors believe is that we can grow our way out of our environmental problems through effective adherence to market principles, entrepreneurial innovation, and corporate responsibility.

Can the government realistically alter the nature of capitalism? How to deal with an economic system that is dynamic, where stockholders demand adequate returns and where many politicians are beholden to corporate campaign contributions? According to Wendell Potter, "By necessity and by law, the top priority of the officers of these companies is to 'enhance shareholder value' . . . that's your top priority" (quoted in Mander 2012, 47). Second, politically chronic and high unemployment offers the potential to destabilize society and may, over time, lead to questions of the legitimacy of the political system as income and wealth inequality continue to grow. Therefore, companies are encouraged by government policy to expand in order to create new employment opportunities so more people can be employed, earning an income to purchase more goods and services, which will lead to more employment opportunities for new labor entrants into the economy. That is, the system is functioning as it was designed to function.

The leadership role of government in funding environmental research is critical since such research is generally unattractive to the private sector if only limited profit is possible, the initial investment is too huge, or the lead time to payoff is too distant. Given this, most environmentalists see the negative consequences of climate change (rising sea levels, shifting rainfall patterns for agriculture, increasingly scarce fresh water supplies, etc.) as inevitable, and thus substantive planning for such future outcomes is paramount. Only governments can provide this critical role, yet the drumbeat by powerful actors is to see the government as a "big government takeover," while political and ideological broadcasts lessen the likelihood of a government/public coalition to design meaningful and effective policies to counter environmental and climate changes.[8] In this libertarian sense and the age of Donald Trump, the common good, paradoxically, is only obtained through the privatized self-interest of each individual and corporation to maximize their utility, and such "natural" efficiency that results cannot but uplift all citizens—"the rising tide raises all boats" principle. The result of this onslaught on the role of government, especially under the former Trump administration, was an attempt to weaken the regulatory ability of the government to enforce regulations (now before the 2024 Supreme Court). The issue of governmental regulation is at the center of ongoing conservative political struggles over environmental protection and sustainability.

Today, entrenched wealth coincides largely with access to or influence over government policies, especially as they relate to the relationship between economy and environment. Fifty years of research by William Domhoff on the American power structure points to the inordinate influence of a corporate elite over government policy. Rather than a pluralist view of competing interest groups and power sharing, Domhoff saw and continues to see government and corporate interests intertwined. In 1967, he wrote, "we conclude that the income, wealth, and institutional leadership of what Baltzell calls the American business aristocracy' are more than sufficient to earn it the designation "governing class"" (1967, 38). Domhoff's research outlines how power is institutionalized, incorporating the wealthy, business elite, and government into a common power elite centered on the organizational and class-based control over, foremost, economic policy. For example, a lawsuit filed in June 2014 by the Sierra Club and other environmental groups accused President Obama of weakening the EPA's power plant wastewater discharge rules. Lawyers for Earthjustice believe the EPA rules were weakened by the Office of Management and Budget to "satisfy the concerns of power companies" (Varner 2014).

The recent trend in skepticism and mistrust in public institutions has led to a weakening belief in the common good. Tea Party-type conservatives, in and out of government, have pushed an agenda to delegitimize the role of government in the belief that any governmental oversight or management of, in this case, natural resources is either corrupt, inept, or illegal. This perspective was most pronounced under former President Trump's administration. The federal government controls millions of acres of Western land under the 1976 Federal Land Policy and Management Act, which many Western states, ranchers, energy companies, and farmers considered a land grab. Their grievances over grazing regulations and high use fees, mining restrictions, and limits on motorized recreational use led to the Sagebrush Rebellion and a push to transfer federal lands to states for open access claims and privatization. In a sense, the Rebellion is the neoliberal expression of a modern enclosure movement like the end of feudalism in Europe. The fact that private use of federal ranch land led to overgrazing, degraded streams, and habitat destruction is not germane to Sagebrushers.[9]

In reality, there is no perfect market or any laissez-faire government allowing Smith's invisible hand to work its magic, but only various groups vying to influence government economic policy for their own interests. Economic wealth and political power merge in the hands of entrenched interests to ensure as much as possible the primacy of economics over all other concerns. Research on the role of business interests and its effects on democracy conducted by Martin Gilens and Benjamin Page surmises that economic interests have disproportionate influence over policy compared to mass-based civil society. Based on their findings, they conclude, "When the alignments of business-oriented and mass-based interest groups are included separately in a multivariate model, average citizens' preferences continue to have essentially zero estimated impact upon policy change, while economic elites are still estimated to have a very large, positive, independent impact" (2014, 575, 577). In other words, moving beyond the rhetoric of conservative ideology, many political observers suggest the United States is a controlled economy influenced by corporate interests and political allies in government.

In American society, an interconnected group of elites exists as a class; that is, an interest group of people who share a common set of statuses, wealth, and the ability to exercise power, not necessarily as individuals but as interlinked institutional actors. It is not the volition of individuals that is important but concerted action taken by a group with shared interests who utilize power in the name of those interests (for instance, the Koch brothers and their Americans for Prosperity organization pushing policy in a more business-friendly direction). It is this group that has influenced policy, economic strategy and operations, and the framing of narratives to the public and politicians. This group—those at the top of the class and wealth structure—are "structurally incapable" of confronting and acknowledging the environmental crisis before us. By structural, Kovel means that the

> behavior of elites cannot be reduced to ordinary motivations like greed or domination. . . . When we are talking of class interest and of how individuals become personifications of great institutional forces, all the innumerable variations that make the human psyche interesting are subject to a few basic rules, and a remarkable uniformity of behavior prevails. (2007, 83)

In a sense, it is not whether the "system" can change but whether those who benefit most from the existing system are willing to change even at limited personal or corporate cost. Long ago Marx understood the nature of capitalism, exclaiming that the drive for profit accumulation is relentless, that capitalism cannot rest and continually whispers in its ear: "Go on! Go on!"

CREATING A NEED AND FILLING A VOID: THE MAGICAL WORLD OF ADVERTISING

Members of all cultures cannot abide a void in the structure of meaning. Stories, myths, and narratives must offer explanations and justifications for the way reality operates and how people fit into such realities. That is, we construct or invent conceptions of life. If traditional stories or narratives lose their power to explain and provide socio-psychic satisfaction, then something must stand in place of the old and provide new ways of thinking and explaining the meaning of things. Advertising has become a major means of developing what is important in consumer society, especially when traditional ways of relating decline. Advertising plays a major role in motivating consumption in peoples" lives. Advertising and marketing people use jingles, images, and commercials to draw a picture of how products can give us a sense of satisfaction and purpose, and of balance between our wants, needs, and desires. The basic message of the consumer narrative is that to be happy, successful, and beautiful, you must have a bounty of things. The narrative gives us a comparison to others with such things. We ask, do we fit in, are we with it, how do we compare? What we own says something, we think, about who and what we are. The conclusion, however, is to encourage persistent insecurities, which require additional acquisitions to address.

The process of encouraging consumption is the role, the only raison d"être, of advertising and marketing. This process of artificially creating the need to consume is important to understand because of its relationship to the production of goods through the continuing and increasing exploitation of natural resources, at one end, of the production cycle to the throughput of wastes, at the other end. The ethos and ideology of dependence on *communitas* and the pleasures of social relationships had to be weakened initially if not destroyed for advertising to offer its version of the play of social relationships, usually in some happy setting such as the beach or pub, laughing with friends, but as individuals, at the joy of life. However, such messages can lead to the vain hope of staving off feelings of insecurity if true life does not measure up to the commercialized ideal life presented.

As suggested, this intimate relationship to material things is not only relatively new in social history but also an artificial, needful creation of modern capitalism. Writing about the beginning of the advertising age, Richard Ohmann notes that industrialists were "looking for a nexus between high-speed, continuous-flow manufacturing and the reshaping of people's habits and lives" and aimed to do so through a "metamorphosis of aspirations and imaginations" of the general population (quoted in Bogardus 1998, 515). In other words, a new narrative, an ideal of life centered on consumption, was being constructed by the manufacturing industry in the late nineteenth and early twentieth centuries. The result leads to the colonization of the imagination with "visions of lifestyle." This was apparent to sociologist Jacques Ellul, who years earlier observed, "The way of life offered by advertising is all the more compelling in that it corresponds to certain easy and simple tendencies of man and refers to a world in which there is no spiritual values to form and inform life. When men feel and respond to the needs advertising creates, they are adhering to its ideal of life" (1964, 407). If the lifestyle is encouraged by advertising, television, and social media, and mediated by the acceptable ownership of things, then lifestyle is one-dimensional and fraught with the uneasy thought of its temporality.

I suggest a negotiation took place over a new definition of the meaning of life, lifestyle, and standard of living, one increasingly influenced by industrial advertising to create new wants and desires. The narrative of desire sees consumption through product imagery as natural. Sut Jhally concurs, stating, "The marketplace (and its major ideological tool, advertising) is the major structuring institution of contemporary consumer society" (2011, 199). This is the atmosphere, increasingly global, in which we are all born and from which we can only with difficulty escape its gravitational pull. Hundreds of billions of dollars are spent promoting literally everything the average individual owns or desires. Jhally recalls that Raymond Williams referred to advertising as the "magic system" offering goods of serious power over people to promise transformation, gratification, and satisfaction. He adds, quoting an ad executive who believed "advertising doesn't mirror how people are acting, but how they are dreaming." From Jhally's point of view, "advertising is ubiquitous—it is the air that we breathe as we live our daily lives" (2003, 202).

Considering television viewing, and now social media, the average preteen watches over 25,000 ads a year while the average adult sees 52,500 ads. Advertising offers the unstated message that the ownership and consumption of things bring us a sense of order and gives us a way to measure if we fit in. In this regard is the idea of relative deprivation, or how we view others and their consumption habits. Wright and Rogers see this as a psychological process "in which the satisfaction one derives from owning something depends in part of one's perception of what other people own" (2011, 136). This pressure relative to others reflects as "induced wants," or referring to Marcuse's one-dimensional man, "false needs."

Ellul believed advertising played a pivotal role in creating the contours of modern life and by extension the "mass man." We are taught from an early age to want to consume. Individuals in consumer society are submerged in the iron cage of corporate needs aimed at developing a new psychological state of being. Consumerism, Ellul felt, is a being devoid of a humane spirituality and authenticity. Through advertising, the individual falls prey to "involuntary psychological collectivization" (1964, 406). Humanity now seeks pleasure and entertainment as a coping mechanism for a diminishing awareness of intimate social life, generally enthralled by technology and the promise it brings of a better life of material progress. Advertisers believe that it is not so much the goods that are being advertised but the meaning of those goods. Hence, the need for the $85,000 Mercedes or the latest high-def LCD/LED flatscreen television—they are employed to help create the dreamworld within which he/she wishes to live, that these things say something profound about who they are and will make us satisfied and happy.

In the next two chapters, we will investigate the role played by the cultural grammar and ideas that give meaning to how we perceive ourselves in our evolving modern world. As we have already discussed, all cultures use myths, rituals, and ceremonies as narratives to tell stories about themselves. These stories organize how we make concrete sense of the world around us. At the beginning of this chapter, we discussed the meaning of human nature and how each epoch encompassed its own ideas about human nature. The method by which culture develops and transmits particular kinds of individuals and modes of thought is through language. Language encodes cognitive models and thus influences thought, behavior, perception, and ultimately, worldview. We are thus socialized into a particular world of thought and action through language and the meaning particular words convey about that world. Many myths and ceremonies encompass the words and ideas of the capitalist narrative, Horatio Alger for example. Alger, a nineteenth-century American writer, wrote a series of books such as Raigged Dick in 1868 where, through hard work and determination, youth of poor beginnings could rise to middle-class success, a rags-to-riches theme. Those socialized within capitalist-influenced culture share a narrative filled with a set of grammar, metaphors, and vocabulary that creates a meaningful world of opportunity that we experience as real, and as real, enduring. The language of advertising and marketing is the modern-day equivalent of long-ago elders sitting around the campfire and, through myth and stories, instructing ascending generations about who they were as cultural beings.

The metaphors and vocabulary that support and portray a capitalist cultural worldview are located publicly in advertising, movies, education, sports, and holidays such as Christmas. Shopping and buying are held in high esteem, pushed by advertising, especially around holidays but infused into everyday life. For example, Lexus' a "December to Remember" ad campaign or advertising for diamonds, "Give her what she is waiting for . . . A symbol of forever." What holiday does not come without a buying quest? Does the gift really say something about love since the excitement and passion of the gift is ephemeral and we move on to the next thing? Yes, many holidays are about giving, but the giving is mediated through the exchange of material objects immersed in monetary value. What does value say about one's emotional commitment to a relationship? It says more about the person's financial well-being. It is a world of competition—on the field, in business, in gift-giving—of spending and buying, of public displays of material well-being, and estimations of self-worth through consumption. The business world of capitalism could not exist without our belief in the symbolic importance of these ideas to mediate our conception of the world.

NATURE AS COMMODITY AND BY-PRODUCT

The principles underlying the global economic system include one of alienation from the natural world as mass production of goods takes precedence. Alienation—the consequence of immersion as a mechanistic part of society and being divorced from a more socially complete human nature, Marx believed—occurs once the natural world is turned into a series of market commodities divorced from any intrinsic aesthetic value. People today are algorithms and statistics and are treated as such by business and government. Forests are not so much habitat for owls or foxes as much as they are valuable standing lumber waiting to be transformed into 2x4s for new homes. A utilitarian approach is applied in which the benefit of exploitation or the ancillary destruction of a habitat or species is, ideologically speaking, for the greatest good for the greatest number of people via the operation of the market. For example, attempts by the U.S. Interior Department to protect open plains sage grouse nesting sites near oil and gas drilling in the Dakotas are seen by the energy industry as a "roadblock," a job killer to fracturing activity. The issue of the sage grouse ecosystem is trampled by the responsibility of meeting adequate returns to shareholders of the company, creating jobs, or providing cheaper energy to consumers. This reflects the classic political trade-off of jobs versus nature and, more importantly, profit over nature.

During the expansive years of the nineteenth century, only a few voices were heard that offered caution and a philosophy for thinking about the land and its resources in a different light. Henry David Thoreau published *Walden* in 1854, and in 1867 John Muir began a career of environmental writings and went on to be a co-founder of the Sierra Club in 1892. Outraged over the slaughter of millions of birds for their feathers, George Bird Grinnell organized the first Audubon Society. Yet, these many individuals were but whispers against the gale of industrial development, new electrified cities, and paved roads.[10] Progress was the watchword of the day, and anything was possible with America on the move. Nevertheless, an environmental approach was slowly put in place by individuals such as Sigurd Olson, Aldo Leopold, and David Brower, challenging economic development in the late twentieth century and culminating with Earth Day, founded by Senator Gaylord Nelson in 1970. Progress has been made; the Environmental Protection Agency was created that same year, but it has been slow and uneven.

Without a basic understanding of the logic that guides economic thinking and activity, our ability to effectively deal with the environmental crisis will be limited, if not futile. Economic growth is dependent upon consumer spending. If we do not spend, businesses cannot grow, and employment cannot be had. Herein lies the environmental challenge. The political-economic need to accommodate increasing numbers of workers (as consumers) has two basic problems essential to the environmental crisis. First, the need to increase consumption in general, which already accounts for considerable economic activity and waste in the United States; and relatedly, with increased spending comes the hiring of more workers due to increased production, who likewise increase their demand for consumer goods. In addition, the basic problem of economic logic for the need to grow also confronts the environmental imperative to pull back from the hyper-exploitation of global natural resources and the release of increasing climate-changing gases into the atmosphere.

Even if economic growth includes greater efficiencies and the use of green technologies, this does not necessarily diminish our ecological footprint for two reasons. One, as Samuel Alexander, writing for the Simplicity Collective blog, states, Although economies are demonstrably getting better at producing commodities more cleanly and efficiently . . . overall ecological impact is nevertheless still increasing, because every year increasing numbers of commodities are being produced and consumed. We might have more fuel-efficient cars, for example, but the rebound effect is that we are also driving more and buying more cars," especially as population increases (2012).

Furthermore, what is produced includes increasingly complex commodity chains, where a simple English muffin involves an intricate series of production steps and each step costs energy.

Second, the need for robust economic growth, what Speth terms the "secular religion" of our times, means that global economic growth is not linear but exponential (if the U.S. economy grows at 2 percent a year, it will double in thirty-five years). Former President Obama understood the need for policies to control the production of CO_2 and other greenhouse gases, yet his options were limited by the need for growth. President Joe Biden claims to be an environmental president offering various climate proposals, but at the same time is pushing for increased fossil fuel production. It's simply a choice between addressing environmental ills or the needs of the economy. For the president it was clear what to do.

Of course, the issue of growth and the increase in consumption are not monopolized by the United States, Japan, and Europe. Continual economic growth will compound as the demand for resources to produce services and consumer items expands by a growing cadre of affluent consumers found in India, Mexico, Brazil, and China. Additionally, as incomes rise anywhere, demand for environmentally friendly products often rises even as affluent consumers recognize their environmental impact. Speth refers to this as the "environmental Kuznets curve" (2008, 56). In other words, the more money one earns, the more one will spend on more commodities, environmentally efficient or otherwise. For example, if I buy energy-efficient lightbulbs to bring my energy costs down, I may end up with my lights on longer because they are efficient. If gasoline prices fall, I may choose to buy a SUV or drive more. In a consumer-based society, the inclination is to consume rather than to save; in many cases, there are those who cannot save, and there is little to save.

The evolution from traditionally oriented, community-based relationships to the values and norms of individualism today mediated by materialism has had a profound effect upon society and the individual. Chapter 6 examines the growth of the ethos of consumerism as a dominant and necessary presence in post-industrial society. In essence, consumer society engages in transformational magic via what it produces. "They can bring instant happiness, and gratification." Jhally tells us, "They act as a passport into a world of fantasy and desire" (1997, 2).

NOTES

1. Tim Ingold argues that the biological search for a "bio-logos," or genotype, is misleading and fruitless that the human genotype is a "fabrication of the modern

scientific imagination" (2006, 273). We do not therefore have free rein over what we wish to be. "But it does mean," he writes, "that there is no way of describing what human beings are independently of the manifold historical and environmental circumstances in which they become—in which they grow up and live out their lives" (ibid). We become, whether we like it or not, a product of history and culture. This, however, is not to say biology is unimportant but is, in most cases secondary to a cultural order that impacts biology.

2. The panel opens its report stating, "unprecedented material affluence" notwithstanding, "more and more young people are suffering from mental illness, emotional distress and behavioral problems," leading to depression, anxiety and suicide (2003, 3, 9; Twenge 2020). They conclude that young people (as well as those of older generations) are drowning in a sea of isolation, meaninglessness, and confusion as social relationships weaken.

3. This is not to suggest such non-market, subsistence-based societies were free of conflicts or personality issues. Conflict did exist and motivations could differ, leading to internal social strife (hence the need among some cultures for witchcraft accusations to exist); but there existed nevertheless a sense of group consensus and orientation. One important role in chiefdoms was to provide the means for conflict resolution, often by means of consensus between individuals or groups, such as the singing duels among various Inuit communities in Alaska and Canada.

4. "In the language of modern sociology," pointing to the difference between the Bunyoro and a European feudal kingdom, Beattie writes, "the relationship between a political superior and his subordinate was "diffuse" rather than "specific;" that is, the chief's "dealings with his subordinates were not restricted to a narrow official sphere but extended over the whole of the subordinate's personal life. Even today many Bunyoro feel that chiefs should be interested in them as persons, and not simply in their tax-paying or working capacity" (1960, 37).

5. Following on his Tanner Lecture at the University of Michigan, Marshall Sahlins outlined the history of wants and self-interest from a Western point of view. He wrote that over time, "possessive individualism was conflated with basic freedom. What St. Augustine had perceived as slavery and indeed divine punishment, man's endless subservience to desires of the flesh, the neoliberal economists . . . take to be the bedrock freedom. Freedom is the ability to act in one's own best interest" (2005, 86–87).

6. More recently, the World Bank has shifted focus to poverty reduction programs and the IMF is now more concerned with climate change issues. In part, they are reacting to various international social movements, such as in Seattle in 1999, that brought the discourse of resistance to the machinations of these institutions into the streets and headlines of newspapers.

7. A case of externality is the 30-year discharge of PCBs (polychlorinated biphenyl) into the Hudson River in New York. General Electric operated two production plants that dumped 1.3 million pounds into the river. Not much was known then about the toxic effects of PCBs, but the point is, the river was a free resource for years before the removal of their waste product. The Environmental Protection Agency declared the river a superfund site with a projected cleanup cost of $2 billion, with GE forced to incur most of the cost of cleanup.

8. The Green New Deal calls for new economic and environmental policies, such as greater public transportation and climate change infrastructure under federal government policies. Critics orchestrated a campaign claiming that private automobiles would be confiscated, hamburgers outlawed, and air travel banned. Cries of socialism accompanied a mocking campaign to discredit the proposal's authors.

9. In 2014, the Sagebrush Rebellion once again erupted when Nevada rancher Cliven Bundy refused to pay overdue grazing fees, forcing a confrontation with federal officials. Bundy felt it was his right to use the land at no cost since he did not recognize federal jurisdiction.

10. The nineteenth century was also, in contradictory fashion, a time of land preservation. Abraham Lincoln took time from the Civil War to sign a bill protecting Yosemite Valley, California. In 1885, the largest land preservation in the East, the Adirondack Forest Preserve, was created by New York State. Congress went on to establish Sequoia National Park and others in 1890. Such efforts at preserving America's wild lands have yet to run their course. President Obama recently added three new national monuments in California to the twenty-two national monuments and other natural resource protections. During his presidency, Joe Biden has added millions of acreage to national monuments and parks, perhaps more than any recent administration.

Chapter 6

Eating Through the Environment

A Question of Consumer Culture

The following two chapters focus on the shift from intimate community to modern society in flux, with individuals unanchored to traditional forms of meaning and identity. The void left behind by progress is filled by a sociopsychological desire for material comfort beyond the basic needs that gives many a sense of identity. This desire therefore has led to the exploitation of resources to produce the consumer goods demanded for a "good life." Our interest in this book, however, goes beyond the specific considerations in this chapter to locate consumption in the expansion of the economy, leading to substantive resource exploitation and environmental degradation. This is in addition to the cultural manifestations of social disruption of postmodern society and identity. Thus, the economic system, our social identity, and sense of worth are interrelated with the deteriorating condition of the global ecosystem that provides the raw material that eventually comprises our identity formation.

The social sciences recognize a social progression of size, complexity, function, and social orientation of society over time. This has been a movement from a little community to mass society, from horizontal to vertical relationships, and from intimate to impersonal social networks and relationships. Galtung summarized this evolving state believing that

> We are at a stage in human history where the problem is not only whether interaction structures between individuals, groups and countries are right or wrong, but whether there is any structure at all; and not only whether the culture defining right or wrong is right or wrong, but whether there is any normative culture at all. (1996, 384)

As we will discuss in the next chapter, within such a transformation the individual becomes unanchored or adrift in a sea of sociocultural relativism in which the individual's self or social identity, as a matter of choice, becomes problematic and subject to uncertainty. For most of human history, the individual, in self and identity, was anchored to an ongoing web of social relationships generations deep but today holds less and less true as we turn to the immediacy of Facebook, Twitter, and Instagram outside the embrace of family and kinship.

Marx, Weber, and Durkheim, the early classicists, focused in their research on the meaning of the jettison of tradition in favor of progress, individualism, and urbanization of mass society. The German sociologist Ferdinand Tönnies decried what he saw as a shift from the intimacy of a community of moral bonds and likeness to one governed by impersonality and individual expediency with his contrast of *Gemeinschaft* (community) and *Gesellschaft* (society). On the other hand, the modernizing world also brought forth personal liberation and ideas of personal sovereignty and achievement. New freedoms of thought, mobility, an orientation toward the future competed with increased bureaucratic control over society, and pressure to conform to an expected regimentation of cultural life. Within this milieu, the social construction of the modern self-developed a mix of rigid beliefs, insecurities, and a growing sense of unlimited potentials and wants.

The world we live in today is a world of relativism and in flux, "there are no hard and fast structures, no class origins one cannot leave behind and no past that refuses to go away or be thrown overboard," as Zygmunt Bauman characterized it, in other words no real sense of Tönnies's community (2001, 61). Unanchored to a communal past, identity is now an unfettered matter of personal choice. But modern life also means living as a stranger amid strangers and increased feelings of alienation and of faceless power centers determining or influencing personal possibilities. In this era of late capitalism, the social construction of self and identity has largely shifted away from the interpersonal and enduring intimate relationships toward an overpowering ethos of consumerism, material possession, and technologically driven personal social media. In this shift, the institutional order of society, according to Peter Berger and colleagues, loses objective legitimacy to the "realm of subjectivity." In this case, Berger realized, "On the other hand, a subjective realm of identity is the individual's main foothold in reality. Therefore, the individual seeks to find his 'foothold' in reality in himself rather than outside himself" (1974, 74). And in the search for identity in this subjective realm, consumption and ownership of things become of essential importance, leaving any sense of the communal past behind. In essence, I am what I am and the insecurities that come with it.

CULTURE AND CHANGE: ENTER THE CONTEMPORARY ERA

The road to late capitalism and its focus on wealth and material possession was perhaps anticipated in 1516 by Thomas More. In his book *Utopia*, the Portuguese navigator Hythloday is uneasy about the future where money and wealth predominate society. He proclaims,

> to speak plainly my real sentiments, I must freely own that as long as there is any property, and while money is the standard of all other things, I cannot think that a nation can be governed either justly or happily. (1997, 24)

More was concerned with a perception of change in European society, where moral and ethical values were increasingly favoring the "greedy, unscrupulous and useless" landlords among the faint whispers of an emerging bourgeoise.

Sociology and anthropology have long been concerned with the process and consequences of social change. Emile Durkheim and Max Weber long ago saw a substantive shift in social orientation from community, with its strong and enduring traditions and standards, to a socially mobile rootless individual in an increasingly bureaucratic and relative world. Peter Berger et al. outlined the sociology of modernization, employing, in *The Homeless Mind*, the term "life-world," to convey a past non-modern social reality of unitary and collective significance. "For the individual this meant quite simply that the same integrative symbols permeated the various sectors of his everyday life" (1974, 64). Regardless of the circumstance, Berger tells us, the individual always existed in and referenced the same "world" of thought, relationship, and behavior. The contemporary world, on the other hand, is one of pluralization of meaning and social experience. Since we are born and socialized in mass society, a multiplication of experience and meaning suggest that we are constantly "traveling" through experience but never possessing an integrated and unchallenged "home world." The case for this is the "urbanization of consciousness" due to vast inputs of information and communications via various media. "The final consequence of all this can be put very simply (though the simplicity is deceptive): modern man has suffered from a deepening condition of 'homelessness'" (82).

Modern consumer society holds as a major value and focus the consumption of goods and services acquired individually on the market. Materialism—the possessive ownership of things—now increasingly central to our daily lives shifts our attention and meaning of life toward a preoccupation with things and the comfort they bring rather than with spiritual or existential matters, as found in traditional societies, as the foundation of reality. The things we buy, for example at Christmas, signify our commitment to each other as well as the happiness we believe such purchase confers upon us. Yet from a social science perspective, most significance is not the purchase itself or how it expresses social stratification, but the emotions and values expressed and how they play into our social identity and larger social behavioral patterns. The maelstrom of holiday advertising implores us to buy in order to give. There is a hollowness to such advertised good cheer compared to the meaning found in O. Henry's 1905 Christmas story, *The Gift of the Magi.*[1]

A cultural ethos has taken hold in which the focus of social life centers on the purchase and individual ownership of ever greater quantities of material possession. Thinking about this, the philosopher Herbert Marcuse wrote in *One Dimensional Man* that the elite industrial class created false needs to integrate all social members, now as consumers, into the production and consumption apparatus (1968). The full effervesce of liberation is limited and defused by a grand bargain in which the lower classes trade freedom for abundance. Marcuse argued that mass media, advertising, and education now created new modes of thought and forms of social control, exemplified by false desires and the need to purchase ever more and newer commodities. Thus was born consumer culture and the consumption society to meet the needs of the capitalist economy for accumulation.

The latter period of the nineteenth century witnessed the growth of economic progress and improved standards of living or at least the potential for such progress. Generally, the publication of the first Sears catalogue in 1888 was the opening salvo for the consumer society. By 1908, Henry Ford was producing the Model T for mass consumption. During this initial phase, the economist Thorsten Veblen, writing at the time, recognized that, "Received canons of knowledge and belief and on the established order of law and custom" have altered ways of living and thinking (1923, 205). The productive capacity of industry was outrunning the demand due to "habits of thought" unchanged to meet new circumstances. The problem, he wrote, was "competitive sellers in a limited market whose purchasing capacity has habitually fallen short of the productive capacity of the industries which supply the marketable output" (286). Veblen pointed out that, in a closed market, to increase profit production costs, it was necessary to apply downward pressure on wages and at the same time increase salesmanship to entice consumers. Additionally, the conservative holdover ideas of "husbandry, handicraft and neighborhood workmanship" in production must give way to the idea of "salesmanship," the art of persuasion of "personal well-being" or "prestige" of the consumer (309). The idea, Veblen understood, was for the general population to model their behavior after the "leisure" class. That is, he wrote, "the conspicuously wasteful honorific expenditure that confers spiritual well-being may become more indispensable that much of that expenditure which ministers to the "lower" wants of physical well-being or sustenance only" (1994, 63; org. 1899). But it was not until after World War II that the consumption of goods had a much greater profound and rapid impact on American culture.

Today, we are awash in a sea of material goods that inhabit our thinking and everyday reality. We, at least in the affluent countries of the West or increasingly in middle upper incomes in the developing South, live in an age of plenty.[2] "Plenty" in every sense of the word: movies and film, novels and magazines, internet and social media sites, and the thousands upon thousands of choices found in supermarkets or Amazon. A smorgasbord of consumer choice is the reality that many people live in. The anthropologist David Mayberry Lewis once asked how much do we need? Answering his own question he replied, as much as we can get. With a degree of abandonment, we have demonstrated his assessment of modern society to be correct.

Modern day equivalent hunters and gatherers haunt the shopping malls, curio shops, and e-retailers, looking for the next trophy to place on a shelf or bookcase. For many people, more things is better than fewer things if only because materialism has significant meaning culturally, economically, and socially. Things say something about who we think we are or wish to be. A society that emphasizes selling, buying, and owning goods and objects as a significant element of life is a consumer society, one that, as Bauman writes, interpolates, that is "addresses them, hails, calls out to, appeals to, questions, but also interrupts and 'breaks in upon' them . . . and expects to be heard, listened to and obeyed" (2007, 52). Although Nicolaus Copernicus was correct that the Earth revolved around the Sun, in late modern society its members revolve around the commodity market. The hegemony of the market leads to the colonization of life, according to Bauman, "the elevation of the written and unwritten laws of the market to the rank of life precepts" or guidelines for how to conduct one's behavior, thoughts, and life (62). Social media supports the market through a "herd" mentality of keeping within the expectations of consumer behavior of Facebook and other social networks, where we are alerted to what our friends are buying or desire. Since many are so immersed within the internet web of life and commerce, computer algorithms play a companion role offering information based on interest, news feeds, and advertisements.

Many commentators, such as Veblen, believe that for consumption to work, basic needs must be turned into new desires and wants.[3] In turn, desires and wants have been folded into ideas of individuality and freedom: the freedom to choose, buy, and possess whatever we wish, and now an elemental aspect of how many thinks about "quality of life." Foster, Clark, and York are correct by cautioning blame solely on the consumer. They argue that it is misplaced blame to focus on the consumer rather than production and capital accumulation. They also maintain that a shift has taken hold in the environmental movement from Malthusian demographics to a Malthusian economics. That is, "In this new Malthusianism the emphasis is not so much on population control, but on consumption control" (2010, 378). They are correct in emphasizing production, for it is production that transforms nature prior to any consumption. But consumer society is an objective fact. There is a dialectical process played out here. Both are complicit in the exploitation and pollution of the environment to produce goods that are to be consumed in a never-ending process. My focus, however, is to move beyond this debate to suggest that material consumption plays a cultural and psychological role in defining the meaning of the "good life" or "standard" of living, which people use to give order and significance to their world.

In *Capital*, Karl Marx emphasized the profound significance of production for the operation and organization of industrial society. Marx recognized the importance of the production of commodities for the capitalist mode of production, writing that "A commodity is, in the first place, an object outside us, a thing that by its properties satisfies human wants of some sort or another. The nature of such wants . . . makes no difference" (1906, 42).[4] Whereas during the mid-nineteenth century of Marx's time production was the focus of socioeconomic change, today many observers see growth of consumer culture as most significant in the interplay between culture and economy. Mike Featherstone sees a growing primacy of consumption, arguing, "it is important to focus on the question of the growing prominence of the culture of consumption and not merely regard consumption as derived unproblematically from production" (1990, 5). Over time, the ability of capitalist production to produce beyond local consumption necessitated the search for new markets. The growth of international European trade of the sixteenth and seventeenth centuries, for instance, as well as the seafaring expeditions elsewhere, were ultimately a search for resources and markets. This continued search in modern times for economic opportunity to accumulate capital is witnessed by the growth of global advertising, easy credit, and the globalization of economy and cultural norms and values.

If capitalism is to continue to accumulate capital and realize profit, the system must continue to produce, trade, and people to want to consume on a consistent basis. For capitalist expansion to continue, then, so too must consumption of the produced goods continue to expand. In the contemporary era, Marx's emphasis on production and labor continues to be relevant but from a cultural point of view consumption must as well be seen as an "engine" of production. The goal of the system, therefore, is to encourage a "buying mood" among the populace, where consumption is the object of obsession and, I argue here, the basis for a postmodern identity and social persona. Ultimately, however, production and consumption are the twin engines for the environmental crises endangering the planet. Given this, we need to ask what happens to global society and culture as we shift toward an expanding international capitalist-oriented consumptive era? The movement of people and ideas through greater communication technologies has witnessed the power of Western-induced social change leading to variant consumer culture and greater conspicuous consumption in many parts of the world. The globalization of consumer culture has given rise to new values and norms including new definitions of social status that are material based yet are transformed into meanings that are culturally understood.

At the beginning of his book *Culture and Consumption*, Grant McCracken borrowed Karl Polanyi's "great transformation" to declare that we are likewise amid a great transformation. Like Polanyi's analysis of capitalism as the catalyst of radical change (helped along by Martin Luther's Protestant break from the Catholic Church as argued by Max Weber), McCracken saw the consumer revolution creating a fundamental shift in Western culture. "The consumer revolution is now seen to have changed Western concepts of time, space, society, the individual, the family, and the state," summarizing what many historians and social scientists think (1988, 3). A major impetus for change was European colonization of much of the Caribbean, North America, and Asia and the production of various commodities such as sugar, cotton, muslin, tea, and spices. Used as a political vehicle by economic elites, new and cheaper goods offered the working class an opportunity to indulge (limited by wages) in consuming like the upper classes (see Mintz's 1985 book, *Sweetness and Power*, on the political–social role of sugar in eighteenth- to nineteenth-century England). This availability of goods was further exaggerated and expanded by the development of the department store and the advent of marketing in the nineteenth century. But it clearly expanded after World War II as hyper-consumerism.

That the presence of capitalist enterprise has infused itself into the social and cultural world is difficult to deny. Social life abounds with corporate logos, advertising, and names on sports stadiums, commercial buildings, and billboards along highways. We are bombarded with commercials on television, radio, and the internet to persuade us what to buy to improve our lives. All regions of the world and all classes from rich to poor are immersed within its grasp as communications technology and culturally sensitive advertising continue to evolve. Those who command the heights of the global system seek to dominate the totality, not only production but the cultural-ideological goods of the global economy. When Jameson characterized postmodernism as the feeling that something fundamental has changed, what changed is the impact of corporate-induced commercial consumption on the nature of contemporary culture, the existential meaning of our humanness consequently, and the relationship between culture and nature including between individuals and community. The capitalist–corporate configuration is future oriented, in which history and stasis are anathema to its being. A new sociocultural and political-economic configuration is at work, changing the structure of society and cultural consciousness in new ways.[5] Capitalism induces a new way of looking and thinking about the world that centers on consumption. Featherstone adds that consumer commodities not only suggest a comfortable lifestyle but are "utilised and renegotiated to emphasise differences in lifestyle which demarcate social relationships" (1990, 8). Goods such as cars and homes can be used to publicly proclaim status differences and contour social identities similar to how occupations can be used to demarcate class position.

In his essay on globalization and identity, Manuel Castells defines identity as the "process whereby people draw on a cultural attribute to build meaning in their lives. People create a cultural construct in referring to something that lies beyond them as individuals, but which also defines them as such" (2006, 62–63). He sees identity built upon personal experience but an experience that is located in a cultural worldview that recognizes history as located in the person. Herein lies the problem: as the elements of history and memory attenuate (or become commercialized) due to rapid sociocultural change, loss of meaningful landscape and experience, an increasingly transient society, and globalization, identity loses the collective and inclusive basis of definition. However, Castells is correct that there is a growing resistance-based self-proclaimed identity found in ethnic communities opposing assimilation, religious fundamental communities, and political action groups. But there are "powerful forces [are] at work," he adds, that are struggling to "impose their will on the planet and wreak profound changes" (ibid, 64–65). We now have, for example, identity-based advertising that uses cultural or ethnic sensitivity to induce consumption among various groups (see, for example, Arlene Dávlia's *Latinos, Inc: The Marketing and Making of a People*, 2001).

Beneath the surface of things, capitalism has been constructing a narrative that the world is indeed a micro-reality of personal responsibility rather than structured by obvious social forces. The focus of social life, in this regard, is not on the structures and processes of corporate institutions that determine levels of poverty or unemployment but on personal volition. In this "deworlding," as Stacy Thompson calls it, we dwell on the micro-ethics of personal responsibility, blame, and solutions to be good consumers and corporate citizens. A recent headline in the *New York Times*, for instance, reads "How What You Eat Affects Climate Change," suggesting that consumers have a great responsibility to watch what they eat and how it affects the environment. From Thompson's perspective, this allows global capitalism to operate "smoothly and efficiently than it could otherwise" by redirecting responsibility toward consumers (2012, 902).

The capitalist story of society is one in which people have desires, the desire to accumulate things at the heart of our alleged nature, one that capitalism fills. In an Antonio Gramscian sense of invisible power, capitalism now occupies our minds and influences our understanding of the world, reality, and our part in it. Unlike most of society's participants, however, some such as Thompson see capitalism for what it is:

> in the face of forces organized globally against us and structuring the shape and texture of the social fabric, we pragmatically and desperately retreat to what, within the social imaginary that capitalism erects, still seems to be within our control: our consumption habits, how we spend our incomes, our carbon footprints. (2012, 915)

The cultural hegemony that Gramsci wrote about is now, for many people, a common sense, where in our daily activities we essentially do the bidding of the existing order established by capitalism—work, spend, and buy. It just seems so natural to work, spend, and buy as if on a treadmill.

In the era of twenty-first-century capitalism, exchange value and the accumulation of wealth are at the center of the world. Even catastrophes brought on by a warming planet, such as the melting of Arctic ice in winter, is seen as an opportunity to explore for oil production. The melting of Greenland's glaciers offers access to billions of dollars' worth of minerals. Global warming not only is a warning about climate change but also provides opportunities for new production and marketing. Capitalism has created an imaginary world to explain itself, one incapable of recognizing its true nature or its broad negative effect upon the planet's environmental health or upon the nature of humanity and society. It is interesting that so many individuals are either indifferent or lack an understanding of capitalism's general contradiction: to create, it simultaneously must also destroy, socially and environmentally. It has so occupied our minds that it is hard to conceive of any other way of organizing ourselves.

THE RISE OF CONSUMER SOCIETY AT THE ALTAR OF CAPITALISM

As much as the ethos of consumerism and material possession seems to consume contemporary society, we of course were not born to consume. It is not human nature to want more than the basic necessities of life. We are born into a conceptual field of norms, values, and wants underpinned by the dynamics of the economics of capitalism. Beyond the subjectiveness of religion or the drive simply for a comfortable life, the contours of our social being is influenced by the hegemony of needs of the economy and the politics that buttress it.

The Premodern World of Social Connection

The cultural history of much of the premodern world centered on community and kinship, between both human and nonhuman. Even within the great premodern empires, community and kinship were significant structural features of their society. To understand contemporary consumer society, it is instructive to contrast it with community-centered indigenous societies.

Every culture has an ethos and worldview that define who they are as a people and from which they derive an identity and find meaning in life. For the indigenous inhabitants of the Trobriand Islands of the Solomon Sea, for example, it was participation in a Kula trading network of prestige items. They could be shrewd traders of practical items, but this was overlaid by a system of reciprocal trade in prestige items that only enhanced the social status of the trader (see Malinowski 1961, org. 1922). It was not the object, which could be held only temporarily, so much as the meaning of the object that was most significant. For the Maori of Zealand (i.e., New Zealand) it was well-organized intertribal warfare and status, for many North American Plains Indians it was the buffalo and spirit quest, and the Mubuti Pygmies of the Congo's Ituri Forest found meaning through kinship, sharing, and the *molimo* (a trumpet-like instrument). Both the Diné (Navajo) and Mexican campesino's world revolved around the symbolic meaning of corn, and among the Quiché Maya it was the *cofradia,* a fraternity of religious leaders, that placed them at the center of their world. Among the Navajo, sand paintings remain an integral curative aspect that expresses the general conditions of existence: the paintings contain "key elements and symbols that people use to locate themselves in physical and social space" and linking an ailing person to the realm of the cosmos (Robbins 2005, 14).

A theme that links most of these precapitalist societies is the nexus of kinship, social obligation and standing, and communally oriented cultural memory. Andrew Oldenquist notes that "community" and "autonomy" (i.e., individualism) are seen as possible values yet they generally conflict in outcome since they contradict each other. He writes that communitarians argue that "humans are complete only when they are socialized into a group with common values and social identities." Otherwise, he continues, social lives are incomplete and experience normlessness and thus generally meaningless lives (1991, 54). In the premodern world the meaning of life, as with one's social identity, was immersed within a web of social relationships and routine in which it was people rather than things that governed society's operation. As Oldenquist continued,

> The world view and conception of the self integral to a culture is, in turn, determined by its traditions, physical environment, religion, and, perhaps, a dominant ideology. A culture is literally an external cause of a person's basic values and social identities. (55)

But he also adds that some individuals might reject their culture's prescriptions, such as "hippies" of the 1960s.[6]

Precontact groups such as Tallness of Ghana, Gabra of Kenya and Ethiopia, Hmong of Vietnam, Lakota Sioux of Dakota, and Panama's Chibchan-speaking Kuna all exhibit a close set of intimate relationships based on community and kinship expressed in various socioreligious rituals. Raymond Firth focused on a small island horticultural society in the Solomon Islands of Melanesia called the Tikopia. As found in most horticultural societies, at the heart of the Tikopian culture was the intimate connection of kinship descent (1936). Such connections and responsibilities were not mutable but an essential foundation of connections between individuals and generations. From a different perspective, Lyle Steadman and colleagues argue for the universality of ancestor worship, that is, ritual communication between the dead ancestors and the living. They add that ancestors are "particularly important to indigenous societies because they are the sources a society's traditions . . . and how to relate to one's physical and social environment" (1996, 73). In this regard, one's identity is a direct expression of one's ancestors. In their review of African family structures, Paul Bohannan and Philip Curtin discuss the importance of the kinship connection. Kinship, they write, provides an enduring web of relationships centering the individual within a context of intimacy and obligation. "African children," Bohannan and Curtin summarize, "grow up in an intense situation of kinship, family, and lineage. They continue throughout their lives to learn and to be bound by their family obligations and family histories" (1971, 115). Marcel Mauss pointed out in *The Gift* that there existed in indigenous communities a moral obligation to exchange goods and services. "[T]here is a series of rights and duties about consuming and repaying," he found among many societies, "side by side with rights and duties about giving and receiving." Such gift giving is institutionalized such that, "In perpetual interchange of what we may call spiritual matter, comprising men and things, these elements pass and repass between clans and individuals, ranks, sexes and generations" (1954, 11,12). The reciprocal gift is a social glue binding social relationships bringing order and structure in a community.

In the 1940s and 1950s, the anthropologist Robert Redfield's research drew upon the ideas of Tönnies, Durkheim, and the Chicago school of sociologists in developing the "folk-urban" continuum. In *The Folk Culture of Yucatan*, Redfield constructed the ideal model of folk culture to one end of a continuum of social organization and cultural change, whereas communities grow disorganization and individualization ensued at the other end (1941). Writing later in *The Folk Society*, he characterized folk society as uncritical and governed by tradition, or *gemeinschaft*: "The members of a folk society have a strong sense of belonging together. Folk sense their own resemblances and feel correspondingly united. Communication intimately with each other, each has a strong claim on the sympathies of others. Moreover, when aware of societies other than their own, they emphasize their own mutual likeness and value themselves higher than others. They say of themselves 'we' as against all others, who are 'they'" (1947).

As time went on, outside the indigenous and peasant community, individuals had to be created anew. The new economy required individuals divorced from supportive communal relationships and alone in approaching the labor market. Peasant farmers and manorial serfs were in the slow process of transforming into workers toiling for a daily wage and more and more alienated from those that traditionally they owed allegiance. The "putting out" system of cottage production transformed over time into factories and independent craftsmen into guilds and eventually quasi employees for long-distance merchants or manufacturers. Time saw the growth of a new social class much more conscious about money, opportunity, and progress. The seat of this evolving and dynamic economy that became the backdrop for much of Europe were the rich burgers of Amsterdam. This rich bourgeoisie

> carried out trade, developed industry, organized Chambers of Commerce, controlled colonial companies, watched over the University of Leyden, endowed the Bank of Amsterdam, and made Amsterdam the financial center of the time . . . for dominating capitalism, for the triumphant bourgeoisie, the geographical horizon of activity is the entire world. (Beaud 1983, 27, 42)

As this process continued, new things or new meaning began to replace older things representing slowly fading symbols epitomizing a continuity of historical and cultural knowledge. In this milieux, the modern individual divorced from intimate social connection began to take shape.

In the sixteenth and seventeenth centuries, the income of landlords, lawyers, officials, urban merchants, and trade financiers rose and with it a demand for more and better quality goods. The twin outcomes of market saturation in Europe on the one hand and elite demand on the other promoted industrial development, international trade, and new investment opportunities especially for Calvin-oriented Protestant merchants. The newcomers to the Atlantic or African shores did not see such cultural understandings but focused on resources that represented opportunity and wealth. The evolving upper class of trader and patrician, freed from the weakening strictures of the moral obligations of feudal Europe, demonstrated their status and superiority through conspicuous consumption and economic investments wherever found such as in the Asian spice trade and the African slave trade to the New World. The trading empire of the Dutch of Amsterdam in the sixteenth century and the English Industrial Revolution beginning in the eighteenth century made available vast quantities of goods to more and more European citizens. The introduction of New World crops, cheaper sugar and molasses from the Caribbean, Asian spices, and cotton make life more comfortable for many people and contributed, in the midst of working-class misery, to the political legitimacy and stability of evolving industrial society.

The Reorientation of the Individual

In his book *The Affluent Society*, Galbraith makes the point that consumer demand is artificial, writing that

> If production creates the wants it seeks to satisfy, or if the wants emerge *pari passu* [at an equal pace or rate] with the production, then the urgency of the wants can no longer be used to defend the urgency of the production. Production only fills a void that it has itself created. (1952, 135)

The individual as consumer is not only necessary for the functioning of capitalist accumulation or political legitimization but an irreplaceable component of capitalism itself. This meant, "We must shift America from a needs to a desires culture," wrote Paul Mazur of Lehman Brothers in 1928, "People must be trained to desire, to want new things even before the old had been entirely consumed. We must shape a new mentality in America. Man's desires must overshadow his needs" (quoted in Lubin 2013).

Urbanization brought forth new institutions, forms of thinking, and behavior. Now largely divorced from private production of food, utensils, and household goods, large department stores such as Gimbel's and Macy's evolved in the late nineteenth century to provide needed merchandise. By 1894, Sears and Roebuck published a mail-order catalog offering hundreds of items shipped to consumers by mail. New lifestyles appeared to differentiate and express different class positions. Veblen argued in *The Theory of the Leisure Class* that in ancient society, as in feudal Europe, there was a bifurcation between the aristocracy and landed gentry who exploited the servant and peasants who produced the goods and services. This, Veblen saw, as a split between the idleness of a leisure class and the exploited activity of the lower classes, underpinned by possession of luxury goods by the former. He coined the term "conspicuous consumption" to refer to the upper classes who used spending wealth on expensive items far beyond basic needs as the basis for social status in society (1994, org. 1899). Victor Lebow wrote in the *Journal of Retailing*, adding to Veblen's insight,

> Our enormously productive economy demands that we make consumption our way of life, that we convert the buying and use of goods into rituals, that we seek our spiritual satisfaction and our ego satisfaction in consumption. We need things consumed, burned up, worn out, replaced and discarded at an ever-increasing rate. (1955)

Henry Ford's assembly line moved from the production of automobiles to the manufacture of a variety of household appliances such as stoves and refrigerators. As the costs came down, the demand for such goods increased. The pent-up demand for consumer goods after the forced savings of World War II brought a new wave of consumption, one encouraged by the development of a series of suburban Levittown housing developments and the need to fill those homes with various goods. In the 1950s and 1960s, labor came to an historic agreement with many industries, trading shop-floor control for greater wages to improve the standard of living of union workers.

Robbins makes the interesting point that contemporary Americans, like the Navajo, also have sand painters who likewise operate to define those elements essential to social meaning and cultural identity in (post) modern life. Navajo sand paintings are symbolic representations of the forces of life. Capitalist sand painters include marketing specialists, advertisers, and public relations specialists create the siren call of desire for material things. They call to the individual to possess material goods as a fetish denoting the standard and meaning of life. They help to develop the contours of culture, according to Robbins, "In which virtually all our everyday activities—work, leisure, the fulfillment of social responsibilities . . . serve(s) as a therapeutic activity," in other words, "the identity of consumer" (2005, 14–15). As a Navajo shaman called upon the deities to heal, center, and reintegrate an individual into the community, advertisers use the allure of consumer goods to bring health ("things go better with Coke"), happiness, and well-being to those looking to fill a social void. Consumption, then, is fundamental to the operation of the cultural and economic system. In affluent society, it occupies a huge portion of our lives—we are born into a world of consuming goods as a fish is born into water.

SYMBOLS, MEANING, AND IDENTITY IN THE POSTMODERN WORLD

"The field of material culture has established a detailed understanding of the symbolic properties that adhere to objects of human manufacture," McCracken wrote. He adds that a goal of many in the social sciences has been to "demonstrate how individuals and communities use inanimate objects to lay claim, to legitimate, and to compete for status meaning" (1990, 31). Understanding the meaning or function of an object or its symbolism requires a deep understanding of the historical period within which a culture exists, a perspective first argued by the anthropologist Franz Boas who believed that rather than universal structures of thought, cultures were complex and needed to be understood according to their own history and particularity (2010). This approach requires that we must differentiate radically different cultural circumstances and historical periods, avoiding presentism in our analysis of precapitalist societies. Among the Mexica, for instance, wealth among the *tecuhtli* class was measured in status and prestige. "Wealth was not pursued for itself; it came as a function of increasing power and official expenses. It was an income and not a capital. The only thing that really counted in the *tecuhtli's* eyes was reputation" (Soustelle 1961, 58). The *tecuhtli* wore parrot feathers as public symbols of their sociopolitical status in Mexica society, not as a sign of wealth to be exploited.

For many traditional societies, values are associated with the nature of social relationships expressed through symbols.[7] Victor Turner pointed out for the Ndembu of Zambia in his book *The Forest of Symbols*, "The symbol becomes associated with human interests, purposes, ends, and means" (1967, 20). For the Ndembu, the milk tree refers in symbolic form various social processes such as the values of social organization, unity, and continuity. For Turner, symbols "instigate social action . . . in that they are determinable influences inclining persons and groups to action" (ibid, 36). Here, we approach symbols and objects in the context of cultural identity. Symbols "stand for" and what they stand for are collective memories, experiences, values, and a way to see the world in relation to all social members such as the milk tree for the Ndembu. This shared understanding of the meaning of symbols and ritual occasions reflect a "sturdiness" of reality, allowing culture's members to take the unity of their world for granted.

In *Consumer Culture*, Celia Lury argues that objects take on a social life of meaning for the users under such circumstances of such material objects. Lury highlights the significance of objects by quoting Igor Kopytoff who wrote, "The life history of a particular object, as it moves through different hands, contexts and uses, leading to the identification of a specific 'cultural biography' of the object" (1998, 19). In precapitalist peasant and tribal societies, symbols had an enduring quality and helped confer a sense of continuity and stability to society for what they represented. In the distinction between such premodern communal societies and contemporary society, our interest is in the communal biographies of objects and associated symbolic social meaning, in contrast to the postmodern idiom of things.

It is not clear that most present-day consumer objects have a life history or a meaningful biography except in special personal circumstances, such as a grandmother's quilt or a recipe passed down through the family. This may be valid for some specific objects such as an old Rolex watch handed down as an heirloom from parent to child. But we argue here that most objects are not objects of memory but function as purely utilitarian, commercialized badges for the projection of public identity of status or, more mundanely, as objects befitting a decor signifying a personal statement. However, even the Rolex's function as biography is a personal story rather than a holder of collective (kinship or public) memory and experience.[8] This is quite different from Malinowski's interpretation of the Kula Ring among the Trobriand Islanders of the Solomon Sea (1961). The Trobrianders traditionally exchanged with trade partners armbands (*Mwali*) and necklaces (*Soulava*) collectively called *vaygu'a*. These items carried long histories of their exchanges through generations of trades. Many were very old with deep, complex histories associated with them and therefore symbols of social process in time. The exchanges were accompanied by ritual speeches denoting the significance of the *vaygu'a*. All participants and bystanders understood the meaning behind the objects, their social biographies as it were, and all were aware of the communal memories that resided within each item. This recognition is collective and is an element of the framework of the cultural identity of the Trobrianders and their Dobuan trading partners.

Under such premodern or traditional circumstances, there is a taken-for-granted aspect that everyday symbolic reality is fixed, shared, and stable from generation to generation (the Kula is still practiced today). Although contentious by some, many anthropological studies have illustrated that small-scale communities tend in self-image, motives, and expectation to be psychologically (and culturally) well integrated where stress and anxiety are relatively infrequent (Erchak 1998, 104–105).[9] The individual is culturally constructed as an extension of the community rather than a "self" unique to the world. But the individual could be individually recognized for special talents, as a great potter or storyteller, for instance. In Western society, especially in the United States, the self stands alone as a monument to modern culture. Erchak reminds us of the significance of norms and values stating, "Individuals control and manage their behavior, selectively expressing or suppressing aspects of their selves, to match appropriate norms in the range of social settings" (21). That is, people are socialized into their social environment, contouring their behavior to meet the expectations of society. When the signifiers that make up culture are relative rather than absolute, open to personal interpretation, and fluid or revealed as meaningless, existential questions come into anxious existence. If social environments are relative or subjective in interpretation, the self becomes disembodied or free of strictures. We see today how such a state can lead to acceptance of fake news or outrageous conspiracy theories that defy logic. The outcome is social disorganization, an alternate reality or chaos. In the premodern world, on the other hand, the solidity of shared meaningful objects, enduring messages of history and experience, gave a sense of permanence to reality and "ontological security."

The sense of ontological security can most obviously be seen in the interaction between person and created object, one produced with intentional symbolism for communication and identity among producer and consumer and acknowledged by the community. Whether pottery or landscape, the meaning placed on these objects can over time induce a potent and emotional sense of belonging and connection. Among the Diné (Navajo), Laguna, and Zuni of what is now New Mexico, *Tsoodzil* (Mount Taylor) was and is a sacred mountain related to various supernatural beings (i.e., Turquoise Boy) that relate to the birth of this world. *Tsoodzil* is a bridge of cultural time linking the present-day viewer to the heritage and identity of what it means to be Laguna or Diné, much more so that a Laguna office worker has the office computer and wildlife calendar in front of her.

Embedded in much premodern objects, such as pottery, spiritual and ritual paraphernalia, as well as physical landscape, are life histories of meaning operated on and passed down through the generations. McCracken notes that objects carry the "culturally constituted world." They are recognized and shared through their public performance in ritual or exchange, which themselves are located within intimate social relations. In all instances, these objects and performances are cultural productions or texts that communicate a shared cultural understanding and worldview. For instance, J. Walter Fewkes wrote in an 1898 edition of *The American Anthropologist* concerning the prevalence of bird feathers in ceremonial and common pottery among the Hopi Indians of the American Southwest from pre-Columbian times to the present (1898). He wrote that bird feathers were (and still are) symbolic elements of power such as a turkey feather to induce rain. Marianne Stoller of the University of Pennsylvania Museum of Archaeology and Anthropology discusses bird feathers in ceremonies as representing clouds and thus rain (associating birds and sky), an important theme in the arid dry-land agriculture of the Hopi (1991, 44). The feathers create a clear symbolic message and memory understood by all tribal members to this day.

Both Fewkes and Stoller see the symbolism of feathers in most aspects of Hopi public and ceremonial life and convey a relationship among humans, animals, and physical elements. Evidence from Sulawesi, Indonesia's Pleistocene past suggest that early humans used animal bones as ornaments of symbolic importance. Brumm and colleagues believe, "inhabitants of LBB (a prehistoric site) used ornaments fashioned from *A. ursinus* bones implies these economically important marsupials may also have acquired symbolic meaning for early human communities on Sulawesi" such as kangaroo fibula used as a "nose-bone" suggesting the "symbolic values to macropods" of the island (2017). In all cases, the symbolism embedded in the objects are "good to think" with, to give fulfillment to the meaning of human relationship to each other and the occupied world of sentient and non-sentient others.

It is in this sense, as Victor Turner pointed out, that humans live in a world of constructed symbols that orient us to the physical features, social relationships, and history of our thoughts and actions. Turner considered symbols in ritualized contexts expressing social order. Participants encountered symbols as elements of public significance that stood beyond the immediate. Thus, all we see and touch are sets of meaning, real or mythic, that in their totality help us give shape to the world we live in. Objects such as pitchers, emblems etched on rock (pictographs), or body art contain symbols that are objectifications of ideas, experiences, and meanings, as forms of communication that have an associative impact on the viewer by the creator of the symbol. Such understandings by the individual, such as totems for example among Australian Aborigines, express a common identity of collective unity and perception. Clifford Geertz once exclaimed that culture is found in public symbols and actions that express a particular worldview. Such symbolic items, such as the landscapes of the Western Apache or the milk tree among the Ndembu discussed by Turner, are living symbols in that they contain deep meaning locating generations of participants in time, place, and event. This dynamic, it is suggested here, differs from the Western Enlightenment narrative that only humans have agency and all else, animals, rocks, and objects, are things "dead" or lacking an ability to communicate except in the most practical or relative of ways.[10] Moreover, in postmodern society, symbolism in objects or physical features take on more personal, ahistorical, or circumscribed meanings that do not travel much beyond the orbit of the individual or his/her social network.

Discussing Jean Baudrillard's ideas on Marx's use of use-value, Lury relates Baudrillard's concerns regarding signs. In contemporary society, Baudrillard argues, objects have lost their symbolic power, seeing them as empty vessels with constantly changing meanings. Lury quotes him stating,

> In terms of signs . . . objects are no longer tied. . . . This is precisely because objects respond to something different, either to a social logic, or to a logic of desire, where they serve as a fluid and unconscious field of significance. (1996, 71)

In a commodified world of individualism and weak social *communitas*, symbols in general are viewed as bankrupt containing only personal depthless meaning, if that.

Following on the ideas of Ferdinand Tönnies's use of *gemeinschaft*, Emile Durkheim labeled traditional, premodern societies as "mechanical" or organized around solidarity of common values and beliefs with generally undifferentiated but routinized deep social relationships. Here, the symbols created were easily understood as visual representations to stand for the social group in time and space, expressed in ritual and ceremony making concrete the element of *communitas* or the sense of community spirit. Created objects functioned as learning tools, as labels, often expressed such solidarity through symbolic design.

For example, the photo of the pitcher with the green iguana and the designs around the pitcher are encoded with symbolism and layers of meaning. Meaning expressed by the maker and understood by the receiver in a reciprocal fashion—who probably engaged in a transaction for the pitcher—was clear since it spoke to their common attachment to a legacy of a bounded cultural and physical world. The pitcher held water and, importantly, ideas about belonging.

Figure 6.1 Old Mexican Water Pitcher with Iguana. *Source*: Author's personal photograph.

In this sense, the pitcher is a living non-commodified object, that is, the embodiment of some significant element of that culture. In other words, in the pitcher is something of the maker as a representative of his/her cultural heritage of meaning. Embedded in both the maker's labor and object are the essence of the creative will of humanity. This is what Marx meant by "species being." While I do not recognize nor understand the narrative expressed by the symbols on this object since I do not know the culture or symbolic "language" used, any member of the culture that produced this item would understand the message or ideas being conveyed. These symbols are a signifier of one's membership in a unified cultural reality of history, kinship, and representations. The symbols on the pitcher, their social meaning, cannot be divorced from the identity of maker, recipient, and others in both time and space.

The pitcher of course offers clues to the meaning and culture of the maker. But there must be a priori understood biography for content to convey meaning. What about the history or relationship of the iguana and the intricate pattern of dots and triangles among the culture that produced the object? What are the symbols trying to express? Do they convey something of the social life of the community in terms of gender or production? In the mystery of the symbols reside clues to the cultural history of which the maker was a member and participant. What is significant here is that the symbols represent an a priori history of remembering. The maker uses memory, linking him or her to a past, when thinking about the representations of the symbols. This very premodern means of communicating a lineage of thought yields a harvest of metaphors writes Paul Connerton in *How Modernity Forgets*. He refers to writing but his comment is applicable to our craftsperson as well:

> the metaphors of writing as "trace," as a "sign" of a lost presence, which nonetheless remains present before the eyes, available, for reflective scrutiny; together with the idea of at the "engraving" upon our minds of lasting "impressions," of "background," of "depth," and of a "layering of meanings." (2009, 145)

Thus, what is made and what is perceived occupy a place in the stream of cultural history and, through the generations, a stream of consciousness and remembering.

David Graeber discusses the idea of the social content of objects in his book *Toward an Anthropological Theory of Value* (2001). Graeber outlines Marilyn Strathern's argument that Western ideology does not recognize the collective in objects but sees only through the lenses of individualism (except the great art masters such as Rembrandt). What the Westerner does, he writes, is to take those objects (that exist apart from the individual) and "appropriate" them socially—"ascribing meaning to them by placing them within some larger system of categories" such as the mind of the idiosyncratic individual, for example abstract art (2001, 39). Are the objects authentic to the individual or are they assigned categories by commercialized interests? The non-modern, non-Western world, on the other hand, sees things differently, less in isolation and more collectively in terms of community and relationship. Strathern sees an object's value in terms of the meaning or importance collective society places on that object. Graeber writes, in contrast "Marxists imply that individuals who produce objects should have the right to determine their meaning." In Mount Hagen, she considers, people do not see things in this way, since they do not see objects as having been produced by individuals. "They see them as the outcome of relationships" in community. In Mount Hagen, among the Tsembaga of Papua New Guinea, metaphorically speaking, a pig is not just a pig, or even a pig, but a meaningful object that in exchange denotes collective identity.

The objects of exchange and the meanings inherent are reproduced and shared by most if not all members of premodern cultures. In this case, as in the Mexican pitcher in figure 1, these objects take on meaning by being assigned in a larger system of social categories. The symbolic nature of the pitcher is to "make visible," as Strathern phrases it, the social relations of identity in the production and exchange that take place and are recognized by a culture's members. The pitcher, in this case, takes on a quality that personifies the web of relationships and cognitive mapping between the maker, the recipient of the object, the broader collectivity, and the sociophysical experiences of the people.

With the development of capitalism, the producer became alienated from his labor since labor became abstract, producing things of practical and exchange value but with limited substantive symbolic cultural meaning.[11] In this process, the laborer becomes an aspect of production, creating "dead" objects without symbolic meaning of kinship, history, experience, and social connection. Marx understood this writing,

> All these consequences are implied in the statement that the worker is related to the product of labor as to an alien object. For on this premise, the more the worker spends himself, the more powerful becomes the alien world of objects which he creates over and against himself.

Furthermore, Marx wrote that the alienation of labor "means that the life which he has conferred on the object confronts him as something hostile and alien" (1932, org. 1844). Over time, the producer becomes the industrial laborer, him/her nothing more than an object, a "disembodied commodity" that can be bought or sold on a market. As capitalism matured, the laborer transforms into a consumer of objects, an object that, so to speak, owns objects. This transformation was at the heart of Marx's ideas concerning commodified labor, "The worker puts his life into the object; but now his life no longer belongs to him but to the object."

Any functional object by the traditional non-object maker expressed the ideas and experiences of group membership representing identity. These objects, such as the Mexican pitcher above, were not "dead" but "alive" in that they expressed a narrative, and by their meaningfulness created a dialogue between maker and recipient in reference to their mutual cultural existence. The Western Apache's place-names to landscape, for example, met this dialogical condition of linking community members in recognition of placed meaning. Such objects operate to provide continuity to culture, but I believe only if the object, such as the pitcher or landscape features, expresses shared meaning felt and accepted by most if not all cultural members. In capitalist society, Marx noted, the product of the laborer is alien to him/herself as he/she becomes alienated to themselves. The indigenous world, however, finds the product of the laborer encapsulated in their own being since the product is not a commodity but the personification of the community and thus the reification of the individual.

Cultural symbolism functions to have social members recall meaning, experience, and recognition in agreed upon direction.[12] Objects have the capacity as coded messages to convey representations of meaning that create a relationship for human understanding in the world. In other words, in the world of kinship and lineage in traditional cultures, many objects were infused with an indelible notation of a way of seeing beyond functionality the experience of the world through human eyes and cognition. The laborer was not estranged from the creation of the object but through his/her consciousness and labor the embodiment of their culture's symbols and meaning is given a broader social expression.

A traditional hunter may engage in the same meaningful activity. The hunter who makes a bow and arrow will encode into the item his/her cultural being that is both personal, possibly representing his kin lineage, and publicly the ontological order of the community. Personal, as what Connerton referred to as personal signatures, are affixed to them. But as a participant embedded in a culture some representations, or shared sentiments, of a broader communal nature cannot but be included as well. The duality of personal and public symbolic representations expresses a sense of personal being but also one of group membership and shared worldview. To give the bow to someone else is to give one's material labor, cultural self, and the ethos of community sharing.

TRAVELING CULTURES AND THE MUTABILITY OF MEANING

Our history and heritage as a people and our sense of place and identity as expressed in our values, symbols, and myths are carried forth through the mechanisms of culture. But culture is not a constructed singularity divorced from a broader reality. Cultures are to a lesser or greater extent organic composites of many ideas, both intrinsic and foreign, ever undergoing revision by its members as circumstances change. Given that this is an accepted truth in anthropology, this does not mean that cultures do not have a deep and significant meaning for their members. Our culture milieu of basic and generally historic values, myths, and rituals is fundamental to who "we" are as distinct from who "they" are. It is, also, difficult to step out of one's culture of attitudes, heritage, perceptions, and worldview and into another. In other words, culture is not like a pair of shoes that we can change at whim.

The notion that culture may have a unitary foundation adhered to by all members, however, no longer holds in the postmodern era as cynicism and relativism take hold in mass society. The relativism of values and myth associated with the subjectivity of is what is meant by postmodernism or liquid times. On the other hand, doubt becomes a significant feature in a urbanized society of strangers as Tönnies long ago foresaw and where the personal "subjectivities" of the self reign supreme in that estrangement that leads to a lack of confidence in social institutions and questions of identity.

Although there appear growing cultural-ethnic localizations and tribalizations, the movement of people and ideas lend to what Jan Nederveen Pieterse has phrased a "global mélange," or a cultural hybridization, a cut' n' mix of "fuzziness" of cultural–ethnic boundaries (2009, 78). Here, Pieterse is referring to cultural mixes such as Chinese tacos, Scottish salsa bands, "Mexican schoolgirls dressed in Greek togas dancing in the style of Isadora Duncan," and so forth, all blending in syncretic ways. He sees a translocal culture that is based on an outward orientation looking vainly for a sense of place compared to traditional culture, which employs an interior accustomed sense of place. The point is that such outward-looking new identities lose a sense of history and lineage leading to the question of upon which foundation is identity linked. Yet what does hybridization give in return to those searching for a more concrete or meaningful station of identity maintenance?

In the modern era, the concept of culture was seen as a mechanism of repetitive and coherent ways of thinking, perceiving, and acting that were relatively stable, agreed upon, and permanent. No longer so, as van Meijl argues, "The meaning of the concept of culture has shifted. . . . A 'culture' is no longer considered to speak with one voice, so to speak, but to be multi-vocal and polyphonous" (2008, 172). In a postmodern world that is under considerable global consumer influence—logos, themes, products, advertisement, education, and politics—culture's foundation is less foundational or linked to history and more in play between the corporation domination of society and cultural members who find themselves floundering in a current of globalization combined with skepticism and subjectivism. This is true today as many question the validity of the basic foundations of society and democracy.

Cultures are "traveling" in two senses of the word, physical and representational. More and more people cross national borders, setting up ethnic enclaves or integrating into host communities with new ideas, customs, norms, and values, changing both themselves and the receiving culture. Rather than assimilation into the dominant culture, immigrants now enter a negotiation as to what they save and celebrate and what they adopt leading to hybrid cultures as ethnic and racial boundaries become fuzzy, as Pieterse characterized it. This hybridity itself, however, must confront and contend with the cultural, economic, and psychological framework of consumerism. Secondly, in a world where consumption is a potent framework of meaning and activity, as new material items are marketed, advertised, and bought, new ways of thinking about one's identity or status changes, especially older traditional status markers such as employment no longer apply (think about social media influencers as persuaders of products or themselves). The advancement of postmodern society and the ethnic enclaves' negotiations with it inevitably leads to a weakening of powerful, immediate role models and cultural/ethnic moral or historical certainties. Such negotiations and social change over time opens public and private spaces to occupation by corporate advertising, changing values, and consumer wish-fulfillment fantasies as a means to develop a sense of completeness potentially now lost.

Critical social science recognizes that such a global movement, and the increasingly profound transfiguration of culture by capitalism, has led to notions of the "deterritorialization" of culture(s).[13] Cultures have lost whatever boundaries once existed between "us" and "them," leading to the flow of cultures—cultures as traveling elements of contemporary human consciousness. Walter Anderson noted, "Symbols of all kinds have detached themselves from their original roots and float freely, like dandelion seeds, around the world" (quoted in Pieterse 2009). This flow is both postmodern and international. The translocalization of liquid culture is expressed in everyday experience in ethnicity, food, entertainment, and social media. Furthermore, the idea of national identity is increasingly informed by global influences and experiences.

Our interest here is what is happening *within* such social arrangements that concerned Pieterse. Ankie Hoogvelt suggests that while no longer expanding, capitalism is deepening itself as a global culture with new communication technologies developing "imagined communities," where "we still have local lives as physical persons, we also now experience phenomenal worlds that are truly global" (1997, 121). It is through time/space compression (a shrinking world), Hoogvelt believes, that a shared phenomenal world of market discipline has taken hold alongside commercialization of social life. This same process that informs global economics also influences the ideas and cognitive mapping of a society's cultural members. In essence, capitalism as transformation "kills all the old gods." If all is fluid, mixing and matching under the influence of capitalism and the power of its narratives, then identity is likewise fluid but now expressed and linked to the transitory and hodgepodge of the commercial postmodern. The ethos of capitalist values and narrative is that consumerism helps to fill in the void, allowing us to express our identity in terms of material possessions.

Argued here, this transfiguration is measured not only by physical distance but also, and in this case more importantly, distance from "things" that convey a sense of heritage, history, and a moral–communal boundary linking past and present, one that act as guideposts for thinking about the future. Distance is also measured by time, that is, the degree of residency that ideas and experiences have in our lifeworld. Connerton considers a hallmark of modernity's effect upon our intimacy with contemporary culture—the condition of time. As he puts it,

> By accelerating time, computer usage immerses individuals in a hyper-present, an intensified immediacy which, by training the viewer's attention on a rapid succession of micro-events, makes it ever more difficult to envisage even the short-term past as "real," since the present comes to be experienced as a narrowly defined time period unlinked from last causes. (2009, 87)

In other words, technology has created the conditions where there is no time to think as we accelerate ever faster into the future. The contemporary condition suffers from information overload and with little time for processing we experience increasing amounts of mind clutter. David Levy remarks on this condition,"This is mind chatter, the incessant and obsessive internal monologue that fills the head with snatches of memories, plans, and stories, very often centered around the self" (2007, 246). In a series of laboratory studies, Timothy Wilson and colleagues at the University of Virginia found that a significant proportion of subjects reported that they did not enjoy just sitting alone and thinking (2014). Their study concludes that "Most people do not enjoy 'just thinking' and clearly prefer having something else to do" including, when isolated, self-administering mild electric shocks, as implausible as that seems (76). People are not used to the uncluttered mind after a lifetime of socialization into the acceleration of life. Life has accelerated faster than most people can absorb it. Many succumb to the tyranny of the inbox, the twitter, and message notifications while at the same time trying to figure out which one of the hundreds of television/radio stations to pause at for a moment. In this sense, objects become dead and are but transitory practical items.

Under the technological, information, social media, and entertainment onslaught, cultures are increasingly "deterritorialized" not only in terms of space but also from time, landscape, memory, and the repositories of history. Jameson made the same point in a lecture at the University of California at Los Angeles) on the disappearance of history in contemporary (American) society. "the way in which our entire contemporary social system has little by little begun to lose its capacity to retain its own past," he remarked, "has begun to live in a perpetual present and in a perpetual change that obliterates traditions of the kind which all earlier social formations have had in one way or another to preserve" (1992).

Figure 6.2 Modern Commercial Vase with Stones. *Source*: Author's personal photograph.

The artistic store-bought object in figure 6.2 has no meaning nor location in history or experience compared to the Mexican pitcher discussed earlier. If one characteristic of the postmodern condition is a defused and undefined anxiety, it is to be found, in part, in the artificiality of images and objects surrounding ahistorical traveling cultures. What does figure 6.2 represent but only an individual's idea of culture. What does figure 6.2 represent but only an individual's desire to fill a space or to match a decor. Unlike the pitcher in figure 6.1 that is expressing something significant publicly, but we do not understand culturally, figure 6.2 is as mute, as Baudrillard's empty vessels, with little of history or heritage.

Modern production and technology have given us a world of objects that are ahistorical, which in their neutrality has robbed us of any narrative of meaning beyond the distraction of superficial connectivity and the immediacy of now. Connerton outlines the slow draining of memory in social life through various institutional and cultural changes. The changes are technological, physical place, and change in the relationship between labor and objects. This results, he writes, "What is being forgotten in modernity is profound, the human-scale-ness of life, the experience of living and working in a world of social relationships that are known" (5). These are the "dead" objects around which we revolve, and in the course of our lives, the intimacy of social relationships weakens and, ultimately, our human connection to each other.

There appear shifts in thinking, worldview, and values without a directional trajectory Cultural erosion and global remixing under the influence of corporate operations and social-psychological relativism is decontextualizing history and meaning, leaving people adrift in a sea of uncertainty. Representation of history and identity at one point was found, as discussed at the beginning of this chapter, in the objects produced in the premodern, traditional work of the laborer in the intimacy of his/her community. With the commercialization of cultural products, the experience of history is lost along with social identity, or as Jameson has phrased it, "The transformation of reality into images, the fragmentation 'me' into a series of perpetual presents are both extraordinarily consonant with this process" (1992, 125). Bauman refers to such shallowness as the "collateral casualty" of consumerism. He quotes J. Livingstone, "The commodity form penetrates and reshapes dimensions of social life hitherto exempt from its logic to the point where subjectivity itself becomes a commodity to be bought and sold in the market as beauty, cleanliness, sincerity and autonomy" (2007, 120).

If figure 2 has a message, it is the lack of history and the lack of any meaningful social relationships between object and viewer. It may have a personal aesthetic value, but it is essentially a "dead" object—it has no social life but is only a playful thing for the individual imagination. It is something to be seen for its own quality or for its harmony to other things. It is what you make of it. Whereas figure 6.1 offers a representation of depth of recognizable meanings, figure 6.2 reflects the apparent emptiness of consumer culture. The world of objects we encounter, Connerton believes, are objects that have no individuality, nuance, or personal meaning, "As we move each day through the sphere of manufactured objects—dishes, cars . . . we do not at each moment consciously perceive that these objects are humanly made" (42). In other words, a postmodernist would argue that the meaning of the figure is not based on social interaction but is nothing more than a meager artificial commodity having merely an objective existence.

Modern people today increasingly are chronically mobile, physically and mentally, experiencing various sorts of displacement, and presumably in search of something to anchor themselves in places such as Facebook and TikTok. Society's members, especially in affluent countries but growing among all global social classes, are now like magnets attracting myriad pieces of flotsam revolving around a consumer-influenced ever-moving macrocosm of advertised commodities. Under the circumstances of a traveling culture of the temporary, the fluidity of the individual within a changing and often confusing social structure, fear, and uncertainty of certitude is ever a concern. Bauman believes that this leads to inadequacy, declaring, "Consumer markets are eager to capitalize on that fear, and companies turning out consumer goods vie for the status of the most reliable guide and helper in their clients' unending effort to rise to the challenge" of overcoming inadequacy (60). People go to the shops and malls to be part of an amorphous group that Bauman refers to as a "swarm." The swarm are those individuals and groups employing similar social patterns of interaction and thinking. Individuals are not only promoters of commodities—tools and guidelines to fit in—but themselves become the commodities they promote. We, in essence, become the walking embodiment of the corporate advertiser's dream.

The penultimate meaning of consumer is the sovereign individual alone in their individuality. It is instructive to quote Bauman at length here on the shift from intimate member of a group, in this case the family as a durable, bonded entity, to the sovereign individual:

> What bonded the diners into a group was the cooperation . . . in the preceding process of productive labour and sharing consumption of what was produced was derived from that. We may suppose that the "unintended consequence" of "fast food," "take-aways" or "TV dinners" . . . to make the gathering around the family table redundant, so putting an end to the shared consumption, or to symbolically endorse the loss . . . which have become irrelevant or even undesirable in the liquid modern society of consumers. "Fast food" is there to protect the solitude of lone consumers. (78)

A testimony to Bauman's "swarm" of consumer aloneness in their conventionality is the exponential increase in ready-made dinners and individualized servings for individuals and families on the go. According to Brittain Ladd writing in Forbes, meal kits are meals already assembled as takeout or delivery to be mixed and cooked by the consumer. The industry's sales are over $3.1 billion in 2018 and estimated to grow by double digits in the next few years. Yet Ladd believes that this industry will be eclipsed by already made complete meals needing no preparation, only to be reheated (e.g., Home Chef Meal Kit Delivery). As an executive of Icon Meals commented, "The mission of Icon Meals is to make food that customers want, when they want it, delivered where customers demand so that customers have one less interruption in their lives" (Ladd 2018). Of course, this trend reflects a class bias favoring the affluent but is nevertheless suggestive: at one time, DVDs were beyond the working class. Nevertheless, the kitchen as hearth now competes with DoorDash ringing the front door with a packaged dinner.

One might ask if preparing a meal or ordering a ready-made one makes any difference. There are two ways to consider this. One is in relation to production in the kitchen, a place not just for production but also a locus for gathering and sustenance. Many onlookers gravitate to the kitchen to help, critique, or share company in the making of the meal. A meal is an outcome of the ideas of the cook, an activity leading to the physical and social nourishment of those partaking of the meal. There are not too many areas in life where individuals engage in the production of anything. The planning and preparation of meals could be considered an expression of *homo farber*, humans as makers. The homemade meal generally, but not always, involves a sense of community in the "breaking of bread" together, the ritual of serving and passing of food in the spirit of *bonhomie*. The meal and the kitchen/dining room table is the modern equivalent of the campfire or hearth of our ancestors. As then, we too surround ourselves in the rituals of eating together. The ready-made meal kit suggests a different dynamic and mindset—one of expediency, satisfying a hunger, a way station on the path to the distraction of other things. One activity means we sit with others and, if necessary, forced, into conversation with table mates. The other allows for eating at the computer or in another room with the television entertaining our mealtime (see, for example, Fresco 2015).

THE VITALITY OF LANDSCAPE AND THE ARBITRARINESS OF CULTURESCAPE

Messages or images of symbolic representation of community commonality are not found only in artifacts such as figure 6.1 but in the physical world as well. In his essay on archaeology and meaning in landscapes, Tim Ingold makes the interesting point that physical features are clues used to discover deeper meaning of human involvement. "Meaning is there to be discovered in the landscape, if only we know how to attend to it. Every feature, then, is a potential clue, a key to meaning" (1993, 172). In his understanding of the significance of the place-names of landscape features, Basso found that place-names represent narratives of distant events made current. He writes,

> when Apache people see fit to speak with place-names, that a vital part of their tribal heritage seems to speak to them as well. For on such occasions . . . participants may be moved and instructed by voices other than their own . . . [and] affected by the voices of their ancestors . . . found in landscape (1996, 101).

"Voices other than their own" also applies to the symbolic message of the water pitcher in figure 6.1.

The postmodern landscape is not the landscape of deep meaning our early ancestors constructed but the fluid and fast-paced "culturescape" of our urban, technological way of life. One could argue that contemporary life, as opposed for instance the Western Apache, is governed by a lack of memory of place as building, houses, employment, and occupants come and go at an increasing pace. Technology has allowed for greater freedom and mobility to substitute for the settled place of our ancestors. "The conquest over the tyranny of distance has helped to free people from the accident of location," Connerton remarks adding, "Place is no longer felt as the force of destiny. It is likely to signify rootlessness: a rootlessness, or loss of place, built into the suburban landscape with its jumble of supermarkets, hamburger joints and criss-crossing highways" (89).

In this case, I use the term "culturescape" to denote its artificiality from the physical world around us as we live in private "bubbles." Today our sense of place is filtered through experiences often indirect or of passing consequence. The architectural boat tour along the Chicago River, for example, is very popular but can be interpreted, as Daniel Boorstin put it, a "pseudo-event," as a performance for the consumer's gaze. The event becomes a commodity of transitory meaning, a temporality of consumption, and a filler of limited significance beyond the experience with little or no direct relationship to the consumer and usually not located in a substantive history.

Culturescape reflect a creative, almost linear purpose, but clearly a delineation separate from the physicality of the natural world. For our purposes, here the creative purpose of contemporary times (via the evolution of capitalism) has been to separate society from nature (and history) thus rendering the landscape, in the sense used by Basso, Ingold, and Connerton, devoid of existential meaning. For example, urban complexes today represent an imaginary of what is technologically or commercially possible and give our imprint on what the world should look like.[14] In place of the symbolism and representation of landscape, we have created a culturescape built of mobile artifacts, techno-excitements, and entertainment possibilities. Megacities under constant architectural rearrangement, advertising and social media moving at superhuman speed, and the complex changing sociopolitical issues have led to an overheated world. Accordingly, we have moved into a world of cultural forgetting of heritage and the natural world.

There is a lack of permanency, at least in the United States, in which buildings and neighborhoods are in a constant state of flux, leading to a diminution of meaning inherent in the newness of things. In the Brooklyn area of South Park Slope, for example, a Polish and Italian neighborhood existed for generations with streets of cafes and shops exuding an ethnicity linking the newness of the immigrants and their children to the heritage of their native culture. Now under (ethnic) gentrification, new condos and apartment buildings are replacing old row houses and stores. The corner bodega selling sausages and old-world cheeses is replaced with a full service pilates gym or Starbucks. These old buildings and stores were repositories of ethnic memories that spoke to identity. Not only buildings change but social change brings in new classes and ethnicities, new ways of life that ultimately erase the past. Such erasure is complete as older community members are dispersed to the suburbs and lose or experience a weakening of ethnic social networks. As Jeremiah Moss cataloged on his blog, *Jeremiah's Vanishing New York*, older ethnic businesses find themselves at the end of changing neighborhood. "In a Times story yesterday," he wrote recently, "Vivian Yee wrote about Eagle Provisions and other Brooklyn businesses 'calling it quits' in the changing city: After decades of anchoring their neighborhoods, these business owners have found that they no longer quite belong" (2015). This story can be replicated in most urban areas as older established working class and ethnic neighborhoods experience gentrification by young urban professionals.

In Chicago, the Pilsen neighborhood has shifted from Polish to Latino over the past several decades even though the complexion of the neighborhood (the buildings, row houses, parks) have remained the same. Now this Latino working-class community has been earmarked for transition. Evan Hague of DePaul University refers to Pilsen as the "gentrification frontier" where two cultures are colliding. He remarks,

> In Pilsen today, there are two neighborhoods in one. Immigrant families struggle to meet rising rents and Hispanic-owned businesses seek to retain their Spanish-speaking clientele, while brew pubs and bars selling craft beers and award-winning tater tots cater to a more footloose, younger, and wealthier population intrigued by the neighborhood's artistic reputation, its proximity to downtown, and hipster appeal. (2015)

Other cities face the same dynamic of change. San Francisco is confronting the gentrification of several historic neighborhoods such as the Mission District and Chinatown as these areas attract more affluent individuals and the condo developers that cater to them (see Zuk and Chapple 2015).

Marc Agué sees a distinction between place defined as "relational, historical and concerned with identity" and if not "relational, or historical, or concerned with identity will be a non-place . . . a world thus surrendered to solitary individuality, to the fleeting, the temporary and ephemeral" (2008, 63, 76–77). In premodern times, as we have discussed, the totality of landscape expression was slow to change. For example, the Cohonina people lived to the west of the Grand Canyon for 700 years, between 500 and 1200 CE, in a landscape that changed little except for seasonal variations. This is not Agué's non-place since the canyon is filled with 700 years of memory and significance. Today change, often rapid or radical, is commonplace, especially in modern landscapes associated with urban space and changing communities. As neighborhoods such as Pilsen undergo change from a degree of permanency to where change is constant (hipster bars come and go, as do so many new business) or where what has changed now expresses a corporate and commercialized—not just sameness—but a purposefully designed corporate intentionality is a non-place that can look and feel like any other place.

While Williamsburg, Virginia. or Mount Rushmore are significant historic places to visit that attract thousands of visitors, what do most think and perceive from their experience? Most Americans, unlike Europeans, share a truncated relationship to the past generally mediated by the need or desire for a tourist "vacation" or conveyed in movies or the ideology of the moment (MacCannell 2013). It is not that we deny the past or the biography of the painting or building but in the rush to an imagined future we see beyond the past, not recognizing it for what it is trying to tell us about ourselves. In both rural and urban America, social change is pervasive: small towns depopulate and essentially disappear while others transform into retirement communities or tourist sites. Where does memory reside except personally under such conditions of change and flux?

As Keith Basso learned from the Western Apache of Arizona, landscape is more than place and space but living, breathing embodiments of a reciprocal relationship between a people, their history, and the physical world. Ingold writes that, in a case such as this, the Apache are not just moving across the landscape, from point to point, since there is no "surface." They are *in* the world rather than *of* it, meaning the Apache (or other indigenous cultures) live and perceive *through* the world rather than *across* it (2006, 14). They are in essence immersed within it. This sense of place brings alive a history of past experience that feeds identity. The places of landscape can be evocative of other times, experiences, and people and create associative memories giving one a sense of place and identity. Unlike the bubble created by the Enlightenment and technology that has us living *on* the world, the landscape for many indigenous cultures has been a dwelling of living *in* the world providing a narrative encompassing shared memory, experience, and a continuity in social identity through perception of the "constructiveness" of the landscape.

Tim Ingold summarizes Basso who argues for an ecology that is truly cultural adding, "one that would attend as much to the semiotic as to the material dimensions of people's relations with their surroundings, by bringing into focus 'the layers of significance with which human beings blanket the environment'" (171). Research on indigenous rock art by Todd Bostwick and Peter Krocek likewise points to the significance of experience and memory in relation to landscape. Their analysis of petroglyphs among the ancient Hohokam and modern Zuni illustrates how rock arts act as cultural repositories as

> records of individual dreams or vision quests; memories of important historical or mythological events; and signs relating to local resources and to the heavens . . . [and] rock art in its landscape encodes events that took place in the past and have the power to evoke that past. (2002, 14)

Perceiving the landscape, Ingold writes, is an "act of remembrance . . . of engaging perceptually with an environment that is itself pregnant with the past" (2006, 189). In these past times, giving names and meaning to places, what Basso calls "place-making," is evocative to later encounters questioning, "what happened here? who was involved? what was it like? why should it matter?" (5). The ability to answer was an expression of one's cultural identity and belonging in time and space.

The point here is that for thousands of years, human groups lived in an intimacy, inhabited by it Basso would say, moving through it with no clear lines of demarcation between people and nature, with the cultural world represented in the landscape of which they lived, experienced, celebrated, developed an identity, and died. As such, we might assume, they were in touch with the rhymes of the world and could not help but give meaning to it that, in turn, reflected who they were as a people and, as Ingold put it, engaged in rituals and stories that, "help to open up the world, not to cloak it." Quoting Inglis, Ingold offers that landscape contains stories "the most solid appearance in which a history can declare itself" because of landscapes's relative permanency (1993, 162). Landscape is there, in the deepness of time, pregnant or encoded with history and meaning for all generations to encounter, engage, and develop a sense of belonging as part of a larger inclusive whole.

How does the power of landscape as it has been experienced by others in prior times apply to an urbanized, changing world of today? The contemporary “culturescape,” infused as it is with fluidity, movement, individualism, and technology provides an all-together different, more encapsulated inversive world. The rootlessness described by Connerton includes a rootlessness of person and perception and, in general, a lack of fundamental questioning regarding place-making of the world. The structural and cultural constraints of postmodern consumer society lead to alienation or estrangement with self or place prompting an edginess to one’s identity. In this case, the self as person cannot be located except in self-idiosyncratic expression or the temporariness of experience but not in the emptiness of culturescape.

In his book *The End of Absence*, Michael Harris believes that the technology and social media surrounding the Internet has produced our non-place bubble and claimed our complete attention (2014). In this information technology age, people are pulled into the vortex of Twitter, Facebook, texting, 24-hour news cycles, and so forth, to the point that we cannot be without our smartphones waiting at our sides. Demands for our attention by our technology smothers us in an intensified immediacy in which the surrounding world and even the present evaporates. Attention is so focused and immersive that the individual becomes, using Connerton’s phrase, “unlinked from last causes.” For example, SnapChat deletes text message by default, erasing histories of conversation and allowing each exchange to be new. Thomas Erickson and Elisabeth Schober in their edited volume on accelerated, overheated social change, *Identity Destabilized*, agrees, believing our attention span is so much more abbreviated. “Life,” they write, “began to stand still at a frightful speed. Your gaze was now fixed at a point roughly one minute ahead” (2016, 14). Because of such acceleration and information overload, we have no time to think and little time to *be*. There is no *querencia* except in the loneliness of the computer screen.

Harris claims that we are so distracted and text-sound bite oriented that we have lost the sense of absence, of being alone with our thoughts. I know that individuals are in constant motion, always having to be doing something. They find the idea of doing nothing, of sitting around and getting lost in their thoughts, incomprehensible if not amusing. Too many people have forgotten the power of daydreaming silence, Harris adds, where “burning solitudes are extinguished” (8). With this idea of filling our days with connectivity, he quotes Gary Small, “Once people get used to this state, they tend to thrive on perpetual connectivity. It feeds their egos and sense of self-worth, and it becomes irresistible” (10). Through our smartphones and computers, we have the world’s accumulated knowledge but also the pings, beeps, and rings of the outside world insistently demanding our attention via Facebook, Twitter, and text message. Notice that many people cannot have conversations or dinner without smartphones being present. Our world is now consumed by online experience, all of which is momentary to be replaced seconds or minutes later with another ping demanding our edgy attention.

With the growth and development of new communication and transportation technologies, as well as the world-wide spread of production, advertising, tourism, and various media, in the wake of globalization came the idea of greater consumption to the rest of the world. Paul James and Imre Szeman in the introduction to their edited volume, *Globalization and Culture*, offer their assessment of the growth of consumer ideology,

> In the almost complete absence of other sustained macro-political and social narratives—concern about global climate change notwithstanding—the pursuit of the "good life" through practices of what is known as "consumerism" has become one of the dominant global social forces, cutting across differences of religion, class, gender, ethnicity and nationality. It is the other side of the dominant ideology of market globalism and is central to what Manfred Steger calls the "global imaginary." (2010, x)

Steger's global imaginary presents an interesting global dynamic. Although there is resistance and transformations to the global forces that move from the global to impact the local, by the late twentieth century a nascent consumerist mode of thinking and living has taken hold in many parts of the world, especially among the young and growing global middle class. The power of things such as the iPhone and branded clothing, especially among those that grow up educated by internationally culturally specific advertising and influenced by peer pressure, is that they alter the relation between civil society and consumers. The new consumer-based technologies operate as a filter or medium through which people begin to think about the world and their place in it. García Canclini, an Argentinian anthropologist, sees identity as no longer an expression of national symbols but informed by Hollywood or Televisa. Many view who they are, García Canclini believes, through media and the consumption of things (2001). In a world of transitory deterritorialized cultures, one of the few means of self-authentication, it appears and depending on the circumstances of ethnic, class, or race, is through the act of consumption of social media informing us who we are and then draping ourselves in the commodities expected of us.

Cultural tradition as expressed through crafts, rituals, customs, and celebrations, such as fiestas or *Dia de los Muertos* in Mexico for instance, García Canclini points out, help to contain the "drift of meanings" (2001, 41; 1993). Depending on the circumstances of place, such cultural traditions expressed in crafts and celebrations are vulnerable to appropriation by tourist expectations, the "tourist gaze." The contemporary impact of globalization has introduced many new cultural commodities and ideas that now have resonance on national and ethnic identity.[15] Changes in cultural traditions such as ritual celebrations and folk crafts by emerging class forces or foreign tourist encounters open the possibility of loss of cultural memory. I have several old handmade clay figurines of cock fights or fruit boat sellers and traditional daily scenes from the Dominican Republic that are the equivalent of landscape in that they hold the memory of a time in Dominican history when peasant culture was pervasive. These old figurines exude an authenticity that is not replicated today. Newer versions of such objects no longer exist or are romanticized and industrially made to meet the tourist "gaze." The global movement of people, goods, and ideas has led to an interfusion of the global into the local. Under such conditions, the unitary force of traditional culture break down under the corporate-led global marketing assault, creating new cultural forms and frameworks of reference associated with the fetishization of purchasing and consuming products. Cultures thus are prone to "deculturalization" and reconstituted as creole or hybrid cultures both in terms of cultural production—ideas, beliefs, meaning, interpretations—and social production such as music, film, institutions, norms, and so forth. For example, the evolving Spanglish, the mixture of English and Spanish, or Halloween and *Dia de los Muertos* beginning to blend as a singular event.

MEANING EXPRESSED IN SOCIAL VALUES

The anthropologist Roy Rappaport once noted that humans developed culture to give meaning to a world devoid of meaning. Culture provides both a metaphysical and a physical understanding of the world and out of these understandings we construct a way of life. The type of society constructed, based on variations of these ideas and meanings, develops a set of values to influence or determine the norms of behavior that a society deems important. Values alert us to what is significant to focus on and guide our behavior in terms of what is good and bad, and right and wrong. If society values individual competition, for instance, members will internalize competition as a good and valuable form of behavior. If wealth is an important value, then Hollywood will find Gordon Gekko proclaiming, "greed is good." Advertisers will, in a world of poverty and inequality, feel that it is entirely proper to offer $300,000 watches and $20 million apartments overlooking the homeless near New York's Central Park.

Values help to organize society by defining what is good, right, just, and proper and are guidelines for how we approach the world. They can also encompass strategies for adapting to various conditions a society faces. For example, among the pastoral Borana of Kenya who inhabit a semi-arid region, one would never withhold where water for cattle could be found. This information would be shared with anyone asking, since all people of this region depend on such information for survival. Among the Gabra, a camel herding group also from Kenya, two important values are called "*dabarre*" and "*irb,*" forms of reciprocal exchange obligating one clan to help another even if the obligation to help is generations old. *Dabarre* and *irb* creates a sense of dependency on others where one can gain access to important resources (such as camels) when no other alternative exists (see Robinson 2009). Sharing through reciprocal exchanges becomes an important value in many premodern societies where social relationships, anthropologists tell us, exemplify kinship affiliation or friendship. Quoting Evans-Pritchard on the Nuer of East Africa, Sahlins suggests that such a perspective is common in the premodern, tribal world: "One cannot treat Nuer economic relations by themselves, for they always form part of direct social relations of a general kind . . . there is always between them a general social relationship of one kind or another" (1972, 186). Such exchanges, even gift-giving, either are a means of distribution, a mode of relationship repair, or a method of dealing with potential conflict, but the gift functions to bind people together. The focus in not on the gift but on the social relationships gift exchange symbolize. Sahlins sums up Mauss's idea on the meaning of the gift, "For the war of every man against every man, Mauss substitutes the exchange of everything between everybody" (168). These transactions are locations of values, embedded with the ideals of group, thus personal obligation and dependency tying morally, religiously, and economically individuals to social groups and social groups to each other.

Consumer goods are appropriated to support one's self-definition even within gift giving to others. Mauss considered gifts as never truly given as in modern gift giving but attaches giver and recipient together morally and socially. He writes, "All of these cultural notions are concretized in goods, and it is through their possession and use that the individual realizes the notions of his own life" (1954, 25). The significance of modern values for social members today is that they allow the individual to adapt to the constraints and opportunities of a pervasive economic market ecosystem. These values not only influence the norms of society—they also provide meanings that are used to strategize the reality of life and to make sense of why we do what we do and give confidence in how we feel about it. Thus, our particular set of values and meanings tell us what it means to be human (from our perspective) and what we can expect of others. In the past, the traditional and premodern worlds referred to values, norms, symbols, and meanings that were recognized by most cultural members as stable and given and that applied to all members (whether all members agreed or not) in time and space. Culture was a scaffolding or an anchor of solid content that offered moral and ethical insight through the ages of one's cultural patrimony. That world, postmodernists would say, is fast disappearing with a new "liquid" sociocultural ballgame now in play with the sovereign unencumbered individual in the lead.

How did all this happen? Why has modernity begun to fade like the burning off of early morning lake mist? Jock Young has asked the same question in his book, *The Vertigo of Late Modernity*, and believes,

> .mass migration and tourism, the "flexibility" of labour, the breakdown of community, the instability of family, the rise of virtual realities and reference points within the media as part of the process of cultural globalization, the impact of mass consumerism, and the idealisation of individualism, choice, and spontaneity

is responsible (2007, 1). The shift is located away from the general formulation of modernity as the loss among its residents to a belief in progress and the promise of such by science. The ideas of progress and enlightenment by the early proponents of modernity have given way to a cynicism or a pessimism of impoverishment brought on by a moral and ideational decline. Considering the cynicism surrounding our institutions where even given reality is affected by "fake news" or suspected of partisan politics, our achievements today seem less a cause for celebration than doubt and misgivings.

In the United States (and increasingly in other countries), through physical mobility, transitory employment and careers, and lack of substantive neighborhood connections, our sense of identity is now more private or through public displays of (competitive) consumption that in and of itself is problematic. It is the fleeting social embeddedness of the person (or its promise) that offers a certitude of an encompassing narrative at once personal and yet publicly social to be acted on by strangers. Late modernity on the other hand, Jock Young writes, agreeing with postmodernists, generates both "economic and ontological insecurity [and] a discontinuity of personal and social narrative" that loses much of its public recognition (17). What is left? Over time our search for personal and social identities, a subject for the next chapter, comes under the influence of a vast wilderness of consumer products and the advertising imperative to think with these goods.

IDEAS AND SOCIAL CHANGE

The difficulty of adapting to the new and growing realities of global climate change and environmental degradation centers on the complexity of culture and more specifically on those ideas, perspectives, and meaning that find expression in a culture's values such as progress.

Conditions of rapid social change may require substantive resilience. The important values are those associated with cultural identity that may need changing, as well as the beliefs that compose standards of living, and the meaning of life itself. These fundamental values and beliefs that we hold to be true ideally say something about our existential being, at least as we see ourselves through the detritus of material possessions. A consumer society is one that values innovation and newness and considers the acquisition of material goods a worthwhile if not cherished endeavor.

The question Tim Kasser and his colleagues ask is, why do people buy into materialist values and consumption in such a fashion (2004)? If not genetically endowed human nature, then what is it that propels the desire to consume on such a consistent scale? As social animals, we are consciously and unconsciously taught what is needed to be a functioning member of a particular culture. "As children acquire language, at the same time they are acquiring knowledge of the statuses and roles which comprise the social order of their society" (Roseman and Rubel 1998, 82–83). This process of knowledge acquisition, enculturation, begins at birth and does not end until death. How an individual as a social member of society views the world is through the filter of a culture's core values and meanings. We are in essence taught to be what our culture needs us to be.

In *The German Ideology*, Marx famously wrote,

> The ideas of the ruling class are in every epoch the ruling ideas, i.e. the class which is the ruling material force of society, is at the same time its ruling intellectual force. The class which has the means of material production at its disposal, has control at the same time over the means of mental production. (1981, 64)

This elite class also has class consciousness concerning their interests. If the system is to work correctly, that is, in the interest of capitalist activity to which they are aligned, then the population must share a set of beliefs and values that benefit the economic system of productive ownership. The elite ruling class must therefore manufacture and promote the ideas important to it. Marx's analysis reveals,

> As they rule as a class and determine the extent and compass of an epoch, it is self-evident that they do this in its whole range, hence among other things rule also as thinkers, as producers of ideas, and regulate the production and distribution of the ideas of their age: thus, their ideas are the ruling ideas of the epoch. (ibid; see Apple 2004)

However important these ideas may be, they must be accepted, even in resistance, by those who are the recipients of the elite worldview. The social formation, then, must not only have elements of social control but, perhaps more importantly, induce the lower classes to buy into the economic system that ultimately works against them. Nevertheless, the industrial and financial systems controlled by this elite class of powerful economic interests can maintain great influence over a system that produces great wealth and power that in turn offer us "stuff."

These ruling ideas ultimately move society over time in the direction of alienation from the bonds of community and the interdependency and intimacy of social relationships toward those of the sovereign possessive lone individual, the market, and the fetish of material things beyond their use value. Labor is no longer the instillation of the human spirit but a necessary performance to purchase needful things. Years ago, William Domhoff spent considerable time analyzing the elites' influence over the structure of American society. An essential ingredient of influence is control over institutions and ideas (and thus people) as Antonio Gramsci once wrote. Much of this is done, he believes, through mass media—newspapers, magazines, televisions, and radio that reinforce "the legitimacy of the social system through the routine ways in which they accept and package events" and while not completely hegemonic are in general successful in shaping public opinion and attitudes (1983, 83, 109, 110).

When we think about economics, however, we must also think about the role politics plays in formulating or supporting the socioeconomic system. It is clear to most people that money and wealth can play a very influential role in determining policy. In his recent book, *Affluence and Influence*, Martin Gilens of Princeton University sees the power of money in political campaigns that go on to influence policy. He writes that "The disproportionate responsiveness to the preferences of the affluent cannot be attributed to their higher turnout rates or their greater involvement with political campaigns. Money—the 'mother's milk' of politics—is the root of representational inequality" (2014, 10; see also Hacker and Pierson 2010). Additional research produced by Martin Gilens and Benjamin Page suggests that wealthy individuals and businesses are relatively more successful at influencing policy than the common citizenry (as Domhoff concluded). They conclude, "The preferences of economic elites . . . have far more independent impact upon policy change than the preferences of average citizens do" (2014, 22). Furthermore, their analysis found, one increasingly clear to many people, that the majority does not have much power to determine outcomes. As polls indicate, several issues organized in elite interests tend to win and the majority loses, for example, income tax laws that tend to favor the wealthy.

In a sense, as Marx and others pointed out long ago, the elites classes have a greater awareness of their class and economic interests than the public, at least in the contemporary era of capitalism and the decline in unionism and labor activism. Resistance today seems more scattershot rather than class based with a theoretical understanding of class struggle. The educational system is not equipped to teach in any patterned way the "emerging contradictions and pressures of our social formation and its mode of production," according to Michael Apple, Professor of Curriculum and Instruction and Educational Policy Studies at the University of Wisconsin, Madison (2004). He maintains that education is a major means through which power and control over ideas is perpetuated by elite and economic interests. At the same time, political discord over dealing with climate change and environmental degradation become litmus tests of political loyalty or rational scientific discourse. How we view our relationship to the natural world plays a central role in our ability to develop policies and strategies responsive to global environmental change. Heyd and Brooks point out that our ability and responses "depend heavily on the extent to which societies see themselves as separate from or part of the wider physical or 'natural' environment" (2009, 269). We thus find ourselves constrained by a structure of problematic logic and values, politicized beliefs, and attitudes that influence our approach to nature and its ecosystems, as well as to ourselves.

As discussed in this chapter, there is good reason to concentrate on the meaning of consumption given its significance for the state of contemporary culture and the exploitation role it plays in various environmental issues. An empirical question that needs further investigation is whether hyper-consumerism and the "personalization" of identity is completely weakening the sense of a collective moral community and loss of historic memory and thus making solving social and environmental problems more difficult. Likewise, Ted Trainer outlined in the Bulletin of the Atomic Scientists, "Simply put. . . . Unless the fundamental structures and systems of modern society are scrapped and replaced, the problems they are causing cannot be solved" (2013).

In the next chapter, we will narrow our scope to focus more sharply on the individual. What has been the effect of contemporary social change on the meaning of the individual under late capitalist culture? The pervasive growth of materialism and consumerism and the weakening of master narratives that proscribe values and social orientation has led to an "empty self." Under previous social conditions, the self had social–psychological boundaries. No longer. Due to the absence or weakness of community and tradition and the growing irrelevance of formally powerful master narratives, the self is alone immersed in itself without social convictions yet a hunger for meaning and connection. The void of the empty self is thus filled by acquisition and consumption. Our possessions become significant symbols that we think relate to who we are. It may be that the only thing we do control is the possessions we own and in this world of traveling cultures and transitory values, this may have a pronounced effect upon how we view ourselves relative to those around us. This suggests how do we reach a sustainable and limited consumerism that leads to environmental rehabilitation given our estrangement from nature and from ourselves? This question will be the focus of the concluding chapter.

NOTES

1. For those not familiar with O. Henry's story, the moral point he made was it is not the gift itself that counts but rather the relationship it expresses.

2. The "age of plenty," however, is not evenly distributed in society but is conditioned by race, ethnicity, and class. Inequality in education, health, and income is much more prevalent in minority communities that face discrimination and prejudice.

3. In the introduction to his book *Land of Desire*, William Leach quotes Artemas Ward on this new world of desire,

> This world seems real only when it answers to our individual touch. Yet beyond our touch, beyond our waking, beyond our working, and almost in the land of dreams, lie things beyond our present thought, greater, wider, stronger, than those we now lay hold on. To each a world opens; to everyone possibilities are present. (1993, 4)

4. In *Grundrisse*, Marx recognized this duality,

> Production mediates consumption; it creates the latter's material; it, consumption would lack an object. But consumption also mediates production, in that it alone creates for the products the subject for whom they are products. The product only obtains its last finish in consumption.

Furthermore,

> Consumption creates the motive for production; it also creates the object which is active in production as its determinant aim. If production offers consumption its external object, it is therefore equally clear that consumption ideally posits the object of production as an internal image, as a need, as drive and as purpose. It creates the objects of production in a still subjective form. No production without a need. But consumption reproduces the need. (1993, 90–91, org. 1857–58)

Ultimately, it is the system of production, as Featherstone comments, "the same commodity logic and instrumental rationality manifest in the sphere of production is noticeable in the sphere of consumption" (1990, 6).

5. In McCracken's brief overview of the history of the development of consumer society, he states that by the nineteenth century, consumption had matured such that it had its own institutional center, the department store. The department store was a physical presence, an edifice of meaning, and a symbol of progress. One went to the store and shared a common public experience. Today however, more people are turning to online "stores" such as amazon.com to purchase goods in a

disembodied digital process, an experience we share with only ourselves as we stare at the computer screen.

6. According to Rasmussen's 1929 research, among the traditional Inuit of the central Arctic region, guilt or innocence was often determined by communal consensus opinion of a "song duel." Judgment was often accepted but could occasionally lead to anger and personal violence (see Eckett and Newmark 1980).

7. Symbols are vehicles of meaning and can be expressed through ritual practices and ceremonies. Symbols are the elements of social processes that link behavior and perception of reality in collective ways. The handprints and animals on the cave walls at Lascaux, France, for example, functioned symbolically to locate the painters' community within a framework of myth and spirituality linked to the physical world, one understood and celebrated by that culture's members.

8. Contemporary objects in which resides collective meaning are often related to catastrophic events such as 9/11. Objects pulled from ground zero are repositories of significant meaning recognized by most society's members. National monuments such as the Lincoln Memorial contain symbolic representation recognized, if superficially, by most people.

9. There are, however, contrasts to Colin Turnbull's research claim in *The Forest People*, of the Mibuti Pygmies of Central Africa as a gentle forest-dwelling people in total harmony with the forest (1962). This may be so, but later research by Turnbull focused on the violent and self-centered Ik of Uganda and Napoleon Chagnon's work on the aggressive horticultural Yanomamo of the Venezuelan Amazon (Erchak 1996, 107–108).

10. In the contemporary modern world perhaps one area where symbolism is most potent, both personally and collectively, is the iconography of religious artifacts. In Christianity, the chalice of wine signifies the body of Christ or a stoup holding holy water, in which one dips fingers as a reminder of baptism and the cleansing of sin. Examples such as these operate as symbolic vehicles to convey a collective relationship to the sacred for the faith community. In this way they are "living" representations of history, legacy, and the supernatural that all members recognize, enduring the movement of generations of worshipers.

11. In *Capital*, Marx remarked,

> The utility of a thing makes it a use-value. But this utility is not a thing of air. Being limited by the physical properties of the commodity, it has no existence apart from that commodity. A commodity, such as iron, corn, or a diamond, is therefore, so far as it is a material thing, a use-value, something useful (2007, 42)

It is not just the pedestrian value of material things but that the material conditions of life are often given meaning by the imprint of cultural experience, that is, a history. It is this meaning beyond the practicality of things that makes us human (that differentiates us from tool using animals). Outside this dynamic resides the alienation of labor that was so much the focus of Marx.

12. Roger Keesing asks, "Do we need to assume that all native actors unconsciously understand deep ritual symbolism to account for the processes of creation, continuity, and change through which such cultural forms emerge and endure?"

(2012, 423). Keesing sees the Kwaio of Melanesia surrounded by symbolism and ritual but believes that most members have a limited and superficial understanding of the symbolism. Not recognizing the dynamism of symbol and ritual does not necessarily mean any rupture with past understandings or relationships. The link between symbol and actor changes but what may remain is the implicit and unconscious recognition that ties the community together with a communal understanding of history and heritage that most members are aware of one way or another.

13. Kale et al. define deterritorialization as "a process of detachment of social and cultural practices from specific places, thereby blurring the natural relationship between culture and geographic territories" (2007, 4). They add that the loss of territorial place and globalization "go hand in hand, for globalization is not simply the coming together of various peoples forming a harmonious tapestry; for many it entails worldwide fragmentation and loss of identity" (9). This of course can lead many to existential crises over the meaning of who they think they are.

14. Urbanism has evolved to estrange society from the broader landscape, surrounded as we are by artificiality, practicality, or fantasy (think Disneyland). In earlier times, urban areas represented Earthly cosmological maps of religious or spiritual belief. Teotihuacán in Mexico and Copán in Honduras were constructed to mirror the landscape of the universe. Such cosmological cities, including those in premodern India and China, operated as connection points between sky (the supernatural world) and Earthly societies. Many cities had cardinal points related to seasonal changes, and among the Maya certain temples also had deep underground rooms in which the sun would shine into certain times of the year and symbolized a connection between the known physical world and the underworld. To enter Copán, for example, was to enter the cosmos in a worldly fashion.

15. There are in many parts of the world cultural revitalizations and ethnic resurgence in resistance to globalized homogeneity. In other cases, foreign ideas are accepted but transformed to meet local conceptions or needs (see, for example, Watson's Golden Arches East (2006).

Chapter 7

I Am What I Own—Or So I Think

Possessions and the Presentation of Me

The previous two chapters suggest that the economic imperative of capitalism created conditions weakening the *communitas* of intense social bonding, releasing the individual to experience the freedom of sovereignty and ascendancy. This chapter examines what this metamorphosis in society means for those living under such changing conditions; that is, has the individual been refashioned or remained the same as in any other era or culture? Anthropologists and sociologists use the term social construction to denote that the sociocultural environment is what shapes an individual's identity, thoughts, and self-concept. In the present period, the self is a dynamic concept played out in a wide variety of social interactions and relationships. Even the psychological realm is conditioned by social and cultural processes that are expressed in the individual as beliefs, behaviors, and meanings applied in different contexts. The moral or spiritual truths passed down through the generations through ritual, ceremony, and myth have given way to a more rational, scientific, and technological way of thinking. Erving Goffman's idea that we play a variety of roles, found in his book *The Presentation of Self in Everyday Life* (1959), essentially different selves, in different situations as if actors on a variety of stages acting out roles are only compatible in complex societies with degrees of freedom, desires, and motivations. In a sense, the individual's identity, sense of self, is considered a "cultural artifact" of modern consumer society. The idea of the dynamic, independent, and unique individual, the modern self, is an articulation incongruous among many traditional world cultures, especially premodern ones.

For much of history, one's sense of self, certainty, and moral worth came from inclusion within a hierarchy of group membership, an immersion in enduring intimate relationships, as much anthropological research has suggested. In the "little communities" discussed by Redfield one did not have to like everyone, but you knew everyone. Even those one disliked provided, unconsciously of course, a degree of psychological security because you intimately knew the person disliked. No one was an unknown given that we are social animals. Whether it was a foraging society or a modern industrial one, to be human is to quest for social bonding. Even in our quest for privacy, we celebrate holidays and special events with those we like, and we go out of our way to be sociable and inviting. But intimate and enduring social bonding with others is made difficult by a cultural environment enthralled by technology, which supports the idea of "me." Personal technologies and social media have made an artificial creation, a bubble in which we are circumscribed in our isolated personal pleasures and controlled connection to others.

THE INDIVIDUAL IN PAST AND PRESENT COMMUNITY

The traveling cultures we have constructed, the physical, social, and cultural mobility of people and ideas, has led to the temporality of things and varying degrees of uncertainty. How might this be so? In *Shades of Loneliness*, Stivers offers one reason for this state of affairs (2004). He argues that the technology of media plays a significant role in shaping experience, by theft of imagination, that influences the modern personality.[1] For example, everyone reading the same novel fills the characters with their own unique mental images. The movie of the novel, however, provides analogous images, where the experience is objectified. Neal Postman argues in *Amusing Ourselves to Death* that television has transformed the way people connect with the world and thus how they think about it. In a reading-based culture, literacy requires time and effort to develop, a complexity extended to the world one learns about once one can read. But television requires no effort and, moreover, encourages viewers to believe that the world is similarly simple and (most troubling of all) that the purpose of politics, education, religion, and so forth is to entertain us in some fashion. The result, Postman writes, "Technology colonizes our experiences, opinions, emotions, and consciousness," leading to a loss of judgment and responsibility that renders us incapable of understanding the nuances of life (2005, 19, 25).

Zygmunt Bauman sees social instability developing as a hallmark of this new postmodern or "liquid" age of transitory structures, institutions, and patterned behavior and thought (2006). Under such nomadic conditions, one's sense of identity is pulled of social relations from their local environments of community, kinship, and family. The totality of rapid social change and the new forms of information and communication technologies now informs so much of contemporary life that it led Nicolas Carr to declare,

> Over the past few years I've had an uncomfortable sense that someone, or something, has been tinkering with my brain, remapping the neural circuitry, reprogramming the memory. My mind isn't going—so far as I can tell—but it's changing. I'm not thinking the way I used to think. (2008)

As Marx so aptly put it, consciousness is conditioned upon the epoch in which it is formed. If cultural experience is liquid and transitory, then so too is one's consciousness of thought and perception. The point is we think cognitively and psychologically different from our ancient indigenous forebears or possibly even from those of fifty years ago.

Many scholars concerned with the weakening of social institutions, changing status sets, and a much more liquid set of ambiguity and relative truths view identity in problematic terms. In tradition-based societies, ambiguity was weak due to strong links to sentiment and experience of the past. Tradition offered social and personal stability to most members who thought and understood the world in the same way. Tradition instructed how to behave and to engage and what was right and wrong according to consensus. This is the foundation for a value base that makes life meaningful. Community solidarity, authority, and custom as direct experience rather than individual choice and freedom took precedence. The rigidity of learned experience and, as Durkheim observed, the mechanical solidarity of sameness gave a sense of psychological security in one's social identity. Identity was not relative but more absolute, an iron cage, and not open to question, and freedom as we know it was constrained by community sentiment.

In *The Division of Labor in Society*, Durkheim believed that the growth of social complexity led to increased social differentiation and a loss of legitimacy, which then led to weaker social relationships and social disintegration and finally to individuals lost in society. If the changes brought about by such broad and pervasive shifts in society's foundations exist, what anchors the individual's location in the social hierarchy on the one hand and provides meaning of self-worth and esteem on the other? Whereas elements of one's social identity were mediated by religion, tradition, and the pressure of socialization for conformity to role expectations, in liquid society it is more a transient question of "who do I want to be?" Tradition is significant in this regard for premodern and indigenous communities. Tradition is the collective memory of a people and as that recedes in memory, to become depersonalized or superficial by commercialism, how do individuals now unanchored know who or what they are?

It is argued here that people today look for tradition in all the wrong places. Due to the internet and social media and the decline in traditional values, social members are released from (intimate) social relations to be restructured "across indefinite spans of time-space," as Giddens believed. People are no longer bounded, as they were in the past, by time and location in part because much of mobile social life is now found articulated through various modalities including social media such as Facebook. Zhang, Jiang, and Carroll theorize that today identity is more "symbolic" rather than infused with emotional and intimate connection or any fixed identity (2012). In this way, identity has been reconstructed through shared values, visions, and interfaced with the internet. But can identity be real in the sense of George Herbert Mead's understanding of how the self is created? If such things, however, are now in dispute, open to different interpretations, or expressed differently, what does this mean for the idea of community? Supporters say Facebook, for example, does provide a sense of community. But this sort of community is virtual, impersonal even when personal, and certainly not transparent nor with any abiding traditions. Individuals can escape their embedded selves through what they elect to present on Facebook as their identity. As a confirmation of the liquid or postmodern world of identity formation, using virtual tools the individual can construct who she/he wants to be. How would a virtual audience know the difference?

Considering the recent development of computer-moderated communications (CMC) such as digital (virtual) communities, the ramifications of their development has yet to meet scholarly consensus. We can view online communities from a more problematic perspective. The construction and presentation of self is purposeful management and self-promoting, framed by questions of deception and authenticity. Traditionally, community included the conception of self, found in face-to-face group membership based on common experience and shared meaning, but this is not necessarily so in virtual communities. Derek Foster quotes Mead who said, "What goes to make up the organized self is the organization of the attitudes which are common to the group. A person is a personality because he belongs to a community" (1996, 25). The package of social interactions through various institutions and roles played in social interaction allows members to develop broader understandings, visions, and empathy toward others, via the looking-glass self, along with guaranteed access to the "public square"—this is what coalesces members into a community. Physical communities in a more general sense involve a degree of transparency of social interactions through schools, church, pubs, long-term interactions, and homes. As Durkheim once pointed out, there is group pressure to conform, to accept the expectations of thought and behavior among members. But this social dynamic requires actual day-to-day physical interactions. The new digital online communities are more one-dimensional, subject to specific interests or issues, in which people come and go in any fashion they desire. Do communications via the internet increase or decrease physical interpersonal relations? Today more and more people are on the internet participating in virtual communities such as chatrooms, Facebook, and so forth. Through these media, one can play with who they want to be, a kind of avatar of self or an invented self. How easy would it be to lose oneself if engaged too much in the virtual world where anything goes?

Online virtual communities allow for a narrower conception of community—one of autonomous individual pursuits increasingly with narrow conceptual blinders. The fear is that this can create the conditions for not only protective isolation but self-absorbed inclinations.

Or as Goffman once put it, "thin and meager" social interactions are a result. In computer modulated communications the computer user is master and in control over the totality of online communications. "Every individual sees himself," Foster quotes Baudrillard, "promoted to the controls of a hypothetical machine, isolated in a position of perfect sovereignty" (27). Hundreds of millions of individuals now have a considerable presence online searching cyberspace, looking for a facsimile of intimacy and connection with strangers that meet their momentary needs or wants. Although in both physical and virtual reality individuals engage in impression management, online management offers greater latitude, that is, sovereignty, since virtual interchanges can be anonymously supported by innumerable digital props easily obtained and used.

The social infrastructure upon which we operate is, as discussed earlier, the capitalist socioeconomic system of values, norms, expectations, and behavior. Socialized by this environment, the generalized individual has become in Roy Baumeister's terms, an "independent, autonomous, self-contained economic agent," where materialism becomes a significant component in one's life and identity (1991, 97). What leads to an overemphasis on materialism and consumption? Research suggests that it is self-doubt, degrees of uncertainty, the need for control, and the feeling of normlessness. Material acquisition, in other words, potentially can act as a coping mechanism. But if needs and desires are to an extent contingent on comparisons (thus competition) with anonymous virtual peer reference groups that are fluid or indeterminate, materialism is a poor coping mechanism, more likely to increase self-consciousness and social anxiety rather than social solidarity. Tim Kasser's research suggests that materialism is associated with egoistic anti-social feelings and self-centeredness and thus a pulling away from the intimacy of social relationships and toward feelings of anomie and thus encourage consumptive behavior (2002).

A central facet of social life, and however weak, remains found within the idea and structure of community, a term of significance for many social scientists as we have discussed. Premodern or traditional communities established moral values, interdependent relationships, and social norms to govern behavior through established codes of conduct, expressed in ceremonies and rituals. For literally thousands of years, our social being was formed through the ideals and moral sentiment lived in intimate group organization. As humans, the search for answers to our existence and place in society, however, was not instituted individually but collectively as communities of face-to-face participants engaged in rituals, celebrations, and ceremonies, for example, coming of age ceremonies into adulthood. Various symbols were employed as grammar to help social groups search for meaning and connection found primarily in tradition. Thinking of the traditional Mayans of the Yucatan, Robert Redfield saw ceremonies enhancing communal awareness, commenting,

> Further details, deeper relationships, emerge to awareness during the ceremonies when the meaning of things is dramatized before him, and if the native is induced to sit and reflect . . . the structure of the world view grows and develops. (1960, 91)

In the reification of this search through ritual and symbolic representation, one's social, collective identity took shape. Identity was group-referential and referred to self—or group image in a culturally historical setting. In kinship-based tribal and peasant societies of previous eras, various social acts were employed to create a "collective consciousness" of *communitas* or community solidarity that offered continuity, belonging, and a sense of place. There was, for the most part, an abiding integration between the individual and the community in which he or she resided.[2]

In the rural communities of Mesoamerica, for instance, "Corporate entities—the communal village, *cofradía*, guild and parish—constituted the largest embodiment and formal support of this set of values: the right to collective use and sharing of resources" was significant for community survival (Voss 2001, 83). Such corporate communities existed among the Mexica of pre-Columbian Mexico, known as *calpulli*. The *calpulli* was a neighborhood/community kinship-based organization that corporately controlled access to communal land and engaged in various socioreligious duties within with the Mexica state (see Soustelle 1961). Although recognizing that all cultures are, at some point, part of larger wholes, through trade for example, Redfield saw the small, local community as a significant and historically a predominant form of social organization. "[T]he unity and distinctiveness of the little community," he wrote in *The Little Community*,

> is felt by everyone who is brought up in it and as a part of it. The people of a band or a village or a small town know each of the other members of that community as parts of one another . . . the community is a round of life, a small cosmos; the activities and the institutions lead from one into all the others so

that to the native himself the community is a list of tools and customs; it is an integrated whole. (1960, 10)

A different form of integration existed among various African and North American indigenous communities. Known as sodalities, individuals as young men (in this case the Masai or Samburu of East Africa) were placed in age-sets that cut across domestic and kinship lines. Each institutionalized age-set composed of members from different kin groups moved through life together into various statuses from juniors to household heads to seniors and elders. According to S. N. Eisenstadt's review of African age-grade societies, "the individual's position within the system constitutes an important index of social status and, to some extent, regulates his behaviour towards all other members of the society (whether seniors, equals, or juniors)" (1954, 101). Eisenstadt outlines such normative behavior functioning as

> The formalization of an age group provides its members with a new focus of identification with the society, a new frame of reference through which they relate themselves to the total society and identify themselves with its values and symbols. (107)

As such, individuals cooperated in mutual help and important community functions and formed solidarity just as they would among family and kinship. The significance of age groups, then, act as an institution educating social values and thus "they serve as important 'reservoirs' of solidarity and identification with the society" (110). In North America among the Crow and Cheyenne, individuals joined military associations and secret societies whose normative behavior oversaw seasonal migrations, collective hunts, and policing duties in their communities. In all cases, they were surrounded throughout life among peers who thought and acted much the same with all being aware of their common roles. For the individual it was clear who they were and how they fit in socially smothered as they were with people almost a mirror image of themselves.

Traditional and kinship-based societies generated predefined roles with stable and relatively fixed identities because they were slow to change in any substantive manner. This is not to say that such cultures were static or in equilibrium. A variety of external factors could come into play such as environmental change, new ideas, or cultural contact. For instance, research by Lauriston Sharp among the Yir Yoront of Australia illustrates that stone axes were the property of men and could be referred to as "my axe," but were nevertheless constantly used by other family members. The significance of the axe, however, involved social relationships that defined the roles and statuses of participants as well exemplifying the clan's mythical ancestors (1952). The axe was the focal point of social structure and its interplay with identity, such as the Mexican pitcher in chapter 6, given that "It can be seen that repeated and widespread conduct centering around the use of the axe helped to generalize and standardize these sex, age, and kinship roles" (19).

In premodern societies, identity was not problematic or something that an individual struggled to ascertain and maintain. There was little ambiguity over how to define oneself since, as many anthropologists have argued, self-consciousness was located within the confines of responsibility and connection to the web of kinship and community relationships, in this case through the axe. In essence, one was born to hunt and gather or herd father's cattle, respect one's elders, and generally that was that; that is, until the arrival of foreign colonial powers and Anglican missionaries toward the end of the nineteenth century, and in 1915 established a mission station on the Mitchell River. Thinking they were helping by providing a more reliable tool, and to attract the Yir Yoront, they indiscriminately handed out steel axes to everyone, women and children, leading to the collapse of their cultural system. "The stress of the collapse of the symbolic and relationship meaning of the axe," Sharp remarks, reaches an intellectual and emotional

> saturation point. . . . With the collapse of this system of ideas, which is so closely related to so many other aspects of the native culture, there follows an appallingly sudden and complete cultural disintegration, and a demoralization of the individual. (22)

The stone axe, which was the foundation to one's identity, disintegrated in meaning, resulting in apathy, alienation, and behavioral problems.

The foregoing is not to suggest that members of these traditional communities all thought alike or were carbon copies of each other, nor were they prisoners of their culture. Agency and experience are important components of how we define ourselves as human beings and the world we live in. The point is one's social location and thus how individuals thought of themselves was through the nexus of social relationships sharing a common cultural or existential grammar. In premodern societies, there was little doubt about who one was and where they fit into the social scheme of things. There was in a sense a symmetry between history, group experience, and the self-encompassing social relationships.

A NEW WORLD OF TRANSFORMATION AND FLUIDITY

In his book *Community and Power* (originally, *The Quest for Community*), Robert Nisbet wrote in 1962 (org. 1953) an understanding prescient for his time. "Competition, individuation, dislocation of status and custom, impersonality, and moral anonymity were hailed," he wrote, "by the rationalist because these were the forces that would be most instrumental in emancipating man from the dead hand of the past" (4). Many believed, in that "golden age" of economic growth and increasing incomes and consumption, that finally the drive for progress was paying off. But Nisbet remarked that this came with a cost in community and social identity. In the opening chapter he commented,

> One may paraphrase the famous words of Karl Marx and say that a specter is haunting the modern mind, the specter of insecurity. Surely the outstanding characteristic of contemporary thought on man and society is the preoccupation with personal alienation and cultural disintegration. (3)

In the contemporary era of globalization, economic transformations, and accelerated technological changes, the individual and sense of self are buffeted by currents not easily understood let alone controlled. In an overheated world, as Thomas Hylland Eriksen and Elisabeth Schober call the twenty-first century, " . . . how can a world that has been ripped apart, whether because of industrial development, migration or the expansion of finance capital, be patched together again so that it appears meaningful and secure?" (2016, 2). That is, my individual sense is not clear with the troubling thought of who I am. Whatever imagined or real world once thought to exist, people perceived clear divisions with narratives and ideologies that appeared solid and stable. The world today, however, is fraught with conflicts, anxiety, and conflicting perspectives that bring prevailing narratives and ideologies into question. If an important element of our social identity is in symbols, memories, and stories of tradition passed down to us, an accelerating world of change breaks or weakens this link. Connection between past and present is easy when there is common agreement and repetition but when there is not clear and compelling agreed upon story linking past, present, and future how can one talk of continuity that is efficacious? More and more, it seems, everywhere is nowhere, or as Gertrude Stein once quipped, there is no there there.

The social and physical fluidity of the contemporary world has made the shared inward or social orientation of the past increasingly difficult if not impossible, weakening the sense of harmony and cooperation in communities now progressively composed of strangers each with their own agenda. In the early days of the modern world, the growing and pervasive bourgeoisie began to proclaim their status through public displays of ostentation as emblematic of status and growing political power. Albert Borgmann tells us that this was a time of public display, where people could meet and proclaim themselves. But over time, "the people who filled these spaces had become silent, passive, and distracted," in their newfound status Borgmann adds, and "eventually, become quiescent observers enjoying the products of others in private spheres of leisure" (1992, 41).

Given such passivity, Bauman argues that over time contemporary culture comprised as it is by strangers induces fear and anxiety in a world of uncertainty and ambiguity (2007, 2013). We are now, as Robert Heinlein once wrote, strangers in a strange land where the wind blows silent and cold. Such fear is a by-product of our embrace of the sanctity of individualism as the greatest of virtues, according to Robert Castel. He believes that

> modern society, having replaced the closely knit communities and corporations which once defined the rules of protection and monitored their application with the individual duty of self-interest, self-care and self-help, has been living on the quicksand of contingency. In such a society the sentiments of existential insecurity and scattered fears of diffuse dangers are, inevitably, endemic. (quoted in Bauman 2007, 57)

One outcome in the development of the modern world of individualism, according to Borgmann, is the accentuation and differentiation of the private from the public spheres of daily life. The sanctity of the privacy sphere is now located in the individual, private consumer, not so much as a family unit, but one of "perfect sovereignty" that Jean Baudillard also wrote about. In other words, the sovereign individual is considered superior to any notion of an organic social community yet leads to various social dysfunctions. As a result, the package of consumer goods operates to "remove or ease the burdens of life that formerly would direct us to our family and community for aid and solace, to give us individual mobility in the pursuit of our ends" leading to consumption that is primarily solitary (1992, 43, 44). The development of private technologically self-sufficient lifeworlds has resulted in a non-integrative society and family alongside changing authority structures, personal technologies, outside and temporary employment, and mobility encouraging weak social relationships.

Along with the changing nature of modern consumer society, the dynamic of globalization and the movement of people creating new diasporas brings a degree of plurality and thus uncertainty to cultural identity. In terms of those identity markers that relate to heritage and ethnic/cultural values and attitudes, that a sojourner brings with him/her undergoes negotiation and construction is understood. Here, however, our interest is in the dynamic and meaning of present-day consumption and its public presentation beyond ethnic culture and heritage. Regardless of ethnic background, in consumption-based societies such as the United States all fall under the sway of assimilation, consumption, and material ownership as a relatively stable means of projecting the self and status in society—stable due to the relentless push by advertising and marketing to convince people that products can change their lives or represent who we are under various circumstances. Ethnic advertising, mentioned earlier, plays a significant role in this regard by using cultural understandings to contour the message, making it receptive to the receiver.

Of the two types of community, one is often rural or ethnic based that retains a significant and observable tightness of social relationships—due either to culture, poverty, and/or discrimination. The other community are those whose members are mobile and affluent and where social networks are not generally located in the physical community but based through work, interest, or income and location. Here, in this community no one is borrowing a cup of sugar from their immediate neighbor. These communities are not like those of *Blade Runner*, of crowded, shoulder-to-shoulder postmodern multiculturalism but sterile communities of strangers focused on status hierarchies and the "coolness of now" in the kinds of jobs, houses, and automobiles they have with a leave-me-alone-and-I-will-do-the-same kind of anonymity. Whereas the former type of community is generally more inward in orientation, due to circumstances the latter is more external (see Carol Stack's classic *All Our Kin* [1975] as an example, due to the intersection of race and class, of such an internal orientation in an urban minority setting, or *The Joyful Community* [1972] by Benjamin Zablocki on the insular Bruderhof farming community of North Dakota). Notice that in the new suburban housing developments, the homes have essentially no front porch unlike the row houses of earlier times. The modern middle-class lifeworld is insular at home, emitting life only by the mild glow of the computer screen, smartphone, or tv. Practically and symbolically, what does this say about public versus private, me versus you?

Mass urbanized societies are structured by rationalized, impersonal bureaucracy and mediated by individual corporatized rationality in both function and structure. There is a pronounced decline in civic consciousness and a deterioration of the public commons coupled with a self-serving ethos such as that found in Robert Putnam's research.[3] Affluence, income, and credit cards create an independence that operates to delink individuals from the need for community and dependence. When the "ontological security," as Giddens phrased it, is missing among strangers, Emile Durkheim's anomie or the breakdown of moral values and a loss of social connection arises. Contemporary social psychologists see this loss of connection in urban, mobile societies leading to various forms of dysfunctional behavior. To be fully human, a sense of self and place within a broader social scheme is of profound importance. If it is not a web of intimate community connection supported by symbolic and ritual representation, then the search for such will lead people in new and different directions: consumerism, social fundamentalism, destructive behavior, or medications.

The twenty-first century has witnessed the continuation of improvements in the standard of living for most Americans and many global citizens but with great and powerful problems that demand complex and difficult solutions. We have accomplished many amazing things and have developed tremendous power to transform the world and society, yet we seem uncertain where such achievements are taking us, into what kind of future. Too many people in advanced consumer societies are oriented inward personally and revolve around their material possessions or concern for presenting public status as the only things they can ostensibly control. The insecurity of status will propel people to think in terms of personal fate or how to meet the expectations of others rather than through collective outcomes and substantive thinking about the future.

This age of uncertainty and subtle anxiety reflects a lack of understanding of those social forces that impact our lives. People are mostly ill-equipped to critically analyze the parameters of their lives. Most information about who we are and what expectations and assumptions that inform our social being comes to us via media, advertising, ideologies of church, education, and entertainment. C. Wright Mills at the cusp of the hypermodern era, offered in his classic, *The Sociological Imagination*, an assessment of the meaning of rapid social change that it is difficult to come to terms with. He wrote,

> Nowadays men often feel that their private lives are a series of traps. They sense that within their everyday worlds, they cannot overcome their troubles. . . . What ordinary men are directly aware of and what they try to do are bounded by the private orbits in which they live; their visions and their powers are limited to the close-up scenes of job, family, neighborhood. (1959, 1)

Given this, most people do not perceive or understand the invisible forces that impact their lives and so vainly try to control something.

Our contemporary culture is influenced and educated more and more by the narrow logic of a marketplace that teaches us that our worth, identity, and value is found primarily in our service to the market through consumption and function and the production of lifestyle. If this is the case, as indeed many think it is, then we are not total or whole human beings, and have no time to think about the meaning of our humanity, and as such are lost and insecure with a limited ability to make sense of the world around us. Wisdom is not conferred by the marketplace or even found in the aesthetic of things but found in the outcomes and lessons of interpersonal experience and traditions enfolded in interdependent community and the rhythms of the natural world in which we walk and live. How can we work together if we are only taught to think in unreflective terms of our individual and autonomous selves in service to a neoliberal ideology that we are little more than aspects of production and consumption and essentially "wards" of the corporate state?

I LOST MY NARRATIVE SOMEWHERE IN LIQUID TIMES

It was the growth and complexity of globalization, technology, and corporate neoliberalism that pushed advanced society (and the rest of the globe in its wake) into the postmodern epoch that concerned Jameson and colleagues. This is the new world of fluid or hybrid cultures of constant change and movement, a period termed by the sociologist Zygmunt Bauman, "liquid times" instead of postmodern (2006). His basic thesis is that social arrangements and their meanings are in flux, de-anchored from history, and full of ambiguity, and less absolute. If this is the case, what happens to identity construction and the meaning behind whatever we construct? Manuel Castells has defined identity as "the process of construction of meaning on the basis of a cultural attribute, or a related set of cultural attributes, that is given priority over other sources of meaning" (2004, 6). The story of who we are is continuously built on a shifting series of attributes and perceptions, and so our narrative of self is reflexive and fraught with ambiguity. Thus, within cultures located in liquid times of constant flux, we find floating identities. As Bauman points out, under such flux comes anxiety and uncertainty, making a coherent life-project difficult if not impossible. He points out that our lives are transient and based more on ephemeral fashions, music, images, various media and entertainment, Baudrillard's simulacra, and our possessions rather than on stable values, norms, and institutions.

If this is the case, then all individuals have left is their ability and freedom to purchase and own material things in a vain attempt to define and represent themselves. The individual is now exposed to a bewildering variety of overlapping lifestyles, conceptual meanings, messages, and definitions so that it is hard to normalize the everyday world. Work as a significant element of the modern narrative, for example, was an activity of great meaning for one's sense of self. Work brought rewards, was recognized for its ability to confer merit, gave satisfaction, was often subjected to loyalty, and offered social mobility. Less and less does the meaning of work today provide a sense of security, enrichment, or solace. Most people work in corporate or market-oriented enterprises with little autonomy or control but under constant performance evaluations. Loyalty no longer exists due to market expediency. Thus, most people live for Verhaeghe's "survival weekend." Thus, the meaning of work has lost much of its power to help us define who we are. It is a world in the turmoil of recombination and hybridity. Does working for Kraken, a bitcoin exchange, or Facebook mean the same thing as it did working for IBM or a lineman for Westinghouse Steel in the 1950s? The social context of such a decentered work world lead, many social psychologists tell us, to pervasive feelings of insecurity and anxiety, as in "will there be a tomorrow."

Do I know who I am when I look at the iguana pitcher displayed in chapter 6 and can understand what the symbols are telling me? Does my knowledge about myself come from empirical evidence around me, as suggested by Descartes? What does it say about me, about you, about us? For the villager, the iguana has a unitary symbolic cultural meaning—a subtle philosophy of life—understood and shared by all members of that community. Can we in postmodern society and as sovereign individuality say the same thing about ourselves, about many of the things around us? We tend to live in subjective worlds with no grand or compelling master narrative to anchor or guide us. In a society that emphasizes and celebrates individuality, originality, and personal freedom, it is hard to find common agreement about symbolic representations such as, for example, the Statue of Liberty or E Pluribus Unum (proposed as the motto of the United States in 1776) since we approach from a multiplex of different perspectives, experiences, attitudes, and ideologies.

For most of human history, individuals made sense of the world through told stories and myths rather than facts and numbers. Narratives can help individuals find a sense of purpose and answers in life, a vision or worldview, but only if they feel it authentic and compelling. One traditional narrative of America was, as David Brooks explains in a *New York Times* column, the Exodus story. Settlers arrived and built a nation out of the endless wilderness, free, and self-sufficient. A new Canaan as promised by Providence. John Winthrop proclaimed that the future undertaking of the Massachusetts Bay colony would be looked at as "a city upon a hill," or as Ronald Reagan phrased it, a "shining city on a hill" (2017). This is the narrative of American exceptionalism, the fulfillment of human history, as Fukuyama's the "end of history." A narrative such as this provides a sense of certainty and allows citizens to coalesce around a national identity and destiny, a sense of who we are. In the contemporary era, this narrative is immersed within the context of modernity's trend toward liberalization, secularization, and the sanctity of individualism, but also includes a turning away from traditionalism. Marx and Engels, looking to the future, recognized the basic essence of modernity as a precursor to the postmodern world, writing in *The Communist Manifesto*, "All fixed, fast-frozen relations, with their train of ancient and venerable prejudices and opinions, are swept away, all new-formed ones become antiquated before they can ossify. All that is solid melts into air" (2010, 31; org. 1848).

In the information-saturated, technologically driven postmodern, liquid world, we are now overwhelmed by the flow of minutia and manifold bits of information that rarely fit a complete pattern that can act as a counternarrative. What counternarrative can accommodate in any personal satisfying way artificial intelligence, algorithms, dysfunctional political partisanship, or the social dysfunction around us? All this is beyond human experience or understanding. Stivers stresses that this leads to a "broken vision of the world," with little memory of history and thus, "It is not morally compelling in the way tradition is; hence, it is easily forgotten" (2004, 39). How to fill in the gaps? This broken vision suggests chaos while humans need order. As we discussed in the last chapter, consumerism and materialism function to offer something concrete and meaningful, giving us a clue to who we are. But is the offering substantive and satisfying psychologically?

Who am I? The psychoanalyst Paul Verhaeghe of Ghent University states that identity "has more to do with becoming than with being" and that in modern society the dynamic of becoming is an ongoing process of questioning (2014, 8). He suggests that much of our early social formation is being told what or how to feel and what to do about those feelings and later what we can or cannot do with ourselves. Here, the sense of self takes hold as we recognize the gaze of Mead's generalized others and begin to manifest self-consciousness. This idea of identity formation in relation to others, however, is like Marx's supposition that we are a product of our historical era. In less ideological vernacular, Verhaeghe shares Marx's conclusion, "Every identity stems from a coherent ideology, a term that I interpret very broadly as a collection of notions about human relationships and ways of regulating them" (26).

Much research among traditional indigenous communities suggests that such insights of interplay between individual and possibilities posed by Verhaeghe are not necessarily the case. In indigenous societies such as age-grade societies, the act of becoming *does* culminate in a social being with little room for variation, questioning, or exploration. There exists a certainty about the self as a social being. Prior to the great transformation, feudal Europe's social life was likewise stable and unquestioned: oneself was generally securely placed with a social structure of history, expectation, and essentially total. Of course, in these societies, people questioned their role or status or perhaps the received truths from their elders or experience. A different cultural-psychological dynamic was at work that substantively integrated the individual in terms of an emergent self and identity with that of Mead's "generalized other." Thinking of the emergent individual during this earlier era, he wrote,

> The attitude of the generalized other is the attitude of the whole community. Thus, for example, in the case of such a social group as a ball team, the team

> is the generalized other in so far as it enters—as an organized process or social activity—into the experience of any one of the individual members of it. (1934, 154)

This was due, he believed, to the intimate and intense social orientation found in, for example, public initiation ceremonies (rites of passage) that followed various forms of adult instruction into the myths, stories, and symbols of that society. It follows, then, by learning in accepted ways that one is integrated into the social process in ways quite like other social members. The "looking glass" upon which one gazed projected the same cultural–psychological persona to all members. The games that children play in traditional society are a form of representation of what they will be later in life, warrior or gardener, father, mother, and so forth. On the other hand, the games played in contemporary society may begin in kindergarten but soon advance to private play via iPad and video games.

Anne Straus's study of Northern Cheyenne ethnopsychology illustrates the overlap and reinforcing relationship between community and social identity. Cheyenne see behavior and the self located not in internal personality traits but rather in a community of social relationships. She writes,

> Within the tribe, they recognize an inalienable connection or relationship, that of blood/heart, which binds all Cheyenne together and renders them sensitive to each other. Because of this inalienable connection among Cheyenne, one's tribesmen have a certain claim on him, their needs and their actions being in some sense the motivating factors in one's own behavior. (1977, 333)

Straus adds that the individual's identity "cannot be understood in terms of the independent, morally autonomous individual" as found in mainstream American culture (355). Recognizing variation on a theme, it is suggested here that the Cheyenne experience is the sociocultural norm of premodern social history.

When did I lose my self, if I ever had a true self? In Western civilization, the social self found in indigenous, traditional cultures has been on a long slow journey toward sovereignty governed by Enlightenment thinking, secularism, and a new market-driven competitive achievement society. Expressing what many observers believe, Gerald Erchak writes in his book *The Anthropology of Self and Behavior* that a "self is not an actual thing that you can see and touch; it is a posited entity . . . a cultural construct." In the West, we are thought of as a unique self, "each person is different, special, never to exist again," an "active agent, the subject of experience" (1992, 8, 10). The Western idea of the self as changeable and pliant on social contexts can be considered, generally, dependent upon the normative expectations of social convention celebrating individuality, which itself is an ongoing process.

Philip Cushman describes an earlier Western shift from "personal moral integrity" based on religious character to a more modern secular conception of being outgoing, liked by others, and searching for personal fulfillment (1990, 602). The need now is impressing others for approval regardless of what might be the morally correct thing to do leads, he says, to the empty self, a decontextualized individual. If accurate, what kind of inner or psychological chaos ensues from such hollowness? In this case, we are constantly evaluating the need to fill this empty self and then, if necessary, change who we are based to a large extent, he believes, on meeting the inducements of advertising or social expectation.[4]

In America, at least, the post-World War II era brought forth, along with new technologies, affluence, and urbanism, a new self. As the family as a cohesive unit weakens, the individual naturally searches for self-actualization and one's potentialities independently, a process without end. It is here that advertising and marketers stepped in to help give content to this new self. The focus moves steadily toward the individual and away from family and community as individual growth, enjoyment, and fulfillment become significant priorities in life supported by new economic entities. These include "The cosmetics industry, the diet business, the electronic entertainment industry, preventive medical care, and the self-improvement industry (containing mainstream psychology, pop psychology, and pop religion) all came into prominence," Cushman believes to help deal with the anxiety of the empty self (604–605).[5]

Social identity theory proposes that identity comes through group social interactions in which we can have several identities, all dependent on group context and membership. What happens when the content and outcomes are conditioned on the interplay of utility, expediency, and the transitory nature of such group interactions? In other words, how stable and intimate are social groups today from which identity formation takes place given that presentations and impressions are now as much located in the fluid movement of digital communications or transitory interactions centered around me? Social groups themselves are located within a rolling traveling culture in an endless process of reinvention and reconstruction made easy and efficient in digital media and encouraged by the marketing of life. Current society, Lauren Langman believes, is a process of "unending spectacles and carnivals, fast food, faster technogadgets and a universalization of consumption; a society which provides ersatz gratifications in a fragmented world of everyday life that is situated in consumption-based routines and lifestyle" (1991, 108). As such, everyday life becomes theater. "This infiltration of mass-produced images has become an essential prop for the articulation of selfhood" (111).

Anthony Giddens goes beyond the interactions of the social group to recognize that experience outside the group has a role to play in the idea of self. He writes that forms of media entertainment such as television while offering escape also provide narratives, "suggesting models for the construction of narratives of the self" (1991, 199). TV programs "offer mixtures of contingency, reflexivity and fate." Giddens adds that these programs do not create aspirations to emulate conveyed television lifestyles but "stories are developed in such a way as to create narrative coherence with which the reader or viewer can identify" and find reassurance by bringing order to the world. Such viewership becomes a form of affirmative culture, as viewers are mollified by what might have once upset them and are offered ways of thinking about contradictions that smooth them over rather than inspire demands for change. Rather than television as a one-dimensional wasteland as many postmodernists see it, others may think of television as structurally similar to older means of myth and ritual, celebrating values and modes of thought leading to a degree of social order. This may be a valid point but what do we learn and how are we affected by this new socially displaced environment? In traditional society, myth, stories, and rituals generally form a coherent whole of narrative speaking to identity, values, and heritage through a common accepted grammar. Whereas at one point we sat around campfires to exchange stories and myth with elders and kin or as spectator listening to tribal elders debate under a baobab tree the merits of a transgression of values, today we sit around a private glowing screen of Facebook, Instagram, and Twitter and communicate within a decontextualized electronic nether world such as Snapchat.

Although research and debate continue over the social effects of social media on young people in particular, researchers such as Brian Primack and colleagues suggest a positive relationship between media use and social isolation among those at critical stages of social identity formation (2017). Social media usage is conducive under certain circumstances (home bound, physical, or mental impairment), but they believe that such use may increase "perceived social isolation," witnessing online people as happier, satisfied, and more connected to others. The result may be that one feels even more isolated by manipulated and unrealistic comparison. Primack and colleagues found in their research, "Finally, instead of accurately representing reality, social media feeds are in fact highly curated by their owners" (6). Who or what, then, to believe?

The changes taking place go beyond the role of technology in contemporary living. All aspects of social life, perception, and structure are affected by postmodern change. Today's families, for example, experience a variety of pressures from financial problems, two-parent occupations, personal technologies, and the changing nature of children growing up.[6] The postmodern family is no longer a "haven in a heartless world," considering that the family is no longer a citadel since the boundaries among home, work, and public life have weakened. Research by M. P. Baumgartner found that children spend considerable time outside a home composed of "loose-knit" relations, where "Family members spend much of their limited time together in passive entertainment, and parents go to great lengths to avoid conflict" (quoted in Stivers 2004, 18). Stivers adds that some see the modern family more akin to a motel composed largely of "moral minimalism" and consequently ambiguous. One could argue that as chauffeur for recreational activities (soccer being most popular today) and providing forms of emotional and physical sustenance, the modern family plays the *role* of family rather than *being* a family.

The family, has lost its centrality, giving way to domestic outsourcing, such as DoorDash for evening meals, of what generally took place within the family. Parenthetically, this social trend toward a weaker family form should not be too surprising. Westerners and Americans in particular are taught to consider themselves, as Clifford Geertz expressed,

> a bounded, unique, more or less integrated motivational and cognitive universe, a dynamic center of awareness, emotion, judgment, and action organized into a distinctive whole and set contrastively against both other such wholes and against a social and natural background. (1974, 31)

The sovereignty of the individual does not lend itself easily, with the help of technology, to the sense of community integration.

A culture's members are "brokers" in this sense, negotiating their integration into culture's norms and expectations even as the members' ideas about themselves are elements of broader cultural constructs. In other words, each individual gravitates toward meeting the appropriate behavior in predictable ways since cultures reward certain behaviors and punish others. More generally as Erchak puts it, "We crave *cosmos*, or order, and fear its evil twin, *chaos,*" that is, we need solid and objective reality found in accepted institutions (116). Erchak's comment reminds one of Peter Berger's "terrors of anomie." His view is that anyone who seeks radical change must offer alternative institutional order otherwise existential aloneness and doubt ensues. In a fragmented liquid culture, the individual's personality will likewise be damaged, considering that the individual is an expression of his/her culture. Whether it is a new economic system, natural disaster, or the stable and smooth social relationships governed by values of kinship or cooperation, over time human behavior will, for the most part, fall in line with the expectations of ideas and attitudes that a culture socializes its members into.

The fact that we live in complex, multifaceted, and mobile societies—traveling cultures, as it were—that are highly socially differentiated in occupation, class, culture, status, and education leads to different behaviors, values, and worldview. This multifaceted world leads modern people to existential thoughts of uncertainty among a process of constantly moving strangers, events, and even landscapes. The question is not only "who am I" but also what does it all mean—our lives, actions, motivations, and the things around us? As confusion sets in regarding the relativism or arbitrariness of everyday conventions, Giddens offers that the chaos, Berger's terror, that threatens "can be seen psychologically as dread . . . the prospect of being overwhelmed by anxieties that reach to the very roots of our coherent sense of 'being in the world'" (1991, 37).

The nation, political ideology, labor markets, and even religious institutions provided stable scripts upon which to develop one's dramaturgical self, and in Giddens's parlance, putting one, however tentatively, in the world of identifiable authority and stable narrative. The characteristics of modern society is a belief in reason, science, and a patterned progress into the future. Brian Ott, thinking about postmodern identity, writes that this circumstance created the rational individual in which identity arose from faith in a circumscribed set of roles and norms within a community or nation state. Such stable identity scripts and the meaning of the enduring institutions and dynamics of life were the anchors of regularity on which to create an identity and accepted prescribed roles, one that may have multiple aspects to it depending upon which stage one entered to engage society. That is until the late twentieth century.

The American narrative of success remains the mantra, if somewhat in doubt today. Many still hesitantly believe the idea that no matter how well off we might be, the future for our children will be better, brighter, and more satisfying. However, doubt and precariousness add to the feelings of insecurity of class position, racism, and tentative social status. This is profound and realistic, especially in such a relative, changing world. Jock Young recognizes the significance of this situation writing,

> Although such a feeling of unsteadiness permeates the structure of society, it is particularly marked in the middle classes . . . those whose lifestyle . . . is so dependent on standard of living. Here fear of falling is fear of total loss of everything—it threatens their loss of narrative, of a sense of modernity where life involves personal progress in career, in marriage, and in the community they choose to live in. (2007,13)

If the old narratives no longer fit the new "liquid" world, what new narrative will replace it since narrative is an essential aspect of the set of scripts telling us and others who we are? The new master narrative may be nothing more than as someone once phrased it in a play on postmodernism, "one damn thing after another," that is, a jumbling of images and impressions without any internal coherence, "of broken narratives and unhinged structures: of a fragmented world where space and culture no longer coincide" (175).[7] There appears to be a relativistic subjectivity to narrative today. But, nevertheless, a narrative must exist as a guidepost for the identity orientation of today's social participants. It appears that given the political and social flux, there are competing narratives, increasingly cynical, nihilistic, and reactionary in their proscriptions. The new narratives under our consumer culture are a smorgasbord, where we pick and choose what we want from social media, orthodoxy, and/or political ideology.

In such a social reality, Young asks, "How, conceivably, can social cohesion and a personal sense of coherence occur in such a fissile world of fragmentation and division?" (176). In a world of hypermobility of thought, values, and norms, who are the contemporary storytellers and "sand painters" of the postmodern world? Who writes the new narrative and tells the story not only of who we are but what we are? Of course, the new social scripts related to our identity and projection of self require a new set of stage props. It is under these psychosocial conditions that a whole industry of self-help and empowerment books has developed alongside Hollywood. Individuals need to take charge of their personal development and "own their power." Books such as *Relentless: From Good to Great to Unstoppable* by Tim Grover focus on the self-interested pursuit of success or *Year of Yes* by Shonda Rhimes that will help you to be your own person. The scripts that make the smorgasbord being written are found in advertising and technology companies, promoted by various media, self-help/fulfillment gurus, and personal desires and encouraged by political-economic interests. It is a search for something we should not have to search for.

Ott makes the point that media can support our identity circumstances by presenting a reality we recognize and accept as valid. Ott uses the example of the TV show, *The Simpsons*, to illustrate this point (2003). The Simpson family is dysfunctional and contains irreverent personal relationships within and outside the family. In the same early years of *The Simpsons*, TV's most popular show, *The Cosby Show*, lost popularity and soon was cancelled. Ott quotes Todd Gitlin's assessment that the cancellation of *The Cosby Show* happened because "[it was] becoming harder to get an audience to believe in family fairyland" (ibid, 59). The Cosbys no longer reflected a reality prevalent in more and more American families: families fractured by weaker interpersonal relations due to technology, outside demands on family members, and growing personal autonomy. *The Simpsons*, on the other hand, may not be a socializing model but the show does mirror a given reality and thus some sort of validation for those caught up in the fragmented world of the modern American family. Ott further points out that viewers can "learn to fashion their identities by watching popular charctersis fashion theirs" providing a truncated TV-based narrative (58).

If the self is contingent and multifaceted and expresses itself according to a set of scripts including associated props, from where do scripts and employed props emanate? Belk and Pollay describe advertising quoting John Berger, "an attempt to make us envious of the selves we might become if only we acquire the product or service advertised" (1985, 394). This feeds into the ideas of consumption for material possession: "advertising attempts to link a sense of self to what we have or what we do. Since the self concept is abstract, having and doing provide tangible evidences of who we are" (ibid). The German psychoanalyst Siegried Zepf adds that at one point advertised products had an instrumental value but today it is experiential values that are most significant (such as Bart or Lisa Simpson). "Commodities are no longer offered solely as a means of meeting certain material requirements; they are now advertised to satisfy needs that are independent of their material usability," and attempt to symbolically fulfill hidden desires (2009, 145).[8] Advertising offer the promise of a better me in a more exciting world if I only partake in buying and using the props. But I submit, this does not negate or supplant social identity theory that posits the interplay between group members in the formation of identity. All social and network members are part of the advertising age, the skepticism of institutions, and the uncertainty of belief in weakened master narratives that no longer provide legitimation or explanation of social history or social function, something advertising cannot overcome. So, we look to each other in non-comprehending ways to determine who we are and what our self-concept and identity might be.

THE REPUBLIC OF FEAR AND THE CONSUMPTION OF DESPAIR

What has this new era of materialism, technology, and advertising wrought beyond insular comfort for some and elusive success or happiness for others? Postmodernists suggest that we live in an age of fear and that there appears to be no permanency and no balance between things and is nothing more than a game of musical chairs of things no longer understood. The perception by many is that we are spinning out of control. In this age of anxiety, of fear, R. Nicholas Carleton, a psychologist at the University of Regina, sees the "fundamental fear" as the fear of the unrevealed. The "one fear to rule them all" as he put it is fear of the unknown, defined as "an individual's propensity to experience fear caused by the perceived absence of information at any level of consciousness" and uncertainty seen as missing or absence of pertinent information in need of answering (2016, 5). Carleton lists a series of criteria outlining conditions of fundamental fears but of interest here that he refers to as FNE (fear of negative evaluation), or fear of how others perceive or judge, especially in negative terms, and how one avoids such appraisals (10). In a competitive and changing world of strangers, the public presentation of one's persona is fraught with danger of not living up to expectations, especially through social media. Is it any wonder that Americans suffer from greater proportions of emotional and physical disorders than found in other affluent societies? From a sociocultural point of view, the one fear—the anxiety it provokes—that rules them all is the fear of the lack of control in one's life, family, and society. Such fear and lack of control, for example, leads many of today's young college students to seek psychological help from anti-depressants and anxiety medication.

Graham Davey, a professor of psychology at the University of Sussex, tells us that along with traditional sources of anxiety such as loneliness and lack of control over ourselves, new sources increase our problem. Most individuals have 24-hour connectivity via smartphones, computers allowing for multitasking, and incessant troubling news notifications. With more and more homes interconnected, including TVs, garage, front doors, and refrigerators, we must be ever alert for hacking, scams, and identity theft. In these daily concerns, Davey sees a world of hassles, anxiety, and fear (2018). Another word for what Davey describes is chaos and disorganization, a topsy-turvy world of fake news, increasing lack of faith in sociopolitical institutions, random violence, and the implications of technology such as artificial intelligence (AI) beyond our grasp. It is largely not that we cannot control, but that we do not even understand that which we cannot control. How does one live in such a world?

What, in essence, do modern individuals control? Possibly nothing or no more than we ever did, considering the strong and often hidden social forces at work, but given a sense of social stability we at least deluded ourselves that we did control our lives. Employment is now transitory and insecure, people argue along with polarized political parties over the relative merits of values and institutions, norms are questioned, subject to domination by bureaucratic rules, regulations, and rigidity that has robbed social life of spontaneity—Max Weber's disenchantment, and the growing impersonality of mass society—none of these do we control. Likewise, seemingly new problems and challenges are now very pronounced such as food insecurity, lack of affordable housing, random acts of mass violence, what is fake and what is "real," terrorism both foreign and domestic, and increasing variety of substance abuse. There appears to be no escape from the subtle chaos surrounding us. Perhaps in earlier times these elements were not controlled either but along with intact or believable master narratives, people could entertain a fantasy that they could control the social environment surrounding their lives.[9] Daily incessant communications technology in our lives no longer afford us any degree of isolation from these issues.

As we surround ourselves with technology and information (the new algorithms of modern life), a new uninvited reality sets in. We slowly but gradually distance ourselves from real intimate social relationships, history, and the physical world. Friends on Facebook, Snapchat, or X substitute for real physical friends; we twitter in 280 words our thoughts and feelings about events around us; and texting is the "best" way to communicate. The inner core of the brave new technology world is a growing loneliness and fear of intimacy.[10] In his study of loneliness, Stivers believes technology abstracts and impersonalizes human relations, conditioned by a sense of a lack of power or meaning in things we have trouble comprehending. "Technology is simultaneously the paramount organizing and disorganizing force in modern societies, it provides a unity in the technological system but leaves in its wake cultural fragmentation," he adds (2004, 142). Ellul understood and foresaw this cultural cul-de-sac. He wrote in the 1960s that modern humankind has been captured by its technology from which there is "no exit," only endurance and dread. There is, he believes, no way to recapture the "ancient milieu" of intimate, bonded community reliant upon its own talents and virtues. The result of the world we now inhabit is that, Ellul concludes, "The further the technical mechanism develops that allows us to escape natural necessity, the more we are subjected to artificial technical necessities" (429). He feared that technology most do not understand would entail a domination of over humanity and social life. Thinking of the role of technology in our lives today, Ellul, writing before artificial intelligence, was percipient stating that we no longer have technology "out there," but is integrated in our lives and will at some point absorb us. What would Ellul think if he could today experience the virtual reality of Zuckerberg's metaverse through the Horizon headset or AI?

Harvard sociologist Robert Putnam published in 2001 *Bowling Alone*, asserting that civil society in the United States is withering away or atrophying as more and more Americans disengage in any substantive manner from community, a several generations growth in the deterioration of civic commitment and the nature and depth of social networks among people. While civic engagement has waxed and waned throughout American history, Putnam adds, the last third of the twentieth century has witnessed civic members pulling apart from one another, less active participation, and more passive spectatorship (2001, 27). Putnam sees the last third of the twentieth century a turning point away from a deep engagement in our communities to a "shelter in place" attitude, a degree of loneliness even though we all stream the same television programs.

The 2021 American Perspectives Survey conducted by Daniel Cox found a growing weakening in social networks, especially close friendships. The major results were increasing rates of social isolation and loneliness due to the decline in the number and quality of close friends. In 1990, 3 percent reported no close friends while the recent survey found 21 percent with no close friends. Thirty-one years ago, 27 percent reported three or fewer close friends. By 2021, the percentage of three of fewer close friends increased to 49 percent of the respondents. About 50 percent of the respondents reported losing touch with a least a few good friends over the past year and 22 percent say that they have not made a new friend in the last five years (Cox, 2021, 2–5; see also McPherson, Smith-Lovin and Brashears 2006). Cox suggests that this decline is not only due to the covid pandemic but also due to structural factors such as geographic mobility, longer work hours, and spending more time with parents. However, during the pandemic, many have also reported making a new friend but primarily online.

It is possible that as the world becomes more alienating and distant it also becomes more frightening, causing people to bunker down in their insular homes connected to the outside world more and more through the enticement of technology. Writing on the *Psychology Today* blog, Peter Gray, a research professor at Boston College, sees one outcome of such fear protective parents who shelter their children from the vagaries of life and work hard to solve for their children the problems and obstacles they confront, known as helicopter parents (2015). Such parents may, ironically, in the end induce in their children anxiety, high levels of narcissism, and an inability to cope with the stresses of life's problems.

The fear and insecurity that pervades our lives manifests in various forms of unfocused resistance. Bruce Levine, a clinical psychologist, sums up this resistance in a recent blog posted on *Salon*. He wrote,

> The reality is that with enough helplessness, hopelessness, passivity, boredom, fear, isolation and dehumanization, we rebel and refuse to comply. Some of us rebel by becoming inattentive. Others become aggressive. In large numbers we eat, drink and gamble too much. Still others become addicted to drugs, illicit and prescription. Millions work slavishly at dissatisfying jobs, become depressed and passive aggressive, while no small number of us can't cut it and become homeless and appear crazy. (2013)

His research concludes that depression and anxiety are growing by-products of such ineffective, futile, and unfocused resistance and, many might add, alienation and loneliness. As Chinua Achebe once remarked, borrowing from William Butler Yeats's *The Second Coming*, things fall apart if the center no longer holds. With the complexity of life and the uncertainty it holds, to continue Yeats, "Mere anarchy is loosed upon the world, the blood-dimmed tide is loosed, and everywhere the ceremony of innocence is drowned" (1989, 200).

Yeats's sentiment is not new. By the early years of the twentieth-century capitalism's effects on culture were increasingly obvious. Published in 1920, *The Acquisitive Society* was R. H. Tawney's criticism concerning changes advanced by the market economy and its focus on the ownership of property, especially the growth of the desire for the acquisition of material goods. Individuals in such a society, Tawney believed, produced, "The motive . . . not the attempt to secure the fulfillment of tasks undertaken for the public service, but to increase the opportunities open to individuals of attaining the objects which they conceive to be advantageous to themselves" (2004, 29).

> By fixing men's minds, not upon the discharge of social obligations, which restricts their energy . . . but upon the exercise of the right to pursue their own self-interests, it offers unlimited scope for the acquisition of riches. (30)

Tawney recognized that the economy produced inequality and wealth to the detriment of society concluding,

> So long will part of the human energy and mechanical equipment of the nation be diverted from serious work, which enriches it, to making trivialities, which impoverishes it, since they can only be made at the cost of not making other things (38)

But in a world of limited access to institutional power, where control over one's life is haphazard at best and where the sociocultural confusions over identity and social place exist, it may be the trivialities that offer a sense of (futile) meaning.

Are our relationships less intimate and more acquaintance based? A study of social isolation over the past two decades by McPherson, Smith-Lovin, and Brashears suggests a shrinking social network of individuals to confide in. The research led them to conclude that broader networks have diminished, replaced by dense, centered ties to spouses and partners. What used to bind to larger networks have narrowly focused on a core grouping. Even among the family, a core group, evidence suggests less strong ties than twenty years ago. Computers and the Internet are partially the reason, promoting individualism as many spent significant time on technological platforms (2006). Such a change is expected by those who see a contrast between the modern and post-modern family. David Elkind, for instance, conceived of the postmodern family as "permeable" and "porous" with less well-defined boundaries between parent–child, public–private life, and home–workplace unlike the standardized family of the 1950s. The outcome is a greater degree of autonomy, whereby "each family member pursues his or her own interests and put these interests before those of the family." Furthermore, Elkind considers "The home and the social relationships that inform it have changed and are no longer the refuge or haven (if it ever was; see *The Way We Never Were* by Stephanie Coontz [2000]) but more like a busy railway station with people coming in for rest and sustenances before moving out on another track" (1995, 13).

In *The Homeless Mind*, Berger et al. describe that one of the family's varied functions was providing life planning since in modern society there are so many choices to confront a pluralization of social lifeworlds. There is a pluralization of subjective meanings to choose the life plan relating to identity, a basic organizing principle that presupposes a degree of stability in family relationships, meanings, and communication. They do caution, however, a degree of instability and unreliability accompanying a "certain loss of reality" as modern society undergoes change (1974, 73, 74). Catching the scent of the approaching transit to postmodern society, the moral imperatives of individual freedom and rights that are taken as a birthright. The consequence of these "moral imperatives" is a growing indifference to a cohesive social identity followed by a decline in any solidarity ethos of commonwealth but instead a growing self-determination. Ultimately, without a deep sense of permanence, in Berger's parlance the modern consciousness becomes homeless.

For instance, schools today emphasize the importance of self-esteem rather than adjustment. The educational system, Elkind argues, has changed as well.

> The new focus on self-esteem makes it clear that competition and individual achievement take precedence over social adjustment. Self-esteem is . . . critical to success . . . reflects . . . family value of autonomy and the need of each individual to be able to go it alone if necessary. (14)

Positive self-esteem is now seen by many as a basic right of all individuals, that promoting one's self-esteem will make one less anxious or frustrated and therefore happier (as self-help books proclaim).

Media's messages can be thought of as a form of pedagogy that teaches us how to comport ourselves as individuals, how to dress and act, and what to consume. As Ott observed, media project what constitutes our accepted culture to use as a guideline to behavior. The focus on important values is glamorized and presented as elements of idealized lifestyles or the general expectations of conventional social arrangements (e.g., how germ free is your kitchen? and what model car do you drive?) that go beyond gender, race, or class. The power of such ideas works to the benefit of those with the ability to promote it. For example, the credit card de-links the individual from dependency upon family and kinship and creates instead allegiance to the issuing bank and concern over one's credit score. This new relationship between the individual and various institutions robs the individual of his/her biography and replaces it with numbers (i.e., social security, credit card, etc.) that fit nicely into various algorithms.

CANNOT BUY ME LOVE: MATERIALISM, THE INDIVIDUAL, AND HAPPINESS

In 1931, Aldous Huxley wrote about a future dystopian society governed by hedonistic impulses, a social hierarchy founded on scientifically based reproduction, and a cheerful yet meaningless consumerism underpinned with drugs and sex. Clearly, *Brave New World* was written as a negative reaction to the call for a technological and consumer-based utopia found during a trip to the United States. Coming from the same era yet writing many years later, Eric Fromm acknowledged Huxley's novelistic trend. Fromm considered the situation today, in *The Art of Loving*, composed of "having fun," which "lies in the satisfaction of consuming and 'taking in' commodities, sights, food, drinks, cigarettes, people, lectures, books, movies—all are consumed, swallowed." This amounts to the "world [as] one great object for our appetite . . . the eternally expectant ones, the hopeful ones—and the eternally disappointed ones." Disappointed, Fromm believed that this amounts to "alienated automatons" who are "utterly alone, pervaded by the deep sense of insecurity, anxiety and guilt" (1956, 73, 72). The environment which provoked Fromm's assessment of the modern human condition has only become more pronounced since he wrote those words.

Several polls and studies have been conducted that examine the relationship between wealth and happiness. Many of these studies find a positive correlation between well-being and affluence. In many cases, respondents responded positively to the statement that more money would improve the quality of life (Myers 2000a; 2000b, 58). However it is phrased—happiness, satisfaction, and well-being—many people believe on the one hand that having more money will lead to a greater sense of being happy with life. Yet other studies find greater ambiguity if not an inverse relationship between greater affluence and well-being. Unfortunately, the consumer can never live up to the idealized media images that confront us or that advertised products or lots of money can make life better and the consumer ultimately happier.[11] Of course, in comparison to the ideal image presented, the consumer finds him/herself painfully inadequate. Media offers representations of ourselves that we can never emulate. Thus, in our search for happiness and contentment in the consumption of things what we generally find is disappointment, unhappiness, and the vague sense that in our lives something is missing. Regardless of what the advertisement suggests, we will never be so thin, pretty, content, or successful no matter how much of the offered product we consume or what our friends say. As social isolation continues to take hold, anxiety about success and happiness increases but especially among heavy social media users (Primack, et al., 2017).

In the world we have constructed, it is hard to ignore the enticements of advertising to improve our lives through consumption. Most individuals in society cannot help but internalize the prescriptions of wealth, success, and consumption. The significance of the family is its potential to provide a loving, warm environment that encourages abilities and self-assurances to attain important goals in life. This is, Kasser says, where self-esteem is generated but such warm and love are problematic today as the structure of the family and relationships undergoes change. There are several social forces that impact the health of the family dynamic. If capitalist society is founded on consuming, then buying, making money, and seeing the monetary worth of things can lead to viewing people the same way. Competition, possessing, and the need for achievement shapes and limits our subjective understanding of others and of ourselves. People become less than what they can be and more what they need to be to be successful and meet family or society's expectations. Fromm's judgment that love is required for good mental health is more conditional or transactional than in previous times. Based on his research on the negative social effects of materialism, Kasser warns that "your spouse may not care as much as you might hope about expressing his or her appreciation for you, about helping you, or about being loyal, responsible, honest and forgiving" (87). It might, he adds, be more about bolstering the partner's self-esteem or getting ahead in life than about you. Kasser's comment reminds one of a quote by Dave Ramsey, "We buy things we don't need with money we don't have to impress people we don't like."

We have discussed earlier how parents are distracted by technology or the changing nature of the parent–child relationship (i.e., helicopter parents, best friends rather than authority figure, etc.). But this also includes the heavy brunt of racism and discrimination to thwart ability and ambition to create a psychology of despair among those disenfranchised. This includes the no-nonsense survival strategies of low-income, overwrought parents working multiple jobs trying to make ends meet. While Stephanie Coontz remarked that the Leave-it-to-Beaver family is a myth, well-adjusted modern families of all varieties are under stress and the distraction of social–economic uncertainty. To fill any potential void of low self-esteem and self-doubt, advertising offers its services via social media and pop psychology to serve up self-help books or distractions from the endless everyday trauma of life.

Research by Kasser and others examined low versus high self-esteem with those of low self-esteem gravitating toward materialistic values (2004, 48–49). Rather than view self-esteem as a binary opposition, esteem runs along a continuum from low to high with most people falling somewhere around the middle of the range. Kasser suggests that other issues surrounding the sense of self-esteem are the discrepancies faced in life. Kasser defines discrepancy as a "function of how far they are from who, what, or where they ideally would like to be" and can apply to our "bodies, personalities, and relationships" (51). Will a tattoo make one more masculine/feminine, alluring, or cool? Is it realistic to think so? Advertising plays a significant and manipulative role in creating or exacerbating these discrepancies by trying to convince that they proclaim the important values, social trends, and standards of society—and have the goods to support such trends and standards—that are constantly changing in the postmodern, liquid world.

Our material objects are used to proclaim who we are in various circumstances. If we do not have close kinfolk, a tight knit community, or intimate personal relationships to help us understand who we are, then props (dead nonsymbolic things) become quite meaningful as personal signs of significance. In general, such props are all most people have. These props are not like the Mexican water pitcher that was intentionally designed to signify lineage, heritage, and a deeper cultural meaning. Material possession is not necessarily linked to issues of self-esteem but to the broader associated conception of identity. In the conclusion of her edited book, *I Shop, Therefore I Am*, April Lane Benson makes the point of how intimate and personal shopping can be. She writes, "To shop is to taste, touch, sift, consider, and talk our way through myriad possibilities as we try to determine what it is we need or desire." Importantly, "Shopping is an interactive process through which we dialogue not only with people, places, and things, but also with parts of ourselves" (2000, 502). Rather than shopping and owning as a frantic search for meaning and control, Benson sees shopping for things as a search for "the external reflections of interior substance" (511). What is problematic regarding reflections of the interior substance is the problem of the empty self that concerned Bauman, Marcuse, and Giddens: what is there to reflect but the aspirations promoted by either anxiety, uncertainty, or the dream world of advertising.

Are only fragile or unstable low-esteem individuals susceptible to these messages? Most people of higher income and education generally surround themselves with material goods that are compatible and proclaim a particular status. These objects act as props for displaying who we are, the social statuses we tentatively hold. Why do I buy a Rolex watch? Because advertising tells me that it is a mark of success and accomplishment. In other words, I confront an external standard of success not necessarily of my own subjective making. Self-esteem, in this case, is "contingent." Kasser defines contingent as a "people's sense of worth [that] depends on meeting particular external standards" (2002, 49). Yes, family is important but as it recedes in our lives, it is replaced by more instrumental or impersonal secondary relationships in which our props become important public symbols of who we present we are.

In the opening paragraph of his edited volume, *Identity Destabilised*, Eriksen offers a litany of the problem of identity in the world of technology, globalization, and capitalism. Where is the modern identity if it is not an inborn trait, as Mead once asked? Is it found in cultural creolization, the politics of identity, hybrid identities, class identity, and intersectionality? In a multicultural environment of rapid change, enumerable categories of personal preference, and presentations in enumerable situations, how can a person truly know who she or he really is? If we live in a shifting world of demands and options, where history is not linked to our present sense of being, where do I find myself?[12] Eriksen, thinking about such issues, writes,

> The work of tracing a line connecting the past to the future, via the present, in a compelling and meaningful way, is easy when there is just repetition, but difficult when these is no clear script relating the past to the future, not story of either continuity or development which is persuasive. (2016, 3–4)

We are, today, essentially on our own.

In both the premodern and early modern era, one's social identity and self was understood and meaningful in a consensus of broad public recognition, that is, group membership and the group rituals and celebrations it entertained. Many Eastern European and Mediterranean dances, for example the *kalamatianos* of Greece, are choreographed in a circle with dancers holding hands or arms linked. The social function of such dances is to express social solidarity and community togetherness, to express an identity shared by all. These dances function in this way because humans are first and foremost social animals. In many traditional West African communities, young boys would be, after being educated into manhood, publicly circumcised as a group (Bohannon 1954; Turner 1967). This was a rite of passage into adulthood, recognized and celebrated by the kindred and community. All boys shared a common identity reflected in each other and sanctified by the community.

Through social interaction with others, we construct ourselves with the building blocks offered by our culture. In earlier indigenous communities, a narrative of kinship obligation and ancestors gave one a location of who they were, an essentialism of being. Today, social status absolutes have given way to degrees of relativism, autonomy, and a sense of "on my own." That is, to be who I want to be but, in essence, imagery without content. Traditionally, since an individual's "structure of his experience in one sphere of life is repeated throughout his experiences in other spheres of life," including meaningful objects, it adds to a completeness of a sense of self. But if those experiences no longer adhere to a particular context, then in this way "conscious life may become 'thin and meagre,' focused as it is upon symbols which are not particularly congenial to it" (Goffman 1959, 98).

Most scholars discuss the relationship between possessions and identity in this functional framework. Some such as Csikszentmihalyi and Rochberg-Halton, in contrast, believe that some individual material acquisitions, referred to as "terminal" materialism, are nothing more than possessions for their own sake, as an end goal (Schrum, et al. 2012, 1183). Tim Kasser also dichotomizes materialism between intrinsic versus extrinsic goals, the latter closely aligned with terminal materialism. Terminal or extrinsic goals reflect a search for happiness, which Schrum and colleagues consider inimical in the long run to one's self-esteem and relations with others. Kasser points out that many social scientists agree that a focus on materialism generally comes at the expense of social relationships (Stivers would agree but adds that it is technology in general that move us away from such relationships (2002). Thinking about consumption, spending, and wealth, Kasser's research concludes that this leads to treating others like objects, which culminates in alienation, or an inability of collective orientation, thus unhappiness (67). Objectivization as such increases an instrumental tendency to use others to bolster one's status or image. Social media such as Facebook present a perfect means using technology as a counterpoint to accomplish the same goals. If happiness is found in the caliber of intimate social relationships, can material possessions act as a proxy for relationship? This question may take on greater significance depending on circumstances such as loneliness, the sacrifice of family for career, and so forth. A growing consensus among social scientists such as Kasser responds with no, there can be no substitute.

One public marker of achievement and status is the display of the things owned such as the Rolex. "Possessions anchor and stabilize identity in space as they configure the world into a place of belonging" (Bardhi et al., 2012, 511). The things owned play both an instrumental and symbolic role in proclaiming status or supporting self-esteem while signaling superficial group membership (living up to the norms of society to consume) as means to deal with the uncertainty of Bauman's liquid times. On a positive note, possessions can provide certainty through common acceptance of the objects' meaning by those around us. But what that Rolex signifies is relative in that it means very different things to different people, from success to vanity or pride to ostentation. "In a desire for certainty about self," Micken and Roberts believe, "[individuals] continue to rely on and require the feedback which comes from others. One approach to ensuring the desired feedback is through the possession and use of objects whose meanings are unambiguous," such as the Mexican pitcher (1999, 514). They agree with Schrum et al. (2012), Chang and Arkin (2002), and Bardhi et al. (2012) that the primary function of possessions is the diminution of uncertainty through group recognition and acceptance of the symbolic meaning of possessions. Certainty relies on unambiguous understanding, yet in the postmodern world individuals cannot rely on memory or assumptions since they may be ambiguous or carry only temporary residence in our thoughts or actions. Some material things have a greater chance of agreed upon meaning and thus make the individual feel more secure. However, the problem is that with constant change, culturally and socially, things likewise shift and change meaning or significance, or just fall out of fashion. Thus, the need to ever possess and consume more stuff or at least different stuff provides some sort of constant in our subjective lives.

Helga Dittmar also believes that possessions relate to our sense of a personal and social identity. Dittmar offers an incident in which when suggested that a person would look good in a particular fashion the individual responded, "that's just not me." She comments further a point we all understand, "Clothes are seen as the outer skin of our personality and identity" (1992, 41). These things we own take on a fetish-like quality of significance being regarded part of the self. Possessions also, research suggests to Dittmar, provide "evaluative evidence" of self-esteem and sense of well-being (47). But there is a caveat as discussed earlier. McCracken, she acknowledges, writes that experiences and identities are social constructs but perceived by people as "possessable." In a society that highly values individualism, identities and experiences "have become 'things' that can be accumulated in the same way one accumulates material possessions, with the belief that our lives are enhanced in proportion to what we gather around us" (107). Identities are not commodities to be bought and worn like a pair of new shoes and does not lead to happiness or any long-term sense of fulfillment and satisfaction but rather anxiety and uncertainty as clothing styles undergo constant change.

It is an orientation and desire for material needs beyond the contours of social relationships or spirituality or needs. Both Dittmar and Zepf ask when did this desire or need for things develop? Zepf clearly sees early childhood development as increasingly devoid of close parental intimacy pushing children toward greater relationships with objects (2010, 147–148). Referring to Winnicott's idea of *transitional object*, Dittmar comments that cuddly toys provide, on the one hand, a sense of comfort and security, while on the other, a role in the "beginning development of a self—other distinction: the cuddly is perceived partly as self and partly as belonging to the environment" (1992, 48). Initially, young children use possessions as expressions of "individuality and self-awareness" rather than an emblematic of an innate need of acquisitiveness (50). As children grow, as with adults, they use possessions both instrumentally as a means to exercise power and control over others, but possessions also provide symbolic importance for personal interests, security, and various sorts of interpersonal relationships (63). Material possessions provide a conduit to developing early in childhood a sense of autonomous self-identity. Possessions provide concrete evidence of who they think or want to be, but do they make us happy?

In 1974, Richard Easterlin famously posited in his paper, "Does Economic Growth Improve the Human Lot?," that increasing the average income did not increase the average happiness and satisfaction, a claim that became known as the Easterlin Paradox. In the complex uncertain world we inhabit, it is no small matter to ask how happy we as a society are. Advertising works hard to convince us that a constant flow of new and improved consumer goods will bring happiness and satisfaction in our lives to our doorstep. Easterlin and those who followed after him suggest that advertising's message is but a false promise playing on our dreams and desires. If advertising image reflects only our desires, then, as Jhally recognizes, "we have only the pleasure of the images to sustain us in our actual experience with goods. The goods thus offer self-validation which consequently emphasize what is possessed rather than what one *is*." That is, from Jhally's perspective, we need to distinguish between *having* and *being*, with the latter now defined through the former (2003, 252). Out of this dynamic, Jhally believes advertising is akin to the supernatural, where commodities identities are magically formed. Out of the rarified air of advertising, we are convinced that anything is possible with the purchase of stuff. The image–world dynamic induces us to believe that life's satisfaction can only be found through the marketplace since, as we have argued, there is essentially nowhere else to go. It may be that the object itself does not necessarily have to be the focal point of happiness but can be a conduit to things that are. A cold beer, advertisers understand, can suggest sexuality or male fraternity or adventure and daring, but always do so by offering a vision or promise. It may not be the cold beer that is important but that it can help get you where you need to be.

In our ever-changing world of fast-paced images, including a liquid cultural landscape of norms, values, and assumptions, the false promise of consumerism is the temporarity of things. Here lies the great irony of consumerism: we can never truly be happy nor find meaningful satisfaction from the ownership of things in such fluid, transitory circumstances. Many researchers have found that materialism and hyper-consumption lead to dissatisfaction and negative feelings of well-being (Kasser 2002; Kasser and Ryan 1993; Roberts and Clement 2007; Super 2007). Those who are materialist-oriented and engage in consumerism far beyond their needs engage in high expectations beyond what those possessions can do for one's satisfaction. Kasser's research suggests that such extrinsic goals as acquisition, image, and status are less satisfying in part due to unrealistic expectations about what those things actually do (2002). Richins's study on possession and expressions of self indicates that those high in materialist orientation describe greater benefits than those low in materialist aspirations. Richins concludes, "It appears that materialistic consumers have greater expectations of what a desired object can do for them than do those low in materialism" (1999, 87). High materialists considered the utilitarian value of objects that enhance their status. In contrast, those low-materialist respondents expressed enjoyment or comfort with the objects or their sentimental value. In conclusion, Richins's research found

> materialists place a higher importance on possessions when judging themselves and others. . . . Thus, they are more likely to use possessions to transmit

information about themselves, and also to decode the status or identity of others through their possessions, than are those low in materialism. (89)

But such satisfaction is often temporary and illusional.

Our discussion has implied but Richins makes explicit David Riesman's depiction of American character as other-directed. Other-directed individuals look to those around them for guidance regarding goals, values, and expression. "An other-directed person pays close attention to the signals from others to determine how s/he should act; s/he has 'an exceptional sensitivity to the actions and wishes of others,'" quoting Riesman (95). Thus, such persons are "acutely aware that they are judged by their external selves (which include their possessions); and, being guided by these others, they are likely to adopt the same standards of judging" (ibid). They are, in essence, inauthentic beings and herein lies uncertainty. Such a psychological disposition feeds into the consumerist ideology promoted by corporate advertising and expressed by those around us. Objects become nothing more than elements in impression management and the presentation of self.

Chang and Arkin point out that their research indicates such fluidity can make one's wealth and possession inadequate that, "In short, materialistic pursuits are essentially endless . . . one cannot afford to stay stagnant while others continue to increase wealth and acquisitions" (2002, 393). In agreement with other researchers such as Kasser, they add that motivations for material acquisition are undertaken to overcome feelings of anomie and self-doubt under conditions of a weak normative structure. The material markers encouraging such consumption patterns are also under constant change and revision, meaning that the individual must constantly strive for more and better possessions. This compares to intrinsic goals or values that focus on comfort, personal growth, and helping others through close connection. "The belief that success can be quantified and determined by explicit material possessions provides one potential norm in their otherwise seemingly normless existence," Chang and Arkin note (404).

As research tends to suggest, the imagined community centered around material possession and ever-consuming consumption has created a false sense of satisfaction and happiness. The competitive demands to succeed and publicly proclaim one's success through displays of material ownership come at a sociocultural and spiritual cost. In a recent article on Salon entitled, "How our society breeds anxiety, depression and dysfunction," Bruce Levine writes that the medical profession sees an epidemic of depression and anxiety in the U.S. population. He cites one report sponsored by the National Institute of Mental Health that during some stage in their lives, "46 percent of Americans met the criteria established by the American Psychiatric Association for at least one mental illness" (2013). The false promise of consumption of desired material goods leads to a lack of fulfillment and sense of stress and more "likely to experience lower self-esteem, lower life satisfaction, and significantly greater discomfort in social settings" (Chang and Arkin, 404). As reported by Hidaka in an overview of depression in modern society, increased depression is likely the outcome of an environment promoting maximization consumption strategies. He states, "In effect, humans have dragged a body with a long hominid history into an overfed, malnourished, sedentary, sunlight-deficient, sleep-deprived, competitive, inequitable, and socially isolating environment with dire consequences" (2012, 211).

The imagined community of consumerism under capitalism has, it appears, in this postmodern era, become a place where antidepressants, alcohol, suicide, and aimless mass killings are expressions of feelings that life has become valueless and disposable. We fruitlessly purchase goods hoping to persuade ourselves to feel better but only accomplish further despoiling of the environment as accomplices to the corporate world. Durkheim, witnessing the further articulation of industrialization in the late nineteenth century, worried about the lack of a moral basis that would lead to anomie and despair. Levels of depression, anxiety, obesity, and other eating disorders have increased, suggesting general affluence is not the answer to our problems.

Thus, we are influenced in our thinking about what we need to feel secure and happy in ourselves by, on the one hand, advertisers and marketers, and on the other with the necessity to fill a void in our loneliness and isolation. In between, we have medicalized the social problems that are outcomes of how we operate. We appear to have a palliative approach to our problems, believing a pill will suffice. We have been taught to buy things as a form of leisure or therapy or to meet the expectations of others. Yet whatever feeling of pleasure or happiness exists, it is fleeting if only because what got you to that point will soon become routine, unexceptional, or superseded by new demands for our attention. The result is a lesser person while indirectly despoiling the environment in the vain hope of finding satisfaction in momentary things rather than people.

Thus far, the issues of concern in this book regarding the environment, the economy, culture, and our social being have been articulated. The journey to this point in time is, I believe, relatively clear if debatable, risky but unavoidable. From different points of view many agree that the Hopi word, *koyaanisqatsi*, is an adequate description of the state of modern things: life out of balance. The more difficult and pertinent question regards what is to be done to get beyond this situation? Many would agree with Gustav Speth, Bill McKibben, and many others that the fate of the Earth, and the human community, depends on how we proceed into the future. If we have lost the sense of community and devolved into a nation and globe of self-serving individual interests, then how will we develop mass social movements that ask for substantive change in how we govern and live our lives and, at the same time, promote a healthy natural environment?[13]

The last chapter will briefly examine a way forward to a new beginning, a new Earth community for conceptualizing human and non-human life on a sustainable planet.

NOTES

1. Recent research on the effects of electronic toys on young children suggests that such toys interfere with child–parent verbal interactions and negatively affect language development (Sosa 2016). On the other hand, traditional nonelectronic toys encourage imagination, more focus attention, and a greater potential for problem-solving. Miller and colleagues see that toy type is significant for child development writing,

> Results from the present study suggest that in the common context of play, different toys may provide different learning opportunities: infants vocalized and gestured more frequently when playing with the traditional toys compared to the feedback toys, parents responded with more contingent responses in the traditional toy context, and infants' sustained attention was longer in the feedback toy context, but they communicated less. (2017, 644)

2. Michael Watts wrote that "communities can be understood as differing fields of power—communities are internally differentiated in complex, political, social and economic ways" (2000, 38). Watts cautions,

> Communities fabricate, and prefabricate through their unique histories, the claims that they take to be naturally and self-evidently their own . . . they always involve forms of fantasy and invention, and they are always shot through with power and authority—some do the inventing and imagining in the name of others who do not. (37)

3. It is important to note a countermovement located at the grassroots level in many marginalized communities. The need to meet local needs will bring communities together for basic security, comfort, and social justice under conditions of poverty and/or racism. See, for example, Pardo's article on Chicano women of East Los Angeles (1990) or Carol Stack's research in a low-income Midwest community.

4. Verhaeghe poises a question long debated among social scientists, philosophers, and many others: is our sense of self based on heredity, that you are born or programmed who you are, or are we products of a nurturing environment. This is the classic nurture versus nature debate. Clearly, we are more than just the sum of our genes and our social environmental impact is extremely comprehensive and begins at the moment of birth. Most agree with Verhaeghe that we are both biological and cultural animals, that as a species we have several innate predispositions that are expressed differently depending on the cultural environment.

5. How do we know the self is empty? The self and its associated personality cannot be objectively seen. What can be observed is behavior. and while not a mirror the behavior is indicative or suggestive on the inner state of being of the individual.

Erchak quotes Levine, an early psychological anthropologist, that "Observed behavioral consistencies do not constitute personality [the self], they are indicators of it, or rather of the internal dispositions that influence overt behavior" (15). Thus, constant shopping and ownership of unnecessary things and the display, pronouncements, and competition over things that overlay weak social relationships may be seen as proxies that say something about the inner self.

6. As one of many coping mechanisms, there are frozen and instant meals, often individually packaged for a dinner of one. One outcome is the weakening of family meals as various demands, obligations, and activities must be met. This change has led to research on the value of family mealtimes on adolescent psychosocial behavior. Research suggests a variety of positive behavioral outcomes from family meals together (see, for example, Cook and Dunifon 2012). Eating with adults, rather than a quick meal alone, and with smartphones off the table informs children an important element of who they are and how to define themselves.

7. The grand narrative not only explains but also legitimizes the social relations and power structures that comprise society. The danger of such totalizing, comprehensive narratives is that they can lead to an intolerance of any deviations from the basic conclusions of the narrative. Alternatively, as social conditions and social forces change the nature of circumstances that inform one's perception, the contradictions that develop between narrative and reality can produce anxiety and fear and a desperate attempt to accommodate or solve the contradiction, often in the form of fundamentalist binary thinking such as yes/no, right/wrong, and us/them with little nuance between them.

8. Zepf believes that the need for meaning in material objects is found embedded in the basic structure of the modern family. He sees the attraction of toys and video games by young children to deal with the absence of parents or insufficient love and care. Things, in this case, lead to a suspension of differences between persons and things as they are embraced to fill a void (148). Advertising is there to offer the means to bridge this difference. "It is this principle of life that seems to protect individuals from being aware that they have been left alone and have become helpless" (149).

9. The difference between then (up until around the 1970s) and now is the amount of information that the computer, social media, and the internet has brought into our lives. We suffer from information overload in that every event and situation, regardless of how distant or slight, now command our attention.

10. In Marc Augé's prologue to *Non-Places: An Introduction to Supermodernity*, he writes of his character Pierre Dupont's process of leaving home to check in and board a flight to a business destination. The whole process did not involve any substantive human contact and only technology but upon putting on his earbuds he proclaims, "alone at last" (2008). How ironic, did he not realize that he had been alone the entire time?

11. We are cognizant, of course, that we are discussing here from a class bias. There are millions of Americans whose lives are far beyond the affluent means to life in a consumer fantasy world. Yet they do confront that fantasy world of consumerism. It may be that rather than anxiety or emptiness many feel anger and frustration. Yet, in either case what may be lurking just beneath the surface is social alienation.

12. Interestingly, in a novel by Peter Robinson, he has a character thinking about who she is at age seventy. Who am I she thought,

> At every stage, she had had to reinvent herself: the selfless career; the diplomat's wife; the ever-so-slightly "with-it" young widow . . . the struggling writer; the public figure with the splinter of ice in her heart. Would that be the last? Which was the real one? She didn't know. (1999, 254)

13. The use of the idea of community is not to imply a harmonious and well-oiled social organization. Many traditional communities did not tolerate deviant behavior but demanded conformity and obedience to community values that most members accepted as nature and appropriate.

Chapter 8

Searching for the Future Meaning of Humanity in the Age of Uncertainty

The convergence of the three great crises gives witness to a great turning point in human history. Out of these fundamental problems, a unique opportunity is presented to rethink who we are and what our relationship to this living planet should be. Under the pressures and demands of a changing world and the need to hold one's life together, do we understand what is at stake? These crises suggest we are in a lifeboat situation, adrift upon a sea of uncertainty and fear that present ways of living untenable and jeopardize the harmony of life, including the geophysics governing the planetary ecosystems. This book is in company with many recent publications, such as Ervin Laszlo's *The Upshift: Wiser Living on Planet Earth*, alerting us to the need to change our way of living and to think about our role in an increasingly uninhabitable Earth (2022). We focused this chronicle primarily on the United States as the most advanced consumer-based, individualist-oriented sociocultural system, but most countries, in varying degrees, follow in our wake and exhibit diverse forms of social transformation to a postmodern, consumer society. In this regard, writing in the *American Psychologist*, Frank Infurna and co-authors note an increase in loneliness and its attendant consequences in England and Mediterranean Europe as they experience similar forms of social change found in the United States (2024).

I believe that at an earlier point in history, two paths were open to us, one older path led to a natural world of integration with all lifeforms and the other, more contemporary, treats the world and its lifeforms, including humans, as resources for exploitation and development. In previous eras, though some animal life had to be eaten for survival and natural resources exploited, they were nevertheless celebrated for their sacrifice and, as resources, carefully husbanded. There was a communion, an integration, between human and animal life since most animals were seen and felt spiritually as sentient fellow travels on the road of life. Most life, accordingly, deserved to be celebrated as living beings trying to find their own way through the journey between life and death, as indigenous cultures saw themselves. There was wonderment and satisfaction in such recognition as witnessed by various rituals and celebrations discussed earlier. Not all is lost in our modern world, however, because many do give witness to the grandeur of planetary life. I am not alone when I see a wedge of geese flying overhead, causing me to pause in wonder of how do they know where to go each seasonal migration and what in their minds tell them when and where to go? They have also figured out what any human cycle racing team understands: those at the front have the job of cutting wind resistance for easier passage for those in the rear. Each honk of a goose in a wedge is alerting, "I am here," and ready to move to the front to relieve the tired leader. I have a Mallard duck pair that for the past ten plus years arrive each season at my bird feeder, tired and hungry, knowing that a meal of bird seed is awaiting them. How do they know how to find my house in the numerous roofs of my sprawling suburban neighborhood? I do not know the answer, but it makes me feel connected and thus alive asking the question as I watch them. This experience, compounded in many ways including my in-house macaw, has given me a new appreciation of life that in a previous time I took for granted. I am now persuaded that to find meaning in our lives, it is not to be found exclusively in our material possessions or 401K plans, but more profoundly, in the intense lifeworld of all shapes, sizes, and species around us. Though often unaware, we are intricately bound as a participant in this world and need to respect our role if this planet of life is to survive.

People cannot be convinced by facts and supporting evidence alone that something is wrong. Fear that the world they live in is in jeopardy because of a way of life we have chosen to construct and celebrate will not work. In other words, how do we move beyond the cul-de-sac of warnings of social and environmental collapse or the hollow pronouncements that we must somehow change our ways? How do we reach the broader public with our understanding of this jeopardy?

This book is a review of how we arrived at this perfect storm of how things fall apart, to borrow a phrase from the great African novelist Chinua Achebe. The difficult question is where do we go from here, what direction should be our efforts, and how do we get there? How do we motivate people that a better world is possible when they are prisoners of this technological consumer world of distraction and misinformation? How to break through the iron cage of conventionality of the present, that while chaotic, is a known and understood phenomenon?

Given the special interests of the political economy, the uncertainty and fear of radical change and its unknown consequences, as well as the lack of imagination that a better, more fulsome way of life is possible, the future is indeed speculative. But radical change in thinking and being is possible. What we need, and is indeed hard to find, is time to think and reflect beyond the practicalities that consume us. Our busy distracted modern lives leave little time to think or gain perspective since we are trapped in the urgency of now. It is thus difficult to understand the maelstrom of messages and images that urge spending and buying that surrounds every waking moment, and which leaves people alone, confused, or misguided about their intrinsic worth to themselves or to the planet. The pronouncements of philosophers and scientists about a world in jeopardy sound hollow to such people even though they desperately look for answers. Unfortunately, for many it is easier to listen to the declarations of political demagogues and faceless social media that offer denialism on the one hand and false promises on the other.

It is presumptuous to say humanity has lost its way, that capitalism only leads to more alienation and loss of what it means to be fully human. But the seductress siren call of progress and consumer betterment beckons with its technological toys of wonder, pulling us ever away from the natural world and each other. The mounting evidence indicates that capitalism, as this book suggests, has transformed both the natural and social worlds in unprecedented ways. The culprit includes a socio-psychological ethos of economic reward, consumer spending, and materialism as the mainstay to an improved standard of living and the "good life." If one thinks about it, however, something is missing. Understandably, many are beginning to wonder that there must be more to life than the unfocused self-centered, sociotechnological world we have created. But to understand this life, one must remember what it is that was lost. In essence, modern humans have forgotten how to live a deep, satisfying, and meaningful life, to embrace a spiritual essence within the web of nature. What is lost is not only the object but the symbolic collective representations of experience, history, and heritage in which resides the building blocks of meaning and identity. The problem is not found in individual psychology but as this book points out, in the structure of society itself. Fear and loneliness are not exclusively inside our heads but in the destruction of what governed social life for thousands of years: communal bonds and a collective ideology of group cooperation for survival. Thus, ever in search of a meaningful life, we look in all the wrong places. We engage in materialist possessiveness in hope that it will provide what we search for. And in this search, we consume that which in production pollutes the planet and undermines life on Earth. This loss of connection to each other includes a disconnect to nature as well.

Thomas Berry, a Catholic priest and cultural historian, understood this, believing humans have a special responsibility, given our consciousness to express and live the grandeur of this living planet. In *The Dream of the Earth*, he wrote, considering what we are,

> Much could be said, too, about the human as that being in whom this grand diversity of the universe celebrates itself in conscious self-awareness. While we emerge into being from within the earth process and enable the universe to come to itself in a special mode of psychic intimacy, it is evident that we have also a special power over the universe in its earthly expression. (1988, 198)

But we do not celebrate this special gift we have. What have we lost? His answer is what this book conveys. "We have in a very special manner lost our presence to the life-sustaining forces of the earth," Berry remarks,

> Whatever our gains in terms of scientific advances or in our industrial economy, neither of these is very helpful in establishing an integral presence to the more profound depths of our own being or into the more powerful forces shaping both the universe and the planet on which we live. (199)

This is what we have lost—we have failed to undertake Berry's belief in ourselves of our special responsibility as the living conscious expression of this Earthand instead, over time, have focused on the self-centered enticements of technology, power, and materialism.

POSTMODERN LIFE IN A RUNAWAY WORLD

In 1967, British anthropologist and provost of King's College, Cambridge, Edmund Leach delivered a series of lectures for the BBC's Reith Lectures about our species' inability to cope with our "Godlike" powers. Leach felt the objectivity of science that we rely on has led to separation, isolation, division, and thus, fear. In his same-titled book, *A Runaway World?,* Leach argued that scientific objectivity as a form of detachment has functioned to alienate society from nature and individuals from each other. "This orderly fragmented way of living," he considered, "serves only to isolate the human individual from his environment and from his neighbors—they reduce him to a lonely, impotent and terrified observer of a runaway world" (1967, 9). The positivism of science and belief in empiricism, numbers, and technology has given a cold understanding of the universe and humanity, most acute in this increasingly secular age.

Even then, the drift of society toward postmodernist nihilism was evident to him. Leach recognized a world of growing flux and uncertainty, which he believed led to alienation or retreat from the perceived disorder gaining ascendancy in social life. He believed fear and isolation were due to our orientation toward things as discrete categories rather than the connections linking all things, human and nature, together. Additionally, the runaway world led to World War II, devastating the planet and killing tens of millions of people, displacing millions of others while destroying countless cities and communities. Afterward, the mass society of recovering affluent countries fell deeper into a self-absorbed, congratulatory fantasy world of consumerism, ultimately leading to a disconnect from the natural world, and today the dire effects of climate change. As an anthropologist, Leach understood the limitations of modern life, commenting on the pitfalls of individualism, "It is significant that most of us are so deeply committed to being alone in a crowded world that we turn the whole problem back to front: we worry about privacy rather than loneliness" (46). The felt aloneness and alienation, he was convinced, inevitably induces fear of the *other* further eroding any real sense of community. Several years later, Christopher Lasch, an historian at the University of Rochester, popularized Leach's sentiments in his book *The Culture of Narcissism* (1979). Lasch wrote that social changes increased a "grandiose of self-conception," of subjective individualism. This narcissism is not about vanity but rather about fear and anguish over a lack of purpose beyond mere existence. This is due, in part, to philosophers or those in the humanities no longer able to explain the nature of things or offer new ways of living, to deal with the collapse of faith and increase in competition and self-centeredness. This trend, he felt, was weakening communal bonds leading to a shallowness of personal social relationships, a "hall of mirrors" confusing and demoralizing people.

America today illustrates the sense of mass confusion, political discord, anti-intellectualism, and in cases, public disengagement sowed by antidemocratic neoconservative corporate interests and misinformation. This is the crisis of postmodern times that concerns many critical social observers. It is within this developing process that climate change has taken on greater urgency. It is difficult to develop and maintain consensus on climate change or any other problem under the conditions of social fragmentation, hyper political polarized discord, and the political-economic hegemony of capitalist first principles. Yet it is hard to convince oneself that there is nothing to worry about.

An element of Leach's criticism of science, given the atomic bomb, is the fantasy that science can control the world for us. Leach sees scientists frightened by a changing unruly society that they cannot control, that scientists, and by extension political and social policymakers, "are concerned with how things are, not with how they ought to be" (14). There are those, however, who do search for some sort of Earthly utopia and ideal society. This is understandable but can also be seen as running away, as defeatism from what we have created. It has been a long journey toward the kind of world where technology and creativity have given varying degrees of humanity a sense of comfort, health, and security. With our powerful technologies in hand, we have become masters of this world, bending reality to our will. But we now realize, fifty years after Rachel Carson's clarion call in *Silent Spring*, that such progress comes at both a physical and spiritual cost. Which choice do we pursue? Is it business as usual based on power, wealth, and materialism or a more decentralized world supported by a different set of values that accentuates the common good and a spiritual connection of "species being," that is, to raise ourselves above Marx's "subjective individuality" and embrace our common bond with ourselves and with nature?

The new promises of artificial intelligence, greater computerization, and continuing advances in technology are offered as if inevitable and awaited with great anticipation. Why not? Looking back over the past one hundred years suggests much improvement in the human condition (except, of course, for those many poor living in the shantytowns, favelas, and barrios of the global South and the United States). If looking back suggests, one might think, such progress, then should not the future also bode well? Many people today continue to have faith in the inevitable linear march of progress into a brighter future, a faith now increasingly dimmed by doubt.

The physicist Michio Kaku exemplifies the current paradigm promoted by those maintaining the path of progress and the techno-science status quo. He believes that we have entered a "golden age," enthralled as he is by science and technology. Kaku believes that humanity's future is to be found in venturing and settling space, beginning with terraforming and, echoes of Elon Musk, building cities on Mars. He remarks in *The Future of Humanity*,

> As we look to the future, we can see the outlines of how science will transform space exploration. Because of revolutionary advances in a wide range of modern technologies, we can now speculate how our civilization may one day move out into space, terraforming planets and traveling among the stars. (2019, 12)

But will anything be different if our way of thinking does not change?

Alternatively, the billionaire Marc Lore proposes a $400 billion high-tech city of the future. While we do need rational and sustainable population centers, how we decide the future should not be determined by a cadre of billionaires and their science-like vision of the future. Lore and Kaku put their faith in artificial intelligence and new technologies, in the cold, dispassionate use of science in building and controlling things in the name of progress, a "new Eden" that Carolyn Merchant has written about. Individuals like Lore, Musk, and Kaku are confident that their new worlds will be different. But without a transformation in values, thinking, and perception, it will be the same humanity in outer space or magic high-tech cities that has brought an alienated world to people and this planet to the brink of destruction. In other words, we cannot solve today's problems using the same structure of thinking that got us into this mess to begin with. A new paradigm shift is called for, to go beyond the conventionality of today's comfort.

Many in the most affluent countries today are beginning to doubt that continued progress is a certainty and that, at a minimum, progress cuts both ways, bringing concentrated affluence but also pervasive poverty, alienation rather than community, and domination instead of communion. To paraphrase M. L. King, who himself paraphrased Theodore Parker, the moral arc of history is long, but it does not necessarily bend in any direction. Those who believe in business as usual—that is, endless growth and unmitigated environmental exploitation, or the technological imperative, consciously or unconsciously believe that the long arc of history is continued techno-material progress and advancement if individuals of ingenuity put their minds and talents to it. Thinking of artificial intelligence, we will have self-driving cars and trucks, smart homes to turn on lights, and internet-linked refrigerators. It is hard for many people to believe we could lose this comfortable way of life—pitfalls yes, but always the promise of progress.

It appears, however, to many who stop, listen, and take the long view that a growing sense of uncertainty and anxiety has infused itself within an unnamed feeling of Leach's foreboding. My argument is that contemporary events of violence and other social ills are associated with a hyper-individualistic society that may be reaching its limits, eventually becoming more dysfunctional than a positive social trait. The impact of technology and materialism on mass society's continued Influence on community, identity, and social relationship appears to revolve today around doubtfulness, uncertainty, insecurity, and social isolation. It is a sad commentary on our times that Elon Musk is willing to invest his fortune on sending a million individuals to Mars by 2050 rather than address how to restructure and save this world.

Echoing the state of world affairs today, in 1925, T. S. Eliot wrote his poem *The Hollow Men* as a reflection of the despondency and disillusionment of the world around him. He wrote,

Our dried voices, when
We whisper together

Eliot, surveying the years after World War I and the ensuring moral decay, is despondent over the human condition of the postwar years. He decries the dimness of modern life, sensing life is spiritually dead, adding that our voices,

Are quiet and meaningless
As wind in dry grass

He ends his meditation with one of the most famous lines in English poem history: "This is how the world ends, not with a bang but with a whimper." There would not be a Berlin Wall moment today but a chronic dismantling of the world we know, a slow slipping away and a receding memory of what was or what should be. From the perspective of today, Eliot appears to be addressing the anxiety of our time.

Leach recognized alienation but could not additionally foresee climate change or a postmodern ethos that threatens to radically upset the world in all its complexity. Of course, there are many NGOs and community activist groups organized to confront social inequality, alienation, and injustice as a backdrop to climate change and Leach's runaway world. There are many earnestly searching for a new more vibrant world of connection. But these are largely piecemeal attempts at change, whereas the problems are emblematic of structural conditions informed by corporate and elite hegemonic power over (global) society and thus require complete structural and cultural transformation based on a holistic understanding of the problem. In a sense, what is needed is a revolutionary social movement in thinking and being, as called for by philosophers such as Berry, to find our heart for the natural world.

HUMAN VULNERABILITY AND ENVIRONMENTAL CHANGE

We have unwittingly entered a new era of human-induced physical dynamics to the Earth's climate system. In the November 2019 issue of *BioScience*, over 11,000 scientists from around the world signed a letter stating that the Earth is facing a climate emergency and that little time remains for addressing the impact of climate change (Ripple et al., 2019). Given this is the case, the issue then becomes what is next, what will be the result if the proposed climate threshold is broached. The collapse of civilization? Total annihilation of the human species? Survivors heading back to the caves or the fortunate sequestered in self-contained fortresses? Or maybe we go the escapist route following Elon Musk and head for Mars.

This book has outlined the close association between global warming and the hyper-exploitation and degradation of the Earth's habitats and ecosystems in the name of consumer progress. The reverberations of the estrangement of nature are all around us, yet we vainly attempt to convince ourselves that all is okay. It is hard to give up a well-worn myth of socioeconomic progress if there is not one compelling enough to replace it. Climate change may be all around us, but its more destructive effects, some think, may be years in the future and easy to dismiss. Environmental degradation of habitat such as wetlands takes place away from our cityscapes or suburban bubbles. The devastating wildfires of 2021–2022 of California and Canada and other catastrophic events may be worrisome but not threatening to those outside the event's field of view.

Between the escapists and climate activists are the modern-day descendants of the Book of Revelations, those who see the apocalypse on the near horizon. In his book, *Going Dark*, Guy McPherson's offers a mood-altering conclusion regarding humanity's fate. Shifting from a cautious pessimism, he wrote in his introduction

> But in June 2012 the ocean of evidence on climate change overwhelmed me, and I no longer subscribe to the notion that habitat for humans will exist on Earth beyond the 2030s. We've triggered too many self-reinforcing feedback loops to prevent near-term extinction at our own hand. (2019, 1)

So much, in his view, for humanity.

Many have given warning over these various crises but generally to little apparent effect. The general response represents what Gaston Bachelard in 1949 referred to as the Cassandra Complex. Cassandra, the daughter of the king of Troy, was given the gift of prophecy but after spurning the god Apollo, as punishment no one would listen to her insights. She knew of events in advance but was helpless to convince others, becoming but a helpless bystander. From a contemporary point of view, the author Isaac Asimov wrote in 1988, "The saddest aspect of life right now is that science gathers knowledge faster than society gathers wisdom." Today it appears that we have fallen into the Cassandra Complex with particular regard to climate change. As Greta Thunberg recently asked Congress to listen to the scientists, the U.S. government and much of the world remain mired in slow-motion response.

Elizabeth Kolbert's recent *Fate of the Earth* lecture on species extinction points out, for example, that extinction events now befalling species of frogs and bats is, in insidious fashion, not caused by humans per se but by pathogens transported globally by human visitors. In so many ways, we have created either intentionally or otherwise a series of domino events changing the face of our planet. As Kolbert acknowledges, "No creature has ever changed it at the rate that we are changing it right now" (2017). Kolbert, a journalist at *The New York Times*, acknowledges that, "No creature has ever changed at the rate that we are changing right now" (2017). In *The Sixth Extinction*, a title that is exceptional given that this extinction process is human-caused rather than a natural force of Earth's geo-physical evolution. She notes, for example, that amphibians are of the ancient world, existing for the last 400 million years and found throughout the world. They are now disappearing at an alarming rate not only in disturbed areas but also in pristine protected areas such as the Monteverde Cloud Forest Reserve in Costa Rica. The global collapse of frog populations is so extensive, many are not known until they vanish. One biologist told Kolbert, "Unfortunately, we are losing all these amphibians before we even know that theyexist" (2014, 10, 201; see also 2015).

The fate of the Earth, one could surmise, is found in Kolbert's visit to the San Diego Zoo's Institute for Conservation Research. There she witnessed stacks and rows of vials submerged in liquid nitrogen. In each vial, the cells of varied species that have gone extinct or soon will be extinct are present. Her host pulled out a vial containing the remaining cells of the pòouli, a black-faced honeycreeper bird. After years of struggle to keep the species alive, the last one died in November 2004. "The windowless room where the pòouli cells are kept alive—sort of—is called the Frozen Zoo." There they are, species now nothing but cells stored in liquid nitrogen tanks. Feeling the weight of the future for many endangered species, she asks, "Does it have to end this way? Does the last best hope for the world's most magnificent creatures—or, for that matter, its least magnificent ones—really lie in pools of liquid nitrogen" (260–261)? Where exactly will the sixth extinction lead us, to what end? Certainly, this is a sad way to think about what our species has done to life on Earth. Quite possibly a more pertinent question, does anyone care beyond a few environmentalists? Are we so blind or indifferent? It should not be so surprising given how we think and treat our own species. Marx himself argued that human nature was more than conditioned by the parochial circumstances of life but by the historical-cultural epoch in which one is born. We are conditioned by our era to be indifferent to the natural world, except when environmental catastrophe hits and then it is but an episodic concern soon to evaporate as we move on to the next big issue.

The underlying questions guiding the analysis of this book are not only the prospects of climate change and environmental degradation for humanity but the condition of humanity itself as it is driven by technology, the misguided pleasures of consumerism, and a nihilistic postmodern alienation of human relationship and community. In her poem *Wild Geese* (2004), Mary Oliver calls to us to let go and be self-aware beyond our parochial concerns:

the world offers itself to your imagination,
calls to you like the wild geese, harsh and exciting

As discussed earlier, awareness of landscape has always played an important role in our history, and she reminds us to be alert to its meaning. She adds that the wild geese are once again heading home in the "clean blue sky," and so, it is our turn to do likewise. Oliver wants us to remember who we are, an inherent member of this wild and exhilarating world around us:

over and over announcing your place
in the family of things

We no longer recognize as a culture, it appears, Mary Oliver's "soft animal," of what we are, nor do we any longer recognize and understand the "harsh and exciting" call of the wild geese. Oliver's evocative poem calls to us to free ourselves from our petty issues and like wild geese to move more effortlessly in this life embracing our true nature to be one with nature and its landscapes and living beings. Denying our inherent nature, she believes, only leads to despair and disappointment.

THE PROBLEMATIC FUTURE OF EARTH COMMUNITY

Robert Hay employed the term "soul sickness" to describe the despondency insinuating itself into Western society. The term suggests a demoralization, a spiritual and psychological poverty of the modern world, where most elements of life appear disconnected, hearing only the faint echoes of lost dreams. This is, as we have discussed, in contrast to indigenous cultures that see things naturally, organically, and clustered together, and as Hay put it, considered synchronous or meaningfully related in time and space (2006). In this book, we have chronicled mass consumer society under capitalism that has replaced meaning found in the symbolism of profoundly abiding cultural elements and relationships, with a commercialized and artificial desire for entertainment, excessive comfort, and self-centeredness. The consequences have led to the weakening of collective solidarity, a loss of deep meaning of a sense of place, time, and the intrinsic value of being. It is argued here that one's "natural" sense of self is found in a profound collective identity of kinship, intimate and abiding face-to-face social relationships enhanced by the symbolic meaning of heritage found in objects, landscape, and the natural world that surrounds us.

There is an old Zulu phrase, *Ubuntu* ("I am because we are"), that serves as a point of departure to what we no longer are. The phrase speaks to personhood and identity found in the relationships of community, built over time through descent bonding individuals and generations together. The essential point of this discussion considers the socioeconomic drift of postmodernism, leading to the "homeless mind," essentially the profound loss of community. As a reaction, Peter Berger et al. sees the growth of a private sphere of social life—a "do-it-yourself" world of "unparalleled liberty and anxiety" but fragile and ultimately unreliable due to the "often severely discrepant world of meaning and experience, a segmentation into a pluralization of life worlds" (64–65).

The growth of hyper-individuation enhanced by internet usage is reconstructing social relationships and the meaning of community. Thus, problems of self-identity, the fragmented self, lead to poor social skills and lack of social intimacy that is expressed in the increase in various social diseases such as depression, anxiety, drug taking, and random acts of violence. Consequently, Jo Griffin writes in her report on loneliness,

> Some observers see a link between our individualistic society and the possible increase in common mental health disorders in the last 50 years. . . . By squandering "social capital" in the individualistic pursuit of greater wealth, or treating social networks as incidental, are we neglecting a part of life that makes us happy and keeps us healthy for longer? (2010, 7)

What kind of human can live in such a plurality of worlds ever morphing into new versions of itself? Only those who allow for the distractions offered by advertising and banal mass entertainment as forms of temporary relief from the unceasing demands placed upon them. This is our corporate dominated consumer society where progress and excess in material things act as salves for the uncertainty and anxiety over life and the future. Many people have little or no understanding of the world, socially or physically, and many lack even the curiosity or concern about it. Many blithely believe in the ideology they have been taught, that it is "all about me" with the world as a series of stages for the presentation of me in my various guises.

The Spanish word *querencia* represents a balanced lifeworld, which denotes heritage, history, and ancestry. It leads to a deep sense of satisfaction and security based on a sense of place and being, where one feels their most authentic self, surrounded by the intimacy of others. It is in *querencia* where memory is not forgotten but lived. *Querencia* is difficult to find in the postmodern world of mobility, relativism, and materialist orientation. Its meaning can be found only at the individual level of relatively stable situations such as the "traditional" family, but here we are focused on the level of an ever-moving "traveling" culture where "home" is situational or transactional rather than permanent. *Querencia* can be thought of as the anthesis of modern life and cannot readily accommodate the modern ethos of progress, utility, and movement. If we thought more systematically about our home planet in terms of *querencia,* we might more effectively confront climate change, habitat destruction, and the psychological discomforts of mass consumer society.

This, then, is the struggle: do we choose the path leading to a more substantive socioecological feeling of *querencia*, what David Korten refers to as Earth Community, or the path of business as usual (Korten's Empire) and embrace the modern world of mass consumption and technology, the mastery of all things?[1] Korten believes the beginning of a "great turning" is emerging to counter industrial Empire's "hierarchies of domination" of social life, where money and power define values and perception (2006). He argues against humans as inherently self-centered, materialist, and competitive. Agreeing with Berry, Rohr, Raskin, and many others, Korten calls for a great awakening of awareness and consciousness for a more "authentic" human nature of communitarianism, where technology is servant supporting spiritual growth and collective well-being rather than the autonomous master of its own ends.

The former path of change to enlightenment and a sustainable humanity and planet is more difficult, far reaching, and revolutionary. But as Einstein once quipped, "We cannot solve problems with the same kind of thinking that created them." Clearly, we cannot replicate the indigenous past, but we can learn from history and different cultures in terms of cooperation and sense of place, including the pleasures and responsibilities of inclusive and abiding relationships with ourselves and with nature. Ecologically, however, indigenous knowledge systems can play a significant role in environmental research and alternative resource management. Most fundamentally, Richard Atleo, an indigenous scholar, considers both science and myths or origin stories concerned with the same thing, that is to understand and explain the nature of existence (Berkes 2018, 33). Berkes summarizes the benefits of indigenous ecological knowledge,

> The remedies may include restoring the unity of mind and nature; developing awareness of the nonlinear and complex nature of our environment; addressing the problem of a self-identity distinct from the world around us; and restoring a worldview based on morality toward nature. (295)

Likewise, Thomas Berry understood this new path believing,

> Our challenge is to create a new language, even a new sense of what it is to be human. It is to transcend not only national limitations, but even our species isolation, to enter the larger community of living species. This brings about a completely new sense of reality and value. (1988, 42)

Berry recognized the difficulty of a new transformation adding,

> It is a bitter moment, also, because the origins of our actions go so deep into our spiritual and cultural traditions, fostering a sense that we are the measure of all things. What we seem unwilling or unable to recognize is that our entire modern world is itself inspired not by any rational process, but by a distorted dream experience, perhaps by the most powerful dream that has every taken possession of human imagination. (204, 205)

In *The Great Work*, Berry continues to feel the presence of the estrangement from nature, "We can no longer hear the voice of the rivers, the mountains, or the sea. The trees and meadows are no longer intimate modes of spirit presence. The world about us has become an 'it' rather than a 'thou'" (1999, 17). We must understand more completely the profoundness of life on this planet as did Henry Beston thinking on the mysteries of nature while walking the shores of Cape Cod in 1928. In *The Outermost House*, he gave thought to our fellow co-inhabitants, writing,

> In a world older and more complete than ours, they move finished and complete, gifted with the extension of the senses we have lost or never attained, living by voices we shall never hear. They are not brethren, they are not underlings: they are other nations, caught with ourselves in the net of life and time, fellow prisoners of the splendour and travail of the earth. (2001; org. 1928)

In many respects, I do not pretend to understand Hatuey, my macaw, whom I have lived with the past twenty-four years. I do not know what goes on behind his eyes, but I do respect him as a complex, sentient being on his own journey with me through life. I frequently catch myself in amazement at how he can negotiate our world so different from his natural world. He has taught me to see the natural world not through the prism of science and facts, but through spirituality, a feeling of the omnipresence of a living, breathing world.

How do we reach that sweet spot and enhance all life? Indigenous societies had such potential but were limited in understanding except in a spiritual sense. Today, we have a storehouse of accumulated knowledge and scientific understanding to move beyond our forbearers. The pertinent questions for an eventual transformation are: How do we get to a world of sustainability, communion with a coequal nature, and the joys of each other's company? Where is the "warm" science to support our inherent need for needful connection and the potential to be more than what we have become? If there is a crying need for a new world, how do we raise the consciousness of humanity to new heights of our "soft animal" awareness of what is important to being human? How do we convince people that the cry of the wild geese overhead is something to stop and celebrate or that Leopold's listening point is more fulfilling and satisfying than the concrete streets of Wall Street, or that Schumacher's "small" is indeed beautiful (1973)? These are difficult questions, but they must be asked. Where or how do we start an inclusive public dialogue?

Many would contend as I do that these questions have no answers in the existing social and economic conditions we have constructed. As argued in this book, we have created dysfunctional societies and communities based on the values of money, competition, wealth, and endless progress. If indeed most people, global or national, regardless of socioeconomic status, feel they are only participants in a never-ending rat race, they may be open to new narratives of human growth centered on social justice, equality, and a willingness to entertain initial steps to new ways of living. The foundation of the new narrative to a new way of life is found in a nurturing relationship of individual development within an intimate community. Healthy communities are environments encouraging face-to-face interactions of cooperation, consensus, and concern for all community members, ensuring basic needs of nurturing, nutrition, and shelter are available to all. Such communities focus on people rather than material things, the careful use and reuse of resources, having enough, and bringing nature into the lives of its members through gardening, local parks, and habitat for animals. The ethos supporting such communities is not so much being modern as being humane and at "home." Such a transformation will not happen overnight given the deep-seated belief by many in the prevailing narrative of empire. The power of the prevailing narrative and the values it promotes while powerful are not absolute. Many people do engage in altruism, sharing, reciprocity, and sacrifice and are motivated by nonmonetary desires and needs. And many are cognizant of the limitations of modern life and wonder if there are not alternatives to the uncertainty of prevailing structures and functions of mass society.

The city of Amsterdam is attempting to implement an urban alternative, referred to as a circular economy in combination with Kate Raworth's so-called doughnut economy, to the market economy governing the Netherlands (2018). The anti-neoliberal principles outlining the doughnut hole economy are, among others, regenerative (reuse and recycle) and, most importantly from a basic thesis of her book, nurturing human nature that promotes diversity, participation, and collaboration by numerous stakeholders (including animals?) including community groups, academics, NGOs, local governments, businesses, and interested individuals working in concert to rethink both economic and social formations.[7] The potential for such inclusive development is to offer a sense of place for community members since they are involved in the process of creating a humane and caring community. Creating a reuse/recycle economy centered on local businesses and small-scale sustainable industry encourages citizen participation in which the economy works on a nongrowth basis. Raworth's approach to economics is like the old anthropological substantive perspective that people are not foremost economic animals but fundamentally social and sharing. The new economy of the doughnut hole functions to nurture and encourage these humane traits through meaningful relationships and a sense of place.[3] The idea is to move away from consumption as a preoccupation to what truly defines quality of life, satisfaction, and security for and with oneself. As this development matures, stress levels weaken and the sense of identity grows based on cooperation, stability, and social satisfaction. Given the three crises discussed in this book and the need for a new path forward, Raworth and Amsterdam's people's centered decentralized socioeconomic model may be the first initial steps into the future not dominated by economic or self-important imperatives.

If we can get beyond the demands of our days and find time to think about what we are, it may lead to a reflection on self and a realization of the need for greater synchronization with the rhythms of the natural world. However, for such a transcendence to take place in society, especially consumer society, there is a need for a new shared story to define and explain reality and the human place. If the future is to be sustainable and in harmony with nature, new organic narratives need to be promoted. The challenge is to break away from the orthodox narrative that wealth is found only by sovereign individuals in monetary terms. More meaningful forms of wealth are healthy, vibrant, yet stable communities founded on intricate webs of social interactions between members sharing a common philosophy of life. Wealth should be measured in who you are rather than what you have, as members of the Gabra of Kenya and Ethiopia would testify.[4] We have bought into the siren call of capitalism, where some have a comfortable yet unsatisfying way of life and where who we are or where we are going remain unanswered. Wealth is also found, I believe, in understanding the call of the wild geese and the exhilaration we feel as they wheel overhead. True wealth is found by reinserting ourselves into the Earth community where all life is a focal point of attention and celebrated.

Many indigenous cultures, and today many ecologists, see human beings as one animal among many, all with a bundle of rights as they cohabit this world equally. Humans are but one expression of the animal kingdom and the sole expression of a conscious awareness of the universe. The many indigenous stories lead us to bear witness to the movement of the stars, the coyote as a wily trickster who sees and knows things we cannot, and the great horned owl who hoots late at night that all is right with the world. Part of the new narrative moves from the empiricism and cold positivism embraced by inevitable progress to one that unleashes our imagination of death and rebirth, in celebration of each other in human solidarity and the ever turning of the wheel of life on Earth. In accepting that the owl is proclaiming the world is okay even when we know empirically this is not so, nevertheless, confers upon the owl that it is more than just a soulless animal, but a being with an inherent right to live, and in his own way, has something to proclaim to the world. This is the challenge of our day according to Berry, "The historical mission of our times is to reinvent the human—at the species level, with critical reflection, within the community of life-systems . . . by means of story and shared dream experience" (1999, 159).

Berry believes that due to our conscious self-awareness we hold a special responsibility to give witness to the grandeur of universal life "the human as that being in whom this grand diversity of the universe celebrates itself in conscious self-awareness." How, then, would we, if we could and must, honor this responsibility? Beyond a new social economics, society in the new world of the Anthropocene needs a recovered Eden that would recognize *terra mater*, where female Earth deities abide (as found in many indigenous origin stories) and replace male gods of the machine and end the separation of culture from nature, as Merchant believes. The Baconian machine would be replaced with a holistic or inclusive tapestry of all life, not as a machine but as a process of being.

Can we step outside our assigned roles in the grand story that we have been educated to accept as natural if not inevitable? Can we change the plot into a different recovery narrative, one at peace with the world? The growing dissatisfactions with modern life overlaid with increasing concern with induced environmental collapse have many individuals thinking about the future. Raskin believes the current conditions offer the potential to entertain fundamental change, "The erosion of faith in orthodox approaches opens psychic and political space for envisioning radically different alternatives." He sees a vast, growing social movement, "a vast cultural and political rising, able to redirect policy, tame corporations, and unify civil society" (2016, 46, 32). There is much in this world to appreciate, and we have done much to honor our accomplishments. While old paradigms and worldviews begin to lose their ability to explain or justify present conditions, it is necessary to think deeply about what we have that encourages liberation, creativity, and new innovations in thinking and action to build upon.

What kind of world is up to us, not God ordained nor will it just happen. But the future, Raskin assesses, "It is a world we are creating for worse if despair disempowers the better angels of our nature, or for better, if we travelers awaken and together set course" (35; Raskin et al., 2002). Raskin may be right that the force of circumstances from climate change, a chaotic social world and habitat loss and animal extinction, may have individuals begin to ask the important existential questions about life and identity and maybe why are there are so few Monarch butterflies or bumble bees than years in the past. Raskin, Korten, and others may be correct that many are ready to venture forth into a new future, but strong countervailing forces remain powerful. However, Marx is correct in his assessment that capitalism is its own grave digger, that its contradictions are not sustainable.

As these crises continue to degrade the viability of the Earth and its inhabitants, human and nonhuman alike, social movements and new ways of thinking about the future can overcome, as history has shown us, the resistance of the powerful. Through education and experience, the struggle for liberation has begun to reform our thinking from the alienating utilitarianism of capitalism to stewardship and the end of seeing the world as nothing more than resources. There is a growing realization among environmentalists, philosophers, and spiritual leaders for renewal and regeneration, one that includes the rights of the animate world of animals as sentient coinhabitants to exist. This realization sees all life as participants in environmental sustainability.

Such a shift in consciousness is possible but it must be recognized and desired. Berry argues at the beginning of *The Great Work*,

> History is governed by those overarching movements that give shape and meaning to life by relating the human venture to the larger destinies of the universe. Creating such a movement might be called the Great Work of a people. . . . The historical mission of our times is to reinvent the human . . . with critical reflection, within the community of life systems.

Ultimately, Berry sees the need to construct a new reality of what it means to be human, "We need to reinvent the human at the species level because the issues we are concerned with seem to be beyond the competence of our present cultural traditions, either individually or collectively" (160). These are calls for a new social movement of discovery and invention, a reaching out to a new world of possibilities.

Our present estrangement clearly is not sustainable. This called-for radical shift in thinking and action will not happen today or tomorrow but is a promise of future tomorrows. The inevitability of a new way of thinking and being is the only means compatible with the age of the Anthropocene, limited resources, and the growing disenchantment with contemporary society that does not feed the human spirit. Berry's call for a spiritual responsibility to the grandeur of Earth can be realized. Humans as agents can create any way of life, if given the knowledge and the understanding of what must be done. There are social experiments and new ways of thinking and connecting. Many people are clearly looking for a more meaningful life, for spiritual insight beyond possessions and wealth. But too many are trapped in Plato's cave, seeing only shadowy images and relying on what they sense immediately around them, our present dysfunctional way of life.

The point of this book is to offer an outline of how we got to this point in history where we now question ourselves. But to know what we should do and in what direction we should attempt, it is important to understand the past. The past can offer possibilities, but it is up to us to step out of the cave of shadows to risk a new ecological, all-encompassing world; many have taken the first steps toward a new world but is it enough? Time is running out as we debate climate change, the use of fossil fuels, and the threatening social-political problems confronting this country and the global community. The question is how much time do we have before we reach the tipping point of no return?

At one point in history, Cristóbal Colón, standing on the Portuguese shore of Palos de la Fronteraores one warm evening in August 1492, gazed at the dark Atlantic and thought about the possibilities venturing forth into the unknown, of what imagined shores awaited him. He remarked, "Following the light of the sun, we left the Old World." We, too, follow in his wake into the unknown of a new world. What confronts us, what is it we seek, and what shall we find? We know that the outcome of his adventure led to conquest and destruction of indigenous cultures and the natural world. Will we repeat in our own way his legacy, the search for a New World but to what outcome?

NOTES

1. Paul Raskin considers three paths or scenarios, "three broad channels fan out from the unsettled present into the imagined future: worlds of incremental adjustment (Conventional Worlds), worlds of calamitous discontinuity (Barbarization), and worlds of progressive transformation (Great Transitions)" (2016, 25). The present three great crises discussed in chapter 1 suggests that incremental change and calamitous discontinuity comprise the prevailing path of business as usual.

2. During the height of Hugo Chavez's Bolivarian Revolution, neighborhood communal councils were empowered to decide the contours of their community development. All community members were encouraged to participate in determining what their community needs were, write grant proposals, and how to allocate and spend the money when awarded. I witnessed several such councils deliberate what was needed, including complex projects, and how to implement once grants were awarded (see also, Martinez et al., 2010; Azzellini 2016). Depending on the leadership, many councils were successful in determining and controlling their own development.

3. From a different perspective, beginning in the 1990s, the slow food movement began in Italy which, in its own way, encourages individuals to view food and eating in a small-scale manner, focused on the moment and the people one is with. Part of the slow food manifesto states,

> We are enslaved by speed and have all succumbed to the same insidious virus: Fast Life, which disrupts our habits, pervades the privacy of our homes and forces us to eat Fast Foods. . . . A firm defense of quiet material pleasure is the only way to oppose the universal folly of Fast Life. . . . May suitable doses of guaranteed sensual pleasure and slow, long-lasting enjoyment preserve us from the contagion of the multitude who mistake frenzy for efficiency. Our defense should begin at the table with Slow Food. (Blog post by Heather Dowd at tourissimo.travel)

There is also a growing farm-to-table movement in which consumers join a farm club to purchase farm produce, generally organic and cage free from the producer without any middle agent.

4. Recall that the Gabra, as in many indigenous and poor communities, measured wealth not exclusively in the number of camels but in old and ongoing relationships of exchange, which one calls upon when in need of help.

References

aaas.org. "Population and Land Use: Mineral Extraction." AAAS Atlas of Population and Environment. *American Association for the Advancement of Science,* 2001. http://atlas.aaas.org/pdf/83-86.pdf

Abel, David. "The Great Melt at the Top of the World." *The Environment Beat Blog,* July 12, 2015. http://davidabelenvironment.blogspot.com/

Achtenberg, Emily. "From Water Wars to Water Scarcity: Bolivia's Cautionary Tale." *ReVista*: *Harvard Review of Latin America* 12, no. 2 (December 2013). https://revista.drclas.harvard.edu/from-water-wars-to-water-scarcity/

Adams, Jonathan, Mark Maslin, and Ellen Thomas. "Sudden Climate Transitions during the Quaternary." *Progress in Physical Geography* 23, no. 1 (1999): 1–36. https://people.earth.yale.edu/sites/default/files/files/Thomas/Adamsetal99.pdf

Aftandilian, Dave. "Animals Are People, Too: Ethical Lessons about Animals from Native American Sacred Stories." *Interdisciplinary Humanities* 27, no. 1 (2010): 79–98. http://sdkay510.yolasite.com/resources/ARTICLE Native American Animal Influence.pdf

Agué, Marc. *Non-Places Introduction to an Anthropology of Supermodernity.* London: Verso, 2008.

Alexander, Samuel. "Questioning the Growth Imperative." *The Simplicity Collective,* 2012. http://simplicitycollective.com

Altherr, Thomas L. "'Flesh is the Paradise of a Man of Flesh': Cultural Conflict Over Indian Hunting Beliefs and Rituals in New France as Recorded in *The Jesuit Relations*." *The Canadian Historical Review* 64, no. 2 (December 1983): 267–276.

Angus, Ian. *Facing the Anthropocene: Fossil Capitalism and the Crisis of the Earth System.* New York: Monthly Review Press, 2016.

Apple, Michael. *Ideology and Curriculum.* New York: Routedge, 2004.

Århem, Kaj. "The Cosmic Food Web: Human-Nature Relatedness in the Northwest Amazon." In *Nature and Society: Anthropological Perspectives*, edited by Philippe Descola and Gísli Pálsson, 185–204. London: Routledge, 1996.

Arnold, David. *The Problem of Nature: Environment, Culture and European Expansion.* Oxford: Blackwell, 1996.

Assadourian, Erik. *The Rise and Fall of Consumer Cultures.* 2010 State of the World. Washington, DC: Worldwatch Institute, 2010.

Augé, Marc. *Non-Places: An Introduction to Supermodernity.* London: Verso, 2008.

Azzellini, Dario. "The Communal State. Venezuela: Communal Councils and Workplace Democracy." In *Moving Beyond Capitalism*, edited by Cliff DuRand, 170–178. New York: Routledge, 2016.

Balée, William. *Cultural Forests of the Amazon: A Historical Ecology of People and Their Landscapes.* Tuscaloosa: University of Alabama Press, 2013.

Bardhi, Fleura, Giana M. Eckhardt, and Eric J. Arnould. "Liquid Relationship to Possessions." *Journal of Consumer Research* 39, no. 3 (1 October 2012): 510–529. https://doi.org/10.1086/664037

Basso, Keith. *Wisdom Sits in Places: Landscape and Language Among the Western Apache.* Albuquerque: University of New Mexico Press, 1996.

Bates, Daniel. *Human Adaptive Strategies: Ecology, Culture, and Politics*, 3rd ed. Boston: Allyn & Bacon, 2005.

Baudrillard, Jean. *Selected Writings,* edited by Mark Poster. Stanford: Stanford University Press, 1988.

Bauman, Zygmunt. *Community: Seeking Safety in an Insecure World.* Malden: Polity Press, 2001.

Bauman, Zygmunt. *Liquid Times: Living in an Age of Uncertainty.* Cambridge: Polity Press, 2006.

Bauman, Zygmunt. *Consuming Life.* Malden: Polity, 2007.

Bauman, Zygmunt. *Liquid Modernity.* Cambridge: Polity Press, 2012.

Baumeister, Roy E. *Meanings of Life.* New York: The Guilford Press, 1991.

Bautier, R. H. *The Economic Development of Medieval Europe.* New York: Harcourt Brace Jovanovich, 1971.

Beattie, John. *Bunyoro: An African Kingdom.* New York: Holt, Rinehart and Winston, 1960.

Beaud, Michel. *A History of Capitalism, 1500–2000.* Translated by Tom Dickman and Anna Lefebvre. New York: Monthly Review Press, 2001.

Beinart, William. "African History and Environmental History." *African Affairs* 99, no. 395 (April 2000): 269–302. https://academic.oup.com/afraf/article-abstract/99/395/269/17395?redirectedFrom=fulltext

Belk, Russell W. and Richard W. Pollay. "Materialism and Magazine Advertising During the Twentieth Century." In *NA-Advances in Consumer Research Volume 12*, edited by Elizabeth C. Hirschman and Moris B. Holbrook, 394–398. Provo, UT: Association for Consumer Research, 1985. https://www.acrwebsite.org/volumes/6422/volumes/v12/NA-12#:~:text=Twentieth Century | ACR-,Materialism and Magazine Advertising During the Twentieth Century, eight decades of this century

Benson, April Lane. "Conclusion: What Are We Shopping For?" In *I Shop, Therefore I Am: Compulsive Buying & The Search for Self*, edited by April Lane Benson, 497–513. Northvale: Jason Aronson, 2000.

Bentz, Barbara, Jacques Régnière, Christopher J. Fettig, E. Matthew Hansen, Jane L. Hayes, Jeffrey A. Hicke, Rick G. Kelsey, et. al. "Climate Change and Bark Beetles of the Western United States and Canada: Direct and Indirect Effects." *BioScience* 60, no. 8 (September 2010): 602–613. https://academic.oup.com/bioscience/article/60/8/602/305152.

Berger, Peter. *The Sacred Canopy: Elements of a Sociological Theory of Religion.* New York: Doubleday, 1967.

Berger, Peter, Brigitt Berger and Hansfried Kellner. *The Homeless Mind: Modernization and Consciousness*. New York: Vintage Books, 1974.

Berkes, Fikret. *Sacred Ecology*. New York: Routledge, 2018.

Bernhardt, Emily S. and Margaret A. Palmer. 2011. "The Environmental Costs of Mountaintop Mining Valley Fill Operations for Aquatic Ecosystems of the Central Appalachians." *Annals of the New York Academy of Sciences* 1223, no. 1 (April): 39–57. https://aspubs.onlinelibrary.wiley.com/doi/abs/10.1111/j.1749-6632.2011.05986.x

Berry, Thomas. *The Great Work: Our Way into the Future.* New York: Bell Tower, 1999.

Berry, Thomas. *The Dream of the Earth.* San Francisco: Sierra Club Books, 2006.

Beston, Henry. *The Outermost House*. Cambridge: Harvard University Press, 2001 (org. 1928).

Bidney, David. "On the Concept of Cultural Crisis." *American Anthropologist* 48, no. 4, Part 1 (October–December 1946): 534–552.

Bidney, David. *Theoretical Anthropology*. New York: Schocken Books, 1967.

Bijma, J., H.-O. Poertner, C. Yesson, and A.D. Rogers. "Climate Change and the Oceans – What Does the Future Hold?" *Marine Pollution Bulletin* 74 (2013): 495–505.

Bloch, Marice. *Feudal Society, Volume 1: The Growth of Ties of Dependence*. Chicago: University of Chicago Press, 1964.

Boas, Franz. *The Social Organization and The Secret Societies of the Kwakiutl Indians.* Washington, DC: Smithsonian Institution and Elibron Classics, 2010 (org. 1897).

Bogardus, R. F. "The Reorientation of Paradise: Modern Mass Media and Narratives of Desire in the Making of American Consumer Culture." *American Literary History* 10, no. 3 (December 1998): 508–523. https://doi.org/10.1093/alh/10.3.508

Bohannan, Paul and Philip Curtin. *Africa and Africans.* Garden City: The Natural History Press, 1971.

Bohannan, Paul. "Circumcision among the Tiv." *Man* 54, no. 1 (January 1954): 2–6. https://www.jstor.org/stable/2795492?origin=crossref&typeAccessWorkflow=login&seq=2

Borgmann, Albert. *Crossing the Postmodern Divide*. Chicago: University of Chicago Press, 1992.

Bosch, K., L. Erdinger, F. Ingel, S. Khussainova, E. Utegenova, N. Bresgen, and P. M. Eckl. "Evaluation of the Toxicological Properties of Ground- and Surface-water Samples from the Aral Sea Basin." *Science for the Total Environment* 374, no. 1 (October 2007): 43–50. https://www.scencedrect.com/scence/artcle/abs/pii/S0048969706009168?via=ihub

Bostwick, Todd W. and Peter Krocek. *Landscape of the Spirits: Hohokam Rock Art at South Mountain Park*. Tucson: University of Arizona Press, 2002.

Bremner, J., D. López-Carr, L. Suter, and J. Davis. "Population, Poverty, Environment, and Climate Dynamics in the Developing World." *Interdisciplinary Environmental Review* 11, no. 2/3 (January 2010): 112–126. https://doi.org/10.1504/IER.2010.037902

British Geological Survey. Groundwater Quality: Ethiopia, 2001. http://www.bgs.ac.uk/downloads/start.cfm?id=1280

Brockerhoff, E. G., H. Jactel, J. A. Parrotta, C. P. Quine, and J. Sayer. "Plantation Forests and Biodiversity: Oxymoron or Opportunity?" *BioDivers Conserv* 17 (April 9, 2008): 925–951. https://doi.org/10.1007/s10531-008-9380-x

Brooks, David. "The Unifying American Story." *The New York Times* (March 21, 2017).

Brosius, J. Peter, George W. Lovelace, and Gerald G. Marten. *Ethnoecology: An Approach to Understanding Traditional Agricultural Knowledge*. Nashville: Westview Press, 1986.

Brown, Lester. *Full Planet, Empty Plates: The New Geopolitics of Food Scarcity*. New York: W. W. Norton, 2012.

Brumm, Adam, et al. "Early Human Symbolic Behavior in the Late Pleistocene of Wallacea." *PNAS, Proceeding of the National Academy of Sciences* 114, no. 16 (April 2017): 4105–4110. https://www.pnas.org/doi/10.1073/pnas.1619013114

Buchmann, Stephen. *What a Bee Knows: Exploring the Thoughts, Memories, and Personalities of Bees*. Washington: Island Press, 2023.

Business in Vancouver. "$5.3 billion B.C. gold mine faces major obstacles." *BIV: Resources and Agriculture* (June 2014). https://biv.com/article/2014/06/53-billion-bc-gold-mine-faces-major-obstacles

Buytaert, Wouter. "Water Resources: The Impact of Glacier Melt." *Grantham Institute*, Imperial College of London, 2021. www.imperial.ac.uk/grantham/research/resources-and-pollution/water-security-and-flood-risk/glacier-melt-and-water-security/

Campbell, Bruce and Ricardo A. Godoy. "Commonfield Agriculture: The Andes and Medieval England Compared." In *Making the Commons Work: Theory, Practice, and Policy*, edited by D. W. Bromley, 99–127. San Francisco: ICS Press, 1992.

Carleton, R. Nicholas. "Fear of the Unknown: One Fear to Rule Them All." *Journal of Anxiety Disorders* 41 (June 2016): 5–21. https://www.sciencedirect.com/science/article/pii/S0887618516300469

Carr, Nicolas. "Is Google Making Us Stupid?: What the Internet Is Doing to Our Brains." *The Atlantic* (July/August 2008) https://www.theatlantic.com/magazine/archive/2008/07/is-google-making-us-stupid/306868/

Castells, Manuel. "The Impact of the Internet on Society: A Global Perspective." *OpenMind BBVA*, n.d. https://www.bbvaopenmind.com/en/articles/the-impact-of-the-internet-on-society-a-global-perspective/

Castells, Manuel. *The Power of Identity*, 2nd edition, Malden: Blackwell Publishing, 2004.

Castells, Manuel. "Globalization and Identity." *TRANSFER, A Journal of Contemporary Culture* 1 (2006): 56–67. https://www.llull.cat/rec_transfer/webt1/transfer01.pdf

Ceballos, Gerardo, P. R. Ehrlich, A. D. Barnosky, A. García, R. M. Pringle, and T. M. Palmer. "Accelerated Modern Human–induced Species Losses: Entering the Sixth Mass Mxtinction." *Science Advances* 1, no. 5 (June 2015). https://www.science.org/doi/10.1126/sciadv.1400253

Chazdon, Robin L. *Second Growth: The Promise of Tropical Forest Regeneration in an Age of Deforestation*. Chicago: University of Chicago Press, 2014.

Chang, LinChiat and Robert M. Arkin. "Materialism as an Attempt to Cope with Uncertainty." *Psychology & Marketing* 19, no. 5 (April 2002): 389–406. https://onlinelibrary.wiley.com/doi/epdf/10.1002/mar.10016

Cheng, Lijing, Kevin Trenberth, John Fasullo, Tim Boyer, John Abraham, and Jia Zhu. "Improved Estimates of Ocean Heat Content from 1960 to 2015." *Science Advances* 3, no. 3 (March 2017). https://www.science.org/doi/10.1126/sciadv.1601545

Christianson, John Robert. *Tycho Brahe and the Measure of the Heavens*. London: Reaction Books, 2020.

Cohen, Joshua and Joel Rogers. *On Democracy: Toward a Transformation of American Society*. New York: Penguin Books, 1983.

Colborn, Theo, Carol Kwiatkowski, Kim Schultz, and Mary Bachran. "Natural Gas Operations from a Public Health Perspective." *Human and Ecological Risk Assessment: An International Journal* 17, no. 5 (September 20, 2011): 1039–1056. https://doi.org/10.1080/10807039.2011.605662

Conklin, Harold. *Hanunoo Agriculture: A Report on an Integral System of Shifting Cultivation in the Philippines*. FAO Forestry Development Paper 12. Rome: FAO, 1975 (org. 1953).

Connerton, Paul. *How Modernity Forgets*. Cambridge: Cambridge University Press, 2009.

Cook, Eliza and Rachel Dunifon. "Do Family Meals Really Make a Difference?" College of Human Ecology, Cornell University, 2012. https://citeseerx.ist.psu.edu/viewdoc/download;jsessionid=8C5455F914120D3AAA26EFFA374DD651?doi=10.1.1.400.8584&rep=rep1&type=pdf

Coontz, Stephanie. *The Way We Never Were: American Families and the Nostalgia Trap*. New York: Basic Books, 2000.

Cornell, Stephen. *Return of the Native: American Indian Political Resurgence*. London: Oxford University Press, 1988.

Cox, Daniel A. "The State of American Friendship: Change, Challenges, and Loss. Survey Center on American Life." *American Enterprise Institute* (June 2021). https://www.aei.org/research-products/report/the-state-of-american-friendship-change-challenges-and-loss/

Crate, Susan and Mark Nuttall, eds. *Anthropology and Climate Change: From Encounters to Actions*. New York: Routledge, 2009.

Cronon, William. *Changes in the Land: Indians, Colonists, and the Ecology of New England.* New York: Macmillan, 1983.

Cronon, William, ed. *Uncommon Ground: Rethinking the Human Place.* New York: W.W. Norton, 1996.

Crutzen, Paul and Eugene Stoermer. "The 'Anthropocene.'" *IGBP Global Change Newsletter* 41 (2000): 17–18. http://www.igbp.net/download18.316f18321323470177580001401/1376383088452/NL41.pdf

Cushman, Philip. "Why the Self Is Empty: Toward a Historically Situated Psychology." *American Psychologist* 45, no. 5 (May 1990): 599–611. https://psycnet.apa.org/doiLanding?doi=10.1037/0003-066X.45.5.599

Daughton, Christian. "Emerging Chemicals as Pollutants in the Environment: A 21st Century Perspective." *Renewable Resources Journal* 23, no. 4 (Winter 2005): 6–23.

Dauvergne, Peter. *Will Big Business Destroy the Planet?* Medford: Polity Press, 2018.

Davey, Graham. "Is There an Anxiety Epidemic?" *Psychology Today* blog, 2018. www.psychologytoday.com/us/blog/why-we-worry/201811/is-there-anxiety-epidemic

Davis, Mike. *Planet of Slums.* London: Verso, 2007.

Davis, Ralph. *The Rise of the Atlantic Economies.* Ithaca: Cornell University Press, 1973.

Dávlia, Arlene. *Latinos, Inc: The Marketing and Making of a People.* Oakland: University of California Press, 2001.

Deloria, Ella Cara. *Speaking of Indians.* Lincoln: University of Nebraska Press, 1998 (org.1944).

Dennett, Daniel C. "Animal Consciousness: What Matters and Why." *Social Research* 62, no. 3 (1995): 691–710. https://www.jstor.org/stable/i40043691

Derber, Charles and Yale R. Magrass. *Capitalism: Should You Buy It? An Invitation to Political Economy.* Boulder: Paradigm Publishers, 2014.

Descola, Phillppe and Gisli Palsson, eds. *Nature and Society: Anthropological Perspectives.* London: Routledge, 1996.

de Souza, Jonas Gregorio, Denise Pahl Schaan, Mark Robinson, Antonia Damasceno Barbosa, Luiz E. O. C. Aragão, Ben Hur Marimon Jr., Beatriz Schwantes Marimon, et al. "Pre-Columbian Earth-builders Settled along the Entire Southern Rim of the Amazon." *Nature Communications* 9 (2018): 1125. https://www.nature.com/articles/s41467-018-03510-7

Diamond, J. M. "The Present, Past and Future of Human-Caused Extinctions." *Philosophical Transactions of the Royal Society B: Biological Sciences* 325 (November 1989): 469–477. https://doi.org/10.1098/rstb.1989.0100

Diamond, Jared. *Collapse: How Societies Choose to Fail or Succeed.* New York: Viking Press, 2011.

Dittmar, Helga. *The Social Psychology of Material Possessions: To Have is To Be.* New York: St. Martin' Press, 1992.

Dobb, Maurice. *Studies in the Development of Capitalism.* New York: International Publishers, 1947.

Domhoff, G. William. *Who Rules America.* Saddle River: Prentice-Hall, 1967.

Domhoff, G. William. *Who Rules America Now?* Saddle River: Prentice-Hall, 1983.

Dowd, Heather. "A Brief History of the Slow Food Movement." *tourissmo.travel* (July 27, 2016). https://www.tourissimo.travel/blog/a-brief-history-of-the-slow-food-movement

Downey, Liam, Eric Bonds, and Katherine Clark. "Natural Resource Extraction, Armed Violence, and Environmental Degradation." *Organization and Environment* 23, no. 4 (December 2010): 417–445. https://doi.org/10.1177/1086026610385

Drouin, Roger. "Wood Pellets: Green Energy or New Source of CO_2 Emissions." *YaleEnvironment*[360] (January 22, 2015). https://e360.yale.edu/features/wood_pellets_green_energy_or_new_source_of_co2_emissions

Dunlap, Riley E. and Arron M. McCright. "Organized Climate Change Denial." In *The Oxford Handbook of Climate Change and Society*, edited by John S. Dryzek, Richard B. Norgaard, and David Schlosberg, 144–160. New York: Oxford University Press, 2011.

Easterlin, Richard A. "Does Economic Growth Improve the Human Lot? Some Empirical Evidence." In *Nations and Households in Economic Growth: Essays in Honor of Moses Abramovitz,* edited by Paul A. David and Melvin W. Reder, 89–126. New York: Academic Press, 1974.

Eckett, Penelope and Russell Newmark. "Central Eskimo Song Duels: A Contextual Analysis of Ritual Ambiguity." *Ethnology* 19, no. 2 (April 1980): 191–211. https://doi.org/10.2307/3773271

Eisenstadt, S. N. "African Age Groups: A Comparative Study." *Africa Journal of the International African Institute* 24, no. 2 (April 1954): 100–113. https://doi.org/10.2307/1156134

Elkind, David. "School and Family in the Postmodern World." *Phi Delta Kappan* 77, no. 1 (1995): 8–14.

Ellul, Jacques. *The Technological Society*. New York: Vintage Books, 1964.

Energy Information Administration. EIA Expects U.S. Energy-related CO2 Emissions to Fall in 2019. U.S. Energy Information Administration (July 15, 2019). www.eia.gov/todayinenergy/detail.php?id=40094

EPA. *A Closer Look: Temperature and Drought in the Southwest.* Washington, DC: Environmental Protection Agency, 2021. www.epa.gov/climate-indicators/southwest

Epstein, Paul R., et al. "Full Cost Accounting for the Life Cycle of Coal." In *Ecological Economic Reviews,* edited by Robert Costana, Karin E. Limburg, and Ida Kubiszewski, 73–98. Annals of the New York Academy of Sciences 1219. New York: Wiley-Blackwell, 2011.

Erchak, Gerald M. *The Anthropology of Self and Behavior*. New Brunswick: Rutgers University Press, 1998.

Eriksen, Thomas Hylland. *Overheating: An Anthropology of Accelerated Change.* London: Pluto Press, 2016.

Eriksen, Thomas Hylland and Elisabeth Schober. *Identity Destabilised: Living in an Overheated World.* London: Pluto Press, 2016.

Erickson, Clark L. "The Transformation of Environment into Landscape: The Historical Ecology of Monumental Earthwork Construction in the Bolivian Amazon." *Diversity* 2, (2010): 618–652. doi:10.3390/d2040619

Evans-Pritchard, E. E. *The Nuer: A Description of the Modes of Livelihood and Political Institutions of a Nilotic People.* Oxford: Oxford University Press, 1969.

Eyerman, Ron. "Modernity and Social Movements." In *Social Change and Modernity*, edited by Hans Haferkamp and Neil J. Smelser, 37–54. Berkeley, CA: University of California Press, 1992.

Evernden, Neil. *The Natural Alien: Humankind and Environment.* Toronto: University of Toronto Press, 1993.

Fagan, Brian. *Clash of Cultures.* Lanham: AltaMira Press, 1998.

Fagan, Brian. *The Great Warming: Climate Change and the Rise and Fall of Civilizations.* New York: Bloomsbury Press, 2008.

Fahey, D. W., S. J. Doherty, K. A. Hibbard, A. Romanou, and P. C. Taylor. "Physical Drivers of Climate Change." In *Climate Science Special Report: Fourth National Climate Assessment, Volume I,* edited by D. J. Wuebbles, D. W. Fahey, K. A. Hibbard, D. J. Dokken, B. C. Stewart, and T. K. Maycock, 73–113. Washington, DC: U.S. Global Change Research Program, 2017.

Fauna & Flora. "Update to An Assessment of the Risks and Impacts of Seabed Mining on Marine Ecosystems." Cambridge, UK, 2023. www.fauna-flora.org

Feagon, Robert. "The Place of Food: Mapping Out the 'Local' in Local Food Systems." *Progress in Human Geography* 31, no. 1 (February 2007): 23–42. https://journals.sagepub.com/doi/abs/10.1177/0309132507073527

Featherstone, Mike. "Perspectives on Consumer Culture." *Sociology* 24, no. 1 (February 1990): 5–22. https://www.jstor.org/stable/42854622?typeAccessWorkflow=login

Feit, Harvey A. "Hunting, Nature, and Metaphor: Political and Discursive Strategies in Ames Bay Cree Resistance and Autonomy." In *Indigenous Traditions and Ecology: The Intervening of Cosmology and Community*, edited by John A. Grim, 411–445. Cambridge: Harvard University Press, 2001.

Fewkes, J. Walter. "The Feather Symbol in Ancient Hopi Designs." *The American Anthropologist* 11, No. 1 (January 1898): 1–14. https://anthrosource.onlinelibrary.wiley.com/doi/abs/10.1525/aa.1898.11.1.02a00010

Fienup-Riordan, Ann. "A Guest on the Table: Ecology from the Yup'ik Eskimo Point of View." In *Indigenous Traditions and Ecology: The Interbeing of Cosmology and Community,* edited by John A. Grim, 541–558. Cambridge: Harvard University Press, 2001.

Firth, Raymond. *We the Tikopia: A Sociological Study of Kinship in Primitive Polynesia.* London: Allen & Unwin, 1936.

FDA. *Pesticide Residue Monitoring Program: Fiscal Year 2017 Pesticide Report..* Washington, DC: Food and Drug Administration, 2017. https://www.fda.gov/media/130291/download?attachment

Foster, Derek. "Community and Identity in the Electronic Village." In *Internet Culture*, edited by David Porter, 23–38. London: Routledge, 1996.

Foster, John Bellamy, Brett Clark, and Richard York. *The Ecological Rift: Capitalism's War on the Earth.* New York: Monthly Review Press, 2010.

Fresco, Louise O. "Why We Eat Together: Communal Dining Is a Quintessential Human Experience." *The Atlantic* (November 26, 2015).

Fromm, Eric. *The Art of Loving*. New York: Harper & Row, Publishers, 1956.

Galbraith, John Kenneth. *The Affluent Society*. Boston: Houghton Mifflin, 1952.

Galtung, Johan. "On the Social Costs of Modernization. Social Disintegration, Atomie/Anomie and Social Development." *Development and Change* 37 (April 1996): 379–413. https://onlinelibrary.wiley.com/toc/14677660/1996/27/2

Garcia Canclini, Nestor. *Transforming Modernity: Popular Culture in Mexico*. Austin: University of Texas Press, 1993.

Garcia Canclini, Nestor. *Consumers and Citizens: Globalization and Multicultural Conflicts*. Minneapolis: University of Minnesota Press, 2001.

GEAS. "One Planet, How Many People? A Review of Earth's Carrying Capacity." *Global Environmental Alert Service*. United Nations Environmental Program, 2012. https://na.unep.net/geas/archive/pdfs/GEAS_Jun_12_Carrying_Capacity.pdf

Geertz, Clifford. "From the Native's Point of View: On the Nature of Anthropological Understanding." *American Academy of Arts and Sciences*, Bulletin 28, no. 1 (1974): 26–43. https://elearning.unito.it/scuolacle/pluginfile.php/218206/mod_resource/content/1/Geertz-dalpuntodivistadeinativi.pdf

Giddens, Anthony. *The Consequences of Modernity*. Stanford: Stanford University Press, 1991.

Gilens, Martin. *Affluence and Influence: Economic Inequality and Political Power in America*. New Haven: Princeton University Press, 2014.

Gilens, Martin and Benjamin Page. "Testing Theories of American Politics: Elites, Interest Groups, and Average Citizens." *Perspectives on Politics* 12, no. 3 (September 2014): 564–581. https://www.cambridge.org/core/journals/perspectives-on-politics/article/testing-theories-of-american-politics-elites-interest-groups-and-average-citizens/62327F513959D0A304D4893B382B992B

Gjerde, K. M., Duncan Currie, Kateryna Wowk, and Karen Sack. "Ocean in Peril: Reforming the Management of Global Ocean Living Resources in Areas beyond National Jurisdiction." *Marine Pollution Bulletin* 74, no. 2 (August 2013). https://doi.org/10.1016/j.marpolbul.2013.07.037

Glacken, Clarence. *Traces on the Rhodian Shore: Nature and Culture in Western Thought from Ancient Times to the End of the Eighteenth Century*. Berkeley: University of California Press, 1967.

Glacken, Clarence J. "Creating a Second Nature." In *The Cultural Geography Reader*, edited by Timothy S. Oakes and Patricia L. Price, 212–219. London: Routledge, 2008.

Glantz, Michael. "Water, Climate, and Development Issues in the Amu Darya Basin." *Mitigation and Adaptation Strategies for Global Change* 10 (January 2005): 23–50. https://link.springer.com/article/10.1007/s11027-005-7829-8

Gleick, Peter H. and Matthew Heberger. "Water and Conflict: Events, Trends, and Analysis, 2011–2012." The World's Water 8. (January 2014). *The Pacific Institute*. https://islandpress.org/books/worlds-water-volume-8

Glickman, Lawrence. *Consumer Society in American History*. Ithaca: Cornell University Press, 1999.

Global Footprint Network. "Species and Spaces, People and Places." *World Footprint,* 2014. www.footprintnetwork.org/en/index.php/GFN/page/world_footprint/

Goffman, Erving. *The Presentation of Self in Everyday Life.* New York: Anchor Books, 1959.

Goldenberg, Suzanne. "Why Global Water Shortages Pose Threat of Terror and War." *The Guardian* (February 8, 2014).

Gray, Peter. "Helicopter Parenting & College Students' Increased Neediness: Researchers Link Helicopter Parenting to Emotional Fragility in Young Adults." *Psychology Today* (October 2015.). www.psychologytoday.com/us/blog/freedom-learn/201510/helicopter-parenting-college-students-increased-neediness?collection=1080494

Graeber, David. *Toward an Anthropological Theory of Value: The False Coin of Our Own Dreams.* New York: Palgrave, 2001.

Green, John C. *The Death of Adam: Evolution and Its Impact on Western Thought.* Ames: University of Iowa Press, 1950.

Griffin, Donald. *Animal Minds: Beyond Cognition to Consciousness.* Chicago: University of Chicago Press, 2002.

Griffin, Jo. *The Lonely Society?* London: The Mental Health Foundation, 2010.

Grover, Tim. Relentless: From Good to Great to Unstoppable. New York: Scribner, 2014

Guelke, Leonard and Robert Shell. "Landscape of Conquest: Frontier Water Alienation and Khoikhoi Strategies of Survival, 1652–1780." *Journal of Southern African Studies* 18, no. 4 (1992): 803–882. https://www.tandfonline.com/doi/abs/10.1080/03057079208708339

Hacker, Jacob S. and Paul Pierson. "Winner-Take-All Politics: Public Policy, Political Organization, and the Precipitous Rise of Top Incomes in the United States." *Politics & Society* 38, no. 2 (2010): 152–204. https://isps.yale.edu/research/publications/isps10-022

Hague, Evan. "Pilsen—The Gentrification Frontier." AAG Newsletter. *Association of American Geographers* (March 2015). www.news.aag.org/2015/03/pilsen-the-gentrification-frontier/

Hall, Anthony. *The American Empire and the Fourth World.* Montreal: McGill-Queen's University Press, 2005.

Hames, Raymond. "The Ecologically Noble Savage Debate." *Annual Review of Anthropology* 36 (2007): 177–190. https://www.annualreviews.org/doi/pdf/10.1146/annurev.anthro.35.081705.123321

Harari, Yuval Noah. *Sapiens: A Brief History of Humankind.* New York: HarperCollins, 2015.

Harding, Steven. *Animate Earth: Science, Intuition and Gaia.* White River Junction: Chelsea Green Publishing Co., 2009.

Harding, Steven. "What Does It Mean to Be Human? Experiencing Our Full Humanity Requires Us to Attenuate Our Self-centeredness by Enfolding It Within a Much Wider Sense of Self in Which We Experience Genuine Love and Compassion for All Beings, Both Living and Non-living." *Center for Humans and Nature* (n.d.). https://humansandnature.org/to-be-human-stephan-harding/

Harkin, Michael E. and David Rich Lewis, eds. *Native Americans and the Environment: Perspectives on the Ecological Indian.* Lincoln: University of Nebraska Press, 2007.

Harris, Michael. *The End of Absence: Reclaiming What We've Lost in a World of Constant Connection.* New York: Penguin Random House, 2014.

Harrod, Howard. *The Animals Came Dancing: Native American Sacred Ecology and Animal Kinship*. Tucson: University of Arizona Press, 2000.

Harvey, David. *A Brief History of Neoliberalism.* New York: Oxford University Press, 2005.

HAVAS Worldwide. "The New Consumer." *Euro RSCG Worldwide Knowledge Exchange,* 2012. https://newconsumer.com/

Hawkin, Paul, Amory B. Lovins, and L. Hunter Lovins. *Natural Capitalism: The Next Industrial Revolution*. New York: Earthscan, 2010.

Hay, Robert. "Becoming Ecosynchronous, Part 2. Achieving Sustainable Development via Personal Development." *Sustainable Development* 14, no. 1 (August 2006): 1–15. https://onlinelibrary.wiley.com/doi/abs/10.1002/sd.257

Heider, Karl. *The Dugum Dani: A Papuan Culture in the Highlands of West New Guinea*. New York: Aldine Publishing Company, 1970.

Heitmann, John A. "The Beginnings of Big Sugar in Florida, 1920–1945." *Florida Historical Quarterly* 77, no. 1 (1998):39–61. http://journals.openedition.org/miranda/2881

Hemler, Elena C., Jorge E. Chacvarro, and B. Hu Frank. "Organic Foods for Cancer Prevention—Worth the Investment?" *JAMA Internal Medicine* (October 2018). https://d3n8a8pro7vhmx.cloudfront.net/yesmaam/pages/680/attachments/original/1540322728/jamainternal_Hemler_2018_ic_180041.pdf?1540322728

Heyd, Thomas and Nick Brooks. "Exploring Cultural Dimensions of Adaptation to Climate Change." In *Adapting to Climate Change: Thresholds, Values, Governance*, edited by W. Neil Adger, Irene Lorenzoni, and Karen O'Brien, 269–282. Cambridge: Cambridge University Press, 2009.

Hidaka, Brandon H. "Depression as a Disease of Modernity: Explanations for Increasing Prevalence." *Journal of Affective Disorders* 140 (2012): 205–214. https://www.ncbi.nlm.nih.gov/pmc/articles/PMC3330161/

Hirsch, Eric and Michael O'Hanlon. *The Anthropology of Landscape: Perspectives on Place and Space*. Oxford: Clarendon Press, 1995.

Hoogvelt, Ankie. *Globalization and the Postcolonial World: The New Political Economy of Development*. London: MacMillan Press Ltd, 1997.

Honorata, Korpikiewicz and Deremiowska Malgorzata. "Listening to Anima Mundi: The Organic Metaphor in the Cosmoecological Perspective." *Lingua ac Communitas* 20 (2010): 13–36. https://repozytorium.amu.edu.pl/items/f450e495-c10a-4f77-ad75-dd29726081a3

Howell, Signe. *The Ethnography of Moralities*. London: Routledge, 1996.

Huesemann, Michael and Joyce Huesemann. *Techno-Fix: Why Technology Won't Save Us or the Environment*. Gabriola Island: New Society Publishers, 2011.

Hurn, Samantha. *Humans and Other Animals: Cross-Cultural Perspectives on Human-Animal Interactions*. London: Pluto Press, 2012.

Hymes, Dell. *Reinventing Anthropology*. New York: Vintage Books, 1974.

IGBP, IOC, SCOR. *Ocean Acidification Summary for Policymakers—Third Symposium on the Ocean in a High-CO_2 World*. Stockholm, Sweden: International Geosphere-Biosphere Programme, 2013.

Infurna, Frank J., Nutifafa E. Y. Dey, Tita Gonzalez Avilés, Kevin J. Grimm, Margie E. Lachman, and Denis Gerstorf. "Loneliness in Midlife: Historical Increases and Elevated Levels in the United States Compared with Europe." *American Psychologist*, 2024. https://www.apa.org/pubs/journals/releases/amp-amp0001322.pdf

Ingebritsen, S. E. "Florida Everglades: Subsidence Threatens Agriculture and Complicates Ecosystem Restoration." In *Land Subsistence in the United States*, edited by Devin Galloway, David R. Jones and S. E. Ingebritsen. U.S. Geological Survey Circular 1182, 1999.

Ingold, Tim. "The Temporality of the Landscape. Conceptions of Time and Ancient Society." *World Archaeology* 25, no. 2 (1993): 152–174. https://quote.ucsd.edu/sed/files/2014/09/Ingold-Temporality-of-the-Landscape.pdf

Ingold, Tim. "Rethinking the Animate, Re-Animating Thought." *ETHNOS* 71, no. 1 (2006): 9–20. https://cspeech.ucd.ie/Fred/docs/IngoldAnimacy.pdf

Ingold, Tim. *The Perception of the Environment: Essays on Livelihood, Dwelling and Skill*. New York: Routledge, 2011.

IPBES. "Nature's Dangerous Decline 'Unprecedented' Species Extinction Rates 'Accelerating.'" *Intergovernmental Science-Policy Platform on Biodiversity and Ecosystem Services*, edited by S. Díaz, J. Settele, E. S. Brondízio, H. T. Ngo, M. Guèze, J. Agard, A. Arneth, et al. IPBES, 2019. www.ipbes.net/sites/default/files/2020-02/ ipbes_global_assessment_report_summary_for_policymakers_en.pdf

IPCC. *Climate Change 2014: Impacts, Adaption, and Vulnerability*. IPCC WGII AR5 Summary for Policymakers. Intergovernmental Panel on Climate Change, Geneva, Switzerland, 2014. www.ipcc-wg2.gov/AR5/images/uploads/IPCC_WG2AR5_SPM_Approved.pdf

IPCC, "Summary for Policymakers." In *Global Warming of 1.5°C*. An IPCC Special Report on the Impacts of Global Warming of 1.5°C above Pre-industrial Levels and Related Global Greenhouse Gas Emission Pathways, in the Context of Strengthening the Global Response to the Threat of Climate Change, Sustainable Development, and Efforts to Eradicate Poverty, edited by V. Masson-Delmotte, P. Zhai, H.-O. Pörtner, D. Roberts, J. Skea, P.R. Shukla, A. Pirani, W. Moufouma-Okia, et al. Cambridge University Press, Cambridge, UK and New York, 2018: 3–24. doi:10.1017/9781009157940.001.

IPCC, Summary for Policymakers. In: *Climate Change 2021: The Physical Science Basis. Contribution of Working Group I to the Sixth Assessment Report of the Intergovernmental Panel on Climate Change,* edited by V. Masson-Delmotte, P. Zhai, A. Pirani, S.L. Connors, C. Péan, S. Berger, N. Caud, Y. Chen, L. Goldfarb, M.I. Gomis, M. Huang, K. Leitzell, E. Lonnoy, J.B.R. Matthews, T.K. Maycock, T. Waterfield, O. Yelekçi, R. Yu, and B. Zhou. Cambridge University Press, Cambridge, UK and New York, 2021. report/ar6/wg1/

IPCC. Climate Change 2022: Summary for Policymakers."In *Climate Change 2022: Impacts, Adaptation and Vulnerability. Contribution of Working Group II to the Sixth Assessment Report of the Intergovernmental Panel on Climate Change,* edited by H.-O. Pörtner, D.C. Roberts, E.S. Poloczanska, K. Mintenbeck, M. Tignor, A. Alegría, M. Craig, S. Langsdorf, S. Löschke, V. Möller, A. Okem, and B. Rama. Cambridge University Press, Cambridge, UK and New York, 2022. https://library.wmo.int/doc_num.php?explnum_id=11359

Jahoda, Gustav. *ages of Savages: Ancient Roots of Modern Prejudice in Western Culture*. New York: Routledge, 1999.

James, Paul, and Imre Szeman. "Global-Local Consumption." In *Globalization and Culture*, edited by Paul James and Imre Szeman, ix–xxix. London: Sage Publications, 2010.

Jameson, Fredric. "Postmodernism and Consumer Society." In *Modernism/Postmodernism*, edited by Peter Brooker, 163–179. New York: Longman, 1992.

Jhally, Sut. "Advertising & the End of the World." In *Media Education Foundation.* Northampton, MA, 1997. https://www.mediaed.org/transcripts/Advertising-and-the-End-of-the-World-Transcript.pdf

Jhally, Sut. "Image Based Culture: Advertising and Popular Culture." In *The Gender, Race,Class and Media Reader*, edited by Gail Dines and Jean M. Humez, 199–204. Thousand Oaks: Sage Publishing, 2003.

Kaku, Michio. *The Future of Humanity: Our Destiny in the Universe.* New York: Anchor Books, 2019.

Kale, Sudhir H., Sangita De, and Robin D. Pentecost. "Homeless Abroad, Homeless at Home: The Conundrum of Globalisation." *ANZMAC 2007 Conference Proceedings*. Griffith University Research Online, 2007. https://research-repository.griffith.edu.au/bitstream/handle/10072/32379/50786_1.pdf?sequence=1

Kasser, Tim. *The High Price of Materialism.* Cambridge: MIT Press, 2002.

Kasser, Tim, and R.M. Ryan. "A Dark Side of the American Dream: Correlates of Financial Success as a Central Life Aspiration." *Journal of Personality and Social Psychology* 65 (1993): 410–422. http://dx.doi.org/10.1037/0022-3514.65.2.410

Kasser, Tim, Richard Ryan, Charles Couchman, and Kennon Sheldon. "Materialistic Values: Their Causes and Consequences." In *Psychology and Consumer Culture: The Struggle for aGood Life in a Materialistic World,* edited by Tim Kasser and Allen D. Kanner, 11–28. Washington: American Psychological Association, 2004.

Keenan, Trevor F., David Y. Hollinger, Gil Bohrer, Danilo Dragoni, J. William Munger, Hans Pete Schmid, and Andrew D. Richardson. "Increase in Forest Water-use Efficiency as Atmospheric Carbon Dioxide Concentrations Rise." *Nature* 499, no. 7458 (2013): 324–327.

Keesing, Roger M. "On Not Understanding Symbols: Toward an Anthropology of Incomprehension." *HAU: Journal of Ethnographic Theory* 2, no. 2 (2012): 406–430. https://www.haujournal.org/index.php/hau/article/view/hau2.2.023

Kharas, Homi, and Geoffrey Gertz. "The New Global Middle Class: A Cross-Over from West to East." In *Wolfensohn Center for Development at Brookings,* 2010. content/uploads/2016/06/03_china_middle_class_kharas.pdf

Klare, Michael T. *Resource Wars: The New Landscape of Global Conflict.* New York: Henry Holt and Co., 2001.

Klein, Naomi. "Capitalism vs. the Climate." *The Nation,* November 28, 2011.

Klein, Naomi. "The Change Within: The Obstacles We Face Are Not Just External." *The Nation,* May 12, 2014, 2014a.

Klein, Naomi. *This Changes Everything.* New York: Simon & Schuster, 2014b.

Kline, Kathleen. *Hardwired to Connect: The New Scientific Case for Authoritative Communities.* Commission on Children at Risk, Institute for American Values, 2008. http://www.americanvalues.org/html/hardwired.html

Kok, M.T.J., and J. Jäger. eds. "Vulnerability of People and the Environment – Challenges and Opportunities." Background Report on Chapter 7 of the Fourth UN Global Environment Outlook 4. United Nations Environment Programme. Progress Press Ltd, Malta, 2009.

Kolbert, Elizabeth. *The Sixth Extinction: An Unnatural History.* New York: Picador, 2014.

Kolbert, Elizabeth. *Field Notes from a Catastrophe: Man, Nature, and Climate Change*, revised edition. New York: Bloomsbury Publishers, 2015.

Kolbert, Elizabeth. "Fate of the Earth." Lecture at the Nation Institute and the New School, 2017. www.occupyearth.art/blog/elizabeth-kolbert-on-the-fate-of-the-earth

Korten, David C. *The Great Turning: From Empire to Earth Community.* Bloomfield: Kumarian Press, 2006.

Kovel, Joel. *The Enemy of Nature: The End of Capitalism or the End of the World?* London: Zed Books, 2007.

Krech, Stacey. *The Ecological Indian: Myth and History.* New York: W.W. Norton, 2000.

Lachmann, Richard. *From Manor to Market: Structural Change in England, 1536–1640.* Madison, WI: University of Wisconsin Press, 1987.

Ladd, Brittain. "Meal Kits are DOA: The Next Big Trends in Food Are Being Driven by Amazon, ICON Meals and Mercatus." *Forbes,* December 2018.

Langman, Lauren. "Alienation and Everyday Life: Goffman Meets Marx at the Shopping Mall." *International Journal of Sociology and Social Policy* 11, no. 6–8 (1991): 107–124. https://doi.org/10.1108/eb013149

Lahren, Sylvester. "A Shoshone/Goshute Traditional Cultural Property and Cultural Landscape, Spring Valley, Nevada." Prepared at the Request of the Confederated Tribes of the Goshute Reservation, Ibapah, Utah, 2010.

Lasch, Christopher. *The Culture of Narcissism: American Life in An Age of Diminishing Expectations*, Reissue edition. New York: W.W. Norton, 2018.

Laszlo, Ervin. *The Upshift: Wiser Living on Planet Earth.* Cardiff, CA: Waterside Productions, 2022

Laurance, William F. "Future Shock: Forecasting a Grim Fate for the Earth." *TRENDS in Ecology & Evolution* 16, no. 10 (2001): 531–533. https://www.sciencedirect.com/journal/trends-in-ecology-and-evolution/vol/16/issue/10

Leach, Edmund. *A Runaway World? The Reith Lectures 1967.* Oxford: Oxford University Press, 1967.

Leach, William. *Land of Desire: Merchants, Poser and the Rise of a New American Culture*. New York: Vintage Books, 1993.

Lebow, Victor. "Price Competition in 1955." *Journal of Retailing,* 1955. https://hundredgoals.files.wordpress.com/2009/05/journal-of-retailing.pdf

Lemaire, Janine, and Bénédicte Sisto. "The Everglades Ecosystem: Under Protection or Under Threat?" *Miranda* 6, 2012. https://doi.org/10.4000/miranda.2881

Levine, Bruce E. "How our Society Breeds Anxiety, Depression and Dysfunction." *Salon,* August 2013. www.salon.com/2013/08/26/how_our_society_breeds_anxiety_depression_and_dysfunction_partner/

Levy, David M. "No Time to Think: Reflections on Information Technology and Contemplative Scholarship." *Ethnics & Information Technology* 9, no. 4 (2007): 237–249. https://doi.org/ 10.1007/s10676-007-9142-6

Lewandowsky, Stephan, James S. Risbey, and Naomi Oreskes. "On the Definition and Identifiability of the Alleged 'Hiatus' in Global Warming." *Scientific Reports* 5, no. 16784, 2015. www.nature.com/articles/srep16784

Liberman, Matthew D. *Social: Why Our Brains Are Wired to Connect*. New York: Oxford University Press, 2015.

Linden, Eugene. *The Winds of Change: Climate, Weather, and the Destruction of Civilizations*. New York: Simon & Schuster, 2007.

Link, Michael, Franzisk Piontek, Jürgen Scheffran, and Janpeter Schilling. "On Foes and Flows: Water Conflict and Cooperation in the Nile River Basin in Times of Climate Change." n.d. https://web.mit.edu/12.000/www/m2017/pdfs/nilebasin.pdf

Locke, John. "The Second Treatise of Civil Government." 1690. www.marxists.org/reference/subject/politics/locke/index.htm

Lovejoy, Thomas, and Carlos Nobre. "Amazon Tipping Point: Last Chance for Action." *Science Advances* 5, (2019): eaba2949. https://www.science.org/doi/10.1126/sciadv.aba2949

Lubin, Gus. "There's a Staggering Conspiracy Behind the Rise of Consumer Culture." *Business Insider,* February 2013. www.businessinsider.com/birth-of-consumer-culture-2013-2?op=1

Ludwig, Fulco, Catharien Terwisscha van Scheltinga, Jan Verhagen, Bart Kruijt, Ekko van Ierland, Rob Dellink, Karianne de Bruin, Kelly de Bruin, and Pavel Kabat. "Climate Change Impacts on Developing Countries—EU Accountability." *European Parliament's Committee on the Environment, Public Health and Food Safety*, IP/A/ENVI/ST/2007-04. Brussels, The Netherlands, 2007.

Lukianoff, Greg, and Jonathan Haidt. "The Coddling of the American Mind." *The Atlantic,* September 2015.

Lury, Celia. *Consumer Culture*. New Brunswick: Rutgers University Press, 1998.

MacCannell, Dean. *The Tourist: A New Theory of the Leisure Class*. Berkeley: University of California Press, 2013.

Macpherson, C.B. *Property: Mainstream and Critical Positions*. Toronto: University of Toronto Press, 1978.

Magdoff, Fred, and John Bellamy Foster. *What Every Environmentalist Needs to Know about Capitalism*. New York: Monthly Review Press, 2011.

Malinowski, Bronislaw. *Argonauts of the Western Pacific: An Account of Native Enterprise and Adventure in the Archipelagoes of Melanesian New Guinea*. New York: E. P. Dutton & Co., 1961 (org. 1922).

Mander, Jerry. *The Capitalist Papers: Fatal Flaws of an Obsolete System.* Berkeley: Counterpoint, 2012.

Mann, Charles. *1494: New Revelations of the Americas Before Columbus*. New York: Vintage Books, 2006.

Marcuse, Herbert. *One Dimensional Man*. Boston: Beacon Press, 1968.

Martin, Calvin. *Keepers of the Game: Indian-Animal Relationships and the Fur Trade*. Berkeley: University of California Press, 1978.

Martin, Claude. *On the Edge: The State and Fate of the World's Tropical Rainforests.* Vancouver: Greystone Books, 2015.

Martinez Carlos, Fox Michael, and JoJo Farrell. *Venezuela Speaks!: Voices from the Grassroots*. Oakland: PM Press, 2010.

Marx, Karl. The Eighteenth Brumaire of Louis Bonaparte, 1852. www.marxists.org/archive/marx/works/1852/18th-brumaire/ch01.htm

Marx, Karl. Economic and Philosophical Manuscripts, 1932 (org. 1844). www.marxists.org/archive/marx/works/1844/manuscripts/labour.htmx

Marx, Karl. *The German Ideology*. New York: International Publishers, 1981 (org. 1846).

Marx, Karl. *Grundrisse: Foundations of the Critique of Political Economy*. New York: Penguin Classics, 1993 (org. 1857–1858).

Marx, Karl. *Capital: A Critique of Political Economy*. New York: Modern Library, 1906 (org. 1867).

Marx, Karl, and Frederick Engels. "Manifesto of the Communist Party, and Its genesis." *Marxists Internet Archive,* 2010 (org. 1848). www.marxists.org/admin/books/manifesto/Manifesto.pdf

Mattick, Paul. *Business as Usual: The Economic Crisis and the Failure of Capitalism.* London: Reaktion Books, 2011.

Mauss, Marcel. *The Gift: Forms and Functions of Exchange in Archaic Societies*. United Kingdom: Free Press, 1954.

McCracken, Grant. *Culture and Consumption: New Approaches to the Symbolic Character of Consumer Goods and Activities*. Bloomington: Indiana University Press, 1988.

McKibben, Bill. *The End of Nature*. New York: Random House, 1989.

McKibben, Bill. "Climate Change—A Rare Opportunity?" *The Ecologist,* February 2007. https://theecologist.org/2007/feb/01/climate-change-rare-opportunity

McKibben, Bill. *Eaarth: Making a Life on a Tough New Planet*. New York: St. Martin's Griffin, 2010.

McKibben, Bill. "Global Warming's Terrifying New Math." *Rolling Stone,* August 2012.

McKibben, Bill. *Falter: Has the Human Game Begun to Play Itself Out?* New York: Henry Holt and Company, 2019.

McNeill, J.R. *Something New Under the Sun: An Environmental History of the Twentieth-Century World*. New York: W. W. Norton & Co., 2001.

McNeill, J.R., and Peter Engelke. *The Great Acceleration: An Environmental History of the Anthropocene since 1945*. Cambridge: Belknap Press. 2016.

McPherson, Guy. *Going Dark*. Woodthrush Productions. Independently published (February 7, 2019).

McPherson, Miller, Smith-Lovin, Lynn, and Matthew Brashears. "Social Isolation in America: Changes in Core Discussion Networks Over Two Decades." *American Sociological Review* 71 (2006): 353–375. https://journals.sagepub.com/doi/abs/10.1177/000312240607100301

MEA. *Ecosystems and Human Well-being: Synthesis*. Millennium Ecosystem Assessment. World Resources Institute. Washington: Island Press, 2005.

Mead, George Herbert. *Mind, Self and Society from the Standpoint of a Social Behaviorist*, edited by Charles W. Morris. Chicago: University of Chicago Press, 1934.

Meadows, Donella, Dennis Meadows, Randers Jørgen, and William Behren. *The Limits to Growth*. Washington: Potomac Associates Books, 1972.

Mekonnen, Mesfin, and Arjen Hoekstra. "Four Billion People Facing Severe Water Scarcity." *Science Advances* 2, no. 2 (February 2016). http://advances.sciencemag.org

Melillo, Jerry M., Terese T.C. Richmond, and Gary W. Yohe, eds. *2014: Climate Change Impacts in the United States: The Third National Climate Assessment.*. Washington, DC: U.S. Global Change Research Program, 2014.

Merchant, Carolyn. *The Death of Nature: Women, Ecology and the Scientific Revolution*. New York: HarperOne, 1990.

Merchant, Carolyn. *Radical Ecology: The Search for a Livable World*. New York: Routledge, 1992.

Merchant, Carolyn. "Reinventing Eden. Western Culture as a Recovery Narrative." In *Uncommon Ground: Rethinking the Human Place,* edited by William Cronon, 132–159. New York: W. W. Norton, 1996.

Merchant, Carolyn. "The Scientific Revolution and the Death of Nature." *FOCUS—ISIS* 97 (2006): 513–533. https://www.journals.uchicago.edu/doi/10.1086/508090

Merchant, Carolyn. *Reinventing Eden: The Face of Nature in Western Culture*. New York: Routledge, 2013.

Merchant, Carolyn. *Autonomous Nature: Problems of Prediction and Control From Ancient Times to the Scientific Revolution*. New York: Routledge, 2015.

Micken, Kathleen S., and Scott D. Roberts. "Desperately Seeking Certainty: Narrowing the Materialism Construct." *Advances in Consumer Research* 26, 513518, 1999. https://www.acrwebsite.org/volumes/8311#:~:text=Materialism Construct

Micklin, Philip. "The Aral Sea Disaster." *Annual Review of Earth and Planetary Sciences* 35 (2007): 47–72. https://www.annualreviews.org/doi/pdf/10.1146/annurev.earth.35.031306.140120

Miller, Jennifer L., Amanda Lossia, Catalina Suarez-Rivera, and Julie Gros-Louis. "Toys That Squeak: Toy Type Impacts Quality and Quantity of Parent-child Interactions." *First Language* 37, no. 6 (June 2017): 630–647. https://journals.sagepub.com/doi/abs/10.1177/0142723717714947

Mills, C. Wright. *The Sociological Imagination.* London: Oxford University Press, 1959.

Mintz, Sidney. *Sweetness and Power: The Place of Sugar in Modern History.* New York: Penguin Books, 1985.

Montaigne, Michel de. *The Complete Essays of Montaigne*, translated by Donald M. Frame. Stanford: Stanford University Press, 1964 (org. 1570).

More, Thomas. *Utopia.* New York: Dover Publications, 1997 (org. 1516).

Moore, Jason, ed. *Anthropocene or Capitalocene?: Nature, History, and the Crisis of Capitalism.* Oakland: PM Press, 2016.

Moore, Omar Khayyam. "Divination—A New Perspective." In *Environment and Cultural Behavior*, edited by Andrew Vayda, 121–128. New York: Natural History Press, 1969.

Mora, Camilo, Rebekka Metzger, Audrey Rollo, and Ransom A. Myers. "Experimental Simulations about the Effects of Overexploitation and Habitat Fragmentation on Populations Facing Environmental Warming." *Proceeding of The Royal Society B* 274 (April 22, 2007): 1023–1028. https://royalsocietypublishing.org/toc/rspb/2007/274/1613

Moss, Jeremiah. "Jeremiah's Vanishing New York." May 28, 2015. www.http://vanishingnewyork.blogspot.com

Mulder, Monique Borgerhoff, and Peter Coppolillo. *Conservation: Linking Ecology, Economics, and Culture.* Princeton: Princeton University Press, 2018.

Myers, David G. *The American Paradox: Spiritual Hunger in an Age of Plenty.* New Haven: Yale University Press, 2000a.

Myers, David G. "The Funds, Friends, and Faith of Happy People." *American Psychologist* 55, no. 1 (January 2000b): 56–67. https://psycnet.apa.org/record/2000-13324-006

Nadasdy, Paul. "Transcending the Debate Over the Ecologically Noble Indian: Indigenous Peoples and Environmentalism." *Ethnohistory* 52, no. 2 (April 2005): 291–331. https://read.dukeupress.edu/ethnohistory/article-abstract/52/2/291/8543/Transcending-the-Debate-over-the-Ecologically?redirectedFrom=fulltext

Nadasdy, Paul. "The Gift in the Animal: The Ontology of Hunting and Human—Animal Sociality." *American Ethnologist* 34, no. 1 (February 2008): 25–43. https://anthropology.cornell.edu/sites/anthro/files/Nadasdy 2007 Gift in the Animal.pdf

Nagourney, Adam, Jack Healy, and Nelson D. Schwartz. "California Drought Tests History of Endless Growth." *New York Times*, April 4, 2015.

NASA. "NASA's Grace Satellites Show Decade of Declining Water Reserves." *NASA Climate Change News.* 2013. www.climate.nasa.gov/news/995

NASA. "World of Change: Athabasca Oil Sands." *Earthobservatory.* 2016. www.earthobservatory.nasa.gov/world-of-change/Athabasca

NASA. "NASA, NOAA Data Show 2016 Warmest Year on Record Globally." Washington, DC, 2017. www.nasa.gov/press-release/nasa-noaa-data-show-2016-warmest-year-on-record-globally

Nash, Roderick. *Wilderness and the American Mind.* New Haven: Yale University Press, 1967.

New York Times. "U.S. Proposes New Rules to Protect Streams from Coal Pollution." July 16, 2015.

New York Times. "'I Don't Know That It's Man-Made,' Trump Says of Climate Change. It Is." October 15, 2018.

Nisbet, Robert A. *Community and Power* (formerly *The Quest for Community*). New York: Galaxy Book, 1962 (org. 1953).

NOAA. "NOAA, Partners: Earth's Oceans and Ecosystems Still Absorbing about Half the Greenhouse Gases Emitted by People." *National Oceanic and Atmospheric Administration.* 2012. www.noaanews.noaa.gov/stories2012/20120801_esrlcarbonstudy.html

NOAA. "Monthly Global Climate Report for December 2022." *National Centers for Environmental Information*, National Oceanic and Atmospheric Administration. 2023. https://www.ncei.noaa.gov/access/monitoring/monthly-report/global/202300

Nordman, Erik. Lobster Gangs and Debunking "The Tragedy of the Commons." *YES! Solutions Journalism* (May 2021). https://www.yesmagazine.org/economy/2021/08/11/the-commons-lobster-maine-elinor-ostrom

North, Douglass C. *Structure and Change in Economic History.* New York: W.W. Norton & Company, 1981.

NRDC. "The Desire to Stop Canadian Tar Sands Transcends Borders." *Natural Resources Defense Council.* 2019. https://www.nrdc.org/stories/desire-stop-canadian-tar-sands-transcends-borders

Oldenquist, Andrew. "Autonomy, Social Identities, and Alienation." *International Journal of Sociology and Social Policy* 11, no. 6/7/8 (1991): 53–80. https://www.emerald.com/insight/content/doi/10.1108/eb013145/full/html

Oliver, Mary. *New and Selected Poems, Volume One*. Boston: Beacon Press, 2004.

Olsen, Sigurd. *The Singing Wilderness*. Minneapolis: University of Minnesota Press, 1997.

Ott, Brian. "I Am Bart Simpson, Who the Hell Are You? A Study in Postmodern Identity Re Construction." *Journal of Popular Culture* 37, no. 1 (2003): 156–82. https://api.mountainscholar.org/server/api/core/bitstreams/de764690-1c82-41f0-aaea-04f8ab7274f5/content

Paleczny, Michelle, Edd Hammill, Vasiliki Karpouzi, and Daniel Pauly. "Population Trend of the World's Monitored Seabirds, 1950–2010." *PLOS ONE* (June 9, 2015). https://journals.plos.org/plosone/article?id=10.1371/journal.pone.0129342

Palmer, Margaret A., and Emily S. Bernhardt. "Mountaintop Mining Valley Fills and Aquatic Ecosystems: A Scientific Primer on Impacts and Mitigation Approaches." *White Paper Submitted for the Record in Senate Hearings.* Washington, DC, 2009. www.epw.senate.gov/public/index.cfm?FuseAction=files

Palmer, Margaret, et al. "Mountaintop Mining Consequences." *Policy Forum Science* 327 (2010): 148–149. https://archive.kftc.org/sites/default/files/docs/resources/mtr consequencesscience2010.pdf

Pardo, Mary. "Mexican American Women Grassroots Community Activists: 'Mothers of East Los Angeles.'" *Frontiers: A Journal of Women Studies* 11, no. 1 (1990): 1–7. https://doi.org/ 10.2307/3346696

Parkman, Francis. *The Oregon Trail*. New York: Penguin Books, 1985 (org. 1849).

Pattberg, Philipp. "Conquest, Domination and Control: Europe's Mastery of Nature in Historic Perspective." *Journal of Political Ecology* 14 (2007): 1–9. https://journals.librarypublishing.arizona.edu/jpe/article/1814/galley/2073/view/

Pearson, Chris. "Dogs, History, and Agency." *History and Theory,* Theme Issue 52, no. 4 (December 2013): 128–145. refreqid=excelsior:b9cc54b29ae1afa6bab9d440a2863e3f&ab_segments=&origin=&initiator=&acceptTC=1

Pepper, David. *The Roots of Modern Environmentalism.* London: Routledge, 1984.

Perlman, Michael. *Farming for Profit in a Hungry World: Capital and the Crisis in Agriculture*. Totowa: Allenheld, Osmun & Co. Publishers, 1977.

Pieterse, Jan Nederveen. *Globalization and Culture: Global Mélange*. Lanham: Rowman & Littlefield Publishers, 2009.

Polanyi, Karl. *The Great Transformation: The Political and Economic Origins of Our Times*. Boston: Beacon Press, 1957.

Pope Francis. "*Laudato sí.* Encyclical Letter on Care for Our Common Home." 2015. https://www.vatican.va/content/francesco/en/encyclicals/documents/papa-francesco_20150524_enciclica-laudato-si.html

Postman, Neal. *Amusing Ourselves to Death: Public Discourse in the Age of Show Business.* London: Penguin Books, 2005.

Power, Matthew. "The Poison Stream: Sacrificing India's Poor on the Altar of Modernity." *Harper's Magazine,* August 2004.

Primack, Brian A., Ariel Shensa, Jaime E. Sidani, Erin O. Whaite, Liu Yi Lin, et al. "Social Media Use and Perceived Social Isolation among Young Adults in the U.S." *American Journal of Preventive Medicine* 53, no. 1 (July 2017): 1–8. https://pubmed.ncbi.nlm.nih.gov/28279545/

Putnam, Robert. *Bowling Alone: The Collapse and Revival of American Community.* New York: Simon & Schuster, 2001.

Rahman, Majeed A. "The Geopolitics of Water in the Nile River Basin." *Global Research* (February 2014). https://www.globalresearch.ca/the-geopolitics-of-water-in-the-nile-river-basin/25746

Rand, Ayn. *Capitalism: The Unknown Ideal.* New York: Signet Books, 1986.

Raskin, Paul, Tariq Banuri, Gilberto Gallopín, Pablo Gutman, Al Hammond, Robert Kates, and Rob Swart. *Great Transition: The Promise and Lure of the Times Ahead.* Stockholm: SEI Stockholm Environment Institute, 2002.

Raskin, Paul. *Journey to Earthland: The Great Transition to Planetary Civilization.* Boston: Tellus Institute, 2016.

Raworth, Kate. *Doughnut Economics: Seven Ways to Think Like a 21st-Century Economist.* White River Junction: Chelsea Green Publishing, 2017.

Redfield, Robert. *The Folk Culture of Yucatan.* Chicago: University of Chicago Press, 1941.

Redfield, Robert. *The Folk Society*. New York: Bobbs-Merrill, 1947.

Redfield, Robert. *The Little Community and Peasant Society and Culture.* Chicago: The University of Chicago Press, 1960.

Reich, Robert. "Why the Share Economy Is Really the 'Share-the-Scraps' Economy." *LinkedIn*, February 2, 2015. https://www.linkedin.com/pulse/why-share-economy-really-share-the-scraps-robert-reich/

Rhimes, Shonda. *Year of Yes*. New York: Simon & Shuster, 2015

Rice, E.F., and Grafton, A. *The Foundations of Early Modern Europe, 1460–1559*. New York: W.W. Norton & Company, 1994.

Richins, Marsha L. "Possessions, Materialism, and Other-Directedness in the Expression of Self." In *Consumer Value: A Framework for Analysis and Research*, edited by Morris B. Holbook, 85–104. London: Routledge, 1999.

Ripple, William J., Christopher Wolf, Thomas M Newsome, Phoebe Barnard, and William R Moomaw. "World Scientists' Warning of a Climate Emergency." *BioScience*, biz088, 2019. www.doi.org/10.1093/biosci/biz088

Ritvo, Harriet. "Border Trouble: Shifting the Line between People and Other Animals." *Social Research* Vol 62, no. 3 (Fall 1995): 481–500. https://www.jstor.org/stable/pdf/40971107.pdf?

Robbins, Richard H. *Global Problems and the Culture of Capitalism*, 3rd ed. New York: Pearson, 2005.

Roberts, Callum. *The Ocean of Life: The Fate of Man and the Sea*. New York: Penguin Books, 2012.

Roberts, James A., and Aimee Clement. "Materialism and Satisfaction with Over-All Quality of Life and Eight Life Domains." *Social Indicators Research* 82, no. 1 (May 2007): 79–92. https://www.jstor.org/stable/pdf/20734447.pdf?

Robinson, Lance W. *Participatory Development and the Capacity of Gabra Pastoralist Communities to Influence Resilience*. PhD diss., University of Manitoba, 2009.

Robinson, Peter. *In a Dry Season*. New York: HarperCollins, 1999.

Rockström, J., W. Steffen, K. Noone, Å. Persson, F.S. Chapin, III, E. Lambin, T.M. Lenton, et al. "Planetary Boundaries: Exploring the Safe Operating Space for Humanity." *Ecology and Society* 14, no. 2 (2009). www.ecologyandsociety.org/vol14/iss2/art32

Rohr, Richard. "Living with the Land." *Center for Action and Contemplation* (October 20, 2021). https://cac.org/daily-meditations/living-with-the-land-2021-10-20/

Roseman, Abraham, and Paula G. Rubel. *The Tapestry of Culture: An Introduction to Cultural Anthropology*, 6th ed. Boston: McGraw Hill, 1998.

Sahlins, Marshall. *Stone Age Economics*. Chicago: Aldine-Atherton, 1972.

Sahlins, Marshall. "Hierarchy, Equality, and the Sublimation of Anarchy the Western Illusion of Human Nature." *The Tanner Lectures on Human Values*. The University of Michigan, Ann Arbor, 2005. https://tannerlectures.utah.edu/_resources/documents/a-to-z/s/Sahlins_2007.pdf

Sahlins, Marshall. *What Kinship Is-And Is Not*. Chicago: University of Chicago Press, 2013.

Salmón, Enrique. "Kincentric Ecology: Indigenous Perceptions of the Human-Nature Relationship." *Ecological Applications* 10, no. 5 (October 2000): 1327–1332. https://www.jstor.org/stable/2641288

Sapir, Edward. *Culture, Language, and Personality*. Berkeley: University of California Press, 1958.

Schrum, L.J., Nancy Wong, Farrah Arif, Sunaina K. Chugani, Alexander Gunz, Tina M. Lowrey, Agnes Nair, Mario Pandelaere, et al. "Reconceptualizing materialism as identity goal pursuits: Functions, processes, and consequences." *Journal of Business Research* 66, no. 8 (August 2012): 1179–1185. https://www.sciencedirect.com/science/article/abs/pii/S0148296312002251

Schumacher, E. F. *Small is Beautiful: Economics as if People Mattered*. New York: Perennial Library/Harper & Row, Publishers, 1973.

Schweickart, David. "Is Sustainable Capitalism Possible?" *Procedia: Social and Behavioral Sciences* 2, no. 5 (2010): 6739–6752. https://www.sciencedirect.com/science/article/pii/S1877042810011547

SciDev.net. "Kenya Starts Drilling Boreholes in Huge Aquifer." Bringing Science & Development together through News & Analysis (April 2, 2014.). www.idev.net/sub-saharan-africa/water/news/kea-starts-drilling-boreholes-in-huge-aquifer.html

Seed, Patricia. *Ceremonies of Possession in Europe's Conquest of the New World, 1492–1640*. Cambridge: Cambridge University Press, 1995.

Sharp, Lauriston. "Steel Axes for Stone Age Australians." *Human Organization* 11, no. 2. (Summer 1955): 17–22. https://web.mnstate.edu/robertsb/306/SteelAxesforStone-Age Australians.pdf

Sheil, Douglas, and Daniel Murdiyarso. "How Forests Attract Rain: An Examination of a New Hypothesis." *BioScience* 59, no. 4, (April 2009): 341–347. https://doi.org/10.1525/bio.2009.59.4.12

Silko, Leslie Marmon. *Ceremony*. New York: Signet, 1978.

Singer, Peter. *Animal Liberation Now: The Definitive Classic Renewed*. New York: Harper Perennial, 2023

Skeptical Science. "What Do the 'Climategate' Hacked CRU Emails Tell Us?" 2015. www.skepticalscience.com/Climategate-CRU-emails-hacked.htm

Smale, Dan A., et al. "Marine Heatwaves Threaten Global Biodiversity and the Provision of Ecosystem Services." *Nature Climate Change Letter* 4 (March 2019). https://pureadmin.uhi.ac.uk/ws/portalfiles/portal/3677164/Smale_et_al_2017_Nature_MHW_impacts_FINAL_main_text_figs_and_tabs_only.pdf

Smith, Adam. *An Inquiry into the Nature and Causes of The Wealth of Nations*. 1776. www.marxists.org/reference/archive/smith-adam/works/wealth-of-nations/index.htm

Sosa, Anna V. "Association of the Type of Toy Used During Play with the Quantity and Quality of Parent-Infant Communication." *JAMA Pediatrics* 170, no. 2 (2016): 132–137. https://jamanetwork.com/journals/jamapediatrics/fullarticle/2478386

Soustelle, Jacques. *Daily Life of the Aztecs: On the Eve of the Spanish Conquest*. Stanford: Stanford University Press, 1961.

Spate, O.H.K. *The Spanish Lake*. Canberra: The Australian National University Press, 2010.

Spencer, Herbert. *The Study of Sociology*. New York: D. Appleton & Company, 1874

Speth, James Gustave. *The Bridge at the Edge of the World: Capitalism, the Environment, and Crossing from Crisis to Sustainability*. New Haven: Yale University Press, 2008.

Spinrad, Richard W., and Ian Boyd. "Our Deadened, Carbon-Soaked Seas." *New York Times,* October 15, 2015. www.times.com/2015/10/16/opinion/our-deadened-carbon-soaked-seas.html?_r=0

Stack, Carol. *All Our Kin: Strategies for Survival in a Black Community*. New York: Basic Books, 1974.

Steadman, Lyle. *Kinship, the Basis of Cultural and Social Behavior*. Department of Anthropology, Arizona State University (Aug 1996). Unpublished paper.

Steffen, Will, Paul J. Crutzen, and John R. McNeill. "The Anthropocene: Are Humans Now Overwhelming the Great Forces of Nature." *AMBIO: A Journal of the Human Environment* 36, no. 8 (December 2007): 614–621. https://bioone.org/journals/ambio-a-journal-of-the-human-environment/volume-36/issue-8/0044-7447_2007_36_614_TAAHNO_2.0.CO_2/The-Anthropocene--Are-Humans-Now-Overwhelming-the-Great-Forces/10.1579/0044-7447 2007 36[614:TAAHNO]2.0.CO;2.short

Steffen, Will, Wendy Broadgate, Lisa Deutsch, Owen Gaffney, and Cornelia Ludwig. "The Trajectory of the Anthropocene: The Great Acceleration." *The Anthropocene Review* 2, no. 1 (January 2015): 81–98. https://journals.sagepub.com/doi/abs/10.1177/2053019614564785

Steinberg, Ted. "Can Capitalism Save the Planet?: On the Origins of Green Liberalism." *Radical History Review* 107 (2010): 7–24.

Steward, Julian. "Basin-Plateau Aboriginal Sociopolitical Groups." *Smithsonian Institution Bureau of American Ethnology*, Bulletin, no. 20. Provo, UT: University of Utah Press, 2002 (org. 1938).

Stivers, Richard. *Shades of Loneliness: Pathologies of a Technological Society*. Lanham: Rowman & Littlefield Publishers, 2004.

Stockholm Resilience Centre. "The Nine Planetary Boundaries—An Update." n.d. www.stockholmresilience.org/research/research-news/2015-01-15-planetary-boundaries---an-update.html

Stoller, Marianne L. "Birds, Feathers, and Hopi Ceremonialism." *Expedition* 33, no. 2 (1991): 35–54. www.penn.museum/documents/publications/expedition/pdfs/33-2/stoller.pdf

Straus, Anne S. "Northern Cheyenne Ethnopsychology." American Anthropological Association. *Ethos* 5, no. 3 (1977): 326–357. https://anthrosource.onlinelibrary.wiley.com/doi/10.1525/eth.1977.5.3.02a00050

Struzik, Ed. "With Tar Sands Development, Growing Concern on Water Use." *Yale environment360*. Yale School of Forestry & Environmental Studies, Yale University, 2013. www.e360.yale.edu/feature/with_tar_sands_development_growing_concern_on_water_use/2672/

SunSentinel. "Sugar Industry Accused of Dodging Everglades Clean-up Costs." *SunSentinel,* June 15, 2014. www.sun-sentinel.com/news/fl-xpm-2014-06-15-fl-everglades-sugar-costs-20140615-story.html

Swift, Anthony. "Tar Sands Tailings: Alberta's Growing Toxic Legacy." *Natural Resources Defense Council* (NRDC). 2017. www.nrdc.org/experts/tar-sands-tailings-albertas-growing-toxic-legacy

Talberth, John, Clifford Cobb and Noah Slattery. "The Genuine Progress Indicator 2006: A Tool for Sustainable Development." *Redefining Progress Research Report,* 2007. www.rprogress.org/publications/2007/GPI%202006.pdf

Tawney, R.H. *The Acquisitive Society*. New York: Dover Publications, 2004 (org. 1920).

Taylor, Paul W. "The Ethics of Respect for Nature." *Environmental Ethics* 3, no. 3 (Fall 1981):197–218.

Terrace, H.S. "Animal Cognition: Thinking without Language." *Philosophical Transactions of the Royal Society of London* 308, no. 1135 (February 1985): 113–128. https://doi.org/10.1098/rstb.1985.0014

The Royal Society. *Climate Updates: What Have We Learnt since the IPCC 5th Assessment Report?* London, England, 2017. www.royalsociety.org/~/media/policy/Publications/2017/27-11-2017-Climate-change-updates-report.pdf

Thompson, Edward P. *The Making of the English Working Class.* New York: Vintage Books, 1968.

Thompson, Stacy. "The Micro-Ethics of Everyday Life: Ethics, Ideology and Anti-consumerism." *Cultural Studies* 26, no. 6 (November 2012): 895–921. https://web-s-ebscohost-com.libweb.ben.edu/ehost/pdfviewer/pdfviewer?vid=0&sid=684c1afd-57a0-4531-8f5e-2db5c52adfa5@redis

Tilman David, Kenneth G. Cassman, Pamela A. Matson, Rosamond Naylor, and Stephen Polasky. "Agricultural Sustainability and Intensive Production Practices." *Nature* 418 (August 2002): 671–677. https://web-p-ebscohost-com.libweb.ben.edu/ehost/pdfviewer/pdfviewer?vid=0&sid=00f217bd-059a-419f-b62f-814ff29cd29f@redis

Trainer, Ted. "Why a Consumer Society Can't Fix the Climate." *Bulletin of the Atomic Scientists* (November 2013). https://thebulletin.org/2013/11/why-a-consumer-society-cant-fix-the-climate/

Turnbull, Colin. *The Forest People: A Study of the Pygmies of the Congo*. New York: Touchstone Books, 1962.

Turner, Victor. *A Forest of Symbols: Aspects of Ndembu Ritual.* Ithica: Cornell University Press, 1967.

Twenge, Jean M. "Increases in Depression, Self-Harm, and Suicide Among U.S. Adolescents After 2012 and Links to Technology Use: Possible Mechanisms." *Psychiatric Research and Clinical Practice* 2, no. 1 (March 2020): 19–25. https://prcp.psychiatryonline.org/doi/10.1176/appi.prcp.2019001 5

Tylor, E.B. *Primitive Culture: Research into the Development of Mythology, Philosophy, Religion, Art, and Custom,* Vol. 2. Cambridge: Cambridge University Press. 2010. (org. 1871).

Union of Concerned Scientists. "Debunking Misinformation About Stolen Climate Emails in the 'Climategate' Manufactured Controversy." 2014. www.ucsusa.org/global_warming/solutions/fight-misinformation/debunking-misinformation-stolen-emails-climategate.html

United Nations. *Second World Ocean Assessment.* Division for Ocean Affairs and the Law of the Sea. New York: United Nations, 2021.

UNDESA. *International Decade for Action "Water for Life" 2005-2015.* United Nations Department of Economics and Social Affairs. New York: The United Nations, 2015

UNEP. *Global Environmental Outlook—GEO-6: Healthy Planet, Healthy People.* Nairobi, Kenya: United Nations Environmental Programme, 2019.

UNEP. *Emissions Gap Report 2021: The Heat is On—A World of Climate Promises Not Yet Delivered.* Nairobi, Kenya: United Nations Environmental Programme, 2021.

Upton, John. "Pulp Fiction, Part 3: The American Trees That Are Electrifying Europe." *Climate Central*. 2015. https://reports.climatecentral.org/pulp-fiction/2/

Urquhart, Ian. *Costly Fix: Power, Politics, and Nature in the Tar Sands*. Toronto: University of Toronto Press, 2018.

USGCRP. *Impacts, Risks, and Adaptation in the United States*. Fourth National Climate Assessment, Volume II, edited by D.R. Reidmiller, C.W. Avery, D.R. Easterling, K.E. Kunkel, K.L.M. Lewis, T.K. Maycock, and B.C. Stewart. U.S. Washington, DC, USA: Global Change Research Program, 2018.

USGCRP. *Fifth National Climate Assessment: Report-in-Brief*, edited by A.R. Crimmins, C.W. Avery, D.R. Easterling, K.E. Kunkel, B.C. Stewart, and T.K. Maycock. Washington, DC: U.S. Global Change Research Program, 2023. https://doi.org/10.7930/NCA5.2023.RiB

van Meijl, Toon. "Culture and Identity in Anthropology: Reflections on 'Unity' and 'Uncertainty' in the Dialogical Self." *International Journal for Dialogical Science* 3, no. 1 (Fall 2008): 165–190. https://ijds.lemoyne.edu/journal/3_1/pdf/IJDS.3.1.13.VanMeijl.pdf

Varner, Kasey. "Environmental Groups Say Obama Administration Watered Down EPA Pollution Rule." *The Huffington Post,* June 24, 2014.

Veblen, Thorsten. *Absentee Ownership and Business Enterprise in Recent Times: The Case of America*. New York: The Viking Press, 1923.

Veblen, Thorsten. *The Theory of the Leisure Class: An Economic Study of Institutions.* New York: B. W. Huebsch, 1994 (org. 1899). https://oll.libertyfund.org/title/veblen-the-theory-of-the-leisure-class-an-economic-study-of-institutions

Verhaeghe, Paul. *What About Me? The Struggle for Identity in a Market-Based Society.* London: Scribe Publications Pty Ltd, 2014.

Vidal, John. "The Sumatran Rainforest Will Mostly Disappear Within 20 Years." *The Guardian,* May 26, 2013. https://www.theguardian.com/world/2013/may/26/sumatra-borneo-deforestation-tigers-palm-oil

Voss, Stuart F. *Latin America in the Middle Period, 1750–1929.* Lanham: Rowman & Littlefield, 2001.

Wallace-Wells, David. *The Uninhabitable Earth: Life after Warming*. New York: Tim Guggan Books, 2019.

Watson, James L. *Golden Arches East: McDonald's in East Asia*. 2nd ed. Stanford: Stanford University Press, 2006.

Watts, Michael J. "Contested Communities, Malignant Markets, and Gilded Governance: Justice, Resource Extraction, and Conservation in the Tropics." In *People, Plants, and Justice: The Politics of Nature Conservation*, edited by Charles Zerner, 21–51. New York: Columbia University Press, 2000.

Weart, Spencer. "The Discovery of Global Warming." In *Center for History of Physics of the American Institute of Physics,* 2017. www.history.aip.org/climate/rapid.htm

Weed, Aaron. "Consequences of Climate Change for Biotic Disturbances in North American Forests." *Ecological Monographs* 83, no. 4 (2013): 441–470.

Weigand, Amy. *Becoming Human: Stories of Animals and Ethics in Biomedicine*. Philadelphia: Temple University Press, 2008.

Whitty, Julia. "The Fate of the Ocean." In *World in Motion: The Globalization and the Environment Reader*, edited by Gary M. Kroll and Richard H. Robbins, 69–90. Lanham: Rowman & Littlefield Publishers, 2009.

Wilson, Timothy D., David A. Reinhard, Erin C. Westgate, Daniel T. Gilbert, Nicole Ellerbeck, Cheryl Hahn, Casey L. Brown, and Adi Shaked. "Just Think: The Challenges of the Disengaged Mind." *Science* 345, no. 6192 (July 2014.): 75–77. https://dtg.sites.fas.harvard.edu/WILSON ET AL 2014.pdf

White, Lynn. "The Historical Roots of Our Ecologic Crisis." *Science* 155 (1967): 1203–1207.

Worsley, Peter. *The Three Worlds: Culture and World Development*. Chicago: University of Chicago Press, 1984.

WMO. "Provisional State of the Global Climate 2022." World Meteorological Organization, 2022. https://library.wmo.int/doc_num.php?explnum_id=11359

WMO. "State of the Climate in 2022." *Bulletin of the American Meteorological Society* 104, no. 9 (2023): S1–S501. https://doi.org/10.1175/2023BAMSStateof theClimate.1

Worldwatch Institute. "The State of Consumption Today." *Worldwatch Institute,* 2013a. www.worldwatch.org/node/810

Worldwatch. "Indonesia's Palm Oil Puzzle." *Worldwatch Institute,* 2013b. http:// www.world watch.org/node/6099.

Worster, Donald. *Shrinking the Earth: The Rise and Decline of Natural Abundance*. New York: Oxford University Press, 2016.

Wright, Albert Hazel. "Other Early Records of the Passenger Pigeon." *The Aux* 28, no. 3. (1911). American Ornithologist Union. https://books.google.com/books?id =wNoUAAAAYAAJ&printsec=frontcover#v=onepage&q&f=false

Wright, Erik Olin, and Joel Rogers. *American Society: How It Really Works*. New York: W.W. Norton, 2011.

Wuebbles, D.J., D.R. Easterling, K. Hayhoe, T. Knutson, R.E. Kopp, J.P. Kossin, K.E. Kunkel, et al. "Our Globally Changing Climate." In *Climate Science Special Report: Fourth National Climate Assessment, Volume I,* edited by D.J. Wuebbles, D.W. Fahey, K.A. Hibbard, D.J. Dokken, B.C. Stewart, and T.K. Maycock. *U.S. Global Change Research Program* (2017): 35–72. doi:10.7930/J08S4N35

WWF. *Living Planet Report 2018: Aiming Higher*, edited by M. Grooten and R.E.A. Almond. World Wildlife Fund, Gland, Switzerland, 2018. https://www .worldwildlife.org/pages/living-planet-report-2018

WWF. *Living Planet Report 2020: Bending the Curve of Biodiversity Loss*, edited by R.E.A. Almond, M. Grooten, and T. Petersen. Gland, Switzerland: World Wildlife Fund, 2020. https://www.wwf.org.uk/sites/default/files/2020-09/LPR20 _Full_report.pdf

Yeats, William Butler and Richard J. Finneran. *The Collected Poems of W.B.Yeats*. New York: Collier Books, 1989

Young, Jock. *The Vertigo of Late Modernity*. New York: Sage Publications, 2007.

Zablocki, Benjamin. *The Joyful Community: An Account of Buderhof - A Communal Movement Now in Its Third Generation.* New York: Penguin Books, 1972.

Zalasiewicz, Jan, Mark Williams, Will Steffen, and Paul Crutzen. "The New World of the Anthropocene." *Environmental Science & Technology* 44 no. 7 (2010): 2228–2231. https://pubs.acs.org/doi/10.1021/es903118j

Zawahri, Neda A. "Governing the Jordan River System: History, Challenges, and Outlook." *Journal of Transboundary Water Resources* 1 (2010). https://www.mdpi.com/2073-4441/14/10/1605

Zepf, Siegfried. "Consumerism and Identity: Some Psychoanalytical Considerations." *Forum of Psychoanalysis* 19, no. 3 (2010): 144–154. https://pep-web.org/browse/document/ifp.019.0144a?index=35

Zhang, Shaoke, Hao Jiang, and John M. Carroll. "Social Identity in Facebook Community Life." In *Technical, Social, and Legal Issues in Virtual Communities: Emerging Environments*, edited by Subhasish Dasgupta, 101–114. Hershey: IGI Global Publishing, 2012.

Zuk, Miriam and Karen Chapel. "Case Studies on Gentrification and Displacement in the San Francisco Bay Area." The Center for Community Innovation, University of California, Berkeley, 2015. https://urbandisplacement.org/sites/default/files/images/case_studies_on_gentrification_and_displacement-_full_report.pdf

Zwick, Detlev. "Consumption As a Practice Of/In Self-Formation: the Neoliberal Politics of Consumption (And Consumer Research?)." In *European Advances in Consumer Research* Volume 9, edited by Alan Bradshaw, Chris Hackley, and Pauline Maclaran, 26–27. Duluth: Association for Consumer Research, 2011.

Index

About the Author

Jack Thornburg received his PhD in development studies and anthropology at the University of Wisconsin-Madison. His research interests include the environment, community development, ecotourism, and postmodern identity. He has conducted research in Cuba, Costa Rica, and St. Lucia. His most recent publication is "Eco-tourism and Sustainable Community Development in Cuba: Bringing Community Back into Development" in the *Journal of International and Global Studies*. "One Earth: Humans, Animals, and the Landscape of Community" will be published in a forthcoming edited volume. He now resides in Guadalajara, Mexico, with a current interest in landscape and identity in modern Mexico.

Milton Keynes UK
Ingram Content Group UK Ltd.
UKHW041312021224
3319UKWH00006B/72

9 781666 958782